The Deconstruction of Employment as a Political Question

Amparo Serrano-Pascual · Maria Jepsen
Editors

The Deconstruction of Employment as a Political Question

'Employment' as a Floating Signifier

Editors
Amparo Serrano-Pascual
Complutense University of Madrid,
TRANSOC Research Institute
Madrid, Spain

Maria Jepsen
Free University of Brussels
European Trade Union Institute
Brussels, Belgium

ISBN 978-3-319-93616-1   ISBN 978-3-319-93617-8   (eBook)
https://doi.org/10.1007/978-3-319-93617-8

Library of Congress Control Number: 2018945060

Cover image: Brain light/Alamy Stock Photo
Cover designed by Akihiro Nakayama

Printed on acid-free paper

This Palgrave Macmillan imprint is published by the registered company Springer Nature Switzerland AG
The registered company address is: Gewerbestrasse 11, 6330 Cham, Switzerland

ACKNOWLEDGEMENTS

The idea for this manuscript emerged following the seminar 'The deconstruction of employment as a political question: Employment as a floating signifier', held by the ETUI (European Trade Union Institute) and the IRL (Industrial Relations School, Complutense University of Madrid) in Madrid on 21 and 22 January 2016.

The purpose of the seminar was to gather together experts from different countries and disciplines in order to discuss and monitor recent developments in the process of deconstruction of employment as a central category for conceiving and regulating the social sphere. This meeting produced some very thought-provoking observations on the political processes involved in the production of new reference categories for under-standing, regulating and problematising employment in today's societies, as well as its impact on different social and gender categories. The meeting not only brought together several different analytical disciplines (sociology, law, economics, social psychology) and additional contributors (research-ers, social and trade-union actors), but also involved experts from vari-ous countries where these processes of deconstruction of employment had taken very different forms with varying degrees of severity. We should like to express our thanks to the European Trade Union Institute, which funded and coordinated the translation work and the meeting that served as a trigger for this joint publication. The ETUI is financially supported by the European Union. Bethany Staunton at the ETUI performed an excellent task of coordinating and revising the translated texts, supported by an exceptional and efficient team of translators.

This publication was also produced as part of a research project (CSO2017-82839-P), funded by the Spanish Ministry of Economy, Industry and Competitiveness. In turn, we should also like to express our great appreciation to the anonymous reviewers of this manuscript, who generously provided some very pertinent input.

Contents

NOTES ON CONTRIBUTORS

Luis Enrique Alonso Professor of Sociology at the Universidad Autónoma de Madrid. He has worked in a variety of areas relating to consumerism, employment and regulation. He has also written on sociological theory, including the work of Pierre Bourdieu, Jean Baudrillard, Zygmunt Bauman and others. He has lectured and published on subjects relating to labour processes, critical management studies, social movements and socio-economics.

Antonio Baylos Full Professor of Labour Law at the University of Castilla-La Mancha (UCLM), Spain. Head of the Department of Labour Law and Social Work. Director of the European and Latin American Centre for Social Dialogue, a research institute of the UCLM. Its main lines of research are European law, transnational labour law, theoretical foundations of labour law and the social state, and analysis of the legal culture of employment and industrial relations.

Jean-Michel Bonvin Professor of Sociology and Social Policy at the University of Geneva. His areas of expertise include social and employment policy, organisational innovation in the public sector and the third sector, the sociology of labour and corporations and theories of justice, including the capability approach. He has recently published *Investir dans la protection sociale: atouts et limites pour la Suisse/Reformieren durch Investieren? Chancen und Grenzen des Sozialinvestitionsstaats in der Schweiz*, Seismo, 2017 (co-edited with S. Dahmen) and *Facing Trajectories from School to Work*, Springer, 2015 (co-edited with H.-U. Otto et al.).

Sarah de Heusch Project Officer for the Development & Strategy Unit of SMart. Currently addressing the issue of social protection and labour market trends (especially atypical employment), she builds partnerships and collaborates with organisations and academics that share SMart's values and concerns. Previously, she was involved in the internationalisation of SMart and addressed issues of professional mobility of artists and cultural professionals (participated in the Open Method of Coordination of the EU, 2009–2010). She was previously Co-founder and Dancer at Transe-en-Dance and Assistant to the Secretary-General at UNICA (Network of Universities from the Capitals of Europe).

Didier Demazière French sociologist. He is a Research Professor at the French National Center for Scientific Research (CNRS) and a member of the French Centre for the Sociology of Organisations (CSO). He is also Editor-in-Chief of the journal *Sociologie du Travail* and Head of Doctoral Studies in Sociology at Sciences Po in Paris. He has recently published two books: *Andrew Abbott et l'héritage de l'école de Chicago* (co-edited with M. Jouvenet), Éditions de l'EHESS, 2016; *Les sociologies françaises. Héritages et perspectives, 1960–2010* (co-edited with D. Lorrain and C. Paradeise), Presses Universitaires de Rennes, 2015.

Jan Drahokoupil Senior Researcher on multinational corporations at the European Trade Union Institute (ETUI). He also coordinates research on digitalisation and the future of work. His broader expertise lies in political economy and development, particularly in the context of Eastern European countries. His book publications include: *Transition economies: Political economy in Russia, Eastern Europe, and Central Asia* (with Martin Myant), Wiley-Blackwell, 2011, and *Globalization and the state in Eastern Europe: The politics of foreign direct investment*, Routledge, 2009.

Brian Fabo Researcher at the Centre for European Policy Studies (CEPS) since February 2015 and the Central European University (CEU) in Budapest. Research areas: The application of web data in labour market research, particularly in the areas of skills mismatch and the sharing/platform economy. He has participated in several research and policy projects as an independent consultant and regularly teaches quantitative and programming classes.

Maria Jepsen Director of the Research Department at the European Trade Union Institute (ETUI) and *chargée de cours* (Associate Professor) in Labour Economics at the Université Libre de Bruxelles (ULB), Visiting Lecturer at the UCL (*Université Catholique de Louvain-la-Neuve*) in European Industrial Relations and Policy Fellow at the Institute of Labor Economics (IZA). Editor-in-Chief of the journal *Transfer*, published by Sage. Her main research fields are the construction and development of social policy at European level and how this interacts with national settings; gender studies; and comparative studies of the impact of welfare states on labour supply, wages and working conditions.

Michel Lallement Professor at the Conservatoire National des Arts et Métiers (Paris), holding the chair of Sociological Analysis of Work, Employment and Organisations, and a member of the Interdisciplinary Laboratory of Economic Sociology, French National Center for Scientific Research (LISE-CNRS). He is a member of the editorial boards of *L'Année sociologique* and *Sociologie du travail*. His main areas of work include changes in work and labour markets, and his latest publications include: *Logique de classe: Edmond Goblot, la bourgeoisie et la distinction sociale*, Les Belles Lettres, 2015; *L'Âge du Faire: Hacking, travail, anarchie*, Seuil, 2015; and *Makers: Un monde social en mouvement*, Seuil, 2018 (with I. Berrebi-Hoffmann and M. C. Bureau).

Margaret Maruani Director of Research at the French National Center for Scientific Research (CNRS) (Paris Descartes University). She is also the founder of the research institute 'Marché du travail et genre' (MAGE). Her main topics of research are work, employment and gender: international comparisons; sociology of employment and unemployment; and history of research on gender in social and human sciences.

Monique Meron Statistician affiliated to the Quantitative Sociology Laboratory (LSQ) of the Center for Research in Economics and Statistics (CREST). She has been responsible for national surveys and has published numerous studies on labour market analysis, examination of statistical tools and the evolution of occupations. She has held various posts, in particular at the National Institute of Statistics and Economic Studies (INSEE), the French Institute for Demographic Studies (INED) and the French Ministry of Employment.

Sofía Pérez de Guzmán Associate Professor of Sociology, University of Cadiz, Spain. Director of the Research Group 'Trabajo, Política y Género' under the Andalucian Research Plan. Research topics: sociology of work and employment; industrial relations; gender; immigration. Her most recent publications include: 'Political exchange, crisis of representation and trade union strategies in a time of austerity: Trade unions and 15M in Spain', *Transfer*, 2016 (with B. Roca and I. Díaz) and 'Políticas empresariales de mano de obra y configuración social del empleo en España: Una aproximación desde los trabajos de investigación sociológica', *Revista Internacional de Sociología*, 2015 (with C. Prieto).

Carlos Prieto Professor Emeritus in Sociology at the Complutense University of Madrid. Assistant Director of the review *Cuadernos de Relaciones Laborales*. Member of the management group of the International Research Group 'Marché du travail et genre' (MAGE). His most recent publications include: *Nuevos tiempos de trabajo: entre la flexibilidad competitiva de las empresas y las relaciones de género*, CIS, 2008; *La calidad del empleo en España*, Ministerio de Trabajo e Inmigración, 2009; and *Trabajo, cuidados, tiempo libre y relaciones de género en la sociedad española*, Cinca, 2015.

Alberto Riesco-Sanz Associate Professor, Complutense University of Madrid. His main research areas are sociology of work and employment. His most recent publications include: 'Trabajo, independencia y subordinación: La regulación del trabajo autónomo en España', *Revista Internacional de Sociología*, 2016, and 'Une indépendance équivoque: Les nouveaux statuts des indépendants espagnols et français', *Revue Française de Socio-Économie*, 2016 (with S. Célérier and P. Rolle).

Vicente Sánchez Jiménez Doctor of Political Economics. Associate Professor and Director of Summer Courses at the Complutense University of Madrid (UCM). Department of Applied Economics, Faculty of Political Sciences and Sociology (UCM). Member of the editorial board for the *Cuadernos de Relaciones Laborales*. His most recent published articles are: 'Influencias entre conductas sociales y decisiones empresariales', *Política y Sociedad*, 2015; 'La redefinición del papel de la empresa en la sociedad', *Barataria*, 2015; and 'Las implicaciones de la economía digital en el sector de la construcción', *Gaceta Sindical*, 2016.

Amparo Serrano-Pascual Professor at the Faculty of Political Sciences and Sociology, Complutense University of Madrid. Her main topics of research and teaching include work and subjectivity; comparative social policy and the European social model. Some of her recent publications are: 'From "employability" to "entrepreneurability" in Spain: Youth in the spotlight in times of crisis', *Journal of Youth Studies* 20(7), 2017 (with P. Martín); *Deconstructing Flexicurity: Towards New Concepts and Approaches for Employment and Social Policy*, Routledge, 2014 (co-edited with M. Keune).

Gérard Valenduc Honorary Professor at the University of Namur and Associate Researcher at the European Trade Union Institute (ETUI). His research areas address the relationships between innovation, work and society. Until 2016, he was a director of the Fondation Travail-Université in Namur.

LIST OF FIGURES

LIST OF TABLES

CHAPTER 1

Introduction: The Political Reinvention of Work in Times of Crisis

Amparo Serrano-Pascual and Maria Jepsen

INTRODUCTION

Changes in the production model, digitalisation processes and economic crisis have exacerbated a breakdown in the terms and assumptions that previously defined and shaped the notion of employment. Given that employment has always been the pivotal issue when it comes to examining the social question in modern Western societies, analysing the changes undergone by this signifier of work makes it possible to address the transformations that have characterised our self-conception as a society. This reformulation of the notion of employment has gone hand in hand with an intensification of the deconstruction of employment as a central category for theorising, problematising and regulating the phenomenon of work (as a field that bears meaning, Donzelot 1984, and as a territory of government, Rose 1996), as well as with a

A. Serrano-Pascual (✉)
Complutense University of Madrid, TRANSOC Research Institute,
Madrid, Spain

M. Jepsen
ETUI and Free University of Brussels,
Brussels, Belgium

© The Author(s) 2019
A. Serrano-Pascual and M. Jepsen (Eds.),
The Deconstruction of Employment as a Political Question,
https://doi.org/10.1007/978-3-319-93617-8_1

1

new understanding of the category of 'worker'. Such categories of thought and political action have allowed us to discuss—and to problematise—vulnerability in employment in terms of unfairness, inequality and inadequate protection. An analysis of the transformation of the 'grammar of the common good' opens up possibilities for conceptualising the market as an entity to be governed and regulated (Rose 1996). The crisis of the category of 'employment' represents a challenge to the main tools (social rights, social protection, workers' organisations, etc.) that have been established in recent history in European societies to deal with social vulnerability. Therefore, the transformation in the meaning of social concepts—as tools for narrating social experience—is not only the result but also the main driver of mutations in the social and production paradigm.

Social sciences currently encounter major obstacles in identifying the main threads of this research topic, namely the changing sense, profile and meaning of work. Deep and far-reaching changes in the organisation of the economy, fostered essentially by the process of its digitalisation and precarisation at work, are leading to a recasting of the category predominantly used for the analysis and regulation of labour in Western societies, namely wage employment (OECD 2016; Degryse 2016). The aim of this collective reflection is to analyse, by means of an interdisciplinary approach, the numerous implications of these shifts in conceptual boundaries and in the semantic contours of the notion of employment. It is a question of analysing new semantic fields and territories that have become available for theorising, understanding and regulating employment; of scrutinising the rules governing the statements that, in a given society, organise what it is sayable and thinkable (Angenot 2010, 21) when speaking of employment. It should not be forgotten that social (and statistical) categories—employment, unemployment, self-employment, inactivity—are, after all, invented and historically contingent institutions (Piore 1987).

The social grammar corresponding to the employment society—the 'common sense' represented by wage employment and its regulation—ensured that the category of wage employment pertained to both representation and action (Demazière, in this volume). This conceptual hegemony promotes technologies to govern employment: insurance (shift from individual lack to social risk, Rosanvallon 1995), collective bargaining (the recognition of conflict of interests as the constitutive backbone of the wage relationship) and labour law (shift from morale to justice). The wage condition becomes the metonymic condition of citizenship (centrality of work). This semantic construction allows European citizens to think of employment from a political angle: recognition of the heteronomy of labour; visualisation of market flaws; construction of asymmetry and intrinsic inequality regarding the wage condition.

However, we are currently witnessing a substantial deconstruction of employment as a political issue. This process is intensified by (but is also the product of) important changes in the values and political identity promoted by the European Social Model (ESM) (the key effort by EU institutions to frame social cohesion), as a political project to deal with current socio-economic challenges (from problematising worker vulnerability to vulnerability of the market) (Jepsen and Serrano-Pascual 2011). These developments, together with the economic crisis and significant shifts in the production model, are intensifying major transformations in the notion of employment and the relationship between employment, citizenship and social cohesion.

A number of authors have analysed changes currently affecting the world of labour, with a focus on various aspects of its reconfiguration: digitalisation of the economy and increasingly heterogeneous modes of performing labour activities (Valenduc and Vendramin 2016); intensification of globalisation of the economy and political reconfiguration in the wake of economic crisis (Huws 2001, 2014); the weakening of labour protection and the increasingly precarious terms of employment and working conditions to which labour forces are subject (Prieto 2014), leading to the rise of a new social class variously termed the 'precariat' (Standing 2011) or 'cybertariat' (Huws 2001; Dyer-Witheford 2015); new models of management organisation and control of work forces ('the entreployee', Pongratz and Voss 2003); the exploration of new forms of labour performance and regulation (Sundararajan 2016; Gold 2004; Schol 2013), etc. In general, these studies have analysed the impact of these wide-ranging transformations in terms of the spread of non-standard forms of work and employment status (OECD 2016) or of a radical reshaping of the nature of work (European Commission 2016; Degryse 2016). Relatively few studies, meanwhile, have examined the transformations accruing in terms of a reformulation of cultural conceptions attaching to wage earning (e.g. full-time jobs, open-ended contracts, regulated employment) and of the deconstruction of the category termed 'employment'.

Studies of shifts in the subjective experience of work and of the under-lying causes of such changes tend to belong to one of two branches of literature, depending on the specific analytical tradition within which they have been produced. In the English-speaking world, studies tend to focus on an analysis of transformations in industrial relations and in ways of understanding and organising work that have come about as a result of radical changes in modes of production (this approach is referred to by different names: the 'sharing economy', the 'gig economy', digitalisa-tion of the economy, the '4.0 economy', etc.). The French-speaking tra-dition, on the other hand, inspired by the work of Desrosières, Bourdieu and Foucault, analyses, predominantly, the reformulation of the catego-ries used for studying and investigating social phenomena. Products of this tradition are the classic studies of the genealogy and social 'inven-tion' of the categories of unemployment and *la question sociale* by several French academics, such as Méda, Castel, Salais, Topalov and Donzelot, among others. An approach aimed at encouraging a merg-ing of these two analytical trends could, at the same time, provide the opportunity for a transcultural, interdisciplinary analysis of how these radical economic, political and ideological changes are producing a reformulation of the conventional wisdom concerning the whole cate-gory of waged employment (aspects previously taken for granted as to the meaning of work and of being 'a worker'), as well as other closely associated categories such as unemployment, self-employment or inac-tivity. The chapters of this book explore different dimensions of the current transformation of the concept of work from a perspective that derives principally from a study of the language and categories used to speak of employment. This approach is aimed mainly at studying a con-ceptual reformulation—constituting a deconstruction of the category of employment—from an interdisciplinary and transcultural standpoint; indeed, the contributors include mainly sociologists (Bonvin, Demazière, Lallement, Maruani, Pérez de Guzmán, Prieto, Riesco, Valenduc), economists (Alonso, Drahokoupil, Fabo, Jepsen and Sánchez), lawyers (Baylos), social psychologists (Serrano-Pascual) and statisticians (Meron), as well as practitioners (de Heusch), from Spain, France, Belgium and Switzerland.[1] On the basis of an analytical focus on the rather hazy and imprecise nature of the concept of employment and the impending dis-mantling of the hitherto prevailing semantic frontiers that defined the area of work, this book sets out to provide tools for analysing associ-ated and simultaneous shifts in the conceptual boundaries affecting the category of 'worker'. To this end, an analysis has been conducted of changes in the way work can be, and is, named, and of the new categories and semantic areas pertaining to 'workers', the purpose of the exercise being to identify new technologies of social subjection and subordination.

ENUNCIATION AND DENUNCIATION: EMERGENCE OF THE CATEGORY OF EMPLOYMENT AS A CONDITION OF ITS REGULATION

This objective will be approached through an analytical process directed essentially towards studying the processes of change and development of employment as a category of thought. This draws its inspiration largely from a rhetorical perspective analysing the performative capacity of words, and interpreting semantic changes as political transformations (which they both promote and result from). It is therefore aimed particularly at identifying the 'word struggles' taking place in the territory of social regulation and their repercussions on the transformation of the social question.

According to this viewpoint, inspired by the linguistic turn that has been applied in the social sciences since the 1970s, the action of naming is treated as an activity that organises, classifies and offers a perspective and a judgement on reality. We do not relate to or perceive real things in the singular, but integrate and classify them in a category, and, consequently, these things will be perceived only as part of a group (Lindesmith, Strauss and Denzin 2006). As a number of authors contributing to this book explore (see, in particular, the chapters by Demazière, Lallement, Maruani and Meron, and Prieto and Pérez de Guzmán), the criteria we use to classify real things (in the case that concerns us here, employment, unemployment or inactivity) are the product of socially and politically constructed cultural conventions through which a society thinks and reflects.

This process of categorisation and classification that characterises language allows us to share meanings and maintain reciprocal perspectives on the objects we encounter, which is a necessary condition for social interaction (Schutz 1999). Depending on the classification criterion, we are faced with different perspectives of perception (Lindesmith et al. 2006) and political evaluation. Therefore, language, as well as permitting social interaction, contributes to its reproduction. As posited by Bourdieu (1985), a central part of the reproduction of the social order consists of the acceptance of classification schemes, divisions, limits, discontinuities and boundaries to what was formerly continuous, and their normalisation (with the arbitrary nature of their foundations being overlooked and legitimised). This exercise in organisation and division (Bourdieu 1985) makes it possible to see connections between objects which, otherwise, we would not see, and defines the scope of what is thinkable and sayable (de Certeau 1990) in a social context. To change concepts therefore means to change perspective. Naming entails an exercise in engineering of the viewpoint.

The emergence of the categories of work and worker were to allow a distinction to be drawn between productive activities and those classified and denominated as unproductive (or the active and inactive population). Although there have always been workers and work, it was only with the emergence of these categories that a meaningful classification was established among activities, depending on their degree of integration into the market—in other words, they acquired significance depending on their exchange value. There were workers before the nineteenth century, but their identity (semantic connotation) was defined according to their guild membership or working conditions. There was also work, but the notions by which it was named, and therefore what it meant, depended on the type of dependence, or the social utility of these activities, or the guild or social group to which one belonged (Meda 1998). The criteria we use to establish categories create territories in thought and in political evaluation and denunciation. Naming therefore implies creating spaces of meaningfulness and territories of thought and political expression.

It is not, therefore, the nature of the task that determines its semantic connotation, nor its space of meaningfulness, that defines whether it is, or is not, work, but the political framework (social and political relationships) within which these activities are carried out and named. Such is the case with the meaning acquired by the notion of employment, more recent than that of work, and the connotation of which will vary according to whether it is framed within the category of the market or that of human rights. While, in the former case, employment will constitute a trading relationship between free, equal subjects, in the latter, it entails the expression of citizenship and of relationships of interdependence. The same applies to the problematisation that has developed around the absence of work in modern societies (what we now call unemployment). As analysed by Cabrera (2001), this situation of economic deprivation may be given various names, and therefore different meanings, depending on the discursive matrix applied: divine punishment, punishment by the market, natural order of things, social injustice, expression of human nature, social issue, mental illness, moral deficiency, equality or laziness and lack of will. These discursive matrices articulate the categories (natural rights, gender, social issue, equality) whereby we understand the meaning of poverty, whereby we establish classifications that distinguish work from non-work, and come up with a diagnosis of the situation and alternatives (or lack of them) to resolve it. Therefore, as Cabrera emphasises, the notions of unemployment, poverty, inequality, etc., do not designate social objects that predate human consciousness, but the connotation they acquire, and the attitude that each society adopts towards these objects depends on the application of certain categories and frameworks with which we construct meaning (Cabrera 2001, 80).

To name work is a performative practice, an activity which produces and transforms social reality and, in particular, an ideological and moral practice. It is ideological insofar as it defines what is considered real, normal and moral: that is, it seeks to define what ought to be done. In identifying these performative functions (Austin 1962), it is important to analyse the differential use of the word by different social groups and at different historical times. Williams (1985) illustrated the major changes in meaning acquired by key concepts, whereby even if they come into being with very specific uses, they go on to embody more general descriptions of areas of thought and experience. This is the case with the notion of work, which shifted from being understood as a (general) verb (doing something) or a noun (something done) to being construed (metonymic shift) as a social relationship (or rather a form of conceiving a social relationship, regular paid employment characteristic of capitalist mode of production and relationship) (Williams 1985). Therefore, notions such as employment, unemployment or inactivity, worker or proletarian, are interpretations and constructions rather than pre-existing metaphysical essences; they are ways of understanding and evaluating social issues. The categories of employment and unemployment were invented in a context of the spread of an economic model, as is the free market, and a model of thought and social awareness characteristic of modernity, which allowed us to imagine and think of ourselves in terms of autonomous individuality.

These categories are the product of a set of social semantics reinforced, to a large extent, by technologies such as statistics (Desrosières 1993), money (as a common measure for objects that makes it possible to trade them, Simmel 2013) or law (legal acts, Castel 1997). These social engineering exercises, into which the social sciences (statistics, sociology, economics, law) have fed, allow us to think of ourselves (and problematise ourselves) in terms of equivalents (Desrosières 1993). Desrosières analyses the historical conditions that shaped the metonymic operation facilitating the shift from part (singular) to all (general), through techniques such as statistics. This operation not only implies a classification but also entails a moral order[2] that recasts the very role of the institutions producing these classifications. For this reason, the author insists that the discipline of statistics is bound to play a fundamental role in the definition of categories, their coding (attributing a case to a category), statistical objectification and the inference of regular patterns from mathematical formalisations.

Hence, the analytical tools that we use to measure the scale and development of major social problems, such as unemployment or precarity, contribute not only to their measurement but also to what they create in political terms, that is to say territories of imagination and political problematisation. Statistical indicators defining the boundaries between concepts (in the case of unemployment, the responsibility—attitudes and availability—of the unemployed person in a situation of exclusion from the labour market[3]) give rise, at the same time, to the spaces of what is thinkable and problematisable in a social context, turning a technical exercise into an act of moral enquiry (differentiation between 'worthy' and 'unworthy' unemployed people/workers, Salais et al. 1986). From this, one may infer the close relationship between statistics and government that has characterised social security societies: Only those jobless people who had access to the category of unemployed were eligible for social welfare (social protection). Unemployment is not, therefore, only the absence of employment: it is also an act of political denunciation. Employment is not only the exercise of a productive activity in exchange for a wage: it is also a social position. Defining the statistical boundaries of unemployment and employment, as described in this book by Maruani and Meron, Demazière, Prieto and Pérez de Guzmán, and Lallement, is proposed not only as a scientific exercise but also as a social and political action.

The conquest of (connotations of) words thus also implies social conquests. The meaning of notions is not to be found in the notions themselves (something with boundaries delimited by perceived reality), but is the outcome of a social relationship, a power struggle. The sign is an important space for political struggle (Voloshinov 1992). Polysemy is a reflection of the existence of different points of view and of different social positions (Serrano-Pascual et al. 2017). That is why the concepts used to name work and solidarity are highly polysemic; they could be analysed as 'floating signifiers' (their meaning depends on the balance of power between different voices).

This situation explains the hybrid nature of these concepts and the ambiguous reappropriation of meaning by those voices with the greatest capacity to impose symbolic power (Bourdieu 1985). This is the case with the notion of market (through which work was named), which takes on a metaphorical connotation with the emergence of liberal societies (a space of homeostatic self-regulation governed by the providential invisible hand). Market demands are transformed into requirements of nature (Bourdieu 1985), thus hijacking politics (Weiss and Wodak 2000; Fairclough 2000). The use of this metaphor is therefore performative: it has ideological effects such as normalisation, erosion of the sense of responsibility and fostering of passivity.

Changes in the meanings and senses of key notions are nothing other than a reflection and a driver of major changes in power relationships. For this reason, the analysis of trends in word use reflects substantial social changes, and, therefore, words represent the expression of and condition for social changes. As Williams says, 'This does not mean that the language simply reflects the processes of society and history. On the contrary, (....) some important social and historical processes occur within language, in ways which indicate how integral the problems of meanings and of relationships really are. New kinds of relationship, but also new ways of seeing existing relationships, appear in language in a variety of ways: in the invention of new terms (capitalism); in the adaptation and alteration (indeed at times reversal) of older terms (society or individual); in extension (interest) or transfer (exploitation). But also, as these examples should remind us, such changes are not always either simple or final. Earlier and later senses coexist, or become actual alternatives in which problems of contemporary belief and affiliation are contested' (Williams 1985, 22). Hence, analysing the changes undergone by the notion of (un)employment involves an exercise in exploring the basic language used in a central area of the current debates on how to reposition solidarity in political terms. It is not possible to understand power relationships without, at the same time, analysing how they are conceived and represented.

Hence, the interest in analysing the social practices (statistics, social intervention policies, administrative data, social regulations) that make up and contribute to changing common sense and knowledge about unemployment and employment (Salais 2006). The current transformation of the key notions with which work and workers' vulnerability has been named and problematised, rather than merely reflecting on the political invention *of new words and notions* (Durand 2007) to reconceptualise the meaning of social cohesion (entrepreneurability, activation, flexicurity, knowledge-based society, etc.), is the result of the colonisation of old notions by neoliberal connotations. Therefore, it is not only a matter of replacing some key terms for articulating political proposals by others (i.e., productivity vs. distribution of wealth, or individual responsibility vs. collective responsibility), but rather of stressing the displacements and subtle changes of meaning taking place in a series of symbolically highly charged concepts, such as employment and unemployment and the appropriation of *social protection language*.[4]

THE DECONSTRUCTION OF WAGE EMPLOYMENT AS A CENTRAL NORM OF MODERN SOCIETY: POLITICAL IMAGINATION UNDER SIEGE?

To a large extent, the current employment crisis is, therefore, a cultural crisis, a tipping point, where society questions itself and queries its regulatory categories and tools. In this cultural crisis, three cornerstones of the wage-earning society would be particularly affected: collectivisation of work (employment designated under a collectivist framework); the boundaries between categories of employment (employment as a metonymic condition for access to citizenship); unemployment as political denunciation (vulnerability as a collective issue).

Firstly, work (wage employment) became a *political issue* that was central to modern societies. This politicisation of work explains why wage disputes were the central axis of social and political conflicts, the quintessentially problematised space (dependence—heteronomy, equivalence—fairness). The centrality of employment makes protected, regulated employment a central social norm (that which we assume is fair and to be expected) (Prieto 2007).

Secondly, wage-earning status came to be a metonym for work and social recognition, making employment a condition of access to citizenship. Boundaries between categories were clearly delimited, which tended to mean that those who fell within the category (males native to the country in their middle years) were regarded as equivalent subjects. This perspective introduced a homogeneity within categories (the risks facing individuals are treated as equivalent) with a probabilistic, statistical angle on vulnerability (Rosanvallon 1995).

Thirdly, and as a consequence of this semantic exercise of category allocation, unemployment and (in)activity came into being, which, in turn, would delimit the relationships and social positions of employed, unemployed and inactive people and their social relationships. The notion of unemployment emerged as something separate from the category of poverty and inactivity (Demazière and Lallement in this volume). These notions embody an order not only among activities (which activities are more worthy, fair, legitimate), but also among groups of people (which kinds of people are acceptable, respectable, etc.) (see chapters by Prieto and Pérez de Guzmán, and Maruani and Meron). This hierarchy of social groups and gender divisions is a reflection of, but also a condition for, a hierarchy of ethical principles and social values (productive vs. life-sustaining nature).

These three axes, which we will cover in greater detail in the conclusions, and which have mapped out the social grammar of employment, are undergoing substantial reformulation in political terms.

Firstly, one of the most prominent examples of this deconstruction of employment is its increasing individualisation and depoliticisation. The notion of employment is being divorced from the collectivist framework through which it was designated, contributing to its precarisation (deregulation of labour law—dismissal protection law, revision of law protecting non-standard employment, etc.) and weakening collective bargaining tools (reduction of labour costs, lack of regulation of working time and wage reforms).

Secondly, working conditions are increasingly being destandardised, contractual statuses proliferating and becoming diversified, and non-standard situations normalised, at the same time as the boundaries between categories are becoming blurred.

Lastly, we are witnessing a major crisis of the category of unemployment and inactivity, new boundaries between employment/unemployment/inactivity and new ways of naming and denouncing the absence of work. Rather than overcoming the dichotomies and inequalities between social groups, the changes and crises in the categories of non-employment are helping to re-establish them, repositioning women and other vulnerable communities in other, subordinate social categories (underemployment or inactivity).

These three axes basically form the pivotal element of the processes of deconstruction of employment as a political category.

KEY THEMES AND STRUCTURE OF THE BOOK

This book is divided into three main parts, which specifically, albeit in an interrelated way, explore each of the dimensions that make up the deconstruction of employment as a political category.

A process of depoliticisation of work is largely the outcome of changes in the model and organisation of production. Part I deals with general trends of the economic and social paradigm, the emergence of new ways of organising production, the changing forms of work and employment and the normative consequences in terms of reformulation of the way work is conceptualised as the key social sphere to be regulated—depoliticisation of work, the meaning of citizenship and its links with employment. In social narratives, new concepts are emerging: uberisation of the economy, digitalisation of the economy, the platform economy, the 4.0 economy, the sharing economy. These new notions cover a semantic field that refers to new production and management technologies, or, more specifically, to an acceleration and intensification of the processes of production, organisation and labour regulation as they have been evolving since the 1980s. This process of depoliticisation of work has been intensified by the recent economic crisis. These developments have contributed to restricting, and legitimising the reduction of, the role of the State as a mediator and an authority that tames the market (deregulation of labour, privatisation of public services, reduction of the levels of welfare provided by the public authorities, etc.; Peters 2001). This entails a growing power imbalance among the various players involved in labour relations, restricting the autonomy of employees (as they are not free from need) and strengthening the authority of employers (who are being freed of social responsibilities; Brown et al. 2003). This is a process that has been accelerated by the participation of the EU institutions in the new social policy model, particularly in those Member States worst affected by the economic crisis. The first part (Part I) of the book describes and illustrates the extent of these processes, the multiple forms they take and their implications for reformulating the political concept of wage employment and depoliticising its regulation (contributions by Jan Drahokoupil and Brian Fabo, Gérard Valenduc, Luis Enrique Alonso and Vicente Sánchez).

Part II analyses the impact of these changes on the redefinition of the concept of employment, and the growing blurring and dismantling of conceptual and regulatory boundaries between labour-related categories—employment/unemployment/underemployment/self-employment, self-employed worker/wage earner, employment/unemployment, standard/non-standard work, formal/informal work, public/private demands. A growing pressure to reduce labour costs (wage reforms, minimum wages for young people, revision of regulations governing redundancies and non-standard employment contracts, changes in unemployment systems, etc.) and to deregulate labour legislation (working time, non-standard employment dismissal protection law) goes hand in hand with the trend to provide the arrangements known as non-standard labour contracts with greater social guarantees (entitlements and protection associated with the status of salaried worker extended to other categories and non-wage workers) (Célérier et al. 2017). Moreover, the borders between wage employment and other forms of gainful activity (self-employment, employer, underemployment, etc.) and the differences between the regulatory and political conditions governing various kinds of contract (self-employed worker/employee; temporary/open-ended contract) are becoming increasingly porous. These developments increasingly call into question the legal protection associated with the status of wage earner and also the condition of dependency, leading to an overhaul of the political and semantic meaning of the wage-earning condition. The spread of market-based frameworks leads to a process whereby the borderline between the public and private spheres with regard to welfare becomes blurred. The user of public services (the citizen) is gradually becoming a customer, while the worker is turned into an entrepreneur, and society as a whole is increasingly understood in terms of market frameworks. An expression of the process of deconstruction of categories is seen in the individualisation of employment contracts and the reformulation of the legal principle of 'labour dependency' that used to be the cornerstone of the wage-earning condition. New categories of self-employed worker (as, for instance, the 'economically dependent' self-employed) and of wage earner (different forms of incorporation in the labour force: apprenticeship, traineeship, distribution tasks such as messenger, home worker, etc.) lead to a multiplication, hybridisation and heterogenisation of occupational statuses which call into question previous labour categories and radically alter and undermine previous understandings of what it means to be a wage earner. Hence this second part focuses on an analysis of the challenges these developments raise in terms of social regulation and on their implications in the context of studying the tandem of the welfare state and the socialisation of risk (and wage employment) (contributions by Antonio Baylos, Alberto Riesco, Sarah de Heusch and Jean Michel Bonvin).

The exercise of deconstruction of employment arises not only from the crisis of the wage employment category (following the dismantling of its boundaries), as discussed in Part II, but also from that of unemployment and inactivity. Part III analyses the crisis of social categories to describe unfairness—unemployment, inactivity—and the emergence of new categories to enunciate/denounce the (problematic) lack of work as well as the consequences in terms of reformulation of gender relations. It discusses the redefinition of the 'social area' as space for action and intervention. Moreover, it deals with the meaning of these conceptual changes from a gender perspective. Traditional categories such as employment and unemployment are being replaced by new categories including 'part-employed', 'self-employed', 'underemployed', or 'semi-unemployed'. This reformulation of the category of wage employment and other related categories such as unemployment and inactivity is also the result of an increasing emphasis on individuals' responsibility to provide their own welfare and security. An increased contractualisation of welfare is observable, replacing the former insurance-related logic that was based on a regulatory framework governed by *entitlement*. This increasing individualisation of welfare has been channelled into a focus on the accountability of the individual (individualisation of interventions—tailored, client-centred intervention services and greater involvement of the beneficiary—revision of the rules governing incentives to work, limits on the level and duration of benefits, penalty mechanisms, tightening up of the terms of eligibility for benefits, Serrano-Pascual and Magnusson 2007). New concepts have emerged (e.g. activation, entrepreneurship, flexicurity), contributing to a reformulation of the interpretative framework applicable to unemployment. Risk management thus becomes individualised, so that a shift in the moral principles attaching to work is taking place, in the direction of strengthened autonomy and entrepreneurial management of the self—the worker becomes the 'employer of her/himself' (Crespo-Suárez and Serrano-Pascual 2011). These developments mean that the traditional analytical instruments used for analysing and assessing social changes, such as the statistical categories of employment, unemployment, self-employment and inactivity, become less useful or relevant for studying changes in the social landscape as it relates to labour activity. Given the fundamental role played in the construction of categories by the tools—i.e. statistics—used to measure these phenomena (Desrosières 1993), the reformulation of the categories 'employed', 'self-employed', 'inactive' and 'unemployed' will be an important factor in determining how these vitally significant conditions are understood. The criteria used to demarcate a statistical category are not politically neutral, but replicate the position of men and women within the social structure. The deconstruction of these categories encompasses different dimensions, some of which would be essentially political in nature, for statistical construction is a highly political exercise, as this book sets out to show. This redefinition of the language of employment and unemployment has important consequences from the standpoint of social and gender relations. These issues, associated with a reformulation of the social and statistical categories used for studying and questioning social reality, are tackled in this part of the book (contributions by Didier Demazière, Michel Lallement, Margaret Maruani and Monique Meron, Carlos Prieto and Sofia Pérez).

After this Introductory chapter, a first chapter in Part I (Chapter 2) by Jan Drahokoupil (European Trade Union Institute, Brussels) and Brian Fabo (Central European University, Budapest) analyses the impact of the outsourcing and offshoring process on the fragmentation and atomisation of work processes and tasks and the weakening of labour market institutions (territorialised by nature, within the company and in the social state at national level), altering the nature of the employment relationship and the meaning of employment. The rise of collaborative platforms, including crowdsourcing services, as well as the expansion of 'sharing economy' services, raises outsourcing to a new level. These online platforms cut transaction costs, disunite and isolate workers (contracting independent contractors) and step up pressure on wages and working conditions, obliging workers to offer their services as just another piece of merchandise for sale. Additionally, the fragmentation of work explains why tasks associated with labour market entry-level positions are becoming increasingly routine and separated from other processes. These developments often lead to a deconstruction of employment relationships through the circumvention of employee representation, collective bargaining systems and labour market regulations in general, which have constituted the main power resources in the hands of the workers for exercising control over working conditions. This weakening of the collective, politically regulated dimension of work has important implications in terms of precarisation of employment. Jan Drahokoupil and Brian Fabo analyse the interplay between outsourcing and the spatial organisation of labour (shift of activities across company boundaries and to more or less distant locations). They provide an overview of different types of process (international production and the use of shared service centres, and the rise of platforms), discuss the different impacts on the nature of employment and identify the relevant strategic issues for workers as well as the possible regulatory responses. Platforms are thus likely to detract from the main collective tools used by employers.

Chapter 3, by Gérard Valenduc (Louvain University) analyses the consequences of the 'digital turn' in the emergence of new forms of work and employment in the digital economy. The diversification of forms of work—virtual work, on-demand work, crowd working, etc.—and the changing meaning of solidarity at work are intensifying a political process of deconstruction of employment and reformulation of the category of 'worker'. This chapter starts by analysing the significant changes in work organisation resulting from the digitalisation of the economy: the new division of labour across globalised value chains; expansion of the two-sided market, a new economic model of digital platforms; the economic capacity to create value from big data; the development of new activities within the informal economy. These changes foster new forms of work and employment: Internet-based virtual work—digitally working at any time and anywhere; on-demand work through digital platforms; crowd working—outsourcing tasks to a worldwide pool of competing individuals with auction-based payment; 'prosumer' work—unpaid tasks carried out by platform users as 'producers/consumers' of data and services; new forms of labour market intermediation—e-recruitment platforms for professionals, freelancing platforms, establishing private arrangements in relation to wage levels, skill profiles, etc. These trends are calling into question some of the foundations of the employment relationship: the concept of workplace (and working conditions); wage formation; the meaning and measurement of working time; blurring of labour hierarchies; representation of workers' interests; and, more generally, the meaning of work and solidarity at work. These developments contribute towards deconstructing solidarity at work.

Chapter 4, by Luis Enrique Alonso, Universidad Autónoma de Madrid, studies the deconstruction of the pillars underpinning social citizenship in its direct link with work. Current changes in production models are having an impact on the employment mechanisms set up in the past to enhance solidarity. The shift to the liberal rationale, accentuated by the economic crisis, has led to the loss of sovereignty of the nation state in relation to the market, and the removal of the Keynesian social state from regulation of the market (the main mechanism of decommodification and worker empowerment), to become a recommercialising factor that stimulates and reinvigorates the market. This change has had major consequences, in terms of the deconstruction of a wage-earning status that was built around social citizenship guaranteed by the State. Homogenisation of waged workers' labour rights has been replaced by horizontal, vertical and temporal fragmentation, deuniversalisation, precarisation and individualisation of contractual labour situations, giving rise to a crisis of the labour citizenship around which the employment norm had been constructed. This situation has resulted in the disappearance of normative conditions and their proliferation ('bogus' traineeships, bogus self-employment, bogus retirees, etc.), and in individual risk management, which drives those concerned to make adaptability to the market their sole safeguard. This model of labour is established around a division between those with good jobs, fixed contracts, investments in housing, etc., and those with high mortgages, poor jobs and precarious positions in society, in different senses. Individualisation and precarity are redefining the meaning of citizenship. A consequence of this transformation of the social state, the facets of which are extensively explored in this chapter, has been the loss of the collective dimension of the wage-earning status and the depoliticisation of employment.

Chapter 5, by Vicente Sánchez Jimenez, Complutense University of Madrid, deals with the replacement of the central role played by work as a social constructor of solidarity and the weakening of collective frameworks of employment. Until recent years, work represented a fundamental component of the link between individual and society, facilitating both personal stability and the construction of a traditional family unit. This was possible thanks to the maintenance of three basic features of stability (material, temporal and spatial) over the past three decades: employment in the same economic entity in the same place over a whole working life. Work has forfeited its central importance as a mechanism of social cohesion/central sphere on which the social question has hinged. The increasingly strong presence of a widening range of different contractual models weakens the traditional boundaries between categories, such as self-employment and waged employment, formal and informal work or employment and unemployment. This drift leads to a weakening of the legitimacy of social rights and collective bargaining practices as a form of protecting workers and regulating the wage conflict, and to changes in the position of work as one of the main sources of security and stability of industrialised societies. This legitimacy of collective action, which has been the fundamental pillar of trade union activity and protection of workers' rights, has been diminishing. This gradual impairment is much more than a reduction in the value attaching to 'work' as a fundamental element of the social fabric, for it is also exerting a strong influence in the whole area of industrial relations, leading to the formation of new types of labour and employment relationships. It causes, in practice, a deterioration of labour law, as well as a more pronounced imbalance between the two intrinsic subjects of the labour market: employer and employee. Flexibility in labour relations prevents the 'model of individual growth' from continuing as it used to in past decades.

Chapter 6, by Antonio Baylos, University of Castilla la Mancha, analyses the blurring of the boundaries of social categories in relation to protection standards (un-/under-/self-employment/employment). This chapter discusses current changes in the regulation and boundaries of wage earners. Wage employment has been the central paradigm upon which social cohesion and access to citizenship have hinged in European societies. The employment relationship has been typically represented as full-time employment for an unspecified term. The assumptions around which this relationship has taken shape have been: the fact that it was a bilateral employer/employee relationship; uniform treatment, despite possibly diverse employment statuses (collective, homogeneous regulations); and a relationship partially opposed, in regulatory terms, to self-employment (the latter being governed by a civil or commercial contract, as opposed to being a subordinate, subject to labour law).

In the past 25 years, these three principles—bilaterality, homogeneity and comparability in the regulatory treatment and collectivisation of work—were to be challenged. This reappraisal of the cornerstones of the category of work has resulted from the concurrence of three circumstances: firstly, employment policies have encouraged the modernisation of labour law and, through this, the proliferation of non-standard jobs (different from the standardised relationship), the diversification of levels of protection and the gradation of, and inequality in, standards of cover (labour segmentation). Secondly, the reformulation of methods of organisation of production (subcontracting) has led to a metamorphosis of business relationships: fragmentation of individual responsibility and replacement of the bilateral relationship of subordination with a complex web of production networks and flows. Thirdly, the austerity policies following the recent economic crisis, combined with the rise in unemployment rates, have contributed to an increase in the precarisation of work and the dismantling of the boundaries that used to separate regular employment from irregular employment. Contractual statuses are expanding, such as those of the 'bogus self-employed person', the 'parasubordinate' worker or the economically dependent self-employed worker, which challenge the established dichotomies between the legal statuses characterising work as an employee and self-employment. The spread of the entrepreneurial reference system into the political arena, which shifts this discussion into the realm of ideologies, is only accelerating this process of political involution.

This combination of circumstances has culminated in the recommercialisation and depoliticisation of employment, through the reshaping of the assumptions that had formed the central reference system of the employer-employee relationship (typical form of waged work): The criteria forming the basis of the categories by which we have conceptualised work have been challenged; there has been a progressive dismantling of the boundaries between standard and non-standard, regular and irregular, self-employed and employed work, and between employment and unemployment (underemployment), etc.; and the collectivist reference systems that formerly protected work have been weakened.

Chapter 7, by Alberto Riesco-Sanz, Complutense University of Madrid, describes (with dissimilar trends in different EU countries) the extent of, and recent changes in, self-employment in Europe as an expression of the deconstruction of the boundaries of the category of wage employment. The strategies of flexibilisation and cheapening of labour costs, and the recent emphasis placed by employment policies on promoting self-employment, are facilitating the spread of this contractual arrangement based on self-employment. This chapter describes some tensions which characterise this form of employment between, on the one hand, the increasing tendency to extend to non-wage employment statuses the regulatory status associated with the wage-earning condition; and, on the other, the reduction of protective mechanisms and social deconstruction of the wage-earning condition. New ways of organising work are substantially hindering the application of the delimiting principle (access criteria) for wage-earning status (principle of legal subordination). The analysis of the ways in which this relationship between self-employed and waged work is being reshaped is proposed as a connecting thread for identifying and discussing other major changes and developments that could have an impact on employment: proliferation of forms of hybrid employment status; extension of wage employment institutions and, at the same time, precarisation of the traditional employment relationship, other forms of mobilisation of productive capacities that are not linked to the traditional wage-earning condition, etc. Given the current blurring of some formerly restrictive theoretical tenets (e.g. the formal distinction between self-employment and wage employment, or strict adherence to the concept of 'subordination' as it is used in law, etc.), self-employment in Europe is an expression of deeper and more far-reaching changes currently affecting the category of employment.

In Chapter 8, Sarah de Heusch (Smart) offers a social economy perspective on the blurring of boundaries of contracts and hybridisation of social status. Right across Europe, the patchwork of contractual forms has been stitched together in a very similar way: The adjustments made are in keeping with the particular sector of work, with specific occupations, or with specific models of operation (temporary or seasonal work). These adjustments have in their turn further diversified the varying levels of social protection and application of labour law, and contribute to confusion on the part of workers as regards their employment status and their access to social rights. We are witnessing a dissipation of the rights of those people whose careers turn out to be nonlinear, or who earn their living by more than one form of work. This chapter discusses this issue with the specific example of a particularly vulnerable category, artists ('project workers'), who have to deal with a diversification of labour status and a wide range of contractual forms of employment. The sharing economy seeks to respond to the challenges posed by this proliferation of contractual forms of employment and ways of working, and by the individualisation of work, and can contribute to the creation of new forms of solidarity. This chapter describes the experience of the social enterprise Smart, which seeks to promote additional tools for solidarity among freelance workers (services to professionals making their living in the 'creative sector', etc.). One important challenge arising in this context is that of finding the right balance between individuals' freedom of enterprise and appropriate forms of social protection. Rather than proposing a single overall response (to fragmented careers and the simultaneous practice of more than one form of work), case-by-case adjustments to the specific needs of particular groups are proposed.

In Chapter 9, Jean Michel Bonvin (University of Geneva) discusses the contribution of the rise of the managerial state to the redefinition of the terms and assumptions of the Fordist notion of employment (security/subordination) and of the welfare state (the governing principle of public services). During the past two to three decades, significant reforms of the public administration have tended towards the introduction of market logic within the public sector ('new public management'). The blurring of employment and regulatory categories is affecting the boundaries between the public (public action) and private (market demands) normative frameworks, as well as the citizen-consumer divide. The rise of the managerial state aims to increase responsiveness of public services in order to respond to the criticism raised by public choice and principal–agent theories, which assume a tendency on the part of 'street-level bureaucrats' to pursue their own interests instead of the public good, resulting in inefficiency. The managerial state aims at reforming the modes of operation of the public administration and the working conditions of public employees with a view to increasing efficiency in the use of public money. By this means, the notion of 'public employment' (as well as the principles governing the welfare state) is significantly deconstructed. Public employment is not to be conceived as a status providing social protection, but as a contract (entitlements are conditional upon reaching certain targets). Market mechanisms (management by numbers and incentives, benchmarking competition with other providers, management by objectives, provision agreements, performance pay, bonuses or penalties, annual evaluations, etc.) are introduced within the public sector to discipline public agents (persuade them to act in an expected way). The introduction of these mechanisms tends to fade the divide between public and private employment conditions and subsequently homogenise the notion of employment in favour of the market criteria for performance and productivity. Public employment is not conceived as a support for solidarity and social rights (civic frameworks) but as governed by a market order (merit and performance). As a result of the blurring of the citizen-consumer divide, citizenship no longer means participating in public debates, but emerges through consumer choice. Public services are not decommoditising tools, but objects of market transactions. As a consequence, the divide between citizen (political and civic logic) and consumer (market logic) is becoming porous, creating the hybrid category of citizen-consumer.

In Part III, Chapter 10, Didier Demazière (CNRS-CSO, Sciences Po, Paris) discusses the boundaries of the notion and category of unemployment as a social category from two perspectives: institutional construction and biographical experience. Unemployment is not only a statistical category (a shared representation) but also a resource for taking action: where classifications are created, phenomena are made visible. Tracing the borders between categories is a social and political act. The work on boundaries is carried out by institutional stakeholders, who define the rules for managing the unemployed, but also by those who actually experience joblessness. This chapter aims to question the current deconstruction of employment, placing the focus of this work on semantic borders. Unemployment is a social (spatially and temporally situated) construct, and not a market phenomenon. Accordingly, these boundaries must be regarded as subject to evolution, fluctuation and process. Demazière analyses work on the borders of unemployment first in its institutional dimension and then in its biographical dimension. The former focuses on the dynamic interplay of rules stemming from the principle of status regulation and entitlement to material resources (unemployment benefits and employment policy measures, in particular). The second considers the experiences and subjective identities that fuel the ways in which the unemployed themselves seek to make sense of their condition (their need to belong to an identifiable group or category) and to devise projects for their own future (jobs to which they might aspire). The chapter shows that these two types of border (institutional and symbolic) actually evolve in opposite directions, narrowing down unemployment on the one hand and expanding it on the other. The boundary operates in two distinct ways (metaphors): one that forms barriers and separates, like a door; and another that opens up space and permits circulation, like a bridge. Their combination signals the joint presence of, on the one hand, the processes of construction and, on the other, those of deconstruction set in motion by unemployment.

In Chapter 11, Michel Lallement (Lise-CNRS, Cnam, Paris) discusses the erosion of the pillars that used to underpin the category of unemployment and the possibility of speaking the language of unemployment based on the French experience. This chapter focuses principally on the cognitive challenge posed by the category 'unemployment'. We have witnessed a step-by-step calling into question of the various criteria that, initially, enabled a distinction to be drawn between unemployment and other forms of labour-related status such as 'of no occupation'. Lallement analyses the changes undergone by the noun 'unemployment' in terms of three linguistic registers: semantics (the criteria used to define joblessness have been called into question: it is neither temporary, nor does it imply a homogeneous category); syntax (changes in the relationship among the categories themselves and the blurring of the boundaries between inactivity, joblessness and employment; spread of ambivalent and intermediate statuses between employment, unemployment and inactivity) and pragmatics (transformation of the measurement tools and of the unemployment statistics by moving those affected into other categories). New indicators have been forged to provide a more accurate or nuanced account of changes in the territory of joblessness (unemployment, employment, inactivity and the many grey areas surrounding them). The constant to- and fro-ing between the search for the right figures and the strategic use made of indicators by institutional stakeholders are an expression of the radical structural changes that, over the decades, have led to deconstruction of the criteria by which, from the twenty-first century onwards, the category of unemployment was delimited (temporary, involuntary, able-bodied). The new elements used today to classify the jobless population hardly lend themselves to the construction of a new reliable, credible category of unemployment. This observation receives further confirmation when, as testified in particular by the rise in the numbers of 'working poor', the boundaries between employment, activity and unemployment are becoming increasingly porous. Has the time come to do away entirely with the term 'unemployment' in favour of an alternative semantic form?

Margaret Maruani (Paris Descartes University) and Monique Meron (INSEE), in Chapter 12, analyse the political nature of the production of (statistical) categories with the specific example of counting the numbers of women at work in France. The statistical criteria used to define the categories of wage employment, unemployment and underemployment actually reflect, but also contribute to establishing, the place of professional and domestic work in the social hierarchy, as well as the respective political strengths of gender groups. By studying the statistics of women's occupational activity over time, it would be possible to learn much about the history of their status. This chapter sets out to develop this reflection through reference to the historical development of ways of naming and codifying women's professional activity in France. Naming is shown to have a performative (or political) effect. Changes in the ways that employment has been named and measured (observed through analysis of the evolution of the statistical categories used for the purpose of labour market administration) have, in the past, made the work of women less visible. At the beginning of the twentieth century, the majority of women worked in the home, in agricultural labour or as the isolated recipients of pay for piecework. As from the beginning of the twentieth century, population censuses illustrate the difficulty of specifying what, in the case of women, counts as, and is referred to as, 'work'. Statistics since the beginning of the twenty-first century have, on the contrary, focused on 'employment at all cost', such being the approach demanded by European policy priorities. Recent changes in the statistical procedures and source questionnaires used serve to alter the official vision of the labour market, in particular where women are concerned. Two dimensions are analysed: firstly, growth of the 'unemployment halo' (individuals who want to work but who are not included in the unemployed category), and secondly, the increase in underemployment and the blurring of its boundaries. Both trends affect women in particular. The new criteria used for classification as 'unemployed' or underemployed cause more women than men to be taken out of labour market statistics. Records of women's labour constitute a major thread for understanding the place of women in society. For this reason, Maruani and Meron underline, definition of the statistical (and linguistic) boundaries of women's employment is, first and foremost, a political issue.

In Chapter 13, Carlos Prieto (Complutense University of Madrid) and Sofía Pérez de Guzmán (University of Cádiz) reflect on the transformation in the meaning of work beyond the institutional sphere from the standpoint of gender relations and differences. This chapter shows how 'naming' does much more than produce 'common sense' on work. It produces, at the same time, a social order, in other words, a definition of norms and a hierarchy of values between active principles (caring, producing) and between groups of people (men and women). Changes in the norm of employment and of care result from the balance of power and they contribute to a strengthening or questioning of the power relationships concerned. The reformulation of the concept of employment (from the wage-led standard to a flexible standard) and of care (from the patriarchal to a more egalitarian one) have not redressed the power *im*balance between men and women. They have, rather, fostered a different imbalance along new lines of fracture and inequality in both the economic realm (concentration of non-standard work amongst women) and in the domestic sphere (diversity of ethics—from 'what ought to be' to 'what is'—of caring according to gender). Two issues are addressed in this chapter in order to develop and illustrate this argument. The contribution describes, first of all, the main lines of change experienced in relation to the concept and social norm constituted by wage employment: from strong employment and low unemployment rates, to precarious employment together with high unemployment and weak employment. An in-depth analysis of changes in any social configuration (norm) of employment additionally requires an analysis of the social configuration of the categories of population among which it takes shape (the hierarchical connections of the domestic social order). These categories distinguish themselves by, among other important features, their different understanding of—and inclination to perform—work. The second focus in this chapter is an analysis of the divergent relationship that men and women establish with work and employment and different meanings they attribute to them. Differing conceptions of—and relationships with—work and employment exist, and are manifested and reproduced within family life. These differences are bound to be reflected in, and to foster, in terms of gender, the social configuration of employment that is evident in the institutional sphere.

In the final part of the book, Amparo Serrano-Pascual (Complutense University of Madrid) and Maria Jepsen (ETUI and Free University of Brussels) (Chapter 14) draw some conclusions, recapping on and discussing the main topics addressed in the book, and putting forward some thoughts on the conceptual and ideological dimensions of these developments, as well as their social and political implications.

Therefore, on the basis of the analytical approach proposed, this book starts out from the principle that changes in the language and grammar of employment result from substantial shifts in the balance of power, while simultaneously entailing important changes in the possibility of thinking about and striving to mitigate social vulnerability. The book seeks to elaborate a meta-analysis of the categories in question and the basic assumptions underlying the discussions that, through an approach that is simultaneously interdisciplinary and transcultural, analyses the modes of theorising and problematising employment and the shifts undergone by the category of 'worker' (destandardisation of the employment norm; recasting of its traditional status as a pivotal element of social cohesion; crisis of the category of employment, unemployment and inactivity and proliferation of new ways of naming social cohesion and its link with employment). This question is of particular relevance in so far as supranational institutions like the European Union see promotion of the digital economy, entrepreneurship and alternative ways of working as an overriding policy priority (European Commission 2016); and yet it would seem utterly impossible to formulate viable policy proposals for tackling issues of vulnerability, precariousness, unemployment and social exclusion on the basis of categories that are themselves in the throes of radical social, economic and political reformulation.[5]

NOTES

1. Most of the issues discussed refer to more general trends permeating European societies, but some of these contributions are more specifically focused on particular countries, especially Spain: It was felt that a study of these processes in a southern European country that was especially seriously affected by the economic crisis allowed us to provide a more salient illustration of the role played by the economic crisis in the process of deconstruction of employment as a political issue.
2. According to Desrosières: 'The word "category" itself is derived from the Greek term "kategoria", which refers to a judgement rendered in a public arena' (1993, 261).
3. The notion of unemployment emerges when it is distinguished from the semantic field of poverty, and, with this semantic shift, the social classification criterion ceases to be personal shortcomings, and shifts to the position of these individuals as seen in terms of the labour market. The problematising exercise moves away from a moralising perspective and towards the operation of the labour market (Gautié 2002).
4. 'Social protection language' refers to terms which define the legitimising discourses of social protection. It is not the objective of this chapter to enter into this prolific debate about the terms that defined this social language and the sociopolitical conditions which favoured the hegemony of these legitimising discourses, but for further information we refer the reader to authors such as Alonso and Conde (1996), Castel (1997), Donzelot (1984), Lecerf (2002), Salais et al. (1986), etc.
5. Translation from the Spanish by Sally Blaxland.

REFERENCES

Alonso, Luis Enrique, and Fernando Conde. 1996. "Las paradojas de la glo-balización: la crisis del estado del bienestar nacional y las regiones vulnerables." *Estudios regionales* 44: 87–124.

Angenot, Marc. 2010. *El discurso social. Los límites históricos de lo pensable y lo decible.* Buenos Aires: Siglo XXI.

Austin John, L. 1962. *How to Do Things with Words.* Oxford: Oxford University Press.

Bourdieu, Pierre. 1985. *¿Qué significa hablar.?* Madrid: Akal.

Brown, Phillip, Anthony Hesketh, and Sara Williams. 2003. "Employability in a Knowledge-Driven Economy." *Journal of Education and Work* 16 (2): 107–126.

Cabrera, Miguel Angel. 2001. *Historia, lenguaje y sociedad.* Valencia: Frónesis.

Castel, Robert. 1997. *Las metamorfosis de la cuestión social. Una crónica del salariado.* Buenos Aires: Paidós.

Célérier, Sylvie, Alberto Riesco-Sanz, and Pierre Rolle. 2017. "Trabajo autónomo y transformación del salariado: las reformas española y francesa." *Cuadernos de Relaciones Laborales* 35 (2): 393–414.

Certeau, Michel de. 1990. *L'invention du quotidien.* Paris: Galimard.

Crespo-Suárez, Eduardo, and Amparo Serrano-Pascual. 2011. "Regulación del trabajo y el gobierno de la subjetividad: la psicologización política del trabajo." In *Perspectivas recientes y críticas en la Psicología Social actual,* edited by Anastasio Ovejero, 246–263. Madrid: Biblioteca Nueva.

Degryse, Christophe. 2016. "Digitalisation of the Economy and Its Impact on the Labour Market." ETUI Working Paper 2016.02.

Desrosières, Alain. 1993. *La politique des grand nombres.* Paris: La Découverte.

Donzelot, Jacques. 1984. *L'invention du social. Essai sur le déclin des passions politiques.* Paris: Fayard.

Durand, Pascal. 2007. *Les nouveaux mots du pouvoir. Abécédaire critique.* Bruxelles: Éd. Aden.

Dyer-Witheford, Nick. 2015. *Cyber-Proletariat: Global Labour in the Digital Vortex (Digitial Barricades: Interventions in Digital Culture and Politics).* Canada: Pluto Press.

European Commission. 2016. "Digitising European Industry Reaping the Full Benefits of a Digital Single Market." Communication from the Commission to the European Parliament, the Council, the European Economic and Social Committee and the Committee of the Regions. SWD(2016) 110 final. Brussels, 19.4.2016 COM(2016) 180 final. http://eur-lex.europa.eu/legal-content/EN/TXT/PDF/?uri=CELEX:52016DC0180&from=EN.

Fairclough, Norman. 2000. *New Labour, New Language?* London: Routledge.

Gautié, Jérôme. 2002. "De l'invention du chômage à sa déconstruction." *Genèses* 46: 60–76.

Gold, Lorna. 2004. *The Sharing Economy: Solidarity Networks Transforming Globalisation.* USA: Ashgate.

Huws, Ursula. 2001. "The Making of the Cybertariat: Virtual Work in a Real World." *Socialist Register* 37: 1–23.

Huws, Ursula. 2014. *Labour in the Global Digital Economy: The Cyvertariat Coms of Age.* New York: Monthly Review Press.

Jepsen, Maria, and Amparo Serrano-Pascual. 2011. "El modelo social europeo. La frágil producción política de un proyecto social europeo." *Pasajes* 35: 53–66.

Lecerf, Eric. 2002. *Le sujet du chômage.* París: L'Harmattan.

Lindesmith, Alfred R., Anselm L. Strauss, and Norman K. Denzin. 2006. *Psicología Social.* Madrid: Centro de Investigaciones Sociológicas.

Méda, Dominique. 1998. *Le travail, une valeur en voie de disparition.* Paris: Champs Flammarion.

OECD. 2016. *New Forms of Work in the Digital Economy.* Directorate for Science, Technology and Innovation Committee on Digital Economy Policy. http://www.oecd.org/officialdocuments/publicdisplaydocumentpdf/?cote=DSTI/ICCP/IIS(2015)13/FINAL&docLanguage=En.

Peters, Michael. 2001. "Education, Enterprise Culture and the Entrepreneurial Self: A Foucauldian Perspective." *Journal of Educational Enquiry* 2 (2): 58–71.

Piore, Michael J. 1987. "Historical Perspectives and the Interpretation of Unemployment." *Journal of Economic Literature* 25 (4): 1834–1850.

Pongratz, Hans J., and Gunter Voß. 2003. "From Employee to Entreployee." *Concepts and Transformation* 8 (3): 239–254.

Prieto, Carlos. 2007. "Del estudio del empleo como norma social al de la sociedad como orden social." *Papeles del CEIC* 2007/1.

Prieto, Carlos. 2014. "From Flexicurity to Social Employment Regimes." In *Deconstructing Flexicurity and Developing Alternative Approaches,* edited by Maarten Keune and Amparo Serrano-Pascual, 47–68. New York: Routledge.

Rosanvallon, Pierre. 1995. *La nouvelle question sociale. Repenser l'Etat Providence.* Paris: Seuil.

Rose, Nikolas. 1996. *Inventing Our Selves: Psychology, Power and Personhood.* New York: Cambridge University Press.

Salais, Robert. 2006. "Reforming the European Social Model and the Politics of Indicators: From the Unemployment Rate to the Employment Rate in the European Employment Strategy." In *Unwrapping the European Social Model,* edited by Maria Jepsen and Amparo Serrano-Pascual. Bristol: Polity Press.

Salais, Robert, Baverez Nicolas, and Reynaud Bénédicte. 1986. *L'invention du chômage. Histoire et transformations d'une catégorie en France des années 1890 aux années 1980.* Paris: Presses Universitaires de France.

Schol, Trebor. 2013. *Digital Labor: The Internet as Playground and Factory*. New York: Routledge.

Schutz, Alfred. 1999. *El forastero. Ensayo de Psicología Social*. Madrid: Amorrortu Editores.

Serrano-Pascual, Amparo, and Lars Magnusson, eds. 2007. *Reshaping Welfare States and Activation Regimes in Europe*. Bruselas: P.I.E. Peter Lang.

Serrano-Pascual, Amparo, Maarten Keune, and Eduardo Crespo-Suárez. 2017. "The Paradoxical Ways of Naming Employment by EU Institutions During the Crisis: The Weakening of Collective Frames." *Stato e mercato* 110: 223–246.

Simmel, Georg. 2013. *La filosofía del dinero*. Madrid: Capitan Swing.

Standing, Guy. 2011. *The Precariat*. London: Bloomsbury Academic.

Sundararajan, Arun. 2016. *The Sharing Economy: The End of Employment and the Rise of Crowd Based Capitalism*. Cambridge: The MIT Press.

Valenduc, Gérard, and Patricia Vendramin. 2016. "Work in the Digital Economy: Sorting the Old from the New." ETUI Working Paper.

Voloshinov, Valentin N. 1929/1992. *El marxismo y la filosofía del lenguaje*. Madrid: Alianza.

Weiss, Gilbert, and Ruth Wodak. 2000. "European Union Discourses on Employment. Strategies of Depolitizing and Ideologizing Employment Policies." *Concepts and Transformation* 5 (1): 29–42.

Williams, Raymond. 1985. *Keywords. A Vocabulary of Culture and Society*. New York: Oxford University Press.

PART I

Rehabilitation of the 'Labour World' as a Locus for Action and Intervention

Outsourcing, Offshoring and the Deconstruction of Employment: New and Old Challenges

Jan Drahokoupil and Brian Fabo

Outsourcing, defined as a shift of activities performed within a company to its suppliers, has become widespread. This diffusion has been facilitated by advances in information and communication technology (ICT). Such advances have also enabled further splintering of work processes into tasks that can then be outsourced or shifted in space, including across borders. Production networks in many sectors have thus become increasingly fragmented. Outsourcing has also been pursued by public sector organisations. Moreover, recent advances in ICT have enabled the rise of so-called online outsourcing platforms, including crowdsourcing services such as Amazon Mechanical Turk and on-demand freelancing

J. Drahokoupil (✉)
European Trade Union Institute, Brussels, Belgium

B. Fabo
National Bank of Slovakia, Bratislava, Slovakia

B. Fabo
Central European Labour Studies Institute, Bratislava, Slovakia

© The Author(s) 2019
A. Serrano-Pascual and M. Jepsen (eds.),
The Deconstruction of Employment as a Political Question,
https://doi.org/10.1007/978-3-319-93617-8_2

33

platforms like Upwork. These developments seem to be taking outsourcing to a new level, in that such platforms enable access to labour directly through self-employment rather than via reliance on subcontractors as in traditional outsourcing.

Cutting labour costs by lowering pay, increasing work intensity and/ or shifting flexibility costs onto workers are just some of the motivations behind decisions to shift work across company boundaries and in space. But these decisions often lead to a deconstruction of the employment relationship through circumvention of labour market regulations and of institutions of employee representation and collective bargaining, which are territorial in nature and also often restricted by the boundaries of the firm. Any change in company boundaries and the geography of work is thus likely to impact on employment, working conditions and industrial relations.

This contribution analyses the interplay between outsourcing and the spatial organisation of work. We provide an overview of different types of process that shift work across company boundaries and in space, discuss the different impacts on the nature of employment and identify the relevant strategic issues for workers as well as the possible regulatory responses. We argue that outsourcing and also offshoring epitomise a variety of mechanisms through which the institutions that have been established to regulate the employment relationship can be evaded, leading to negative effects on pay and working conditions. In this context, technology plays an important role not only in helping to undermine the political basis of the employment relationship, but also in weakening its economic rationale. More specifically, the use of technology reduces the transaction costs involved in accessing labour through the market mechanism and in coordinating activities across space. As evidenced by the example of platforms, technology can also address market failures that provided the economic rationale for the employment relationship. Finally, given the territorial nature of existing regulatory mechanisms, the spatial dimension is key to understanding the impact of outsourcing, as well as the possibilities for addressing such practices through regulatory responses.

We start with a discussion of the variety of processes involved in traditional outsourcing and offshoring, present evidence of their prevalence and their impact on working conditions and employment relations, and consider the mediating role of institutions and the strategies pursued by trade unions and other employee representatives. Following the same structure, we then consider the role played by online outsourcing platforms.

This allows us to assess the extent to which they represent a new challenge requiring new regulatory responses.

Outsourcing and Offshoring: Challenging Institutions Regulating Employment

Outsourcing and offshoring refer to a number of related, yet distinct, processes involving restructuring of work organisation and a shift of activities across company boundaries and in space. First, defined as shifting of activities performed within a company over to its suppliers, outsourcing can be related to very different types of company restructuring. On one end of the spectrum, an integrated company may decide to spin off activities that can be relatively independent from other lines of business. Similarly, a multinational corporation may decide to supply markets in some regions through independent resellers, or indeed to leave a market entirely. Further, outsourcing may involve vertical disintegration of the value chain when a company focuses on a narrower segment of activities and transfers such activities as production or distribution to other companies. Then, on the other side of the spectrum, there is outsourcing of primary value creation activities within core business areas (so-called strategic outsourcing). This also includes the unbundling of business support processes such as IT, customer services, invoicing or accounting. This kind of outsourcing can also involve relying on workers hired through labour market intermediaries (agency workers) or on the self-employed to perform core activities. It is this side of the spectrum that is likely to directly impact on working conditions and employment relations and where the decision to outsource is often motivated by the desire to sidestep labour market institutions and achieve savings by lowering the quality of working conditions.

The second distinction to consider is that between outsourcing and offshoring (see Table 2.1). Outsourcing refers to externalising in-house activities to suppliers (the 'make or buy' decisions), who may be located in the same country (or even on the same production site) or abroad. Offshoring refers to the relocation of activities to other (lower-cost) countries, although the foreign suppliers may be part of the same company as the outsourcer.

Both outsourcing and offshoring influence the effectiveness of existing worker representation structures and collective bargaining

Table 2.1   Outsourcing and offshoring

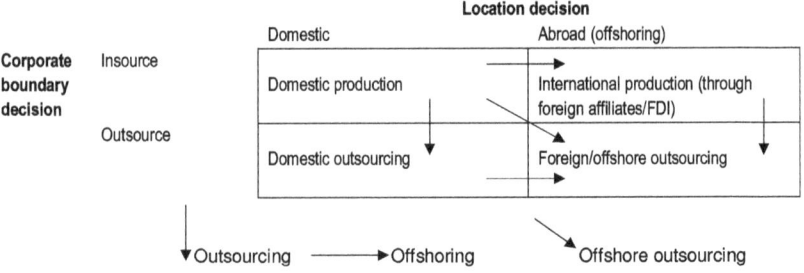

Source Drahokoupil (2015a), adapted from Sako (2005) and Olsen (2006)

institutions and hence the ability of workers to exert control over their working conditions. While outsourcing involves the transfer of activities and workers to outside the scope of company-level employment relations institutions, offshoring goes one step further, involving a shift to a different regulatory regime. Transnational employment relations institutions, such as European works councils (EWCs) and transnational company agreements, where they exist, become relevant in the case of offshoring to foreign subsidiaries.

Outsourcing decisions are often directly motivated by the attempt to circumvent company-level employment relations institutions and/or national labour market regulations (Batt and Nohara 2009; Crouch et al. 2009; Doellgast et al. 2009; Holst 2014; Drahokoupil 2015b). The weakening of worker representation structures and the undermining of trade union strategies through restructuring by outsourcing can exacerbate the negative impact of outsourcing and offshoring on working conditions. In the US context, Weil (2014) demonstrated that businesses, and 'lead firms' in particular, have used subcontracting, franchising and supply chain management to cut labour costs by ridding themselves of the responsibilities inherent in managing their workforces (see also Kalleberg 2013; Warhurst et al. 2012, arrived at similar findings on the basis of evidence from across the world).

Offshoring and outsourcing can limit the bargaining power of workers in multiple ways. The spectre of restructuring can be used by managements to obtain concessions in collective bargaining by threatening job losses (e.g. Doellgast and Greer 2007; Flecker 2009). In such situations, trade unions sometimes choose to protect core workers by allowing the use of peripheral workers, typically employed under inferior conditions with weaker employment protection. The use of agency workers as a flexibility buffer is now widespread in the automotive sector. Other mechanisms include a strategic deployment of markup across the production network of the firm in order to undercut rent extraction potential in affiliates where workers enjoy stronger bargaining power, as has been the experience in the North American automotive sector (Sly and Soderbery 2014).

Finally, the effects of outsourcing and offshoring in terms of their implications for industrial relations and the applicability of labour market regulations become blurred when outsourcing is used to import workers from abroad. Subcontracting to transnational labour market intermediaries has been used to circumvent host-country employment regulations and to arbitrage between different regulatory environments (Lillie and Wagner 2015; see also Bernaciak 2015). The challenges involved in integrating migrant workers into national industrial relations structures have limited effectiveness of the national institutions (e.g. Danaj and Sippola 2015).

Such 'double mobility' (Altreiter et al. 2015) is a particular challenge for employment relations. While the threat of relocation gives employers the upper hand, labour mobility provides access to skills and hence undermines the 'power of the place', leaving workers divided and willing to accept inferior conditions and pay. Such a configuration facilitates 'hyper-Taylorist' work practices, extensive working hours, extended control over workers and extreme numerical flexibility. 'Double mobility' is enabled by outsourcing to labour market intermediaries providing access to workers from outside the location. These also 'immobilise' foreign labour through specific accommodation arrangements.

THE EXTENT OF OUTSOURCING AND OFFSHORING

The extent of outsourcing and offshoring differs substantially across countries. This reflects the fact that the decision by companies to engage in outsourcing and offshoring reflects national institutional opportunities and constraints. Companies in different countries thus resort to different forms of flexibility in accordance with national conditions (e.g. Flecker 2009; Lallement 2011). Studies confirm substantial national diversity, but they have not found a dominant pattern explaining this diversity (e.g. Mol et al. 2014).

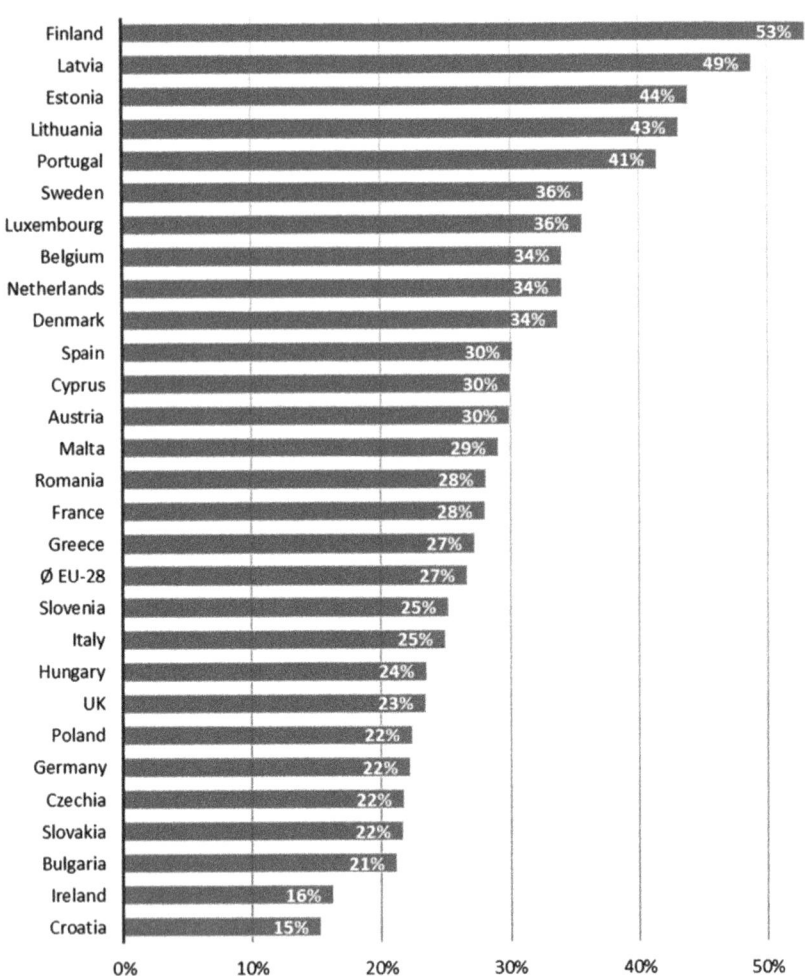

Fig. 2.1 Outsourcing of production of goods or services in the EU-28 (*Note* ECS 2013, own calculations, weighted by establishment; *N*: 23, 326; chi2 P=0.0000; countries in ascending order of percentages; excluding public service cases)

The analysis by Kirchner (2015) enables a comparison of differences in the extent of outsourcing in EU member states and between individual economic sectors. The analysis draws on the 2013 European Company Survey, a data set that allows a unique comparison across all member states. It shows that the extent of outsourcing is high in Nordic

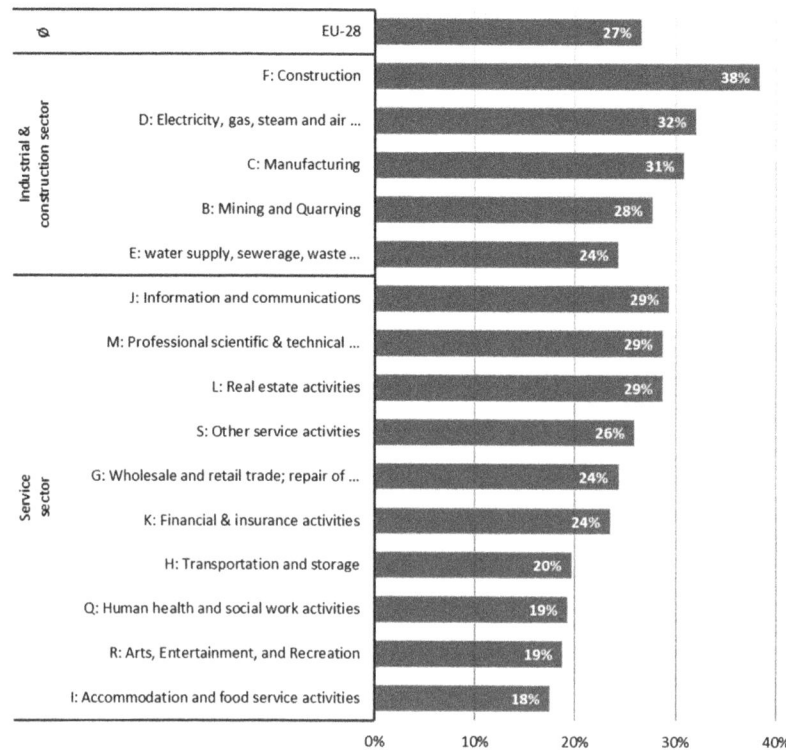

Fig. 2.2 Industries and the outsourcing of the production of goods or services in the EU-28 (*Note* ECS 2013, own calculations, weighted by establishment; N: 23, 326; chi2 P = 0.0000; excluding public service cases)

countries and the Baltic States and low in Central and Eastern Europe, whereby the latter seems to remain primarily a European offshoring destination (see Fig. 2.1).

The differences between countries remain even when controlled for company size, skill content and industry composition. In fact, outsourcing levels across sectors in a given country are closely related. The manufacturing, ICT and construction sectors tend to outsource the most (Fig. 2.2). The overall picture is thus of highly country-specific outcomes, apparently shaped by national institutions and regulations.

These, for instance, structure incentives for companies in terms of access to alternative flexibility arrangements.

THE IMPACT ON EMPLOYMENT AND WORKING CONDITIONS

Popular attention has for the most part been devoted to offshoring processes because they involve a direct transfer of jobs abroad. The impact of offshoring, or offshore outsourcing, on employment, inequality and productivity has been studied extensively, with most studies showing an inequality-enhancing effect, consistent with the theoretical expectation that trade will increase the relative wages of high-skilled workers. Workers exposed to offshoring experience substantial income losses as a result of unemployment (see an overview in Hummels et al. 2016).

Empirical evidence suggests that low-skilled workers are the losers from offshoring in many countries (e.g. Feenstra and Hanson 1996; Geishecker et al. 2010; Hijzen et al. 2005). For instance, Hummels et al. (2013) demonstrate on the basis of Danish data that low-skilled workers displaced from firms that are hit by an offshoring shock lose 21% of earnings in the year after displacement, while five years after displacement these workers are still substantially below their pre-displacement earnings. Some studies also show a negative impact on high-skilled workers, especially in services,[1] while the evidence regarding the overall demand for labour remains inconclusive. The productivity effects of offshore outsourcing reveal no clear pattern, with somewhat greater positive effects in services (Olsen 2006).

The impact of domestic outsourcing has been studied less extensively because it is more difficult to measure. Documenting a dramatic growth of domestic outsourcing in Germany since the early 1990s, Goldschmidt and Schmieder (2015) showed that wages in outsourced jobs fall by approximately 10–15% relative to similar jobs that are not outsourced. Their study also found evidence that the wage losses associated with outsourcing stem from a loss of firm-specific rents, suggesting that labour cost savings are an important reason why firms choose to contract out these services. Outsourcing has also contributed to the increase in German wage inequality, with outsourcing of cleaning, security and logistics services alone accounting for around 10% of the inequality increase since the 1980s.

The impact of outsourcing and offshoring on working conditions and industrial relations has featured less prominently in outsourcing/

offshoring research. Available evidence is based mainly on comparative case studies. ETUI's outsourcing project has collected international comparative case-study evidence providing an overview of the impact of outsourcing in a range of sectors, including logistics and food, customer service in public services, IT departments in health call centres in telecommunications, public services construction, meat processing and shipbuilding (Drahokoupil 2015b). The studies consistently reported a deterioration of employment terms and conditions, including a negative impact on job quality, increased risk of stress in both the sending and destination locations, less satisfying job content with fewer opportunities for learning, and declining pay and working conditions for lower-skilled workers and those who were more easily outsourceable.

As discussed above, the decline in job quality is often related to the avoidance of firm-level bargaining (or public sector collective agreements) and national industrial relations institutions, as well as to benchmarking and concession bargaining. At the same time, reorganisation of labour processes is in fact a key mechanism through which outsourcing and offshoring may directly impact working conditions and job quality. In this context, a distinction between outsourcing and the integration of work processes is useful (see Table 2.2). It is particularly relevant for understanding the outsourcing of such business services as IT or the creation of shared service centres (business process outsourcing).[2] Profound transformation of the labour process is required to allow certain tasks to be separated from others in the sending location (Ramioul and Van Hootegem 2015).

In fact, companies may decide to centralise some activities without actually outsourcing them, aiming to achieve economies of scale and/ or specialisation benefits. This can have a similar transformational impact

Table 2.2 Outsourcing and integration/transformation of the labour process

		Organization of the work process	
		Do not transform	Integrate/transform
Corporate boundary decision	Insource	In house, disintegrated	Integrated service provision (in-house service/activity centres)
	Outsource	Outsourced, disintegrated	Outsourced integrated services

Source Drahokoupil (2015a), adapted from Gospel and Sako (2010)

on work processes and job quality to outsourcing itself, whereby activities remain in-house, though possibly shifted to another location. At the same time, companies may outsource and shift activities such as HR-related processes without necessarily integrating them. Such separation is also likely to affect labour processes and job quality, and it may represent a first step towards creating an (external) integrated services centre (cf. Gospel and Sako 2010).

THE ROLE OF INSTITUTIONS AND WORKER STRATEGIES

The factors and processes that condition and mediate outsourcing and offshoring outcomes, including the role of institutions and actors, remain understudied. Quantitative evidence is particularly limited and somewhat mixed. For instance, Kramarz (2008) found on the basis of French data that wages are higher in firms with stronger unions, with offshoring variables having no statistically significant effects on wages. At the same time, these firms experienced decreases in employment and increases in offshoring during the period 1986–1992. Milberg and Winkler's (2013, 190–204) analysis of OECD countries from 2000 to 2008 showed that public expenditure on labour market protection increased the positive impact of offshoring on the share of employee compensation in gross value added (labour share), and that employment protection legislation had no effect in this context (although it had a negative impact when the period from 1991 onwards was included). Their analysis also demonstrated that offshoring is associated with less economic insecurity (and a higher labour share) in countries with more supportive labour market institutions (i.e., the 'Rhineland model', including Belgium, Germany, Austria and Sweden, and the 'flexicurity model', including Denmark, Finland and the Netherlands). Union density had positive effects in all these authors' models, except for the Mediterranean countries. The positive effect of unions appeared stronger the more flexible were the labour market institutions.

Geishecker et al. (2010) observed the effect of labour market institutions in their comparison of offshoring's impact on wages in Denmark, the United Kingdom (UK) and Germany. International outsourcing had little impact on wages in Denmark, where they were quite rigid in contrast to employment protection; hence, adjustments were expected to mainly concern labour quantity as opposed to price. In the UK, with its flexible labour markets, wages for both high- and low-skilled workers were reduced by outsourcing to Eastern Europe, while skilled workers benefited from outsourcing to (more advanced) non-Eastern European countries. In Germany, high-skilled workers were negatively affected by outsourcing to Eastern Europe, while low-skilled workers faced reductions in wages as a result of outsourcing to non-Eastern European countries.

Comparative case-study evidence shows that effective worker involvement in outsourcing decisions, planning and implementation is a key precondition for satisfactory outcomes for workers (Drahokoupil 2015b). Moreover, their involvement is often crucial for the success of the outsourcing processes also from the perspective of the company (Giustiniano et al. 2015). Worker voice thus represents a collective good in many respects. However, effective worker involvement institutions are challenged by changing company boundaries and increasing production network fragmentation.

Trade unions have a key role to play in ensuring that the institutional base for effective worker representation remains relevant. However, experience underlines the need to employ innovative strategies to reach peripheral workers and to organise and mobilise across company boundaries (Drahokoupil 2015b). There are examples of successful strategies that managed to extend collective representation and legal protection to externalised groups, often by availing of non-traditional tools such as public shaming. However, in the end, some campaigns proved to be more effective than others. Many successful campaigns relied on the historic bargaining power of unions in incumbents to negotiate limits on externalisations (Doellgast et al. 2015). The underlying problem is a lack of effective institutions that could enable representation of workers across firm and national boundaries.

The examples of effective worker representation in fragmented value chains typically combine effective organising with a reliance on supportive institutions and regulations at national and European levels. The successful solutions included the use of collective agreements to re-regulate employment relations through insourcing (albeit often at the cost of concessions) and public policies such as minimum standards, rigorous checks on self-employment and extended contractor liability for offences against national insurance/labour law as found in the construction or cleaning sectors. Strong sectoral bargaining institutions can be effective in mitigating the effects of workplace competition, but these can be found only in a limited number of sectors and countries.

The increase in outsourcing also makes the effective regulation of agency work, self-employment and the transfer of undertakings particularly relevant. Such regulations are an important resource for trade unions and employee representatives. Experience has also revealed that the effective enforcement of such legal standards often requires well-oiled worker voice institutions. Although agency work and the transfer of undertaking are regulated at EU level, the evidence shows that these regulations have failed to consistently guarantee worker rights. The degree to which the principles of EU directives have been transposed in individual member states varies significantly (Drahokoupil 2015b).

Ultimately, however, effective European worker participation institutions are needed to address restructuring through outsourcing, given that it commonly occurs in a cross-border manner. Transnational institutions such as EWCs, and international company agreements need to be used to set common standards and limit the room for concessions related to workplace competition (Doerflinger and Pulignano 2015).

Finally, employment of migrant workers through labour market intermediaries has become a standard in many sectors, most notably construction. However, the formation of the pan-European labour market has not been matched by the introduction of regulatory and enforcement mechanisms able to effectively protect workers' rights. Posting of workers is regulated by EU legislation (Directive 96/71/EC), but the enforcement of the rules is hindered by the complicated mix of home- and host-country legal standards. Violation is thus hard to detect, and the enforcement options of labour inspectorates are limited (Lillie and Wagner 2015). Extension of chain liability provisions could address some of these regulatory failures. Moreover, effective worker voice in the sectors with the most mobile labour markets requires the establishment of a transnational trade union organisation (Danaj and Sippola 2015).

ONLINE PLATFORMS: THE ULTIMATE OUTSOURCERS?

Thinking about contemporary outsourcing dynamics necessarily includes consideration of the impact of technologically driven change of labour organisation, particularly in connection with the rise of the role of the Internet in labour market matching (Askitas and Zimmermann 2015). While the role of the World Wide Web in labour matching was already thought about at the turn of the century (Autor 2001), the importance of its function has increased dramatically since then. Originally, the

Internet was used as a bulletin board for efficient dissemination of vacancies among jobseekers. This is still the case to an extent and we can learn a lot about the labour market from the analysis of vacancies published online (Mýtna-Kureková et al. 2015), however, the true role of the web is much broader (Lenaerts et al. 2016). One of the most curious new developments is the appearance of *online outsourcing platforms*, which have transcended the role of the Internet as a mere bulletin board and incorporated it into the organisation of work as such. To put it simply, an Uber driver or Upwork web designer are likely not even aware where the organisation they work for is physically located. What is important for them is the virtual platform, which assigns work and manages payment of earnings.

Yet, the understanding of platforms is still in its infancy. In June 2016, the European Commission published a Communication on a 'European agenda for the collaborative economy' (European Commission 2016), where 'collaborative economy' is a term used to refer to online platforms for facilitating temporary access to assets, including labour outsourcing. The supporting document included a rather vague definition referring to the collaborative economy as 'business models where activities are facilitated by online platforms that create an open marketplace for the temporary use of goods or services often provided by private individuals'. Such a broad definition gives us very little to work with in terms of understanding the impact of this new economy on society. Moreover, the Communication notes that there is not yet unity even in the use of terminology. The collaborative economy is also sometimes referred to as the *sharing economy, peer-to-peer economy* or *on-demand economy* and many other names. Clearly, these are very loaded terms pointing in different directions. Unfortunately, the Commission continued using the confused term 'collaborative economy' also in the consultation on the challenges of access to social protection for people in all forms of employment in the framework of the European Pillar of Social Rights (European Commission 2017).

Collaboration or interactions between peers obviously represent something different from sharing, and they are certainly different from the meaning associated with the concept of 'on demand'. In a similar fashion, the concept of 'collaboration' does not typically relate to a 'marketplace, where use of goods and services is facilitated'. Moreover, major outsourcing platforms in fact represent standard market transactions that would be better described as 'renting' rather than 'sharing'.[3] Therefore, we propose speaking about a 'platform economy', given that the underlying phenomenon is the use of online platforms that decrease the transaction costs of labour outsourcing and temporary access to assets. Outsourcing platforms provide a matching service, linking demand for labour with its supply. They thus enable the organisation of access to labour through the market, even in contexts where the use of a matching service proved to be too costly or where market failures required a reliance on institutions such as the employment relationship. Three aspects are thus important. First, platforms provide an algorithm that enables an effective matching of labour providers and users. Second, technology reduces transaction costs to the extent that platforms can also facilitate microtransactions. Third, platforms provide services that diminish or manage risks involved in market transactions, hence addressing market failures such as incomplete information about the labour provider or the risk of cheating. These services include reputation and monitoring systems, as well as standard insurance mechanisms and legal services against fraud.

The key concept of our understanding is thus the lower transaction costs, because we see the key value added of this new economy in the potential for making it easier for firms and individuals to access assets and workers exactly when they are needed, rather than in some abstract notions about collaboration or sharing. As a result of this lowering of barriers to entry, the platform economy can expand to previously informal/non-market spheres, for example, by making pet-sitting a paid job (De Groen et al. 2016).

In order to fully appreciate the variety of services that fall under the concept of online platforms and to fully grasp their impact, we must also consider the variety of existing platforms. The first distinction is between platforms that facilitate access to goods or property and those that enable access to self-employed workers or services. Thus, on the one side of the spectrum, there are virtual marketplaces such as eBay and property rentals such as Airbnb. On the other side of the spectrum, there are platforms such as TaskRabbit and TakeLessons that match labour providers with users. However, there is no clear-cut line between the two types, and some physical-goods platforms may have important labour market consequences. Consider the example of Airbnb, a major platform allowing users to rent out their private residences (as a whole or even just a single room in an inhabited house). At first sight, such a platform has very little relevance for the labour market. However, the platform

Table 2.3   Structure of work platforms

	Low/medium-skilled	High-skilled
Virtual/global services	CrowdFlower, Amazon Mechanical Turk	Upwork, 99designs, GoPillar
Physical/local services	Uber, Deliveroo, TaskRabbit	TakeLessons

Source De Groen et al. (2016)

itself has admitted that many of the users do not in fact use the platform to supplement their income by occasional renting of their house,
rather they rent out a number of uninhabited housing units as a sort of
mini-hotels (Fabo et al. 2017b).[4] Such an arrangement requires various
forms of labour: cleaning, accountancy and maintenance, for example,
which can be provided by the owner himself, but indeed are often outsourced to another person, who then might be someone doing the work
themselves, or might also be an intermediary.

The second distinction is that between platforms that organise local
labour markets or goods exchange and those that organise or create markets on trans-local and/or global scales. Indeed, while companies like
Airbnb and Uber are international corporations in their own right, many
of the platforms operate on a local scale only; for example, ListMinut,
which can be used to procure services in a range of categories, such as
plumbing, tutoring and pet-sitting, but only in Belgium. A special case is
the 'pure' web platforms, such as Amazon Mechanical Turk, TaskRabbit,
or Upwork, which have no offline component and where the work, such
as data entry, programming or website design, is done purely over the web.

Finally, it is useful to differentiate between platforms that facilitate
access to low- to medium-skilled work (such as data entry or taxi driving) and those mediating high-skilled activities (such as interior design).
Table 2.3 presents a categorisation of online platforms divided according
to skill level and local vs. virtual nature of the work.

HOW WIDESPREAD IS THE PLATFORM ECONOMY?

The growing importance of the platform economy is apparent. The taxi
service Uber has grown from an upstart local company to a global corporation with a market valuation of over $60 billion in just five years,
making it the fastest growing start-up in history (Steinmetz 2016).

And the popularity of platforms has not been limited to equity investors. Traditional companies have also invested into platforms that may challenge their business models. For instance, FedEx has acquired DoorDash and car2go is now owned by Daimler. Such influx of capital has fuelled the fast growth of the platform economy. A widely cited PricewaterhouseCoopers report (2015) foresees a growth of revenue in the key sectors of the 'sharing economy' from $15 billion today to $335 billion in 2035. It goes without saying that such a far-forward-looking prediction is of limited use and that not all sharing economies are Internet platforms and not all platforms are sharing economies. Nonetheless, there is very broad consensus on the idea that it is a very fast-growing field. The estimates by the European Commission on the size of the 'collaborative economy' are broadly in line with this—the revenue of these platforms in Europe is estimated at a sum of about $17 billion, and 17% of EU citizens have used services offered through these platforms at least once (European Commission 2016; Eurostat 2016).

There are, however, large differences between countries. Knowledge of these platforms is most widespread in France, Croatia and Estonia, while it remains very low in Cyprus, Malta and the UK. Interestingly, there tend to be more workers than users on platforms, likely suggesting that the customers are quite often companies rather than individuals (Fig. 2.3).

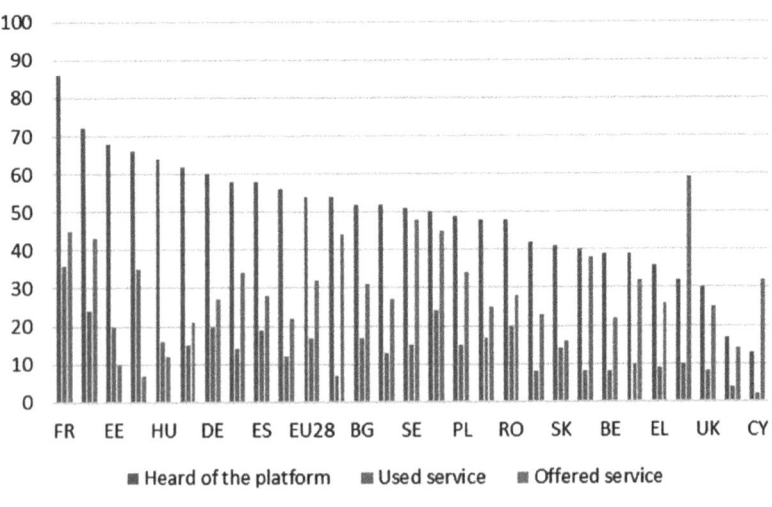

Fig. 2.3   Knowledge and use of online platforms (*Source* Eurostat 2016)

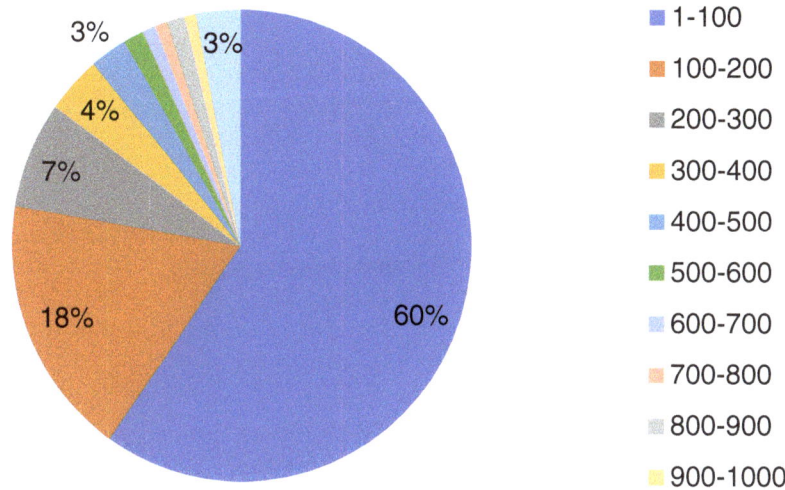

Fig. 2.4 Distribution of earnings on the ListMinut platform (*Source* De Groen et al. [2016]. *Note* Unspecified shares are 1% or less)

In general, the platforms appeal to younger, more educated and urban demographics (Eurostat 2016).

Nonetheless, serious questions remain regarding the intensity of the work. Empirical evidence suggests that engagement on the platforms is often a one-off thing for prospective workers, who register on the application, might take a job or two—and then leave forever (see example of the ListMinut platform in Fig. 2.4). Perhaps some of the quitters try their luck on some other platform, but many might be gone forever. According to the Eurobarometer survey, only 15% of workers on the platforms offer services regularly, while 28% offered their services only once (Eurostat 2016). The question of the sustainability of work platforms past the time when people are attracted to trying something new is still open.

The Impact of Online Platforms on the Labour Market

The variety of platforms discussed implies a number of different impacts on the labour market. The distinctions between the types of platforms discussed above are useful also for understanding different types of impacts.

First, platforms can enable organisation through self-employment of activities that traditionally relied on the employment relationship. This would be, perhaps, the most radical transformatory impact that deserves attention from policymakers. However, so far, the successful platforms have rather reorganised sectors that already relied on some forms of self-employment. Uber is the major example, but platforms such as GoPillar (formerly known as Cocontest) also seem to be limited to services that have relied on self-employment (e.g. architects) (see Maselli and Fabo 2015).

Second, platforms may facilitate remote provision of services. They thus may lead to offshoring of work from local labour markets. The examples of such effects include Amazon Mechanical Turk, which matches workers from around the world, or the Belgian platform for interior designers, GoPillar, which happens to match, among others, Serbian designers with clients in Italy (Ipeirotis 2010; Maselli and Fabo 2015; Berg 2016). Interestingly, PwC (2015) identifies local services such as transportation, eating out, hospitality provision and art/entertainment among the fields where the sharing economy is likely to grow, suggesting that the effect of offshoring might not be crucial at least in the short run.

Figure 2.5 plots some of the major platforms in relation to the two key distinctions that broadly correspond to the offshoring/outsourcing differentiation. There are platforms focusing on reorganising the

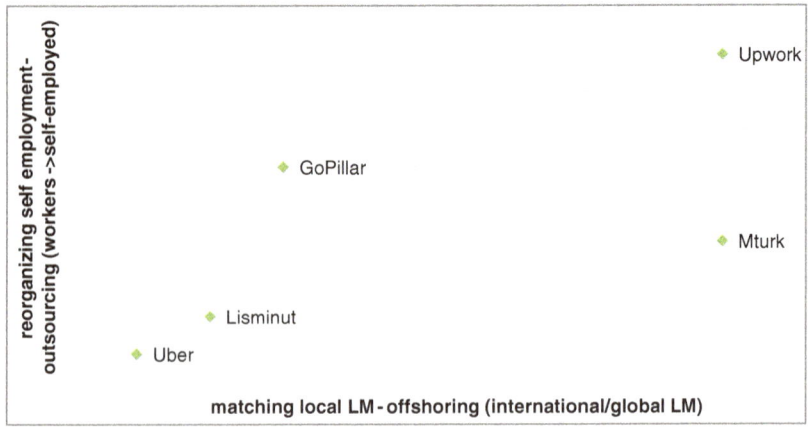

Fig. 2.5 Platforms, the variety of impacts (*Source* Own elaboration)

matching of activities that are already organised on a self-employment basis, while remaining local (most notably Uber); then there are those that actually offshore work that would traditionally be done in a local labour market by workers in employment relationships to self-employed workers in a low-cost location (Upwork). It is notable that the upper-left quadrants remain empty, as the successful platforms do not seem, as of yet, to reorganise local labour markets from employment relations to self-employment.

Third, platforms increase competition by lowering barriers to entry even if they do not transform employment into self-employment, hence creating pressure on pay and working conditions. Such is the case of Uber, which places professional drivers in competition with students or people on parental leave seeking an occasional top-up of their income.

Fourth, the reputation mechanisms used by platforms further contribute to the marketisation of the world of work. The *begging and bragging* rituals associated with modern academia, freelance journalism or art creation are prominent features of working on these online job platforms (Boyce et al. 2007; Huws 2014).

Finally, platforms may facilitate increased breakdown of working activities into individual tasks, which are then differentiated between those that require creative and highly skilled work by 'heads' and those that can be left to 'hands'. While the work of 'heads' comes with a very high level of employment quality in terms of pay and other perks, the 'hands' are constantly threatened by offshoring and automatisation (Huws et al. 2009). This can take very extreme forms on some online platforms, particularly Amazon Mechanical Turk, where users commonly perform tasks such as identifying objects in a picture for as low as $0.01.

Platforms thus may contribute to the precarisation of work. Indeed, there is much about this new economy that is strikingly familiar to researchers of precarious employment. For instance, the common use of euphemisms such as 'partners' (Uber) when referring to workers is a standard sign of a practice long known as *bogus self-employment* (Jorens and Van Buynder 2008). Workers are expected to constantly present themselves as a 'valuable good' to a wide range of customers and to offer themselves for individual jobs in order to be picked by a customer like a product from a catalogue, while remaining stuck in the trap of precarious, stigmatised, dead-end jobs (Boyce et al. 2007; Huws 2014).

The fast growth in the importance of the platforms might potentially also lead to increased setting of employment standards on the basis of the platform economy practices (De Groen and Maselli 2016). An even more radical vision was presented by Sundararajan (2016), who sees employment relationships, as well as the platforms themselves, being replaced in the future by virtual peer-to-peer interactions, displacing the rigidities of the currently existing forms of capitalism.

While such a scenario might seem far-fetched, we can in fact already see such new forms of organisation of work. A qualitative research study conducted by the Oxford Internet Institute on Asian workers providing technical skills to Western employers through platforms found that a rather complex network of individuals in the developing world with various skill levels has emerged to exploit the opportunities provided by this new form of work (Lehdonvirta et al. 2015). Besides the technically skilled workers capable of working on the platform, such networks commonly include persons capable of efficient communication with the clients and various other individuals providing services to the platform worker in exchange for a claim on a part of the earnings. It is thus not surprising that particularly the purely virtual, borderless platforms have captured the imagination of scholars. Degryse (2016), for example, talks about capital being empowered by the platforms to a degree, which would allow it to override all boundaries of national regulatory frameworks and taxation.

Regulating Online Platforms

The impact of the rise of online platforms will depend on the reaction from policymakers. Due to the quick growth of the on-demand/sharing economy and the increased politicisation of the platforms manifested in protests against Uber and Airbnb, in particular, there is a growing pressure to end the current largely *laissez faire status quo* and regulate the industry (Fabo et al. 2017a). At the same time, some countries, such as France in 2008, have introduced laws promoting self-entrepreneurship that have arguably facilitated growth of these forms of work. Low pay and, somewhat paradoxically, a lack of control over their working time are by far the top grievances of platform workers (see, e.g., Berg 2016). Lack of insurance is a major concern for those delivering food. Accidents, including serious injuries, are common among cyclists. The regulatory response thus needs to address the issue of pay and working conditions.

It is thus not enough, for instance, to ensure portability of insurance systems. Portability cannot bring security, particularly if the problem is low pay.

The key aspect of the debate is that of the nature of platform work, specifically whether it constitutes employment or not. Here, the Commission takes the view that employment is, in principle, every working relationship, according to three criteria: the subordinate relationship, the nature of the work, the remuneration provided. The Commission specifies that many of the common arguments made by the platforms, such as that workers are not constantly monitored and that the work does not take place continuously, are not sufficient in order to avoid classification of platform work as a working relationship (European Commission 2016).

However, given the precarious position of platform workers, one could go one step further and argue that they represent a category of workers in need of special protection, similarly to the regulatory provisions for part-time, fixed-term and agency work. In addition, policymakers should consider an extension of collective agreements to wider categories of workers than only employees, thus also including platform workers.

At the same time, workers who do not qualify as employees should be protected through regulations on self-employment, or through a platform-specific protection. At the moment, the self-employed do not have access to social protection systems with a comparable level of social protection as enjoyed by the standard workers (see OECD 2015).

For truly occasional work, as De Groen et al. (2016) show, there are already specific employment statuses in many European countries, typically limited by maximum allowed income, special registration or other conditions. Consequently, it can be argued that, for truly occasional workers, there are in many cases already legal ways to ensure that the employment relationship is not overly regulated given the casual nature of work.

Moreover, the self-employed (platform) workers should be allowed to organize and conduct collective bargaining. In the European Union, organizing of self-employed persons is in principle not permissible under Article 101 TFEU. EU case law has excluded 'false self-employed' from the applicability of Article 101 (Case C-413/13). The decisions by national courts of whether the platform-workers should be considered an employee, self-employed or false self-employed determine the scope to regulate salaries and working conditions via collective agreements but they will have to evaluate the cases in the light of EU competition rules. Instead, collective agreements should be possible to extend to wider categories of worker than 'employee', with a view to including platform workers. At this moment, legislation in many member states does not include possibility for self-employed persons to conclude a collective agreement or to be covered by one.

The preliminary experience with regulatory responses has clearly demonstrated that platforms, particularly those operating in the local labour markets, are not beyond the reach of existing regulatory frameworks. Matching platforms that set pay and contract conditions, such as Uber or Deliveroo, are most compatible with protection that approximates to, or fully complies, with standard worker protection. In fact, Uber pays a guaranteed minimum wage per hour in a number of markets. In Belgium, Deliveroo workers benefit from an agreement, negotiated by the agency Smart, that includes a minimum hourly pay rate, minimum working time, insurance against injury at work and social insurance. However, a regulatory framework is required to extend such provisions to wider groups of workers.

Platforms that reorganize local markets are also easiest to regulate as both customers and suppliers come under one jurisdiction. The oligopolistic tendency which comes with the network effects also makes it easier for the regulator to target the handful of dominant platforms—such has been the experience of Airbnb and, in some cases, Uber. Here, platforms in fact provide an opportunity to regularize undeclared activities, as their model allows for an efficient monitoring of microtransactions as well as for their incorporation into insurance and tax systems.

On the other side of the spectrum are platforms, such as CrowdFlower and Upwork, that facilitate the remote provision of services, thus potentially leading to the offshoring of work from local labour markets, often across borders. This is one reason why an EU-wide framework would help, but additional solutions need to be sought for outsourcing across the globe.

Finally, platforms, such as Upwork or Mechanical Turk, that allocate work through various types auctions or "contests"—which remunerates only the winners while competing bidders do a job without getting paid at all—call for new institutions of protection to address contest-specific issues, such as a lack of grievance mechanism in case of non-payment, or unfair practices in specifying work content. Again, decent pay is the main challenge.

CONCLUSION

Outsourcing, whether it is on the traditional 'offline' basis or based on an online outsourcing platform, is associated with a set of challenges. The most pressing ones are linked to employment relations. The fears that the outsourcing dynamics can lead in many cases to increased uncertainty and precarisation among workers appear to be justified.

In particular, the shift towards 'on-demand' workplaces undue pressure on the workers, who face a serious lack of certainty about their future earnings and employment that strongly benefits the employers. This effect can be reinforced further when outsourcing is coupled with offshoring, fuelling a race to the bottom.

The second important change associated with outsourcing is work-content reorganisation. This can be associated with the breakdown of jobs into tasks, which are then performed by different workers, sometimes in different parts of the world. Alternatively, it can take place through an increase in the 'begging and bragging' requirement at the expense of the actual work. The effects of these changes represent an under-researched topic, which deserves attention in future studies.

Finally, particularly the growth of the online outsourcing platforms comes with the risk of strengthening marginalisation and stigmatisation of vulnerable groups such as youth, minorities or migrants. This comes with a responsibility to ensure that the workers on the platforms retain their dignity and rights, rather than becoming a part of global exploited cybertariat, with potentially grave social and political consequences.

The increased politicisation of the issue opens up windows of opportunity for relevant actors, including trade unions, representatives of traditional and new industries and, naturally, the authorities to create the 'rules of the game'. This process will necessarily entail a thinking about the barriers between the market and society, between encouraging sharing and commercialising public space, between profit and welfare. As a result, the debate on the platforms might very well drive the much broader normative debate about the type of society we want to live in.

NOTES

1. For a detailed overview, see Winkler (2013).
2. On the same logic and with similar implications, one could also make a distinction between offshoring and the integration/transformation of the labour process.
3. Also see http://olivierblanchard.net/stop-calling-it-the-sharing-economy-that-isnt-what-it-is/.
4. This phenomenon has also been covered by the media, see for example http://www.bloomberg.com/news/articles/2016-02-25/airbnb-says-it-removed-1-500-listings-in-new-york-before-data-release.

REFERENCES

Altreiter, Carina, Theresa Fibich, and Jörg Flecker. 2015. "Capital and Labour on the Move: The Dynamics of Double Transnational Mobility." In *The Outsourcing Challenge: Organizing Workers Across Fragmented Production Networks*, edited by Jan Drahokoupil, 67–87. Brussels: European Trade Union Institute.

Askitas, Nikolaos, and Klaus F. Zimmermann. 2015. "The Internet as a Data Source for Advancement in Social Sciences." *International Journal of Manpower* 36 (1): 2–12. https://doi.org/10.1108/ijm-02-2015-0029.

Autor, David H. 2001. "Wiring the Labor Market." *The Journal of Economic Perspectives* 15 (1): 25–40.

Batt, Rosemary, and Hiroatsu Nohara. 2009. "How Institutions and Business Strategies Affect Wages: A Cross-National Study of Call Centers." *ILR Review* 62 (4): 533–552. https://doi.org/10.1177/001979390906200404.

Berg, Janine. 2016. "Income Security in the on-Demand Economy: Findings and Policy Lessons from a Survey of Crowdworkers." ILO Working Paper. http://www.ilo.org/travail/whatwedo/publications/WCMS_479693/lang–en/index.htm.

Bernaciak, Magdalena, ed. 2015. *Market Expansion and Social Dumping in Europe*. London: Routledge.

Boyce, Anthony S., Ann Marie Ryan, Anna L. Imus, and Frederick P. Morgeson. 2007. "'Temporary Worker, Permanent Loser?'A Model of the Stigmatization of Temporary Workers." *Journal of Management* 33 (1): 5–29. https://doi.org/10.1177/0149206306296575.

Crouch, Colin, Martin Schröder, and Helmut Voelzkow. 2009. "Regional and Sectoral Varieties of Capitalism." *Economy and Society* 38: 654–678.

Danaj, Sonila, and Markku Sippola. 2015. "Organizing Posted Workers in the Construction Sector." In *Organizing Posted Workers in the Construction Sector*, edited by Jan Drahokoupil, 217–235. Brussels: European Trade Union Institute.

De Groen, Pieter Willem, and Ilaria Maselli. 2016. "The Impact of the Collaborative Economy on the Labour Market." SSRN Scholarly Paper ID 2790788, Social Science Research Network, Rochester, NY. http://papers. ssrn.com/abstract=2790788.

De Groen, Willem Pieter, Ilaria Maselli, and Brian Fabo. 2016. "The Digital Market for Local Services: A One-Night Stand for Workers? An Example from the On-Demand Economy." CEPS Special Report ID 2766220, Centre for European Policy Studies, Brussels. https://papers.ssrn.com/abstract=2766220.

Degryse, Christophe. 2016. "Digitalisation of the Economy and Its Impact on Labour Markets." SSRN Scholarly Paper ID 2730550, Social Science Research Network, Rochester, NY. http://papers.ssrn.com/abstract=2730550.

Doellgast, Virginia, and Ian Greer. 2007. "Vertical Disintegration and the Disorganization of German Industrial Relations." *British Journal of Industrial Relations* 45 (1): 55–76. https://doi.org/10.1111/j.1467-8543.2007.00602.x.

Doellgast, Virginia, Rosemary Batt, and Ole H. Sørensen. 2009. "Introduction: Institutional Change and Labour Market Segmentation in European Call Centres." *European Journal of Industrial Relations* 15 (4): 349–371. https://doi.org/10.1177/0959680109344366.

Doellgast, Virginia, Katja Sarmiento-Mirwaldt, and Chiara Benassi. 2015. "Union Campaigns to Organize Across Production Networks in the European Telecommunications Industry: Lessons from the UK, Italy, Sweden and Poland." In *The Outsourcing Challenge: Organizing Workers Across Fragmented Production Networks*, edited by Jan Drahokoupil, 199–216. Brussels: European Trade Union Institute.

Doerflinger, Nadja, and Valeria Pulignano. 2015. "Outsourcing and Collective Bargaining in the Recent Crisis: Implications for Employment in Multinationals." In *The Outsourcing Challenge: Organizing Workers Across Fragmented Production Networks*, edited by Jan Drahokoupil, 255–276. Brussels: European Trade Union Institute.

Drahokoupil, Jan. 2015a. "Introduction." In *The Outsourcing Challenge: Organizing Workers Across Fragmented Production Networks*, edited by Jan Drahokoupil, 9–21. Brussels: European Trade Union Institute.

Drahokoupil, Jan, ed. 2015b. *The Outsourcing Challenge: Organizing Workers Across Fragmented Production Networks*. Brussels: European Trade Union Institute.

European Commission. 2016. "Communication on a European Agenda for the Collaborative Economy." COM(2016) 356. Brussels: European Commission. http://ec.europa.eu/DocsRoom/documents/16881.

European Commission. 2017. "First Phase Consultation of Social Partners under Article 154 TFEU on a Possible Action Addressing the Challenges of Access to Social Protection for People in All Forms of Employment in the

Framework of the European Pillar of Social Rights." Consultation Document COM(2017) 2610. Brussels: European Commission. http://ec.europa.eu/social/blobServlet?docId=17614&langId=en.

Eurostat. 2016. "Flash Eurobarometer 438: The Use of Collaborative Platforms." http://ec.europa.eu/COMMFrontOffice/PublicOpinion/index.cfm/ResultDoc/download/DocumentKy/72885.

Fabo, Brian, Jovana Karanović, and Katerina Dukova. 2017a. "In Search of an Adequate European Policy Response to the Platform Economy." *Transfer: European Review of Labour and Research* 23 (2): 163–175. https://doi.org/10.1177/1024258916688861.

Fabo, Brian, Silvia Hudáčková, and Arthur Nogacz. 2017b. "Can Airbnb Provide Livable Incomes to Property Owners?: An Analysis on National, Regional and City District Level." AIAS Working Paper 168. http://www.uva-aias.net/en/working-papers/aias/2017/can-airbnb-provide-livable-incomes-to-property-owners.

Feenstra, Robert C., and Gordon H. Hanson. 1996. "Globalization, Outsourcing, and Wage Inequality." *American Economic Review* 86 (2): 240–245.

Flecker, Jörg. 2009. "Outsourcing, Spatial Relocation and the Fragmentation of Employment." *Competition & Change* 13 (3): 251–266. https://doi.org/10.1179/102452909x451369.

Geishecker, Ingo, Holger Görg, and Jakob Roland Munch. 2010. "Do Labour Market Institutions Matter? Micro-Level Wage Effects of International Outsourcing in Three European Countries." *Review of World Economics* 146 (1): 179–198. https://doi.org/10.1007/s10290-009-0039-9.

Giustiniano, Jan Luca, Lucia Marchegiani, Enzo Peruff, and Luca Pirolo. 2015. "Business Outcomes of Outsourcing: Lessons from Management Research." In *The Outsourcing Challenge: Organizing Workers Across Fragmented Production Networks*, edited by Jan Drahokoupil, 47–65. Brussels: European Trade Union Institute.

Goldschmidt, Deborah, and Johannes F. Schmieder. 2015. "The Rise of Domestic Outsourcing and the Evolution of the German Wage Structure." Working Paper 21366, National Bureau of Economic Research. http://www.nber.org/papers/w21366.

Gospel, Howard, and Mari Sako. 2010. "The Unbundling of Corporate Functions: The Evolution of Shared Services and Outsourcing in Human Resource Management." *Industrial and Corporate Change* 19 (5): 1367–1396. https://doi.org/10.1093/icc/dtq002.

Hijzen, Alexander, Holger Görg, and Robert C. Hine. 2005. "International Outsourcing and the Skill Structure of Labour Demand in the United Kingdom." *The Economic Journal* 115 (506): 860–878. https://doi.org/10.1111/j.1468-0297.2005.01022.x.

Holst, Hajo. 2014. "'Commodifying Institutions': Vertical Disintegration and Institutional Change in German Labour Relations." *Work, Employment and Society* 28 (1): 3–20. https://doi.org/10.1177/0950017012464423.

Hummels, David, Jakob R. Munch, and Chong Xiang. 2013. "Globalization, Labour Market Institutions and Wage Structure." *Nordic Economic Policy Review* 1: 75–98.

Hummels, David, Jakob R. Munch, and Chong Xiang. 2016. "Offshoring and Labor Markets." IZA Discussion Paper 9741. ftp.iza.org/dp9741.pdf.

Huws, Ursula. 2014. *Labor in the Global Digital Economy: The Cybertariat Comes of Age*. New York: Monthly Review Press.

Huws, Ursula, Simone Dahlmann, Jorg Flecker, Ursula Holtgrewe, Annika Schonauer, Monique Ramioul, and Karen Geurts. 2009. "Value Chain Restructuring in Europe in a Global Economy." http://uhra.herts.ac.uk/handle/2299/14452.

Ipeirotis, Panagiotis G. 2010. "Demographics of Mechanical Turk." CeDER Working Paper 10-01. http://archive.nyu.edu/handle/2451/29585.

Jorens, Yves, and Tineke Van Buynder. 2008. "Self-employment and Bogus Self-employment in the European Construction Industry." http://efbww.org/pdfs/Annex%2010%20-%20Final%20report%20Belgium.pdf.

Kalleberg, Arne L. 2013. *Good Jobs, Bad Jobs: The Rise of Polarized and Precarious Employment Systems in the United States 1970s to 2000s*. New York, NY: Russell Sage.

Kirchner, Stefan. 2015. "Who Performs Outsourcing? A Cross-National Comparison of Companies in the EU-28." In *The Outsourcing Challenge: Organizing Workers Across Fragmented Production Networks*, edited by Jan Drahokoupil, 25–45. Brussels: European Trade Union Institute.

Kramarz, Francis. 2008. "Offshoring, Wages, and Employment: Evidence from Data Matching Imports, Firms, and Workers." *CREST-INSEE Mimeo*. http://www.crest.fr/ckfinder/userfiles/files/pageperso/kramarz/Offshoring072008.pdf.

Lallement, Michel. 2011. "Europe and the Economic Crisis: Forms of Labour Market Adjustment and Varieties of Capitalism." *Work, Employment & Society* 25 (4): 627–641. https://doi.org/10.1177/0950017011419717.

Lehdonvirta, Vili, Isis Hjorth, Mark Graham, and Helena Barnard. 2015. "Online Labour Markets and the Persistence of Personal Networks: Evidence from Workers in Southeast Asia." http://vili.lehdonvirta.com/files/Online%20labour%20markets%20and%20personal%20networks%20ASA%202015.pdf.

Lenaerts, Karolien, Miroslav Beblavý, and Brian Fabo. 2016. "Prospects for Utilisation of Non-vacancy Internet Data in Labour Market Analysis—An Overview." *IZA Journal of Labor Economics* 5 (1): 1–18. https://doi.org/10.1186/s40172-016-0042-z.

Lillie, Nathan, and Ines Wagner. 2015. "Subcontracting, Insecurity and Posted Work: Evidence from Construction, Meat Processing, and Ship Building." In *The Outsourcing Challenge: Organizing Workers Across Fragmented Production Networks*, edited by Jan Drahokoupil, 157–174. Brussels: European Trade Union Institute.

Maselli, Ilaria, and Brian Fabo. 2015. "Digital Workers by Design? An Example from the on-Demand Economy." CEPS Paper 11030, Centre for European Policy Studies. https://ideas.repec.org/p/eps/cepswp/11030.html.

Milberg, William, and Deborah Winkler. 2013. *Outsourcing Economics: Global Value Chains in Capitalist Development*. Cambridge: Cambridge University Press.

Mol, Michael, Chris Brewster, Geoffery Wood, and Michael Brookes. 2014. "How Much Does Country Matter? A Cross-National Comparison of HRM Outsourcing Decisions." In *Human Resource Management and the Institutional Perspective*, edited by Geoffery Wood, Chris Brewster, and Michael Brookes, 200–220. London: Routledge.

Mýtna-Kureková, Lucia, Miroslav Beblavý, and Anna Thum-Thysen. 2015. "Using Online Vacancies and Web Surveys to Analyse the Labour Market: A Methodological Inquiry." *IZA Journal of Labor Economics* 4 (1): 1–20. https://doi.org/10.1186/s40172-015-0034-4.

OECD. 2015. *In It Together: Why Less Inequality Benefits All*. Paris: OECD Publishing.

Olsen, Karsten Bjerring. 2006. "Productivity Impacts of Offshoring and Outsourcing: A Review." STI Working Paper 2006/1, Organisation for Economic Co-operation and Development, Paris.

PwC. 2015. "The Sharing Economy." https://www.pwc.com/us/en/technology/publications/assets/pwc-consumer-intelligence-series-the-sharing-economy.pdf.

Ramioul, Monique, and Geert Van Hootegem. 2015. "Relocation, the Restructuring of the Labour Process and Job Quality." In *The Outsourcing Challenge: Organizing Workers Across Fragmented Production Networks*, edited by Jan Drahokoupil, 91–115. Brussels: European Trade Union Institute.

Sako, Mari. 2005. "Outsourcing and Offshoring: Key Trends and Issues." Available at SSRN. Rochester, NY: Social Science Research Network. http://papers.ssrn.com/abstract=1463480.

Sly, Nicholas, and Anson Soderbery. 2014. "Strategic Sourcing and Wage Bargaining." *Journal of Development Economics* 109 (C): 172–187.

Steinmetz, Katy. 2016. "Exclusive: See How Big the Gig Economy Really Is." *Time*, January 6. http://time.com/4169532/sharing-economy-poll/?xid=homepage.

Sundararajan, Arun. 2016. *The Sharing Economy: The End of Employment and the Rise of Crowd-Based Capitalism*. Cambridge: MIT Press.

Warhurst, Chris, Françoise Carré, Patricia Findlay, and Chris Tilly, eds. 2012. *Are Bad Jobs Inevitable?: Trends, Determinants and Responses to Job Quality in the Twenty-First Century*. Basingstoke: Palgrave Macmillan.

Weil, David. 2014. *The Fissured Workplace: Why Work Became So Bad for So Many and What Can Be Done to Improve It*. Cambridge, MA: Harvard University Press.

Winkler, Deborah. 2013. "Services Offshoring and the Relative Demand for White-Collar Workers in German Manufacturing." In *The Oxford Handbook of Offshoring and Global Employment*, edited by Ashok Bardhan, Dwight M. Jaffee, and Cynthia A. Kroll, 72–99. Oxford: Oxford University Press.

CHAPTER 3

New Forms of Work and Employment in the Digital Economy

Gérard Valenduc

During the past two years, plenty of articles have been published in newspapers and magazines about the so-called uberisation of work, new forms of work in a sharing or collaborative economy, the flood of flexible mini-jobs in the 'gig economy', the uncertain future of wage employment, etc. Throughout both printed and digital media, the feeling has become increasingly widespread that the forthcoming tsunami of digital technologies—whether this is named the second machine age, or the third or fourth industrial revolution—will deeply question the employment relationship.

The aim of this paper is to analyse how some recent innovations in the digitalisation of the economy are intertwined with emerging forms of work and employment; and to what extent the accelerated development of digitalisation contributes to the political process which is deconstructing the concept of employment and reformulating the category of 'worker'.

In the first part, the paper will focus on some significant characteristics of the 'digital turn' which might contribute to changes in work

G. Valenduc (✉)
European Trade Union Institute and Chair Labour-University (UCLouvain), Namur, Belgium

© The Author(s) 2019
A. Serrano-Pascual and M. Jepsen (Eds.),
The Deconstruction of Employment as a Political Question,
https://doi.org/10.1007/978-3-319-93617-8_3

63

organisation patterns, occupations and forms of employment. In the second part, four emerging forms of work and employment will be considered: Internet-based virtual work; on-demand work through digital platforms; crowd working; and prosumer work. The third part will capture some recent transformations of the basic components of the employment relationship. The paper is based mainly on a recent review of changes in work in the digital economy prepared for the ETUI (Valenduc and Vendramin 2016) and other exploratory research in cooperation with trade unions (Vendramin and Valenduc 2016).

THE 'DIGITAL TURN' AND THE LABOUR PROCESS

A first question regarding the forthcoming wave of information and communications technologies (ICT), more fashionably renamed digital technologies, concerns how we might characterise such a development (Holtgrewe 2014). The 'digital turn' is a mix of, on the one hand, a continuation and an amplification of existing trends (the information society, the knowledge-based economy, the net economy) and, on the other hand, a significant breakthrough in the organisation of the global economy, linked to rapid and exponential performance growth in a new generation of innovations, reputed to be 'disruptive'. The purpose of this paper is not to assess the extent to which technological performance can be really disruptive, but to highlight how the labour process can be transformed, in a wide range of economic activities covering manufacturing and services. Four trends are analysed: the use of ICT to enable a renewed international division of labour across globalised value chains; the expansion of the business model of digital platforms; the rapidly growing capacity to collect 'big data' and to generate economic value from this; and the 'digital renewal' of the informal economy.

ICT, Value Chains and the Global Division of Labour

Over a long period there have been theories about the restructuring of the global value chain in the information age, although some authors have recently suggested that the analytical framework needs to be adapted to the transition from the information age to the Internet age which occurred between 2000 and 2010 (Huws 2013). Indeed, over the past few years, several authors have analysed the fragmentation of the value chain at the global level as one of the key features of current globalisation processes (Flecker 2007; Huws et al. 2009). Fragmentation involves, first, the splitting of different business functions for both tangible and intangible goods along numerous value chains: research and development; design; prototyping; production (including subcontracting and assembly); logistics and distribution; sales and marketing; and maintenance and servicing. Second, it involves the restructuring of these functions as part of a new international division of labour. ICT facilitates the conduct of intangible tasks anytime and anywhere, as well as the development of processes which codify and commoditise knowledge. 'Fragmentation (…) provides an apt metaphor for the new human division of labour whereby units of human skill and knowledge are broken down into increasingly standardisable and interchangeable units and can also be reconfigured in new permutations and combinations, spatially and across other dimensions' (Huws 2007, 1).

Fragmentation entails a global offshoring of certain functions, particularly, the mass production of tangible and intangible goods, while other functions are relocated to be closer to centres of decision-making or to consumer markets. The new generation of digital technologies, including communicating objects and learning robots, will strengthen this trend, at the same time as potentially altering the balance of power. For example, Brynjolfsson and McAfee (2015) suggest that the relative advantages of relocating operations to low-wage countries may be neutralised by the decreasing cost of robots able to outperform a low-skilled workforce.

The New Business Model of Online Platforms

Online platforms, which have been described by economists as 'two-sided markets' (Wauthy 2008), are becoming increasingly present in consumer as well as in business-to-business markets. Here, products and services are delivered to two distinct user groups at the same time—the two sides of the market—through a platform which can be accessed from a computer, smartphone or tablet. One side of the market is made up of consumers who benefit from access to low cost or free services and positive network externalities, since the services become more attractive as user numbers grow; by accessing these services, however, and whether they realise it or not, they are supplying the platform with sets of data on their personal profile, location and consumer habits. The other side of the market comprises economic players which are involved in the provision of platform-based services and which also benefit from positive network externalities in proportion to the size of the consumer base. The value of a service for the actors on one side of the market correlates to the number and the quality of the actors on the other. Economists refer to such phenomena as 'cross network externalities' and regard them as a typical feature of two-sided markets (Blomsel 2007). Platforms of this kind are funded by levies on the transactions between the two sides of the market, but the information which is collected is also valuable to the actors on both sides, representing not only a source of data but also a body of knowledge. The platform itself is, therefore, the primary location of value creation for both sides. Examples of platforms which correspond to this description include Google, Booking.com, Uber, Amazon and many others; while the superficially 'free' nature of their services (Google when used by individuals, for example) is, in reality, merely a manifestation of the optimum pricing model for one side of the market.

Online platforms have not only been developed in the area of the trading of goods and services but also in the labour market, as intermediaries in the demand and supply of fragmented work. This paper will also consider these developments.

The Increasing Capacity to Extract Value from Big Data

Developments in the field of cloud technologies have led to the emergence of the large-scale physical infrastructures of data centres and high-speed connections. The recent exponential growth in the performance of data mining and modelling software makes it possible to analyse vast quantities of digital data as a basis for activities such as consumer profiling, behaviour modelling and movement tracking, as well as the mapping of interactions and the diagnosis of machine breakdowns or human illness. The big data industry relies on the 'four Vs' principle: volume; velocity; variety; and value. The predictive power of big data software is improving apace thanks to its capacity to handle volumes of data at the same time, going beyond current levels of human understanding. By way of an example, machine translation tools now draw on a huge corpus of digitalised texts in every conceivable language rather than using linguistic algorithms alone (Brynjolfsson and McAfee 2015).

Big data software is increasingly coupled with other, recently widespread, technological innovations such as the geolocation of people (now currently embedded in smartphones); the geolocation of products (embedded in RFID chips); mobile apps, allowing ubiquitous access to online services and social networks; and the 'internet of things'— communications protocols facilitating the exchange of data between physical or virtual objects equipped with sensors, telemetry tools, QR codes and embedded apps in computers, smartphones or robots.

From a work-related perspective, big data collection and analysis has implications in terms of surveillance and monitoring in the workplace and the tracking of employee activities. Big data modelling solutions are making it even easier to use quantitative and qualitative performance standards as a basis for individual benchmarking and performance profiles; these are not new weapons in the managerial arsenal, but the tools now available for their implementation are increasingly powerful. The use of consumer-generated big data is also transforming working practices in the fields of commerce, marketing and financial services; more generally speaking, the same applies to all client-facing activities where the aim now is to customise products and personalise services (Valenduc and Vendramin 2016).

The Digital Renewal of the Informal Economy

Networks for exchanging services in the informal economy are not a new phenomenon as such, but they have become both more visible, thanks to their development first into websites, and more efficient, thanks to the online platform model. This model provides new opportunities for not-for-profit exchanges over collaborative platforms or peer-to-peer networks for services in areas as varied as DIY, car sharing, babysitting, equipment pooling, domestic help, etc.—the so-called 'sharing economy'. This denomination, however, covers a very wide spectrum of activities. At one end of this spectrum, there are networks allowing individuals to share or pool goods and services, either without monetary exchange or via the use of alternative currencies at the local level. At the other end of the spectrum, some online platforms, which were initially designed as 'sharing' or 'collaborative', have rapidly succeeded in capturing the value created on both sides of their market and have become very profitable businesses, positioning themselves as market leaders, such as the case of AirBnB. At the same time, the business model of platforms also facilitates alternative forms of trade, such as direct sales from farmers to consumers, fair trade, short distribution circuits at the local level, etc., while it also refreshes the debate about "common goods" that can be shared at very low marginal cost. Indeed, digital commons, such as open-source software or creative commons publishing licences, are shifting the boundaries between property and use (Coriat 2015).

This wide spectrum reflects two significant changes: first, the digital renewal of the informal economy; and, second, the increasingly blurred boundaries between the formal economy and the informal economy—and consequently, between formal and informal work.

EMERGING FORMS OF WORK IN THE DIGITAL ECONOMY

ICT-Based Mobile Work and Digital Nomadism

Digital nomads are characterised by two specific work practices. First, they make extensive use of computers, smartphones, cloud services, the Internet and email in the course of their professional activity. Second, their working time is not spent solely on the premises of the employer (and neither is it spent on their own premises if they are self-employed) as they work mainly from other locations such as their home, client premises, external sites, modes of transport, hotels, co-working spaces or any other (Eurofound 2015).

ICT-based mobile work may also be virtual. In some cases— geographically dispersed virtual teams, computer-based video-conferencing, virtual meetings bringing together avatars of real people, remote monitoring of industrial facilities, remote maintenance, etc.—real-life mobility is less important than the ability to be present in multiple virtual locations. By allowing people to be present everywhere in virtual form without physically relocating, digital technologies are fostering the emergence of new virtual forms of work organisation (Valenduc and Vendramin 2016).

According to the European Working Conditions Survey (EWCS), the proportion of workers (wage earners and self-employed) spending at least one-quarter of their working time outside their usual workplace rose from 7% in 2005 to 24% in 2010. There were, however, considerable variations among EU countries: from more than 40% in Nordic countries and the Netherlands to between 25% and 30% in Belgium, France, Germany and the UK, 20% in Spain and less than 15% in other Southern or Eastern countries. They are mostly men (65%), higher education graduates (56%) and aged between 35 and 49 years (45%). The proportion of digital nomads is highest among executives and professionals (45%) and, to a lesser extent, among intermediate professionals (33% of technicians, assistants, supervisors and paramedic occupations). Focusing only on salaried workers, those working mainly on client premises, external sites, home or elsewhere accounts for 23% of men but only 11% of women.

The campaign 'New World of Work' (NWOW), initiated by Microsoft in 2005 and launched in its national subsidiaries during the period around 2010, provides an interesting example of employers' strategies to foster the development of digital nomadism. The purpose of the campaign is to promote new flexible, autonomous and mobile work organisation patterns—and obviously to promote the new generation of the online and cloud-based tools of Microsoft. With such tools, enterprises can free their employees from fixed workplaces, allow them to work from anywhere at any time and develop a new work culture. Each subsidiary of Microsoft is charged with building up a national NWOW coalition. In Belgium, for example, the coalition (launched in 2012) gathers high-tech companies, public administration bodies and consultants in human resource management, and provides coaching and support services for enterprises or administrations interested in the implementation of NWOW initiatives (Vendramin and Valenduc 2016).

To some extent, digital nomadism could be considered as an extension of telework. However, most national collective agreements implemented after the European framework agreement on telework in 2002 are restricted to telework at home, considering that other forms of distance working, such as remote offices, hired offices, itinerant work or work on client premises are, respectively, covered by specific other collective agreements. Most national or sectoral collective agreements considered the different forms of distance working separately, while nomadic work organisation patterns combine all of them. Several authors consider that current legislation or agreements on telework do not cover the full range of working situations with which digital nomads are confronted (Eurofound 2015; Mettling 2015; Popma 2013).

The development of ICT-based nomadic work entails several consequences for the employment relationship. While the employment relationship classically relies on clear definitions of working time and working place, the various patterns of nomadic work are dissolving both of these. The NWOW campaign clearly aims at this dissolution while describing it as 'new work culture'. Moreover, company practice in ICT-based mobile work reveals that flexible working time and flexible workplaces are often being coupled with an increasing role for wage flexibilisation, for instance, flexible remuneration according to targets, performances or results, and the introduction of extra-wage benefits (Popma 2013).

On-Demand Work Through Online Platforms

On-demand work relies on a continuous employment relationship with an employer but without the employee having a continuous job, pre-defined working hours or volume of remuneration; the employer calls on the worker only when needed. According to a Eurofound report on new forms of employment, which draws a detailed picture of the contractual varieties of on-demand work across Europe (2015, 55–61), two main categories of employment contracts can be found: either the well-known 'zero hours' contract or a minimum threshold contract. In the first type, which exists in the UK, Ireland and the Netherlands, no volume of work is guaranteed by the employer, while only the Irish legislation makes provision for financial compensation when the number of worked hours falls below one-third of a full-time job. Under a minimum threshold contract, the volume of work and remuneration are only guaranteed for a basic number of working hours (generally between one-quarter and one-third full-time equivalent, depending on national legislation) although, in some particular cases, such as the 'min–max' contract in the Netherlands, both a lower and an upper threshold are fixed which, in practice, leads to a variable part-time contract.

On-demand work has existed for a long time. Its development is related to the expansion of flexible work practices in the 1990s, and the British case of zero-hours contracts was mentioned in most research reports on flexibility at this time. On-demand work is different from intermittent work, for instance, in the case of artists or seasonal workers. In intermittent work, the nature of the economic activity is factually not continuous (for instance in artistic jobs) whereas, in on-demand work, working hours are adjusted only to the needs of the employer.

What is new is the combined utilisation of online platforms, geolocation and mobile apps on smartphones to match employers' requests and workers' availability (time availability and optimal physical location) and to fine-tune the on-demand process. This new pattern of work organisation is named 'work on demand via apps' (De Stefano 2016) or 'online platforms for on-demand work' (Eurofound 2015; Vendramin and Valenduc 2016).

The development of such online platforms for on-demand work is mainly observable in economic activities characterised by continuous, but variable, demand: domestic and care activities, including for children and seniors; extra-school activities for children; organisation of events of any kind; office support; retail trade; express delivery; truck driving; etc. In many cases (care, technical, cultural, sales or office skills, specific professional licences), a specific skill or training may be required although in others no specific skill is needed. From the point of view of employers, the basic principle of the on-demand employment relationship fits the requirements of such activities: the continuous character of the business allied to a need for specific skills justifies a continuous employment relationship, while the discontinuous volume of business justifies a variable volume of remunerated working hours carried out by a pool of available workers. However, according to a recent ILO report, the development of online platforms and apps is progressively shifting the nature of on-demand work from specialised work (e.g. mobile nurses, child carers, audio–visual technicians, accountants, secretaries) to low-skilled "gig" jobs (De Stefano 2016).

To sum up, the employment relationship—which still exists in contractual form—is becoming mainly characterised by extremely flexible working time, extended availability and highly variable wages, while working time is becoming disconnected from the work contract. The undermining of the contractual relationship not only concerns work but also everyday life which, in turn, is being subordinated to the demands of increasingly unpredictable work schedules.

Crowd Working

Crowd working (or the crowd sourcing of work) refers to work carried out through online platforms which allow organisations or individuals access to an undefined and unknown group of other organisations or individuals prepared to solve specific problems or supply specific services or products in exchange for payment (Green et al. 2013). Work is "externalised to the crowd". Different types of crowd working platforms are currently operating at the global level (Drahokoupil and Fabo 2016; Vendramin and Valenduc 2016):

- *Crowd working on fragmented virtual micro-tasks.* The pioneer in this field is Amazon Mechanical Turk, set up in 2006. This type of platform establishes a market place for micro-tasks in areas including web development, design, software development, photo/video image recognition, data replication, translation, audio transcription, data-based research and the submission of bids for creative tasks (such as designing a logo). Although Amazon qualifies those tasks as "human intelligence tasks" (HITs), they result from a typical process of "virtual Taylorism", separating design from execution and fragmenting the work process into elementary units that can be outsourced to the global crowd. Tasks can be outsourced to anybody, amateur or professional, without any control over skills. As written on the Mechanical Turk home page: "We give businesses and developers access to an on-demand, scalable workforce. Workers select from thousands of tasks and work whenever it is convenient". Prices are set by auction. Work is only paid if well done. Workers are rated by the platform—and their rating is displayed when they apply for a task.

– *Crowd working on freelance tasks.* Other platforms, such as PeoplePerHour, are only open to freelance professionals who must be agreed by the platform and provide professional credentials. Freelancers publish their daily or hourly rates and those requiring labour select them according to profiles and prices. These platforms mainly manage virtual tasks, which can be carried out anywhere using digital tools: web design and development; copy writing; translation; multimedia production; public relations; community management in social media; tutorials for mobile apps; etc.

– *Crowd working for material tasks and services, executable at local level.* Such tasks are not at all "virtual" and consist mainly of "gigs": errands; baby-sitting; watching cats or dogs; gardening; home repair; and a wide variety of tasks that do not require professional skills. TaskRabbit is a well-known example, and has "subsidiaries" in many countries; indeed, such platforms can be multinational companies but they must operate at local level.

Crowd workers' profiles vary from skilled professional to unskilled amateur. According to a recent survey carried out in the UK, about 21% of the population aged 16–75 had sought a job on crowd working platforms during the past year, but only 11% had found one: 3% had done so at least once a week and 4% had found at least one a week. The survey reported that 88% were looking for online tasks while 12% were looking for off-line ones. For only one out of four crowd workers did the income from crowd working represent at least one-half of their income; most crowd workers are young people (51% are younger than 35) looking for extra income (Joyce and Huws 2016).

Concerning the employment relationship, most crowd working platforms deny any employer responsibility. Their websites display general terms and conditions of use and legal disclaimers, leaving to workers all responsibilities for settling their taxation, social status, social and professional insurance. In the case of platforms for freelancers, the deal is rather clear: workers are supposed to have freelance status (self-employed or other) in the country where they live. Other platforms are less explicit. For instance, the disclaimer of the Belgian platform Listminut declares that 'The relationship between service demander and service provider is an independent relationship. Most providers are individuals who provide services only on a casual basis. This kind of service provision does not need to comply with the social status of self-employed' (Vendramin and Valenduc 2016).

Crowd working has other damaging effects. Platforms using a bidding system for payments for online tasks are really promoting a worldwide race to the bottom. The system of rating workers may lead to the unilateral disqualification of workers who have no means to contest or mount counter-claims. The fragmentation of tasks can also spill over into freelance work; for instance, the platform PeoplePerHour launched in 2012 a pricing system named "hourlies", in which freelancers are invited to describe what tasks they are able to realise in one hour of remuneration.

Crowd sourcing platforms are obliged to comply with general legislative provisions in the form of commercial law, consumer protection directives, the civil code and data protection regulations, but specific legislation on crowd working has not yet been collectively defined at European level. Their terms and conditions generally dictate all the details (such as pay, working conditions and intellectual property), but workers effectively have no clear status.

Prosumer Work

The business model of digital platforms has introduced the concept of 'prosumers' or, in other words, individuals who both produce and consume digitised information. They are rarely paid, but prosumers carry out work by supplying data and services for which salaried employees were previously at least partly responsible, such as amateur reviews of services or products, the rating of services, supplying user-generated content and data entry. In a less explicit way, a wide range of our daily digital activities as users of social networks, mobile apps, search engines and connected objects contribute to the production of economic value which is captured by the platform owners. According to Cardon and Casilli (2015, 12–14), such activities could be considered as "work" if they comply with three conditions:

- They produce value for economic players.
- They are subject to a minimal level of contractual agreement, usually accepted by clicking on an agreement message, defining property ownership of data and user-generated content, privacy standards and consumer rights.
- They provide performance indicators: indicators of reputation, quality assessment and popularity measurements; that services are rated by lay people instead of experts, etc.

This kind of work is theorised by some authors as "digital labour" (Scholtz 2012). In some cases (e.g. clicking "like" on a Facebook page), these tasks can be considered as low-intensity and low-expertise, exploited by data mining algorithms; in other cases (e.g. rating a travel service or a movie), tasks can be considered as cognitive within informal activities, captured and appropriated in a market context through the mediation of digital systems (Cardon and Casilli 2015).

Prosumer work exists quite clearly outside any kind of employment relationship.

TRANSFORMATION OF THE EMPLOYMENT RELATIONSHIP

This section proposes a synthesis of the main features of the challenges to the employment relationship which are coming from emerging work forms in the digital economy. It then draws some pathways for further research into the development of an 'in between' work status operating between employment and self-employment.

Challenges for the Employment Relationship

Several dimensions of the employment relationship are called into question by the trends mentioned in the preceding section: the concept of the workplace (and its aspects related to working conditions);

the meaning and measurement of working time; the formation of wages; a blurring of the manager–employee relationship; and the representation of workers' interests.

Both digital nomadism and crowd working question the definition of the workplace—which is historically a basic concept in labour contracts and agreements. Digital nomadism relies on multiple workplaces and workers moving between them, although being always digitally 'present' on the company network; consequently, digital nomadism is not correctly covered by the existing legislation or collective agreements on telework. The concept of the workplace is absent from crowd working platforms, although it is a key point of reference for working conditions and health and safety at work. There are, however, several risks associated with crowd working (EU-OSHA 2015). Workers suffer from a lack of social protection, information asymmetry and an absence of reliable dispute resolution mechanisms. Workers are also likely to suffer boredom, due to the undemanding and repetitive nature of the tasks; social isolation; the stress of being solely responsible for organising their work; and, finally, a blurring of the boundaries between work and home and potential intrusions into their private lives.

The concept of working time is as much under threat as the concept of the workplace. In ICT-based mobile work, project-based work in focused teams is the predominant pattern of work organisation. Here, time is related to workflow, milestones and deadlines, beyond the classical definition of working hours; it allows for greater individual autonomy and flexibility but within a framework imposed and controlled by the employer. In on-demand work, working time (and consequently the volume of wages) is left to the full discretion of the employer. In crowd working, time becomes a unit of the fragmentation of tasks, a process which leads to piecework wages. In all these work forms, there is an increasing blurring of the boundaries between working time and private time (De Stefano 2016; Degryse 2016).

The formation of wages is at the core of all emerging new forms of work. In the 'new work culture' promoted by NWOW campaigns, wages should become increasingly flexible, in line with individual benchmarks and performance indicators. In on-demand work, the irregular volume of working hours leads to variable and often unpredictable wage levels, entailing uncertainty about the future and income precariousness when the activity becomes too infrequent. In crowd working, wages are low or rock bottom, payments are not guaranteed and workers are systematically put in competition with other workers, even on a world-wide scale in the case of online tasks; while piecework becomes the general rule and social protection is disconnected from work (De Stefano 2016; EU-OSHA 2015).

Consequently, the manager–employee relationship is becoming increasingly blurred. Emerging forms of work are developing a 'self-employment logic' among employees, who are put in competition in project teams, by internal tendering within companies and by the individual benchmarking of performance. At the same time, the expansion of freelance work generates new groups of economically dependent self-employed workers who then develop a wage-earning logic in trying to develop more stable contractual relationships with their core clients. The category of 'economically dependent self-employed worker' thus emerges as a potentially new category, in between salaried employment and self-employment (Drahokoupil and Fabo 2016; Mettling 2015; OECD 2016).

The representation of collective interests is also under threat since structures of worker representation and social dialogue are mostly absent in the world of on-demand work and crowd working. Some interesting attempts are, however, being made to reconstruct structures of collective representation. On the one hand, some Western trade unions are setting up new internal structures in order to affiliate economically dependent self-employed workers and to provide them with collective assistance, legal advice and reference points concerning remuneration standards in their profession (Degryse 2016). On the other, crowd workers are creating platforms to share their experience, rate themselves and their employers and build online solidarity such as, for instance, the Dynamo platform setup by Amazon Mechanical Turk workers (Salehi et al. 2015).

Pathways for Future Research: Towards a New Work Status?

The dilemma can be summarised as follows: in order to occupy the vacant space and improve the coverage of freelancers and platform workers, we might either elaborate a new status between salaried work and self-employment; or, alternatively, we might enlarge the respective scopes of wage-earner status and self-employed status.

The first approach relies on a new hybrid status of 'economically dependent self-employed worker'. This should concern itself with self-employed workers who receive a major share of their income from stable relationships with a limited number of contractors (Jolly and Prouet 2016; Mettling 2015). Such an intermediate status has already existed for more than 20 years in Italy and Spain, but the workers involved are frequently nevertheless dissatisfied as they are often maintained in an uncertain or precarious situation and are seldom offered stabilisation prospects in a real career. Furthermore, trade unions are also dissatisfied as those with such intermediate status contribute to a weakening of the standard work contract. Improvements are needed. According to a working document of France Stratégie, 'Intermediate status should, at the same time, recognise the autonomy of the worker (autonomy of selection of contractors, autonomy in work location and working time, which should be excluded from the scope of the contract), and recognise his/her economic dependence by means of guaranteeing basic rights in connection with collective bargaining, accidents and occupational illness, income loss and training' (France Stratégie 2016, 7). Another option might be to reclassify freelance work as a wage relationship with an intermediate agency, such as practised by SMart (cf. the contribution of Sarah De Heusch, this volume).

This first approach raises other questions: will the status of 'economically dependent self-employed worker' be able to cover all the currently emerging work forms, including crowd working? What should be the financial contribution of contractors or platforms to the funding of guarantees for workers? And is there a risk of the further destabilisation of existing statuses?

The second approach consists of a broadening of the scope of both existing statuses. Wage-earning status should be adapted to cover increasingly diverse individual trajectories characterised by multiple transitions between different statuses (fixed-term contracts; periods of part-time employment; temporary leave; self-employment as a main or complementary status; time spent in training; subsidised contracts; etc.). This would be done by establishing the concept of sustainable and continuous social rights. Meanwhile, self-employment status, initially designed for entrepreneurs or regulated professions, should be enlarged to encompass freelance workers and the casual self-employed. In this approach, every new form of employment in the digital economy should be separately scrutinised in order to elucidate the extent to which it could belong to an existing form of regulation. The examination of each case should start from the initial presumption of an employment relationship and then establish how it could be connected to existing legislation or collective agreements in the European Union: either part-time work or temporary work for an agency; or posted work (working in another country than where the contract was established). If none of these regulations could be applied, then it should be considered as self-employment.

This second approach also raises other questions: to what extent could those situations, where the contractor has no control over working time, work location and working conditions be assimilated to an employment relationship? To what extent could work in respect of which remuneration is fixed by a platform involving thousands of workers be assimilated to self-employment? How might we establish legal criteria for distinguishing the work done by professional workers, in the course of an employment relationship, from the income generated by people using a platform to gain value from their possessions and personal skills (car, apartment, linguistic skills)? (France Stratégie 2016).

In this debate, researchers have recently suggested that greater attention should be paid to the status of the employer rather than that of the worker (Prassl and Risak 2016). According to these authors, five main functions characterise the role of an employer: starting and terminating the employment relationship; providing work and its remuneration; receiving labour and its results; managing the enterprise's internal market (control and task allocation); and managing the external market (getting benefits and return on investment). In the case of crowd working, those employer functions may be distributed among three categories of actor: the platform owner; the crowd sourcer; and the crowd worker. Each crowd working case should be examined according to these functions. In some cases, like Uber, it is the platform only which assumes these five functions. In other cases, like TaskRabbit, the functions are spread among several actors and the employment relationship is something akin to temporary agency work (for employees) or a representation agency (for intermittent workers).

All these questions remain largely open to further investigation and require closer cooperation between researchers, practitioners, public authorities and trade unions.

CONCLUSIONS

The development of the digital economy is characterised by significant changes in work organisation: a new global division of labour across value chains; the new business model of online platforms, reflecting the increasing capacity to extract value from big data; and a digital renewal of the informal economy. These changes are fostering new forms of work and employment, notably ICT-based nomadic work, on-demand work through online platforms, crowd working and prosumer work. All these emerging forms of work put deeply into question the foundations of the employment relationship: workplace and related working environments; working time; wage formation; the manager–employee relationship; and forms of collective representation. Questioning the employment relationship opens the dilemma either of elaborating a new work status in between wage employment and self-employment, or broadening the respective scopes of both statuses in order to cover intermediate working situations. Both these potential responses raise more questions than answers and should, therefore, open pathways of future investigation.

REFERENCES

Blomsel, O. 2007. *Gratuit! Du déploiement de l'économie numérique.* Collection Folio actuel. Paris: Gallimard.

Brynjolfsson, E., and A. McAfee. 2015. *Le deuxième âge de la machine. Travail et prospérité à l'heure de la révolution technologique.* Paris: Odile Jacob.

Cardon D., and A. Casilli. 2015. *Qu'est-ce que le digital labor?* Paris: INA éditions.

Coriat, B., ed. 2015. *Le retour des communs. La crise de l'idéologie propriétaire.* Paris: Les Liens qui libèrent.

Degryse, C. 2016. "Les impacts sociaux de la digitalisation de l'économie." ETUI Working Paper 2016.02, European Trade Union Institute, Brussels.

De Stefano, V. 2016. *The Rise of the "Just-in-Time" Workforce: On-Demand Work, Crowd Work and Labour Protection in the Gig-Economy.* ILO Conditions of Work and Employment Series 7. Geneva: International Labour Office.

Drahokoupil, J., and B. Fabo. 2016. "The Platform Economy and the Disruption of the Employment Relationship." ETUI Policy Brief N°5/2016, Brussels.

EU-OSHA. 2015. *A Review on the Future of Work. Online Labour Exchanges or Crowdsourcing: Implications for Occupational Safety and Health.* Discussion Paper of the European Agency for Safety and Health at Work, Bilbao.

Eurofound. 2015. [Mandl Irene et al.] *New Forms of Employment.* Luxembourg: Publications Office of the EU.

Flecker, J. 2007. "Network Economy or Just a New Breed of Multinationals?" *Work Organisation, Labour & Globalisation* 1 (2): 36–51.

France Stratégie. 2016. *Nouvelles formes du travail et de la protection des actifs.* Documents Stratégie 2017–2027.

Green, A., M. de Hoyos, S.-A. Barnes, B. Baldauf, and H. Behle. 2013. *CrowdEmploy: Crowdsourcing Case Studies. An Empirical Investigation into the Impact of Crowdsourcing on Employability*. European Commission Joint Research Centre. Institute for Prospective Technological Studies. JRC Technical Reports EUR 26351. Luxembourg: Publications Office of the European Union.

Holtgrewe, U. 2014. "New 'New Technologies': The Future and the Present of Work in Information and Communication Technology." *New Technology, Work and Employment* 29 (1): 9–24.

Huws, U., ed. 2007. "Defragmenting: Towards a Critical Understanding of the New Global Division of Labour." *Work Organisation, Labour & Globalisation* 1 (2): 1–4.

Huws, U. 2013. "Working Online, Living Offline: Labour in the Internet Age." *Work Organisation, Labour and Globalisation* 7 (1): 1–11.

Huws, U., S. Dahlman, J. Flecker, U. Holtgrewe, A. Schönauer, M. Ramioul, and K. Geurts. 2009. *Value Chain Restructuring in Europe in a Global Economy*. WORKS Report, HIVA, Leuven.

Jolly C., and Prouet E., eds. 2016. *L'avenir du travail: quelles redéfinitions de l'emploi, des statuts et des protections?* France Stratégie. Document de travail 2016-04.

Joyce, S., and U. Huws 2016. *Crowd Working Survey: The Size of the UK's Gig Economy Revealed for the First Time*. University of Hertfordshire, FEPS and UNI-Europa, February.

Mettling, B., dir. 2015. *Transformation numérique et vie au travail*. Rapport pour la Ministre Myriam El Khomri. Paris: La Documentation Française.

OECD. 2016. *Automation and Independent Work in a Digital Economy*. Policy Brief on the Future of Work. Paris: OECD Publishing.

Popma J. 2013. "The Janus Face of 'New Ways of Work'—Rise, Risks and Regulation of Nomadic Work." ETUI Working Paper 2013.07.

Prassl, J., and M. Risak. 2016. "Uber, TaskRabbit & Co: Platforms as Employers? Rethinking the Legal Analysis of Crowdwork." *Comparative Labour Law and Policy Journal* 37 (3): 619–651.

Salehi, N., L. Irani, and M. S. Bernstein 2015. "We Are Dynamo: Overcoming Stalling and Friction in Collective Action for Crowd Workers." *Proceedings of the 33rd Annual ACM Conference on Human Factors in Computing Systems*. ACM, 2015.

Scholtz, T., ed. 2012. *Digital Labor: The Internet as a Playground and Factory*. New York: Routledge.

Valenduc, G., and P. Vendramin. 2016. "Work in the Digital Economy: Sorting the Old from the New." Working Paper 2006.03, ETUI, Brussels.

Vendramin, P., and G. Valenduc. 2016. *Le travail virtuel*. Rapport pour la CSC dans le cadre du mécénat de la Banque nationale, Bruxelles.

Wauthy, X. 2008. "Concurrence et régulation sur les marchés de plateforme: une introduction." *Reflets et perspectives de la vie économique* XLVII (1): 39–54.

CHAPTER 4

The Deconstruction of Employment and the Crisis of Citizenship in Europe

Luis Enrique Alonso

INTRODUCTION

The financial crisis, which forms the main frame of reference for understanding the meaning of life in society today, has led to a particular focus on a trend that began in the economic cycle of the 1980s, with a major change in patterns of state intervention in the economy. Public measures to restore the solvency of financial systems and limit their indebtedness have recently led to the effective abandonment of any public policy to sustain employment and, at the same time, effective containment of all wage claims. This is the development of 'supply-side policies', intended to break down any barrier to market operation, even where that might result in misallocation and obvious social inequalities: supply-side policies that were used in boom times (theoretically) to foment growth, although, paradoxically, they are now also being used as a virtual remedy for panic, the crisis and the widespread recession, always supposedly to boost the activity and confidence of the markets themselves.

L. E. Alonso (✉)
Universidad Autónoma de Madrid, Madrid, Spain

© The Author(s) 2019
A. Serrano-Pascual and M. Jepsen (Eds.),
The Deconstruction of Employment as a Political Question,
https://doi.org/10.1007/978-3-319-93617-8_4

Since the financial crisis that began at the end of the first decade of this century, the rhetoric of state *managerialism* has served to bring about a systematic deformalisation of the historical concepts on which the social responsibility of European governments used to be based (Bauman 2015; Le Goff 2000). Many of the social policies were implemented in the Keynesian cycle, based on the idea that public resources and social rights were guaranteed by the direct action of the state. Now, however, they are justified and managed by means of a powerful corporatisation of supply (with consequent dematerialisation of the public sector), coordination with the market sector in the provision of (duly scaled down) traditional services, and, above all, maximum subordination of state public intervention measures to the assessments and approvals of international financial agents, which have turned into anonymous, super-legitimated *markets* (Alonso et al. 2015). We have moved on from the governmental practice as implementation, on behalf of the state (hence management of civil rights), of measures politically guaranteeing the economic rationale of a society, to the omnipresence of the concept of *governance* as the proposition for the simple public coordination of private and business-based social initiatives that has come into being in urban or regional territories and contexts (Rose 1999).

In the following pages, we will study how the disintegration of the traditional form of labour market, and of the set of civil conventions of which it used to consist throughout Europe, has come about. We shall see that we have moved on from the use of a legally shaped category of employment, regulated by specific laws that tended towards the harmonisation of general rights and legal conditions of work, to a progressive, cumulative dualisation and institutionally organised fragmentation of contractual employment situations, resulting in a process of progressive weakening of the conditions of protection, security and rights assured by the classic idea of European labour citizenship. Thus we can see how, since the 1990s, the European Union has been acting more as a disciplinary monetary agency than a body championing the collective guarantees of the wage-earning society. In this current European framework, social citizenship is buckling and turning into a new kind of liberal citizenship, with sole reference strictly to individual political freedoms.

THE CRISIS OF THE PURPOSE OF WORK

In the last major historical cycle of the market economy, we experienced a demonstrable decline in the mass production model and the *visible hand* (a legal framework for economic regulation, as well as recognition and greater visibility of defined and predefined employment rights, particularly, in the context of large companies), associated with the demand for large volumes of production and the achievement of industrial economies of scale of a fundamentally *national* nature. This model has been replaced by the organisational and ideological hegemony of a *flexible company*, characterised by rapid innovation and speedy technical change, dedicated to adapting to the differences and segments of a particularly fragmented global market, where the corresponding economic logic is the search not so much for economies of scale, but for economies of organisation and management of new competitive resources and financial profitability derived in the short term and at *international* level (Alonso 2001). And in this transition, many of the legal certainties that used to constitute labour standards have become obscured and weakened to vanishing point, and, with this, pay and incentive systems, the duration of contracts and the structure and agents of collective bargaining have exploded into a highly complex set of dynamics that tend towards fragmentation, and even personalisation, and to a large extent the loss of the links and activities of the production chain, collective references and institutional labour protection mechanisms (Le Goff 1999).

Employment is becoming separated from its public, or simply collective, frame of reference, and its legal certainty is being limited by the rhetoric of the intrinsic perversity of intervention of any labour law safeguard, which now conflicts with the strict orthodoxy of competition, focus on trade and deregulation. The *work culture*, as a set of standards and values of the world of work derived from the wage ratio underlying it, which in the long term creates a model for a lifetime project, is dissolving into a constellation of jobs taken as micro-contracts for individualised services, adapted by volume and time to companies' business needs (Du Gay 2007). Thus, the public deficit becomes the dimension most severely penalised by the globalised, anonymous and volatile international financial markets that dictate possible economic policies within territories. With this, social policies of all kinds (from employment to health, through pensions and unemployment benefits) always appear as the first element to be reduced and minimised in governments' processes of surgical cuts, rationalisation and economic adjustment. Under this *new spirit of capitalism* (Boltanski and Chiapello 2002; Du Gay and Morgan 2013), Keynesianism as a policy, and the Keynesian pact, as a state of order negotiated between the corporate representatives of the employment process, have been declared to be definitive barriers to maintaining the competitiveness of nations, and ineffective in achieving the flexibility essential to joining the global economy's profitable groups.

In short, the Keynesian-Fordist world of work has shattered along numerous horizontal, vertical and temporal lines, always tending towards the individualisation and depoliticisation of labour relations, leading to partial deactivation of the traditional mechanisms of collective bargaining, and thereby of the trade union organisations that found stable form and became institutionalised in that world (Jessop 2008). The horizontal breach has opened up between the centre and the periphery of employment, between the corporate nucleus of companies and subcontracted work, between internal and external markets, in a broken line that imposes barriers and differentiated, unequal labour relations between good jobs and bad jobs. A dualisation that attacks industrial and middle-management jobs, to defend and shield highly qualified jobs in financial intermediation, technological innovation or business strategy, while downgraded jobs in both the direct services sector specifically, and under the general convention whereby all jobs in this band are regarded as a contract for work and services, without any further commitment or obligations, are proliferating and being weakened. There is therefore little left of the Fordist occupational scale, defined as a continuum with pay increasing as a person rises up it, but with formal rights practically identical throughout the scale (Graeber 2015).

The weakening of the social, legally constructed meaning of work is a process coinciding with the centrifugation of labour relations with a view to removing as much of the workforce as possible from the collective bargaining process, which also imposes a break in the line of incentives. This immediately verticalises, establishes a hierarchy and increases inequality between positions in the work process. Thus, at the top, the technical specialists (who, in the Keynesian era, built alliances with the historical class organisations through their dynamics of training and defence of collective interests in negotiations) are now distancing themselves from the pact, in the form of '*symbolic analysts*', who determine the use of information, take financial decisions and devise flexible company strategies (Reich 2015), seeking entirely individualised promotions and incentives and embarking on aggressive careers which, while securing their own improved position in the organisation, tend to worsen the position of others, particularly the weakest and those who cannot defend themselves through their qualifications or status in the company.

Lower down, the generalised, institutionalised precarisation, mobilisation and insecurity make sheer survival the central, albeit clearly perverse, incentive, which individualises and fragments the world of work. The volatility and absence of macroeconomic organisation of the post-Fordist model (a disorganised capitalism that operates in terms of disciplinary randomness as the absolute neoliberal rationale (Laval and Dardot 2013) ultimately form two kinds of social flexibility—*internal flexibility*, which individualises, relaunches and applies market situations restricted to professionals, who endeavour to separate their human capital from other kinds of social capital of production, in order then to enhance its profitability in line with the business cycle; and an *external flexibility*, which is the pure application of social Darwinism to the most elemental, troubled, insecure forms of contracted employment, lying between structural unemployment and cyclical misemployment and generating very low cognitive and qualification requirements, wherever traditional stable occupations can be eliminated. In any event, it is in this disorganised capitalism that the rhetoric of flexibility comes to the fore as the *engineering of subjectivity* (Serrano et al. 2012) and replaces any shared commitment as a mechanism for regulating work behaviours and occupational development.

Lastly, the generational split in the labour market entails the fragmentation of personal life cycles in relation to work. The Fordist production structure life cycle was a continuum running from relatively early integration into regular work, and again a relatively late retirement from working life, on a gently rising trajectory within one company, or with minimal changes between very homogeneous categories. The post-Fordist landscape is very different. At the top levels of employment, rotation and switching companies is increasing, as the idea of a profession is largely being decoupled from the idea of a stable organisation, on a path that initially turned people working in the liberal professions into functional professionals (working for a large economic organisation), and from those functional professionals we have moved on to hired professionals (selling strategies in the short term from one organisation to another), but quantitatively, it is at the lowest levels of the occupational scales or in the *external* markets where working life cycles are being disrupted and fragmented, with people constantly joining and leaving regular employment, putting their lives on hold, with partial relationships with the regulated occupations (Durand 2013).

Thus, we see the glory of unstable work, with constant changes of job and ambiguous, or downright fraudulent, uses of regulations and contract terms (bogus traineeships, bogus self-employment, bogus unemployment on benefits, bogus retirees, etc.), all circumscribing a 'Balkanised' market that is institutionally disorganised and generates permanent social *risks* (unemployment, social exclusion, disaffection or new poverty, as the loss of stable relationships with society). This situation is presented as natural to the human condition, and something that a competent individual should be able to internalise and manage by him—or herself, expediting his or her availability and adaptability to the requirements of the new, changing world of work (Castel 1997, 2010).

THE DESTRUCTURING OF FORMS OF EMPLOYMENT

There is, therefore, another side to the new promotional, disciplinary culture (Sennett 2006) of the beneficiaries of post-Fordist deregulation, defiscalisation and privatisation, with a strong increase in elitist, self-promoting, ostentatious and trophy kinds of consumption: that of the socially unstable, the excluded, and those surviving on 'socially undesirable' jobs (occupied by people in the most vulnerable sectors of society, including immigrants, refugees, displaced persons or indeed, in other respects, by the disabled) and with lifestyles not so much of material or static poverty, but of dynamic exclusion or unequal access and limited capacities in the social order. Lifestyles that, with any unstable incomes they may have, can sustain actual levels of consumption, but which are in some way stigmatising, as they are categorised as unbranded, undiscerning consumption or *functional poverty*, a form of existence of those who are surviving with no future plans other than remaining on the margins of the labour market day after day (Castel 2013; Paugam 2007).

The proliferation of *divergent* paths of employment on the labour market comes up against the very contradictions that engender the public and private defensive strategies established as a way of escaping from the impasse of unemployment. Thus, improvements in the educational level, whether in the form of statutory education or private investments in human capital, can immediately relieve the pressure on the labour market (and the unemployment statistics), generating the parking effects we know well—studying because there is no work available—but, at the same time, the lines of desirability of jobs and the social normality of work are drawn, leaving aside manual and industrial jobs or traditional trades that are looked down upon, compared with the stereotypical image of working in finance or an academic profession as the only occupations that satisfy job aspirations and the status level carved out by an education system modelled, in turn, on the idea of a professional career. The class-based honour acquired through study means that jobs failing to meet the status expectations created are undesirable (Bauman 2010, 2011).

The high levels of unemployment in the socially weakest age groups, and the concentration in these age groups of precarious, temporary or seasonal work, are an expression of the practice of postmodern organisation of fragmenting and breaking down the social bases of work until the most favourable conditions for profitability are achieved for the individualised pseudo-contracting of resources, appearing in the freest possible (least socially protected) form. Only some successful careers, based on the class origin, special meritocratic values or cycles of major business growth, break through the shield of the internal job markets and protected professional careers (Alonso et al. 2012, 2016). The rest play out from the ostracism and minimisation of traditional workers' working lives sustained by family solidarity, to placement en masse in precarious underemployment or on subcontracts as a provisional form of livelihood, and bogus social lengthening of 'official' youth, via working lives of complete marginalisation or spent in *successive approximations*, in other words passing through successive positions in the production process (often with periods of unemployment between jobs) on the basis of trial and partial error, which end up as an increasingly long period of instability, extended study and support from the family, approaching the corporate cores of organisations in a drawn-out process of constantly competing for posts defined by their fundamental instability, against the clock, and with the constant threat that each move could cause one to drop completely 'out of the market' (Alonso et al. 2011).

In short, the post-Fordist employment crisis (which began with heavy unemployment that has continued throughout the period, extending into loss of stability and quality of actually existing employment) indicates a change in the economic uses of work, where the relationship between growth and quantitative and qualitative job creation is being lost and destabilised in a combination of haphazard dynamics depending on the chaotic 'anti-laws' of the financial markets (Alonso 2009). In this deregulation and dejuridification of work, turning it into individualised employment competed for by people in the various job queues for the labour market, the socially weakest groups have shouldered the costs of a model of high profitability and low security, and thus the age ranges socially construed as youth, together with other especially vulnerable groups (workers aged over 50, women with family responsibilities, immigrants and expellees) have been reproducing, in an amplified way, according to their particular socio-economic status, the conditions of dislocation, Balkanisation and precarisation of the post-Fordist labour market. Even the very idea of work has exploded once and for all into highly differentiated occupational paths based on the quotas of human, social, economic, cultural and relational capital that are extremely varied depending on the different social groups of reference, membership and origin.

GOVERNANCE OF THE CRISIS

Thus, from the principle of socially regulated, legitimate authority, typical of the social-democratic cycle of governability, based on the concept of *governance*, one moves on to the interchange of interests and resources between public and private spheres, legitimated by increased efficiency and profitability for all parties. This change in legitimation models is justified in terms of post-political management of public affairs, and recasts the image of the network (of public and private associations, the tertiary sector and businesses), this time as activator of the interchange and mobilisation of basically economic resources. Hence, the state, in this function of *governance* (yet another reincarnation of the theory of liberal civil society) now takes on the role only of a facilitator of alliances and relationships of partnership between social and economic actors (taken as equal, autonomous and horizontal, and committed to generating public wealth on the basis of seeking to achieve individual objectives and further individual interests).

The impact of the new concepts of *management* has not been long in coming at state level, and, from the 1980s onwards, states have been changing the direction of their intervention: we are seeing less and less of a *welfare state* strictly speaking, and more the configuration of a *workfare state*.

In other words, we are experiencing the transformation of a welfare state based on the social, productive or employment policies to a performance state, fundamentally based on the policies of technological, financial and monetary profitability. With this kind of change in intervention philosophy, far closer to a liberal state than a social state, public policies of building up the productive and social fabric are replaced by policies of monetary recovery, individualised training and mobilisation of human resources, control of social demands and facilitation of operation of the major economic powers under the 'technical' argument of their support for the market as a synonym of competitiveness, modernisation and development. For all these reasons, it is argued that the state can no longer support excessive social costs, but is obliged to prioritise profitability and facilitate what the market requires, because, if this line were not followed, any territory would miss out in the race for international markets, leading to backwardness and poverty (Anisi 1995, 2010). In the West, the state is, therefore, turning from a state that decommoditise the social area into one that commoditise, or even recommoditise it (through privatisation); from a social state based on the socio-occupational ownership models to an 'agent' state based on the economic and financial ownership models.

Universal access to social services is becoming increasingly problematic, due to simple elimination, privatisation, deterioration and/or abandonment—'neo-beneficence'—or through the reconstruction of a system of additional payments for their immediate funding, as is the intention of user fees, charges and indirect taxes. Strategies along these lines may be combined: public services directly provided under the state are neglected, ignored, starved of cash and eroded, and, at the same time, subsidised or unsubsidised private services are boosted, with claims of their better quality and accessibility, even though frequently the public authorities directly or indirectly become the principal funder of private services (Cingolani 2015). Highly current examples could be postal services, police, education, healthcare services and even private pensions. From the state as a universal benefactor and producer, it is, therefore, possible to move to a client state publicly collecting taxes to allow private businesses to operate securely around them.

In the final analysis, the process of public management as privatisation or as a process of market recovery, that is to say general social recommoditisation, amounts to *the institutionalisation of the risk society and the precarisation of work*. Leaving work constantly at the mercy of market activity cycles means that there is no job stability over one's lifetime, and acknowledges that citizens are divided into those who are stable and those who are unstable (Alonso 2007). Thus, in the most economistic rhetoric, citizenship has become a label of 'financial normality' rather than a right to recognition of the public nature of social affairs. In this vein, we are seeing a complete reformulation of the state as a protector, benefactor and producer: we have moved over to the state being fundamentally a monetarist, pro-entrepreneurial enabler, with stimulating the market as its chief mission. In many cases, the state no longer has the role of rationaliser and holder of the reins of the market (creator of positive or public freedoms), but fundamentally, it is the greatest champion of the market's overlap with social affairs, maintaining only its role as guarantor of negative or private freedoms (Harvey 2007). It also implies the danger, already present and proven (Piketty 2015), that fairly obvious social inequalities and costs will arise.

We are witnessing a dramatic change in the intervention policies of the contemporary state. Thus, we are moving away from the preponderance of openly decommercialising intervention policies—generating public areas not directly regulated by the laws of value and profitability—now regarded as passive, to recommercialising state policies, generating the bases and means of profitability for the private sector, now redefined as *active policies*. The state is not so much an instrument or agent of an all-encompassing, indefinable power, as the product of the conflicts between social classes and groups, and, as the balance of forces and bases of action of these groups has changed, so has the purpose of their action (Heilbroner 1976; Galbraith 1984). In this way, the strategies of social intervention are becoming ever less universal, and social rights are becoming more differentiated between particular groups, in the same way as they are being taken on board in very different ways, according to different territorial situations.

Austerity Welfare

It is a recognised fact that austerity imposed on the cost of labour, the freezing, cutting or even partial or complete dismantling of important areas and services of the welfare state, and the heavy focus on technology in the production process and parallel increasing legal flexibility, have caused the typical redistributive effects classic to Keynesian policies to be replaced by the anti-distributive effects of the supply economy.

Spurred on by deregulation, forms of elitist consumption and a new financial euphoria emerged and were encouraged: new forms of speculation on the stock markets, mergers and acquisitions of companies, bullish behaviour on the property market, etc. The expansion of the financial economy and the creation of a type of more or less specialised, highly paid job in the management apparatus of this financial, speculative economy served to consolidate a new level of elites and upper strata of society with a renewed promotional, individualist culture. As well as occupying the main decision-making posts in politics and the media, they have succeeded in socially asserting the narrative of sacrificing whatever is collective, public and shared to the markets, the only bodies that have true power and self-legitimation (Aglietta and Orléan 1990), as the one and only possible rational policy. The financial crisis has not only failed to erode the power of these economic elites but has given them carte blanche to take part in the decisions of national democratic governments.

With this, we have experienced, first, the decline in social policies, with the limitation of services and benefits created in a universalist spirit, and at the same time the beginning of a maximum possible cutback in public expenditure, blamed for all the ills and evils of the crisis. And, secondly, we are seeing the boom in financial policies, which is where state interventionism takes on special vigour and where the current policies of economic adjustment, restructuring and realignment come in. An example of these policies is the support and use of public resources for the winding up and financial rehabilitation of indebted organisations with excessive toxic liabilities (Fine and Dimakou 2016).

The latest episodes in the cruel crisis we are undergoing presuppose the culmination of progress from an interventionist state which has therefore turned into an agency that is more than 'redistributive' (in the sense of the Keynesian era), into a lever of reallocation and recommoditisation, where its economic efficiency has to transcend any of its social objectives. Moreover, and first and foremost, it must be *cheap*, in the sense of not draining resources away from the revival of economic growth, using the dogma of displacement of the private initiative through the excessive growth of the public sector—or *crowding out*—as a political justification for minimising the state's social functions. Thus, we have seen the partial transformation of the criteria organising the welfare field and the controversial conversion of universal public policies into elements of an *assistentialist* state with a preresidual focus, based on the application, in this area of social action, of the economic rationality criteria prevailing in the market. This minimisation of public policies on welfare, and application of the corresponding criteria of efficiency and market rationality, bring to the fore a model of *austerity welfare*, the rationality and efficiency of which are measured in terms of resource savings. There is an ethos that corresponds to this parameter: the ethos of scarcity and frugality of services (Gil Calvo 2009, 2013).

FINANCIAL CONTROL AND SOCIAL DISCIPLINE

In its various guises, the European welfare state always operated to generate a universal culture of the public sector, which had become synonymous with the very idea of citizenship, supporting a series of growing rights, in terms of both the number of individuals covered by them, and their depth and the benefits included under generic ownership. However, the trend has now been inverted, and what can be discerned is a kind of *selective* state intervention. In this way, as regards its social aspects, state intervention at the centre of society is taking place ever more scarcely.

The general recommoditisation of the post-Keynesian (or more precisely anti-Keynesian) era means that risks have to be assumed and managed personally, forming part of the package of purchases of the consumer society itself, according to one's private purchasing power, with these elements of risk management, in the form of private health, pension plans, life annuities, all kinds of individual insurance, etc., thus reinforcing the market and financial structure of dematerialised capitalism (Klimecki and Willmott 2012). However, for especially vulnerable and weak groups, which cannot assume the risk with a degree of financial solvency, new styles of social policies, described as *de minimis* policies, are appearing: social policies for intervention in the margins of the system, associated, basically, with what might be called an attempt to avoid social collapse and disintegration in peripheral and premarginal groups in the social system.

This represents the decline of the social policies of full citizenship and their replacement with highly *focused* assistential policies, almost always linked with groups unrelated or only loosely related to work, making them immediately capable of isolation and stigmatisation as 'abnormal' groups, with normality regarded as a stable, fluid relationship with the market as a purchasing entity. They are *palliative* policies for what could be called the excessive social costs that can arise from a private-sector-based and absolutely commercialist model of overall social management (Ruesga 2002); they are precarious policies for a socially precarious period that are increasingly deinstitutionalised and confused, seeking a new *governability* in the social management of risk, between commoditisation of assistance and endorsement of responsibility falling on personal solidarity or the public's sense of charity.

In another different, but clearly related, aspect, we can state that not only is there a generic decline in social policies, but also, at the same time, a trend, almost general throughout Europe, is emerging, according to which social or employment policies, as they grow scarcer, are becoming more territorial and are linked with administrative units below the national government. The status of citizen is thus caught in a paradoxical dilemma: the more the media and the economy are globalised, the more the condition of social citizenship tends to take refuge in local communities, as an area of *minimal* resistance where a scaled-down social pact may possibly be established (small is beautiful), but also where costs can be externalised to other territories with less capacity to compete. Accordingly, to a large extent, social policy, in its generic profile, no longer tends so much to be a policy of universal national citizenship, but rather one of management focused on at-risk groups (and of maintenance of these groups in a situation of a certain minimum, functional social integration), and of territorialisation associated with actual competition between regions and the resulting border effects.

It is symptomatic, along these lines, that post-liberal employment plans are meticulous transpositions from *managerial* literature, and in general the policies that we have seen in the past few years in this field are either policies of a fundamentally individualising character, tending to provide individuals with solutions in the form of personal information, training or specific meritocratisation in relation to 'job-seeking' (Lazzarato 2012); or they are policies of subjection of premarginal individuals in the secondary labour markets, with these margins being established as a more or less stable element of the social structure model. We are therefore witnessing a de facto separation between employment policies and social policies, with the subsequent decline in the '*conventions and justifications*' that used to bind social and employment policies together, based on the idea of a normalised, universalised wage-earning lifestyle, and social welfare rights derived from collective labour rights.

PRECARIOUS CITIZENSHIP

The practice of this post-Keynesian *austerity welfare* has cut off at the root the assumptions that made it possible for the previous welfare cycle to develop. These days, the dominant economic rhetoric, taken up by the most conventional political management, has pushed service universality and growth to turn into service *selectivity* and reduction. The economic and social rights of citizens have become financial property rights, and the internalisation of the social costs of economic growth has turned into the elimination of the supposed perverse effects of state intervention. In short, caveats about shortcomings of the market have been withdrawn, and it is now proclaimed that inefficiencies are the product of distortions of the state (Graeber 2012).

In this context, the neoliberal proposition was always accompanied by the hymn to civil society as an abstract alternative to the ill effects caused by public policies in the field of citizens' social rights. *Self-help* is, therefore, the proposition that family or community should take charge of dealing with temporary problems of social welfare. At root, it is suggested that any social problem can be rapidly internalised if the person concerned really has a positive, normalising attitude that is not deviant or pathological, since the market will always provide wealth and welfare to those who do not want to be social parasites. Thus, the triumph of the autonomy of civil society over dependency caused by welfare state bureaucracy is proclaimed (Damon 2013). This would be the rhetoric to legitimate policies of containment or cutbacks of social expenditure as a response to social needs falling outside organised economic channels, which would amount to relocating the field of need in a *residual—* 'pre-welfarist'—space, and would reopen an assistentialist field for associations (commercial, voluntary or agreed partnerships), closer to nineteenth-century charity than to the social justice of a constitutional social state.

The formal separation between social and employment policies is especially relevant. Once shrinking, declining employment rights are separated from social rights, the latter tend to be regarded in a partial (compensatory) and non-distributive manner (they must not modify the income structure or reallocate funds in a strong economic sense). In the *workfare state*, social rights have to sign up to the universal code of the market, regarded as the prime regulator (Standing 2013). Only once disturbing effects have actually been detected (extreme poverty, increased inequality, uncontrolled migration, family breakdown, etc.) is intervention tolerated to contain the conflict, lay down the limits or create a 'safety belt' for the welfare society (no longer the welfare state), but with interventions that still do not cause economic distortion (cheap), presented as socially enabling or resorting directly to measures of public policy (Foucault 1990).

Implementation of the *workfare* philosophy by means of 'social liberalism' or notions of 'flexicurity', promoted, through the ideas disseminated by the European Union, in many arenas, from the Luxembourg summit at the end of the 1990s to date, is aimed at a new form of management of localised minimal social policies intended for marginal groups, and employment policies of a productivist stamp targeted at the individualised search for jobs or niches, sources of work or autonomous forms of employment (Standing 2014).

The formula of 'work for those who can, security for those who cannot', championed by the entire post-neoliberal front that came to power in much of Europe at the end of the 1990s, implies the philosophy of the new commitment to 'prepare' people for technological change, with their maximum adaptability to the requirements of the labour market, using the euphemistic formula of increasing '*employability*'. At the same time, social policies are being restricted to controlled assistance for the social margins (like a safety belt for the central system), within which the diffuse circle surrounding the new post-industrial society is stabilised: those without documents, those without a fixed wage, those without a computer, those without nationality, those without qualifications—in short, 'those without' all kinds of things. The era of precarity, not only of employment, but also in social and survival terms, has been institutionalised, condoned by the highest institutions of the European Union (Paugam 2007).

We are seeing the development of employment policies of a competitive personal stamp, intended for the integrated internal core of society, which require (in exchange for a socially 'entrepreneurial' intervention by the public sector) that state measures be governed by pragmatism and financial probity. The meticulous checks on diminishing social benefits are intended to bring the compulsory nature of job-seeking together with inducements for self-employment or any other form of detachment from the stable wage ratio. We are faced with *de minimis* social policies for the citizens at the bottom of the scale, those who can neither manage nor individually commercialise their own risk prevention and, in a dependent and subordinate fashion, resort to a public sector which is more assistential than redistributive.

The policies of overexposure to the risk of this integrated dual society breach concepts that were so obvious in other eras, such as the regulation of employment. Thus, the wage-earning society is dissolving into thousands of increasingly personally and particularly fragmented strategies for integration into the labour market, or for support in one's protective groupality, historical community or ethnic status, as forms of survival. Accordingly, the models of social intervention deploy compensatory strategies that correspond less to universal social rights or laws than to particular protocols, created for localised groups and individuals with poor social and labour integration. The assistentialisation of social policies is now indissolubly linked with its *focus*—in other words its 'deuniversalisation'—and also with its increasingly territorialised and localised management (Taibbi 2015).

The danger of this new intervention, if it occurs, is that it can be increasingly stigmatising and demeaning. The state, when it intervenes, must place its seal on the incapacity of the individuals resorting to it in the race for social competitiveness. It is the state of those who 'cannot go private and so have to rely on the state'. This style of social intervention for the needy and the incompetent (those who can no longer compete) may impart certain characteristics to the current, shameful social state that are very similar, albeit in a different context, to those of the pietistic state of the poor, with no collective project.

This stigmatising, passively assistential public sector would be merely a remedy for possible situations of social disorder or conflict that might be generated by the potentially growing number of those marginalised by and expelled from the market sector (Stockhammer 2009). This situation coincides with the parallel process of heightened aggressiveness in market rhetoric: rhetoric that makes the market not only the idyllic, cosy world of the inclusive, carefree consumer society of the past, but also the necessary and often painful step for people's competitive future, whether in the form of the purchase of education, technology, or through the means and merits for individual adaptation to the labour market. This assistentialisation is also becoming the complement to the underemployment and vulnerability of broad occupational groups, whose wage ratio is becoming ever less socialised and hence politically disjointed. The dangers of creating a crystallised, strengthened dual society are clear, along with the tendency to place social policies, the very existence of which presupposes the automatic, generalised stigmatisation of users of these social benefits, in a shameful context. By this means, Fordism's typical labour culture has been breaking down and becoming segmented into divergent personal and group paths.

CITIZENSHIP AND DEMOCRACY IN THE EUROPEAN CRISIS

We have seen how relationships between the economic system and the political system have changed in the context of the past few decades of European society. Furthermore, this trend should, in turn, be placed within a general dynamic of transformation (or possibly deterioration) of Western democracies, as the latter is passing through periods of anxiety, pressure, doubt, malaise and, indeed, overt crises that are currently placing the classic concept of democracy itself in a de facto area that is confused, paradoxical and difficult to sustain (Flores D'Arcais 2013; Galli 2013). For the peripheral countries of southern Europe, the difficulties have been amplified by their debt crisis in recent years, in that they have lost their clearly autonomous, sovereign systems of government not only to the major political powers dominating the European Union, but also to pressure from international financial groups that predetermine the policies of authorities at all levels.

Regarding the concept of democracy and its derived citizenship model, we can say that the current international financial crisis has stoked up almost to the limit the polemics about the very pertinence of the concept to describe our current forms of government, where universal suffrage, the competitive party system, the election of indirect political representatives and the guarantee of *negative* liberty, as Isaiah Berlin (1998) called it (that is, the freedoms that guarantee the individual's sphere of activity and autonomy), are clearly maintained as sacred principles. However, disaffection with these representatives on the part of citizens is constantly growing; the dependence of professional politics and its decisions on the economic powers is undeniable and obvious to any averagely well-informed observer; as is the deterioration in quality of democratic life, in the form of an increasing perception of loss of transparency, trivialisation of *accountability* as the obligation to answer to citizens for political decisions, and a significant decline in the integrity and independence of the management processes of current systems of government (Revelli 2015).

As regards the social rights associated with advanced democracies, the collapse is still greater, and the crisis has dealt a final blow to the idea of the constitutional social and democratic state that had become the central narrative of legitimation in Europe since the end of the Second World War. The impact has been so great that there is even talk of a *crisis of rights*—including human rights—and absolute regression, to return to Berlin's definition, of the idea of positive liberties, or of civil rights to obtain public services and goods enabling people to enhance their well-being, dignity and quality of life, the fundamental axis of the idea of the welfare state and the very concept of citizenship (Balibar 2012).

More than an economic crisis, this set of circumstances appears to circumscribe a new regime of *governance* associated with the neoliberal order, which the British sociologist Colin Crouch (2004), with his usual farsightedness, describes as *post-democracy*—a political situation in which, although all the formal mechanisms of electoral (and importantly *only* electoral) participation and political alternation are nominally used, we see a massive reinforcement of the power of performance politics and the media, the power of the major global economic and financial corporations to impose their interests, the decline in sovereignty of the nation state and its capacity to formulate public policies, and the market assault on the basic elements of social citizenship and typically Fordist labour rights (Todd 2010). Along these lines, the rebellion of the international financial and technological elites of the neoliberal cycle that started in the 1980s drained and voided many of the effects of the Keynesian model's political, social and participatory pact. The crisis served to increase the compulsory nature and disciplinary sense of this social shutdown to the point of making the rhetoric on the needs for financial recovery and the income levels of market agents the basic condition for the functioning of political life as a whole (Hibou 2012).

This post-democracy, which in some of its dynamics bears a similarity to an elitist pre-democracy with despotic traits (albeit now in the form of economic and technological despotism), has tended to eliminate what, back in the 1970s, the well-known report of the Trilateral Commission (Crozier et al. 1975) on the governability of democracies (although it was rather concluded that they were ungovernable) judged to be an excess of participative and distributive democracy in the Western nations. According to this argument, the excess disrupted the parliamentary political system (the market of votes) and the economic system (the market of prices), which ultimately sowed panic among the traditional economic elites at the very functioning of democracy, as the distinguished Italian political scientist Norberto Bobbio (1985) summarised critically in his day.

Along these lines, the path towards a new *governmentality*, understood to be the combination of institutions, procedures, calculations and tactics enabling the exercise of power in a *specific, complex* manner (Foucault 2006, 2009), was opened up, and from the outset rights that were not strictly parliamentarian were limited, powers of representation of social organisations and movements (starting with trade unions) disabled and lifestyles and forms of social reproduction individualised and fragmented.

With the debt crisis at the start of the second decade of this century, the Keynesian pact was not only definitively ruptured, but also rendered politically impossible by the rhetoric of *total financialisation* (Alonso and Fernández 2012, 2013). The same thing happened to social democracy, without any real room for manoeuvre, as in the Spanish case, with budget orthodoxy and political neglect of the social sphere in favour of the financial sphere, rendering impossible the typical decommodising political exchanges that acted as a guarantee in the Keynesian era, and even, now dwindling, in the neoliberal cycle that was in the ascendant before the current crisis. The characteristic processes of the Keynesian pact that used to enrich political democracy, from generalised collective bargaining to income agreements, via social control of the legally regulated market and a certain positive redistribution of income and risks, are now regarded with suspicion, and all kinds of ill effects on the market competitiveness of national economies are attributed to them. Thus, we have post-democracy, for a fragmented, precarised, individualised postmodern society, with social and employment rights in decline, and where the increase in social inequality and the erosion of the middle classes have now been laid bare (Gaggi and Narduzzi 2006; Hernández 2014).

But while this post-democracy is a general trait of post-Fordist financial capitalism, the impact of the crisis has been especially severe and socially disciplinary in the peripheral European democracies. For them, the European Union has ceased to be the main modernising vehicle financing their infrastructure and business activities and has turned into the fiercest guardian of financial orthodoxy and budgetary austerity (Koch 2011). Increasingly, remote from its founding principles (and with the content of its compensatory social policies trivialised), the European Union as an institution has become an unwavering champion of monetary stability for the euro, Germany's economic interests and the most blatantly neoliberal economic thinking, passing on the pressure of its austerity and social cutback policies to southern Europe. Along with this, a rhetoric of economic terror and guilt campaigns against the poor is emanating from the European institutions; in which, moreover, all the clichés about the earnestness and efficiency of Protestantism and its work ethic compared with the profligacy and almost congenital inefficiencies of Latin societies (exploited, wasteful, light-minded) are being deployed.

The idea of making societies as a whole pay, particularly, those that are most vulnerable because of the indebtedness caused by their politicians and financial managers, was bound to tarnish the legitimacy of the European institutions. The Greek crisis and the successive interventions and total or partial 'rescue packages' for the peripheral European economies have given rise to a particularly authoritarian cognitive framework for the crisis. The ideas of paying for what one has squandered, having lived above one's means, facing up, first and foremost, to the external debt and expiating the excesses of flawed, inefficient economies have become discursive conventions that have had highly antisocial practical results in the form of national policies of cutbacks, recommoditisation and privatisation of the public sector (Gil Calvo 2013; Dufour 2012). The socialisation of the costs of private bank financial debt, driven and enforced by the institutional machinery of the European Union, entailed a particular harshness and depth of the crisis in southern Europe, entrapped within the monetary rigidity of the euro, the financial penalties of the markets, imposed *austerity* and hence forced recession, without any possibility of expansionary policies, resulting in plummeting economic activity, credit paralysis and massive, growing unemployment (Stuckler and Basu 2013).

The crisis of legitimacy and the loss of perception by large sectors of the population of the social mission of the European Union (one of its historical characteristics) has put an end to many of the pacts and understandings that constituted it over the long term. If the elites of the European political bureaucracies have opted quite distinctly for defending primarily and almost exclusively the interests of the major European (and especially German) economic and financial groups, the peoples of Europe have responded in different ways, but fundamentally imbued with Euroscepticism, remoteness from official policy and distrust of the European institutions (Maurin 2009).

The rising pre-fascist and nationalist right-wing populism and the various versions of social protest that has taken place betray a major difficulty in maintaining the ideological consensus on, and unwavering acceptance of, the European Union. The idea for the absence of real effective policies with social content or even on economic action, other than those that are strictly monetary and financial-control-oriented, masked by technocratic rhetoric, could have been taken from the policy of the European Union itself (now merely an agency representing the interests of the economic elites). However, the policy is still being supported by citizens in very diverse, sometimes paradoxical and contradictory, ideological forms, but which highlight the loss of engagement with and trust in European institutional policy and its official agents.

CONCLUSION: THE DEMISE OF SOCIAL CITIZENSHIP?

Clearly, the electoral market, with the political establishment competing over it, and in the actual rivalry among parties for votes, tends to introduce a second dynamic for the well-timed distribution of social rights, explained rather by the strategy of legitimation and maintenance of parties in power than by essentialist reasons or reasons of recognition of inalienable rights deriving from historical citizenship.

Thus, actions that also tend to fragment and reposition social policies have been taking place throughout Europe, leaving a very large group of these policies (those that have very few electoral benefits) in an enclosed, well defined, almost segregated space, as is the case with actions taken in the context of combating social exclusion and the 'new poverty'. Epitomising progress in the market since the 1980s and its costs (in the form of the increase and institutionalisation of particularly weak, vulnerable social bands), social policy in recent years has restructured its regulatory framework, modelled on a reorganisation aiming to maintain commercial competitiveness at the centre of society and provide a certain minimum level of security at its peripheries, avoiding excessive social breakdown and aligning the basic commercial motivation of the social system with a certain cohesion *in extremis* (Peugny 2009).

In actual fact, the process that we have been and still are experiencing has proved to be more complex than one of the simple recommercialising measures. It is not a case of the dismantling of the welfare state, but of a process of radical restructuring and limitation. This latter process has actually been the result of both supply-side policies and recommercialising initiatives of a liberal or neoliberal type, and of the counterpressures and social resistance actions, defending the maintenance and modified consolidation of the Keynesian consensus, not forgetting the political impossibility of achieving its total elimination, breaking down the remains of the post-war democratic and institutional model (Chavel 2006).

Thus we have experienced tensions which, without destroying the wel-fare state as a whole, have radically transformed it (Rosanvallon 2012). Democracies themselves, especially in Europe, have generated a structure of political, institutional and organisational opportunities that have not succeeded in eliminating (in order to avoid breaking with their own politi-cal legitimation narrative) certain basic social elements of the intervention-ist state, elements that could not be removed or dismantled as a whole, but which have indeed been transformed. We have been able to observe this in the subsequent deployment of new-style paradoxical public policies, strengthened and increased to levels which, in the current financial crisis, appear almost irreversible, the sole purpose of which is to destroy the very idea of social citizenship with positive rights and liberties (Ricoeur 2003).

We are also witnessing, not the end of or decline in traditional employment—as some of the liberal, neoliberal or managerial propa-gandists would have us believe—but the conversion of the wage-earning society into a set of highly unstable employment and quasi-employment cultures; increasingly differential personal working cycles and journeys of integration into the world of work in varying, sometimes directly clash-ing, employee status situations, within an increasingly chaotic contract-ing system; and, in short, the formation of a turbulent universe of hazy work identities, only subject at its periphery, at the most, to policies of particular assistentialisation designed to avoid the excessive social dis-locations of the weak regulation model established by financial post-Fordism (Cowen 2014). Thus it is striking how the post-Fordist mode of regulation introduced by the European Union since the end of the last century, having regard to the codification and convergence of Fordist social-democratisation, is, as a matter of principle, fundamentally weak and socially disorganised, but, on the other hand, highly effective in gen-erating potential gains for the major international economic and finan-cial groups (Sassen 2015). Social justice, pursued as a prime objective by national states—a typical rhetorical point, but a central one, in post-war commitments and those associated with European citizenship—has ceased to be one of the prime forms of regulation of political conven-tions, and has become an explicit absence or an implicit enemy in the *managerial* policy of states, only to be introduced, partially, as an effect of instances of a market self-regulation or cybernetic couplings of com-bined flows of information and economic management. In short, social justice as a limit, or as an unintended cognitive consequence, rather than as an objective of a globalised socio-economic system.[1]

NOTE

1. Translation from the Spanish by Sally Blaxan.

REFERENCES

Aglietta, M., and A. Orléan. 1990. *La violencia de la moneda*. México, DF: Siglo XXI.

Alonso, L. E. 2001. "New Myths and Old Practices: Postmodern Management Discourse and the Decline of Fordist Industrial Relations." *Transfer: European Review of Labour and Research* 7 (2): 268–288.

Alonso, L. E. 2007. *La crisis de la ciudadanía laboral*. Barcelona: Anthropos.

Alonso, L. E. 2009. *Prácticas económicas y economía de las prácticas. Crítica del postmodernismo liberal*. Madrid: La Catarata.

Alonso L. E., and C. J. Fernández Rodríguez, eds. 2012. *La financiarización de las relaciones salariales. Una perspectiva internacional*. Madrid: La Catarata.

Alonso, L. E., and C. J. Fernández Rodríguez. 2013. *Los discursos del presente*. Madrid: Siglo XXI.

Alonso, L. E., C. J. Fernández Rodríguez, and R. Ibáñez Rojo. 2011. "Del consumismo a la culpabilidad: en torno a los efectos disciplinarios de la crisis económica." *Política y Sociedad* 48 (2): 353–379. https://doi.org/10.5209/rev_poso.2011.v48.n2.8.

Alonso, L. E., C. J. Fernández Rodríguez, and R. Ibáñez Rojo. 2012. "Las identidades de ocio y consumo de los jóvenes en la era postlaboral." In *Los nuevos problemas sociales: Duodécimo Foro sobre tendencias sociales*, edited by J. F. Tezanos, 453–479. Madrid: Fundación Sistema.

Alonso, L. E., C. J. Fernández Rodríguez, and R. Ibáñez Rojo. 2015. "From Consumerism to Guilt: Economic Crisis and Discourses About Consumption in Spain." *Journal of Consumer Culture* 15 (1): 66–85.

Alonso, L. E., C. J. Fernández Rodríguez, and R. Ibáñez Rojo. 2016. "Entre la austeridad y el malestar, discursos sobre consumo y crisis económica en España." *Revista Española de Investigaciones Sociológicas* 155: 21–36.

Anisi, D. 1995. *Creadores de escasez: del bienestar al miedo*. Madrid: Alianza.

Anisi, D. 2010. "Capitalismo y democracia." *Economía a contracorriente. Antología de David Anisi*. Madrid: La Catarata.

Balibar, E. 2012. *Citadinanza*. Turín: Bollati Boringhieri Editore.

Bauman, Z. 2010. *Living on Borrowed Time*. Cambridge: Polity Press.

Bauman, Z. 2011. *Daños colaterales*. Madrid y México: Fondo de Cultura Económica.

Bauman, Z., et al. 2015. *Management in a Liquid Modern World*. Cambridge: Polity Press.

Berlin, I. 1998. *Cuatro ensayos sobre la libertad*. Madrid: Alianza.

Bobbio, N. 1985. "La crisis de la democracia y la lección de los clásicos." In *Crisis de la democracia*, edited by N. Bobbio, G. Pontara, and S. Veca, 9–38. Barcelona: Ariel.

Boltanski, L., and È. Chiapello. 2002. *El nuevo espíritu del capitalismo*. Madrid: Akal.

Castel, R. 1997. *La metamorfosis de la cuestión social*. Buenos Aires: Paidós.

Castel, R. 2010. *El ascenso de las incertidumbres: Trabajo, protecciones, estatuto del individuo*. Buenos Aires: Fondo de Cultura Económica.

Castel, R. 2013. "De la protection sociale comme droit." In *L'avenir de la solidarité*, edited by R. Castel and N. Duvoux. París: Presses Universitaires de France.

Chavel, L. 2006. *Les classes moyennes a la derive*. París: Seuil.

Cingolani, P. 2015. *La précarité*. París: Presses Universitaires de France.

Cowen, T. 2014. *Se acabó la clase media*. Barcelona: Antoni Bosch Editor.

Crouch, C. 2004. *Posdemocracia*. Madrid: Taurus.

Crozier, M., S. P. Huntington, and J. Watanuki. 1975. *The Crisis of Democracy: Report on the Governability of Democracies to the Trilateral Commission*. New York: New York University Press.

Damon, J. 2013. *Les classes moyennes*. París: Presses Universitaires de France.

Dufour, D. R. 2012. *Le divin marché. La révolution culturelle libérale*. París: Gallimard/Folio.

Du Gay, P. 2007. *Organizing Identity: Persons and Organizations "After Theory"*. Londres: Sage.

Du Gay, P., and G. Morgan, eds. 2013. *New Spirits of Capitalism? Crises, Justifications, and Dynamics*. Oxford: Oxford University Press.

Durand, J. P. 2013. *La cadena invisible. Flujo tenso y servidumbre voluntaria*. México, DF: FCE/Universidad Autónoma Metropolitana.

Fine, B., and O. Dimakou. 2016. *Macroeconomics. A Critical Companion*. Londres: Pluto Press.

Flores D'Arcais, P. 2013. *¡Democracia¡* Barcelona: Galaxia Gutemberg/Círculo de lectores.

Foucault, M. 1990. *Tecnologías del yo y otros textos afines*. Barcelona: Paidós.

Foucault, M. 2006. *Seguridad, territorio, población: Curso en el Collége de France (1978–1979)*. Buenos Aires: Fondo de Cultura Económica.

Foucault, M. 2009. *Nacimiento de la biopolítica: Curso en el Collége de France (1978–1979)*. Madrid: Akal.

Gaggi, M., and E. Narduzzi. 2006. *El fin de la clase media*. Madrid: Lengua de Trapo.

Galbraith, John K. 1984. *Anatomía del poder*. Barcelona: Plaza y Janés.

Galli, C. 2013. *El malestar de la democracia*. Buenos Aires y México: Fondo de Cultura Económica.

Gil Calvo, E. 2009. *Crisis crónica. La construcción social de la gran recesión.* Madrid: Alianza.

Gil Calvo, E. 2013. *Los poderes opacos: austeridad y resistencia.* Madrid: Alianza.

Graeber, D. 2012. *En deuda: una historia alternativa de la economía.* Barcelona: Ariel.

Graeber, D. 2015. *La utopía de las normas. De la tecnología, la estupidez y los secretos placeres de la burocracia.* Barcelona: Ariel.

Harvey, D. 2007. *Breve historia del neoliberalismo.* Madrid: Akal.

Heilbroner, R. L. 1976. *Business Civilization in Decline.* Nueva York: W. W. Norton.

Hernández, E. 2014. *El fin de la clase media.* Madrid: Clave Intelectual. Madrid.

Hibou, B. 2012. *La bureaucratisation du monde à la ère neoliberal.* París: La Decouverte.

Jessop, B. 2008. *El futuro del Estado capitalista.* Madrid: La Catarata.

Klimecki, Robin, and Hugh Willmott. 2012. "De las altas finanzas a la debacle: un relato sobre dos aspirantes a bancos." *Cuadernos de Relaciones Laborales* 30 (2): 305–325.

Koch, M. 2011. *Capitalism and Climate Change. Theoretical Discussion, Historical Development and Policy Responses.* Basingstoke: Palgrave Macmillan.

Laval, C. H., and P. Dardot. 2013. *La nueva razón del mundo. Ensayo sobre la sociedad neoliberal.* Barcelona: Gedisa.

Lazzarato, M. 2012. *The Making of the Indebted Man: An Essay on the Neoliberal Condition.* Los Angeles, CA: Semiotext(e) Intervention Series.

Le Goff, J.-P. 1999. *La barbarie douce. La modernisation aveugle des entreprises et de l'école.* París: La Dècouverte.

Le Goff, J.-P. 2000. *Les illusions du management.* Paris: La Découverte.

Maurin, E. 2009. *La peur du déclassement.* Paris: Seuil.

Paugam, S. 2007. *Le salarié de la précarité.* Paris: Presses Universitaires de France.

Peugny, C. 2009. *Le déclassement.* Paris: Grasset.

Piketty, T. 2015. *El capital en el siglo XXI.* Barcelona: RBA.

Reich, R. R. 2015. *Saving Capitalism, for the Many, Not the Few.* New York: Alfred K. Knop.

Revelli, M. 2015. *La lucha de clases existe...¡y la han ganado los ricos!* Madrid: Alianza.

Ricoeur, P. 2003. *Amour et justice.* Paris: Seuil/Points.

Rosanvallon, P. 2012. *La sociedad de los iguales.* Barcelona: RBA.

Rose, N. 1999. *Powers of Freedom: Reframing Political Thought.* Cambridge: Cambridge University Press.

Ruesga, S. 2002. "Desempleo y precariedad laboral en Europa." *Acciones e Investigaciones Sociales* 14: 5–33.

Sassen, S. 2015. *Expulsiones. Brutalidad y complejidad en la economía global.* Buenos Aires: Katz.

Sennett, R. 2006. *La cultura del nuevo capitalismo.* Barcelona: Anagrama.

Serrano-Pascual, A., C. J. Fernández Rodríguez, and A. Artiaga Leiras. 2012. "Ingenierías de la subjetividad: el caso de la orientación para el empleo." *Revista Española de Investigaciones Sociológicas* 138 (abril-junio): 41–72.

Standing, G. 2013. *El precariado. Una nueva clase social.* Barcelona: Pasado y Presente.

Standing, G. 2014. *Precariado. Una carta de derechos.* Madrid: Capitán Swing.

Stockhammer, E. 2009. "The Finance-Dominated Accumulation Regime, Income Distribution and the Present Crisis." *Papeles de Europa* 19: 58–81.

Stuckler, D., and S. Basu. 2013. *Por qué la austeridad mata. El coste humano de las políticas de recorte.* Madrid: Taurus.

Taibbi, M. 2015. *La brecha.* Madrid: Capitán Swing.

Todd, E. 2010. *Después de la democracia.* Madrid: Akal.

CHAPTER 5

The Decline of the Worker as Collective Subject

Vicente Sánchez Jiménez

INTRODUCTION

As a significant number of authors (Alaluf 1999; Alonso 1999; Prieto 1999) have asserted, work has lost its central role as a mechanism of social cohesion and establishment of collective solidarities. This is demonstrated by its replacement to a large extent as an element unifying the individual and society. In practice, this goes hand in hand with the undermining of labour rights and an ever-increasing imbalance between the two collective subjects intrinsic to the labour market: employer and employee. This manifests itself in the appearance of an ever wider range of contractual models and the weakening of traditional boundaries between categories, such as self-employment and waged employment, formal and informal work, employment and unemployment.

Until a few years ago, work was perceived as an essential precondition for pursuing other goals of a more personal nature, while it also constituted an indissoluble component of the process of socialisation. Particular evidence of this fact is the hitherto customary concept of

V. Sánchez Jiménez (✉)
Complutense University of Madrid, Madrid, Spain

© The Author(s) 2019
A. Serrano-Pascual and M. Jepsen (eds.),
The Deconstruction of Employment as a Political Question,
https://doi.org/10.1007/978-3-319-93617-8_5

107

'stability' in labour relations. Stability means that a person spends most of his or her life embedded in a single workplace with a set of people varying little in its composition. This is clearly illustrated by large industrial factories, the transport sector, education, healthcare or indeed public administration.

Accordingly, work was a basic component of an individual's interaction with society, fostering his or her personal development, as well as the establishment of the traditional family unit. This was possible with the maintenance in past decades of three basic enabling characteristics of stability: material, temporal and spatial. Material inasmuch as it is understood that developing a working life allows a minimum standard of living to be maintained, sufficient remuneration to be obtained and, most importantly, certain revenues to be received when the worker withdraws from the labour market, particularly entitlement to a lifelong pension. As regards the temporal aspect, the labour market, albeit with a large number of unemployed people, particularly in this country, provides continuity from the time of integration into the world of work until the point of leaving, having reached old age, including periods of non-employment covered to some extent by unemployment benefits. Following on from this, spatial stability facilitates the common option of establishing one's habitual residence in a single location, in so far as the workplace remains substantially in the same place. In this country, this is associated, among other things, with the culture of buying a house to live in as part of a safe investment.

The model of the welfare state that prevailed in Europe during the second half of the twentieth century is giving way to flexibility in labour relations, which prevents people from formulating a model of individual growth, as they used to previous decades. However, the displacement of work's role as a social backbone and anchor is not attributable solely to this change in employment conditions, but also to the emergence of other concepts that are given priority status in contemporary society, such as consumption and leisure (Veblen 2008; Galbraith 2012); and to the consequences of the current economic crisis (Barroso 2013).

THE DIMENSIONS OF FRAGILITY OF THE SOCIAL QUESTION

A study of the quality of wages, the instability of plans for a person's working life and the fragility of social protection mechanisms should shed light on the changes that have occurred in the composition of the labour market, the characteristics of employment and labour relations themselves. Moreover, this should make it possible to find the connecting link between these three questions and the progressive decline of the worker as a subject. Likewise, it is useful to bear in mind the deterioration in the welfare model that prevailed in Europe after the Second World War, with, for instance, tax revenue deriving from constant improvement in production from the second half of the twentieth century onwards, which ultimately implies a model of rebalancing among social classes. Public expenditure cuts have been underway since the 1980s, although it is with the current period of economic uncertainty, starting in 2008, and the consequent change in the economic cycle, that there has been a further impairment of its main characteristics, and unexpected consequences have emerged.

Similarly, changes are occurring in what we know as the contemporary constitutional social and democratic state, with the modification of its three fundamental pillars as regards the world of work: the right to form and become a member of a trade union, the right to strike and the right to collective bargaining. An example of this is the Spanish labour market, a model that, while largely combining the basic characteristics of the European social contract, has been suffering from greater pressure in the past few years due to the severe crisis of 2008 and the political and economic decisions taken thereafter. This state of affairs has, moreover, been aggravated, first, by the unresolved chronic persistence of a high degree of precarity in employment and, second, by the weakness in welfare and social protection systems compared with the countries of central and northern Europe. Third, it is important to emphasise the imbalances traditionally existing in the Spanish production model and the successive employment reforms for job creation at any price, which have resulted more or less in a series of failures, as attested by Asenjo and Cebrián (2015).

In certain aspects, there is a need to make comparisons with other European countries, as we are doing here, to help us better understand all the changes that have occurred and the dynamics of the decline of labour in the current political and social circumstances.

ASYMMETRY IN THE WAGE-BASED CONTRACT: PRESSURE ON WAGES AND IMPOVERISHMENT OF THE WAGE-EARNER

Since the consequences of the crisis began to take effect in the economy itself, from 2008 onwards, the total wage bill as a percentage of gross domestic product (GDP) has fallen continuously. That year, the figure for income distribution was higher for wages, amounting to 50.1% of

GDP (INE 2015). Between 2008 and 2010, the share of the total wage bill as part of GDP remained above 50% on average. This figure plummeted from 2012 onwards, coinciding with three key factors: first, the implementation of a new labour reform, which, among other things, had the effect of reducing the importance of sectoral agreements compared with intra-company negotiation; second, wage restraint, leading to the gradual reduction of wages due to the continuing economic crisis, on the pretext of an attempt to maintain levels of competitiveness and, accordingly, the maximum number of jobs; lastly, the upswing in unemployment data, serving as a justification for the two previous measures.

In 2013, wages dropped to 46.7% of GDP (INE 2015). In other words, the share of income from employment as part of wealth distribution continued to fall, while that of income from capital and profit margins increased. From 2008 to 2013, wages fell by EUR 54,500 million, while the gross operating surplus increased by more than EUR 31,000 million. This also includes another variable that is hidden behind the macroeconomic figures: the drop in the total of waged employees and the growth of the self-employed workforce, since the latter falls under operating surpluses and mixed income. This latter factor is particularly clearly reflected in the construction sector.[1] While before the crisis, in June 2007, when the highest number of people were employed in construction, the number of wage-earners was more than 1.9 million, and that of self-employed workers almost 540,000, or 21.6% of the total, by the end of 2015 this figure had altered substantially to 690,000 wage-earners and 365,000 self-employed workers. In other words, the proportion of self-employed workers rose from just above 20% to almost 35% (SS 2015).

Still on the subject of the reduced share of wages in the economy, it may be observed how, between 2007 and 2013, according to data from the Agencia Tributaria [Tax Agency] (AEAT 2016) on figures for the total wage bill, based on the personal income tax (IRPF) returns, the average wage dropped in nominal terms by 1.8% among the population in the 36–55 age bracket, whereas this decline was as much as 9.7% if one considers the earlier age group comprising younger workers up to age 35.

In the time that has elapsed since the outbreak of the crisis of 2008, two clearly distinct periods may be identified. Between 2009 and 2011, the purchasing power of wages continued to rise by more than two points. However, it was between 2012 and 2014 that the reduced share of wages was observed, since the agreed wage increase was 1.3 points below the consumer price index (CPI). The fact is that wages are losing their purchasing power, inasmuch as average pay in Spain increased by a nominal 3% between 2009 and 2013, entailing a 5.8% drop in purchasing power given cumulative inflation over that period. This factor lessened between 2014 and 2015, but even so, in the past five years, there has been a cumulative reduction of 4.5% in average pay, equivalent to EUR 912 less a year (INE 2015).

In this respect, it is also interesting to be able to observe the drop in unit labour costs in terms of competitiveness. This factor should make it possible to determine whether wage devaluation corresponds only to amounts received for the same volume of activity, or on the contrary whether wages are depreciating even further due to a greater increase in productive capacity. This is reflected in the unit labour cost, since this adds the productivity factor to wages. Between 2009 and 2014, the cost of labour rose by 3.1%, but productivity increased by as much as 9.6%, resulting in a reduction of 6.5% in the unit labour cost. This shows how work intensity has been stepped up very significantly, since companies are cutting their workforce during the crisis period by more than the decline in production. While GDP has fallen by 7%, waged work has dropped by 19% (INE 2016).

These data are more alarming if, in addition to the unequal distribution of income between employers and employees, we note the growth, during these years of crisis and economic recession, of poor workers, understood to be the number of people in work but whose earned income is not sufficient for them to sustain a minimum standard of living. According to data from the Labour Force Survey (LFS 2015), the workers who earn the least are receiving gross monthly income of EUR 355 in 14 instalments, which amounts to EUR 4970 a year. Indeed, around 4.5 million wage-earners earn less than EUR 1000 a month in 14 instalments, which is approximately 24% of the total.

This confirms the existence of a progressive wage devaluation that prevents people from taking individual actions of the kind that occurred in past decades, such as having access to housing, and the possibility of accumulating sufficient income to permit a certain level of savings or maintenance of an average standard of living, to name but a few. Even before the current period of economic recession, authors such as Alonso (2001) and Navarro (2004) were already warning of the weaknesses of employment and the gradual precarisation of employment conditions.

The portion of income earmarked to reward wage-earners is being reduced to increase company profits, leading to a complete reformulation of the profit ratio, inasmuch as during the period following the outbreak of the crisis in 2008, the wage bill was reduced to increase profits. This accumulation of wealth at the expense of earned income has serious consequences in terms of fairness and social justice, and also in the capacity for real growth in the economy (ILO Global Wage Report 2014/2015).

Indeed, the trend in tax bases is a faithful reflection of the economic crisis. While earned income is shrinking, state benefits are sharply increasing. By way of example, it may be observed how pensions account for 123,208 million euros of the personal income tax base (AEAT 2016), 25.9% higher than before the outbreak of the crisis and 69.9% up on a decade ago. Similarly, unemployment benefits have increased by 25.9% and 105.7%, respectively.

Alongside these questions, it should be stressed that inexorable adherence to the monetary rules of the euro makes structural measures through the mechanism of currency devaluation impossible, which is conducive towards internal devaluation of wages with the alleged objective of regaining competitiveness against other economies. Among these proposals are restraint on wages, pensions and unemployment benefits, the purpose of the latter being to support income when people are unemployed. In this vein, a more detailed analysis of the temporal variable, as carried out below, is needed, in that we are faced with a process of ongoing wage devaluation underpinned by the adjustment programme for the Spanish economy.

The situation of loss of income from work does not only lead to migratory processes both inside and outside the borders of a given state, but also makes it difficult to maintain stability in a given location. The impossibility of maintaining a sufficient financial contribution and for it to be, in some way, constant over time has a knock-on effect, in terms of the loss of those possessions that help people plan for personal and collective development in an economic model of growth, such as access to housing.[2]

Insecurity and Loss of Control over One's Working Life

The current economic situation entails a loss of earned income. This wage devaluation is, in turn, caused by the deterioration in the labour market, which, together with precarity, goes hand in hand with labour turnover and part-time working as a key factor in this progressive impairment of the necessary stability to plan ahead, individually and socially. Questions such as the temporary nature of jobs, which prevents normalisation of a person's plans for his or her working life, or the generalisation of part-time contracts that do not cover the maximum agreed working hours, with the consequent reduction of income, are essential to gauging a progressive deterioration in the conditions of stability in employment. Likewise, the analysis of unemployment cover must take account of whether people aspiring to work can sustain their livelihoods at times when the labour market cannot meet their expectations of finding employment.

In April 2016, employment, measured through affiliation to Social Security (SS), amounted to 17,463,836 contributing members, 402,996 more than in April of the previous year, representing an increase of 2.68%. However, the number of contributing members remains at 2011 levels, which, to provide further context, are moreover actually similar to those of 2005, due to the precarity of contracts. Indeed, if we take as a baseline the period before the effects of the 2008 financial crisis hit the actual economy, the figures still show a loss of approximately two million affiliations to the general scheme. In other words, affiliation would have to increase by more than 10% to produce figures similar to those of 2007 and 2008.

If the low employment rate in the past few years compared with the period of growth before the crisis, with all that this entails for public finances, is also observed in terms of temporary work, one of the most remarkable characteristics of the Spanish labour market compared with the other countries of the European Union, this continues to be one of the main difficulties. The rate of temporary work in the European Union (Eurostat 2016a) was 14% in 2014, identical to the 2005 annual average figure, which remained very stable over the years. In Spain, this figure was as high as 34% in 2006. With the outbreak of the crisis, a significant number of these jobs were lost, since in the first stages of a crisis it is precarious jobs that are cut in the highest numbers, and a pronounced drop to 31.6% was observed in 2007, 29.1% in 2008, and 25.2% in 2009. That was the year when the decline continued, but far less steeply, and bottomed out in 2013 at 23.1%. From that year onwards, it increased to 24% in 2014, and the forecasts for 2015 were that it would remain at 24.2%. In the case of young people up to 24-years-old, these figures spiked to as much as 69.1% in 2014, with a forecast to exceed 70% in

2015, whereas in Europe the figures for these years are 43.3% and a forecast for 45% (Eurostat 2016b).

Although a drop in temporary work may be seen during the first years of the crisis, it begins increasing again as from the stabilisation of the employment data from 2013 onwards. This fact demonstrates that recovery of the employment situation entails temporary work as its main characteristic. Moreover, temporary contracts with a duration of over 36 months are excluded, which, on average, amounts to 4% of all temporary contracts.

The challenges that a high level of undesired temporary workplaces on the labour market are intensified by the shorter average duration of temporary contracts (Eurostat 2016c). It is important to stress that average contract duration has been falling since 2008. In 2008, the average duration of temporary contracts in days was 77.1%, in 2011 it was 61.6% and in 2014 it was 57%. At the end of 2008, 27% of temporary contracts were part-time, a percentage that remained stable until the end of 2011. From 2012 onwards, it began to rise steadily, reaching 32.7% in December 2014, reflecting an increase of 5.7 points higher than in the period prior to the outbreak of the crisis. In the case of permanent contracts, in December 2008, 31.8% of contracts were for part-time employment. The trend continued, rising steadily, to reach 41.7% in December 2014, 10 points up on 2008.

The increase in temporary employment and the reduction in average contract duration conflict with the desire to obtain full-time work, and the presence of the phenomenon known as involuntary part-time work, whereby people are obliged to take up contracts for shorter working hours due to the impossibility of obtaining full-time contracts, has increased in the labour market. At the end of 2014, this latter position represented 63.2% of part-time workers employed, compared with 35.5% in 2008. In other words, involuntary part-time working doubled in barely six years. This implies that, for the period in question, of the almost 2.4 million people on temporary contracts, more than 1.6 million are in this position because they cannot find full-time work.

However, these data should be weighed against the duration of customary average working hours per week per full-time worker. From 2008 to 2015, this was over 41 hours a week, with only minor variations. Likewise, the customary average working hours per week per part-time worker are more than 18 hours on average over this same period of time.

Similarly, it is worth ascertaining how, in periods when a person is unable to find any job at all, there is a reduction in income from unemployment insurance to offset the lack of earned income. In this respect, unemployment benefit amounts to approximately EUR 7800 a year on average per unemployed person, whereas in 2008, it was around EUR 9500. The reason for this drop of 17.2% is that, currently, recipients of unemployment benefit are accessing the benefit with a more precarious and shorter working life, attributable to temporary work, increased part-time working and rotation in the labour market.

The rate of unemployment cover, being the percentage of unemployed people receiving a benefit as a proportion of the total number of unemployed people (INE 2015), has been in constant growth since the years comprising the period of the crisis up to 2011, as shown in Table 5.1.

This information is supplemented by the long-term unemployment rate, in terms of the number of jobless people who have been seeking work for more than a year as a proportion of the total active population. In 2014, the average for the European Union (Eurostat 2016d) was 5%. In Spain, this rate dropped to 1.7% in 2007, after which it started to rise and was above 10% in the last three years recorded: 2012, 2013 and 2014. This figure is twice as high among young people: in 2007, it was 1.8%, whereas in the last three years recorded, it was over 20% on average (Table 5.2).

The highly unstable nature of the labour market, and, in particular, of contract duration, goes hand in hand with an upswing in the at-risk-of-poverty rate (Eurostat 2016e). Whereas this rate was 24.5% in the EU-28, in Spain it was as high as 29.2% in 2014. The rate declined until 2008, when it bottomed out at 23.8%, 21.6% in the European Union. From the following year, the percentage increased, as shown in Table 5.3. Alongside this, there was an increase in social protection expenditure (Eurostat 2016f). In the European Union, this was 29.5% in 2012; in Spain, it settled at a few decimal points above 20% of GDP

Table 5.1   Rate of unemployment cover. Percentage values

2006	2007	2008	2009	2010	2011	2012	2013	2014	2015
23.9	25.2	29.3	38.3	41	37	36.3	34.3	31.1	28.2

Source INE (2015). Author's compilation

Table 5.2   Long-term unemployment rate. Percentage values

	2007	2012	2013	2014
Total	1.7	11	13	12.9
Young people	1.8	18.9	21.9	21.5

Source INE (2016). Author's compilation

Table 5.3   At-risk-of-poverty rate. Percentage values

	2008	2009	2010	2011	2012	2013
Risk of poverty	23.8	24.7	26.1	26.7	27.2	27.3

Source Eurostat (2016e). Author's compilation

between 2000 and 2007; in 2008, it reached 22.2%, and from 2009 to 2013, it rose to an average of 25.7%, and up to 25.9% in 2012.

FRAGILITY OF SOCIAL PROTECTION MECHANISMS

This heading relates to the substantial decline in mechanisms available to individuals within the labour market in their status as wage-earners to defend their rights, albeit also in periods outside employment, but where income continues to be linked with the labour market, such as unemployment benefits. In particular, it is embodied in the threefold rights available to workers as a whole for the legitimate defence of their interests: the right to collective bargaining, the right to strike and the right to form and become a member of trade unions.

The economic crisis has not only caused working conditions to deteriorate, as may be seen above, but it has also had a profound impact on the characteristics of the constitutional social and democratic state itself, with particular reference to the world of work. Indeed, the need to stimulate a labour market that was not sufficiently dynamic in terms of job creation was cited in order to justify a new labour reform (Royal Decree-Law No. 3/2012 of 10 February 2012 establishing urgent measures for reform of the labour market), which radically reformulated the regulatory standards governing employment.

This latter regulatory change directly affects the configuration of the labour relations framework prevailing until the date of adoption of the employment reform, by altering the balance among the social stake-holders in collective bargaining. This has become possible because the primacy hitherto given to sectoral agreements over company-level agreements has changed. The levels of protection of collective agreements at the sectoral level, principally those with nationwide status, but also those of more limited geographical scope, such as the autonomous region or province, can be replaced by deals reached within companies.[3]

Given the characteristics of the Spanish labour market, where, of the total number of companies registered with the general Social Security scheme (SS 2016) in March 2016, 40.2% consisted of a single worker, 37.6% had between 2 and 5 workers, 19.8% between 6 and 50, 1.2% between 51 and 100, 0.9% between 101 and 500, and only 0.13% more than 500, the level of contractuality in the labour market is very uneven if the only agreements considered are those signed within the company context. According to these data, almost 78% of companies are SMEs or micro-SMEs, which to date have in many cases been governed by sectoral agreements establishing minimum levels (Table 5.4).

The contractual power of workers is declining, as they do not have a sufficiently stable critical mass to face up to their counterparty. In this respect, the regulatory change sanctions a draining of their contractual power, in that sectoral agreements no longer have the highest authority and are losing their status of laying down a minimum that company-wide agreements must, in all cases, improve upon; such that the appearance of a large number of new trade unions is directly related to the option that companies have to enter into agreements at levels below the sectoral agreement, without any need to establish opt-outs for reasons of their financial situation.

This circumstance gives rise to two fundamental questions. The first is the percentage representativity that trade union organisations must have to be able to negotiate sectoral agreements. The second is the weakening of agreements reached by the social stakeholders, since

Table 5.4 Number of companies, total and by number of workers, Spain

Total companies	1 worker	2–5 workers	6–50 workers	51–100 workers	101–500 workers	Over 500 workers
1,461,550	588,052	550,822	289,743	17,682	13,211	2040

Source Social Security (2016). Author's compilation

the above-mentioned employment reform took place only a few days after these stakeholders had signed a new State-Level Agreement on Collective Bargaining, which was therefore left without any kind of legitimacy, and the application of which, as guidelines for the whole body of collective agreements negotiated in Spain, principally by the organisations that go to make up the CEOE, CEPYME, CCOO and UGT, has effectively been blocked.

The attempt to reduce the contractual power of the weaker side in labour relations goes hand in hand with the pressure being exerted on the class-based trade unionism represented by the two majority trade union organisations,[4] the CCOO and the UGT, signatories to this kind of agreement. In this respect, an intensive campaign is being waged by the aforementioned Spanish trade union confederations for a derogation to Article 315.3 of the Penal Code, under which the activities of informational pickets organised for a strike day are subject to prosecution.

This circumstance is not an exclusively Spanish phenomenon, in that pressure to curtail this right may be observed in the latest reform adopted in the United Kingdom, or the stance of the employer side within the ILO. Evidence of this is the global day of action called by the International Trade Union Confederation on 18 February 2015 in support of the right to strike. This trade union confederation, the largest in the world, which represents 176 million workers in 162 countries and has 328 national trade union organisations, was obliged to make this appeal because of the pressure that the group of employers' associations and some governments were exerting within the ILO to amend Convention 87 on trade union freedom, calling into question the right to strike, as well as attempting to limit the role of the international organisation's own supervisory bodies.

Pressure on trade union organisations is also a reason for the decline in trade union membership. Data provided by the Organisation for Economic Co-operation and Development (OECD 2015)[5] reveal a continuous loss of membership for the period 2001–2011, the last decade for which figures have been published. Whereas average membership in the OECD countries was 19.9% in the year when this period began, this figure had dropped to 17.5% 10 years later. In the case of Spain, it is below the average for the OECD countries, at 15.9% in both 2001 and 2011. This is explained by the significant increase in membership during the years of economic growth and the decline in tandem with the rise in long-term unemployment over the years (OECD 2015).[6]

The loss of membership, and pressure against the counterweight being exerted by trade union organisations for a change in the social concertation model, as in the case of Spain, combined with the characteristics of the labour market after the 2008 crisis, have resulted in circumstances that, before the outbreak of the crisis, were not perceived to be as virulent as they are currently revealing themselves to be.

The constant labour reforms undermining the position of the weaker side in the labour market, as the previously existing correlation between the sectoral contractual framework and that of the company has changed, show the diminished importance of labour law, understood as the broadest and most homogeneous regulatory framework possible. The deconfiguration of occupational categories is a good demonstration of the breach between a labour market that inherited the victories secured principally after the Second World War, and the new labour market emerging from the process of globalisation that we have been experiencing in the past few decades: that is to say, between those workers who experience their departure from the labour market through retirement with 'guaranteed' payments, and those generations who are joining the world of work with the belief that these rights are disappearing.

In Spain, for instance, the number of people living off income from the work of previous generations, whether through the extension of benefits such as a retirement pension or from rent, as with housing, is increasing significantly. For this reason, it would seem that the idea of realising a labour market that permits sufficient income through an increase in the national minimum wage, and also the securing of a guaranteed minimum income, for which there is a Popular Legislative Initiative promoted by the CCOO and the UGT, with a view to eliminating in-work wage poverty and social poverty, is gaining greater traction.

THE POLITICAL FRAGMENTATION OF THE COLLECTIVE SUBJECT

The International Labour Organization (ILO 2015) still refers to four non-standard forms of employment, namely: temporary employment, temporary agency work and other contractual arrangements involving multiple parties, part-time employment, and ambiguous employment relationships, as in the case of economically dependent self-employed workers. However, the labour market trend demonstrates a wide range of contractual mechanisms which, in some cases, fall outside employment relationships as such and are located within parameters more in keeping with trading, with the consequent fragility of the collective subject.

As Bernard and Dressen (2014) point out, one of the main characteristics of the reformulation of work is the progressive 'hybridisation' of employment statuses, in particular, the mixture between the formerly more limited categories of waged employment and self-employment. This has led to the reformulation of both categories, in such a way that we are currently observing the major reconfiguration and deconstruction of the wage-earner's legal status, propelling it towards increasing crossover with other categories, such as the 'entrepreneur' or the 'independent worker', thus creating ever more heterogeneous contractual situations and new forms of labour flexibility, as indicated by Caveng (2014) and Menoux (2014).

From the four emerging forms of work and employment, which are web-based virtual working, on-call working through digital platforms, crowd-working and working as a prosumer, set out by Valenduc and Vendramin (2016), we can see how we are immersed in a debate which leaves behind, as obsolete, the traditional boundaries between the employed worker and the freelance worker, in other words, Fordist-style waged work and self-employed work. The changes that have come about due to the new technologies and 'Revolution 4.0' technology, all embryonic forms of what still today is the potential of the digital economy, place us in a scenario, where the political fragmentation of the collective subject has become an intrinsic part of this development of the economic market.

Thus, there has been a transformation of the political subject that goes far deeper than a mere modification of the conditions of waged work, making it a dispensable element in the new models of employment. Ultimately, this implies the emergence of a veritable contractual juggling exercise, tending towards the most extreme heterogeneity, the basic principle for a unique approach to contractual relationships which makes it possible to encompass the whole wide spectrum of cases that has developed in the past two decades, which has been strengthened with regard to the categories of the self-employed worker and the bogus self-employed worker.

Self-employment has become established as a response to increasing unemployment, turning into a way of devaluing the labour market and making it more flexible, accentuated by the creation of statutory frameworks in all European countries, as indicated by Abdelnour (2013).

Indeed, although the degree of implementation of the main directives in each Member State varies considerably, as with the regulations on self-employment and agency working, practice demonstrates the need for a greater degree of participation by workers so that working conditions can be guaranteed, as argued by Drahokoupil (2015).

In any event, the ongoing renewal of class-based trade unionism has become necessary, as proposed by Bernaciak et al. (2012), in order to face up to the changes that the economy, politics, technology and society are undergoing, which, moreover, are accentuating and accelerating the transformation of the labour market and employment; this will permanently affect people entering it, principally the young. The traditional structures are proving insufficient to withstand the break with the traditional wage-earning model and the transition from a wage-earning society to another, with a set of paradigms based more on individual cases.

For all these reasons, there has been a radical transformation of the political subject in the past few decades, implicitly involving the depoliticisation of work, a fact highlighted by Keune and Serrano (2014). Thus, the changes that have occurred in the world of work entail the increasing political decline of the worker, moving from the cohesion provided by the community to a situation of individualism, not only from the viewpoint of labour relations, but also from parameters that involve the very composition of the role that was hitherto attributed to the wage-earning society over the course of history.

Conclusions

The main drivers for the reformulation of the meaning and notion of work are intimately linked to the concept of deconstruction of employment as a political question. The impairment of employment law as a protector of the weaker side is a good demonstration of this statement. This situation is leading to the reformulation of the role of work as a fundamental part of the social process, a question that can be seen from both the collective and the individual point of view.

Not long ago, securing a job was regarded as essential to achieving one's individual development in society, and it was, moreover, regarded as a fundamental aspect of socialisation. This point is particularly well illustrated by the concept of 'stability' in the regulation of work and in employment relationships themselves, which meant that a person spent the majority of his or her adult life in one and the same environment, with specific people around them, arising from the resilience of labour referred to above.

However, work is currently losing much of its capacity for socialisation and development of individuals, based on the parameters we have expounded. The prevailing model in the Europe of social welfare is being displaced in favour of flexibility in employment relationships, which are increasingly frustrating the idea of a wage-earning society in which social cohesion is integrally linked with work.

As a result of these circumstances, situations that were thought to have been largely eradicated until just a few years ago have resurfaced, such as that of the poor worker. This phenomenon, which may be observed throughout the European Union, is seen more acutely in Spain. This context gives rise to the debate on the need for a basic income providing a minimal revenue for any adult lacking other means of support, given the incapacity of the labour market to maintain the standards of living of past decades, as affirmed by Groot (2016).

Likewise, within the framework of labour relations themselves and of the way businesses are interlocked with society, we are moving from a stage where labour disputes were a fundamental pillar for securing improved rights, to another where this situation shares space with an increasing appeal to the 'goodwill' of companies, primarily multinationals, through what is known as corporate social responsibility.[7]

Accordingly, constant change is occurring in social habits and customs, as we note in the case of the configuration of employment, perhaps because it used to be considered that the welfare state itself would be bound to respond, combining invariable rules to frame an improved balance between social groups, particularly between workers and the business world, from the point of view of the area that concerns us.

This goes hand in hand with the reduced share of traditional manufacturing sectors, such as industry, in European economies, an issue that has been observed since the 1980s in terms of the percentage of GDP. The relocation of large factories, with continuous processes and high concentrations of workers, to emerging or developing countries, means that there is a loss of stable sectors, at the same time as a reconfiguration of the wage bill itself. The new production sectors that serve to help maintain employment do not offer the same conditions as the former industrial sectors did, as is the case with all aspects of what is known as the digital economy, as outlined by Drahokoupil and Fabo (2015). Hence, also, in line with an increase in workers in these sectors, there is constant attrition of the purchasing power of wages. This assessment derives not only from

the change perceived in the actual configuration of manufacturing processes, but also from the reappraisal of the social state which we have had
until now in the societies that combine parliamentary democracy with a
market economy. Likewise, commercial agreements are gaining strength,
and are serving to supplement or indeed replace the previous regional
pacts. In all of these, one notes a significant gap that demonstrates the key
concept of this study: the loss of work as a means of articulating the social
question and social protection mechanism, in that the organisation of the
world of work is left to the mercy of economic development, as may be
seen from the absence of employment regulation frameworks in this kind
of accord, including those that are still to be implemented, such as the
future Transatlantic Trade and Investment Partnership (TTIP).

In conclusion, in an economy undergoing constant change and evolution, which has never been so interconnected and globalised, the collective dimension of the wage-earning status is being weakened, as testified
by Keune (2015b). Questions relating to the labour market or indeed
employment rights are increasingly disappearing from public debate, at
the same time as existing conditions are being weakened, as mentioned
in the preceding sections, inasmuch as *the decline of the worker as collective subject* is becoming more pronounced. In this way, something that
is coming to be regarded as inevitable is registering as legitimate in the
collective consciousness.[8]

Notes

1. Affiliation to SS. Calculations for CNAE93 [National Classification of
   Economic Activities, class 93], code 45; calculations for CNAE09, codes
   41, 42 and 43.
2. The cutting of millions of jobs, and the deterioration in the purchasing
   power of wages, leads to a very significant increase in eviction processes. In
   2008, 26,748 eviction notices were registered by the Servicios Comunes
   de Actos de Comunicación y Ejecución [Common Services for Acts of
   Communication and Enforcement] (CGPJ 2016); this figure increased to
   33,918 in 2009, 47,809 in 2010, 62,121 in 2011 and 70,257 in 2012.
   In other words, in just four years, the number of dwellings affected by an
   eviction process almost trebled. In 2013, there was a slight drop to 65,182
   evictions, but in 2014 and 2015 the figure stabilised at over 69,000, specifically 69,233 in 2014 and 69,631 in 2015.
3. This matter is considered in greater detail by Maarten Keune (2015a) in
   his article: *Less Governance and More Inequality: The Effects of the Assault
   on Collective Bargaining in the EU.*

4. The most telling case is that involving eight trade union members working for AIRBUS (seven with the CCOO and one with the UGT), for whom the public prosecutor is calling for a total of 66 years' imprisonment for taking part in the pickets of the 2012 General Strike. It is worth recalling that the last major trial involving class trade unionism was 'Trial 1001', with the incarceration of the CCOO leadership. Judicial pressure is currently not confined to the workers mentioned here, but, according to data from the trade unions themselves, there are 300 trade union members with proceedings in progress or trials already held for exercising the right to strike.

5. Membership data for the countries of northern Europe are worthy of note in that they show indices well above average. Thus, the figures for Iceland are approximately 79.4 and 88.1%, respectively, for Finland 70 and 74.5%, for Denmark 68.8 and 77.9% and for Sweden 67.7 and 77.3%. The following figures are of particular interest, at 19.3 and 22.4%, respectively, for Portugal, 18.5 and 23.7% for Germany and 18.2 and 21.2% for the Netherlands. However, these are in no way comparable with those presented in two of the most liberalised economies in the world: the USA and South Korea. Membership data are particularly remarkable in these two countries: for the former, the figure is 11.3 and 12.9%, respectively, whereas for South Korea, it has fallen below 10%, at 9.75 and 11.5% (OECD 2015).

6. Trade union persecution combined with the characteristics of the labour market, and, as a consequence of the Spanish Constitution of 1978, the low level of development of the Spanish trade union model towards more advanced parameters in terms of representation, like those in other European Union countries, where trade union and employers' organisations manage many of the benefits arising from industrial relations, mean that membership levels are not very high.

7. Corporate social responsibility constitutes a movement that aims to overcome the dichotomy between employers and employees, proposing to dilute the role of workers' representatives together with other interest groups, because of the impact of their activities on the company's performance (Sánchez and Puente 2016).

8. Translation from the Spanish by Sally Blaxland and the Peer Group.

REFERENCES

Abdelnour, Sarah. 2013. "L'entrepreneuriat au service des politiques sociales: la fabrication du consensus politique sur le dispositif de l'auto-entrepreneur." *Sociétés contemporaines* 89: 131–154.

Agencia Estatal de Administración Tributaria. 2016. http://www.agenciatributaria.es/AEAT/Contenidos_Comunes/La_Agencia_Tributaria/Estadisticas/Publicaciones/sites/irpf/2013/home_parcialf1bdabb08a8166b07fc4bd-d679ad9625100bcdbfb.html.

Alaluf, Mateo. 1999. "Evolutions démografiques el rôle de la protection sociale: le concept de cohesion." Rapport Préliminaire (DGV/ULB). Bruxelles: Commission Européenne.

Alonso, Luis Enrique. 1999. *Trabajo y ciudadanía. Estudios sobre la crisis de la sociedad salarial.* Madrid: Trotta.

Alonso, Luis Enrique. 2001. *Trabajo y postmodernidad. El empleo débil.* Madrid: Editorial Fundamentos.

Asenjo, Almudena, and Inmaculada Cebrián. 2015. "Precarización y empobrecimiento de la población trabajadora en España." *La precariedad del empleo como factor estructural de la pobreza laboral.* Madrid: Fundación 1º A0de Mayo.

Barroso, Durao. 2013. *Discurso sobre el estado de la Unión.* Bruselas: Comisión Europea.

Bernaciak, Magadalena, Rebecca Gumbell-McCormic, and Richard Hyman. 2012. *El sindicalismo europeo: ¿de la crisis a la renovación?*, en Colección Cuadernos nº40. Madrid: Fundación 1º de Mayo.

Bernard, Sophie, and Marnix Dressen. 2014. "Penser la porosité des satatus d'emploi." *La Nouvelle revue du Travail. Indépendance el salariat, parasité des status.* http://nrt.revues.org/1823.

Caveng, Rémy. 2014. "Institutionnalisation el usages d'un salariat libéral." *La Nouvelle Revue du Travail. Indépendance el salariat, parasité des status.* http://nrt.revues.org/1823.

CGPJ. 2016. Consejo General del Poder Judicial. http://www.poderjudicial.es/cgpj/es/Temas/Estadistica-Judicial/Informes-estadisticos-periodicos/Datos-sobre-el-efecto-de-la-crisis-en-los-organos-judiciales—Datos-desde-2007-hasta-cuarto-trimestre-de-2015.

Drahokoupil, Jan. 2015. *The Outsourcing Challenge: Organizing Workers Across Fragmented Production Networks.* Brussels: European Trade Union Institute.

Drahokoupil, Jan, and Brian Fabo. 2015. "Outsourcing, Offshoring and the Deconstruction of Employment: New and Old Challenges in the Digital Economy, the Outsourcing Challenge." In *Organizing Workers Across Fragmented Production Networks*, edited by Jan Drahokoupil. Brussels: European Trade Union Institute.

Eurostat. 2016a. http://appsso.eurostat.ec.europa.eu/nui/show.do?dataset=lfsq_etpga&lang=en.

Eurostat. 2016b. http://appsso.eurostat.ec.europa.eu/nui/show.do?dataset=lfsq_etpga&lang=en.

Eurostat. 2016c. http://appsso.eurostat.ec.europa.eu/nui/show.do?dataset=lfsq_
eppga&lang=en.
Eurostat. 2016d. http://appsso.eurostat.ec.europa.eu/nui/show.do.
Eurostat. 2016e. http://appsso.eurostat.ec.europa.eu/nui/show.do?dataset=ilc_
peps01&lang=en.
Eurostat. 2016f. http://appsso.eurostat.ec.europa.eu/nui/show.do?dataset=spr_
exp_sum&lang=en.
Galbraith, John Kenneth. 2012. *La sociedad opulenta*. Madrid: Planeta.
Groot, L. 2016. "*¿Algo a cambio de nada?*" Madrid: El País, 11 de septiembre de.
ILO. 2015. *Las formas atípicas de empleo*. Ginebra: Organización Internacional
del Trabajo.
INE. 2015. Instituto Nacional de Estadística. http://www.ine.es/prensa/
np917.pdf.
INE. 2016. Instituto Nacional de Estadística. http://www.ine.es/jaxiT3/Tabla.
htm?t=9376&L=0.
Keune, Maarten. 2015a. "Less Governance Capacity and More Inequality:
The Effects of the Assault on Collective Bargaining in the EU." In *Wage
Bargaining Under the New European Economic Governance*, edited by Guy
Van Gyes and Thorsten Schulten, 283–296. Brussels: ETUI.
Keune, Maarten. 2015b. "Shaping the Future of Industrial Relations in the
EU: Ideas, Paradoxes and Drivers of Change." *International Labour Review*.
Geneva: International Labor Organization. http://onlinelibrary.wiley.com/
doi/10.1111/j.1564-913X.2015.00225.x/abstract.
Keune, Maarten, and Amparo Serrano Pascual. 2014. *Deconstructing Flexicurity
and Constructing Alternative Approaches. Towards New Concept and
Approaches for Employment and Social Policy*. London: Routledge Advances in
Sociology.
LFS. 2015. *Informe cuarto trimestre de 2015*. Encuesta de Población Activa.
ine.es/daco/daco42/daco4211/epa0415.pdf.
Menoux, Thibaut. 2014. "Indépendants subordonnés oy salariés autonomes?"
La Nouvelle Revue du Travail. Indépendance el salariat, parasité des status.
http://nrt.revues.org/1823.
Navarro, Vicenç. 2004. *El Estado de Bienestar en España*. Madrid: Tecnos.
OECD. 2015. *Union Members and Employees*. Paris: Organisation for Economic
Cooperation and Development. stats.oecd.org/Index.aspx?Datasetcode=
U_D_D.
Prieto, Carlos. 1999. *La crisis del empleo en Europa*. Germanía: Valencia.
Sánchez, Vicente, and Mónica Puente. 2016. *Responsabilidad social empresar-
ial y participación de los trabajadores: un estudio crítico del marco normativo-
institucional actual*. Gijón: Congreso Nacional de Sociología.

Social Security. 2015. www.empleo.go.es/es/sec_trabajo/autonomos/econo-mia-soc/autonomos/estadisticas/2015/4trim/Publicacion_RESUMEN_RESULTADOS.pdf.

Social Security. 2016. http://www1.seg-social.es/ActivaInternet/groups/pub-lic/documents/rev_anexo/rev_035194.pdf.

Valenduc, Gérard, and Patricia Vendramin. 2016. "Work in the Digital Economy: Sorting the Old from the New." Working Paper 2006.03, ETUI, Brussels.

Veblen, Thorstein. 2008. *La Teoría de la clase ociosa*. Madrid: Alianza Editorial.

PART II

Blurring of Boundaries Between Categories (Self-Employed Worker and Wage-Earner; Employment and Unemployment, Typical and Atypical Work, Formal and Informal Work)

CHAPTER 6

The Employment Relationship, Atypical Forms of Employment and Protection Standards in the European Union

Antonio Baylos

The Employment Relationship and Employment with Rights

Human labour makes a key contribution to the production of goods and services that forms the basis of the free enterprise economic system. The significance of free, productive human labour may be evaluated from a variety of primarily economic, social or political perspectives. This paper will approach the issue in terms of its legal regulation and its political and democratic import.

In the 'immense accumulation of commodities' that characterises our society and lifestyle, when work is performed and serves to create goods and services within the framework of a corporate organisation, it is regarded as 'salaried employment' or 'subordinate employment'. These are the customary ways of describing the performance of productive human labour for a company. In other words, the work performed

A. Baylos (✉)
University of Castilla-La Mancha (UCLM), Ciudad Real, Spain

© The Author(s) 2019
A. Serrano-Pascual and M. Jepsen (Eds.),
The Deconstruction of Employment as a Political Question,
https://doi.org/10.1007/978-3-319-93617-8_6

131

within the organisation and under the direction of a company constitutes salaried employment and is in all cases subject to employment regulations.

In principle, subordinate, salaried employment is, therefore, a legal construction subject to a protection framework fundamentally defined by state regulation and collective bargaining. This is because the contractual basis of the individual's employment relationship, i.e. their contract of employment, does not allow individual workers full autonomy to directly determine their own employment and working conditions. Instead, its main function is to enable the 'legal categorisation' that determines the existence of an employment relationship 'subject to labour law'. Inclusion within this category entitles workers to a range of rights establishing universal protection standards with regard to employment and working conditions and collective and trade union rights. These form the basis of the economic and social status of labour by providing for its representation and for collective action for its advancement and improvement.

This employment relationship exists alongside a public law relationship with the social security system, which provides for the protection of employees who meet the relevant employment law conditions for the different sectors of economic activity. The system is funded through compulsory employer and employee contributions, with employer contributions bearing the larger share of the corresponding financial burden. In other words, it is compulsory to contribute to the public system of social security benefits that are guaranteed as subjective rights to workers who meet the relevant requirements in terms of their employment category and payment of contributions. Accordingly, employment underpins the social protection instruments that enable social citizenship, i.e. the provision of support to address the hardship and employment risks experienced by people belonging to a subordinate social condition.

Employment regulations are overseen by the public administration, which is responsible for carrying out inspections and imposing the relevant penalties in the event of a breach of labour law. Employment rights are upheld by the courts, which rule on cases involving disputes about the application or interpretation of the legal regulations. In some cases, the law even treats the most socially damaging behaviour as a criminal offence.

The concept of the legal regulation of employment is a political model that became progressively established in tandem with the concept of the welfare state, leading to the European social constitutionalism of the post-war period that marked the downfall of the fascist, Nazi regimes and eventually also replaced the southern European dictatorships that persisted in Greece, Portugal and Spain during the Cold War. Social con-stitutionalism thus regards the key role of employment and the associ-ated collective and individual rights as a central part of the democratic system.[1]

It also reflects the establishment of a 'European social model' enshrined in the region's charters of rights, from the European Social Charter to the Charter of Fundamental Rights of the European Union. However, as we will see later on, this approach is in stark contrast to the de facto principles that govern the European Union based on the great economic freedoms. Finally, at an international level, it has taken on the role of a universal model in the shape of the ILO's 1998 Declaration on Fundamental Principles and Rights at Work.[2] This resulted in the 'most highly developed' notion of decent work[3] as a civilising principle that transcends the incorporation of the ILO conventions and international treaties into national law, advocating that labour rights should be treated as fully-fledged human rights.[4]

The important thing about this model is that work constitutes a fun-damental political value that incorporates people into the free enter-prise economic system and acts as a means of ensuring social cohesion and preventing any global, political challenges to the capitalist political and economic system. In exchange for accepting the free market system in a market economy, people are granted recognition of individual and collective rights derived from their work, establishing a social citizen-ship that includes the representatives of labour as well as the principle of the progressive achievement of substantive equality that characterises social democracy. As the basis of material reproduction and the starting point of the social lives of most men and women, work is thus a social and political phenomenon as opposed to a private matter. Moreover, it underpins the legitimacy of the Constitution in a material sense, i.e. the concrete functioning of social life and the balance of power within soci-ety (Galli 2013, 143). It is at the root of the progressive compromise between the rationality of capitalism and the protection of labour that is embodied in the welfare state and it gives rise to the social figures that represent labour and defend its interests both at the level of relations between employers and employees and at a political and social level, rec-ognising conflict and collective autonomy as fundamental aspects of this endeavour.

As well as a deeply embedded institutional model, this political and democratic dimension of the legal regulation of work has created a culture that has become widespread among collective actors—especially the trade unions—and key social actors. These actors have established practices and rules in collective bargaining and the social dialogue that are predicated on these fundamental assumptions. However, the economic, social and cultural changes that started to occur in the developed world during the last quarter of the twentieth century have led to major transformations in the very nature of work and thus in the notion of citizenship and how workers understand themselves (Crespo et al. 2009). The progressive decline in the fundamental importance of work's social value has come about due to the crisis of the model of stable employment as a condition of citizenship which, in terms of the technical legal regulation of employment relationships, entailed a preference for permanent contracts and the establishment of mechanisms to protect people from redundancy (Pérez Rey 2004). This particular aspect deserves closer examination.

THE DEFINITION OF A WORKER

The services provided by a worker under their employment contract can be summarised as the performance of productive labour—carried out voluntarily or freely—that is remunerated by the employer in the form of a salary and is undertaken on behalf of and in a dependent relationship with said employer. The law, primarily case law, plays a pivotal role in the definition of employment by establishing whether the 'fundamental assumptions' of an employment contract have been met. In this context, certain rules exist concerning the presumption of the existence of a contract of employment and proof thereof, and the fact that a ruling that defines a contract as an employment contract cannot be changed by a declaration of intent on behalf of the parties to the contract. When the courts make a ruling on the employment status of the work relationships existing in the real world at a given point in time, in effect they are attempting to identify the fact pattern by subsuming or fitting certain key elements of it into the generic concepts established by the law—the concepts of subordination, being in the employ of another and dependence—or, conversely, by applying analogous criteria or the standard assumptions that the relationship between employer and employee is based on.[5] These are the questions facing the judge when, based on the detailed description of a specific job, they are asked to give a binary response—yes or no—to the question of whether it constitutes employment, as well as justifying their decision and thus constructing the discourse on the general concepts. However, this 'Praetorian definition' (Wolmark 2007) as to whether a relationship characterised by subordination or working on another's behalf exists in the case in question is based on the unstated presumption that permanent, stable jobs carried out in a company should be regulated by a permanent contract and that fixed-term or temporary contracts should only be used under exceptional circumstances requiring a specific reason or justification.

Two factors come into play here. Firstly, the fact that a complex and diverse range of employment relationships exist for different job descriptions should not prevent them from receiving the same treatment under the auspices of the employment contract category. Indeed, one of the features of the employment contract's historical development is its adaptability (Alaluf 2002, 26; Bavaro 2018, 7). Secondly, when a job is ruled to be subject to an employment contract, the relevant general standards must be applied with regard to working and employment conditions. These are the same for everyone and are determined by sectoral collective agreements or, less commonly, company agreements. These agreements establish collective, homogeneous standards relating to pay, working time and the type of work performed, through the collective regulation of the employment relationship. Ultimately, if the court rules that a job constitutes employment, this will result in the application of a standard employment relationship (SER[6]), which establishes a framework of rights that guarantee a decent job, traditionally associated with permanent contracts.

The progressive development of the European Union into a single market and monetary union has an important bearing on this issue, for two main reasons. The first is the establishment of a European regulatory level over and above the nation state level, based on the European Union's fundamental economic freedoms. This regulatory level overrides national regulations and has its own institution for interpreting and applying the law—the European Court of Justice—which plays an important part in the creation of European law by guiding and shaping the regulations and case law of the member states. The second is that the establishment of this 'area without internal borders' necessitates the removal of obstacles to the free movement of goods, persons, services and capital. In this context, 'persons' refers to 'economically active' individuals who move from one place to another to engage in activities that generate income either through subordinate or salaried employment or through self-employed or freelance work (Giubboni and Orlandini 2007, 11). In legal terms, this is made possible thanks to the principle of non-discrimination 'based on nationality between workers of the Member States as regards employment, remuneration and other conditions of work and employment', although this principle may be overridden on the grounds of public policy, public security or public health.[7]

Based on a simple interpretation of the freedom of movement principle, the European Court of Justice defines a 'worker' as 'any person who temporarily or permanently performs services for another in exchange for remuneration'. This is a broad concept, where the essential point is that 'the person *provides services during a given time for and under the direction of another in return for remuneration*'. And although it varies depending on its area of application—for instance, it isn't necessarily the same as the definition used for inclusion in the social security system—the fact that it is connected to one of the fundamental freedoms means that this broad concept tends to occur widely in European legislation (Pavlou 2016; Casas Baamonde 2017).

In the twenty-first century, the questioning of the content of employment regulation that began during the 1980s would find expression in the debate about the modernisation of labour law. This debate intensified following the onset of the economic and financial crisis of 2008 and the enthronement of the new governance of the European Union and eurozone. However, this process did not in principle affect the definition of the employment relationship itself—i.e. the 'point of entry'. Instead, it focused further down the line on determining what protection should be afforded to people who have been defined as workers. Put another way, although efforts to interpret the regulations concentrated on establishing what protection labour law should grant workers as parties to an employment contract, this did not imply that the level of protection provided by employment regulations should be the same or constant for everyone defined as a worker under labour law. Today, this diversification of protection levels has become a structural element of labour law that cannot simply be put down to differences between permanent and temporary work or the 'special status' of certain employment regimes within the overall category of employment. In fact, it can be traced back to the debate that began in Europe in the 1980s on the application of different levels of protection to workers in direct relation to employment policies and linking them to economic growth and job creation targets.

The result is that the figure of the worker defined as a party to a contract of employment is no longer treated as a single, unified concept. Instead, we see the same fragmentation that exists in the labour market, which translates into an asymmetrical graduation of employment guarantees and the protection level provided by the social security system. Consequently, determining the characteristics of the work performed under an employment contract does not only involve fitting the social concept of salaried employment into the regulatory categories that define and regulate it by establishing the presence of a series of clues or indicators relating to working time, pay, how the work is performed, membership of an organisation, subordination to the employer, technical autonomy, hetero-directed cognition, etc. (Zoppoli 2006, 21). More crucially, it also involves classifying the fragmentation of the protection afforded by employment regulations in terms of the system of employment guarantees and the level of social protection.

SEGMENTATION AND FRAGMENTATION IN THE EMPLOYMENT RELATIONSHIP

Pressure resulting from rising unemployment and changes in public labour market policy led to the progressive introduction of certain forms of 'atypical' employment into the regulatory frameworks of most European countries. The justification put forward for doing so was that it supported economic and business recovery and was just a provisional, 'emergency' measure in response to the current crisis. In fact, however, these atypical employment forms have subsequently become established as an inescapable reality in the structure of employment relationships. Atypical forms of employment are associated with the flexibility that businesses require to recover and consolidate their market position. They are also seen as a means of generating employment and are thus directly linked to job creation. Another important aspect of these forms of employment, which equate atypicality with flexibility, is that the new jobs being created today lack the full range of high employment standards enjoyed by full-time, permanent jobs.

Although the consequences have varied depending on the political and social coordinates of the different nation states, atypical forms of employment can be said to have resulted in the segmentation of countries' workforces, creating a divide between 'stable' and 'precarious' workers and leading to the replacement of permanent employees with temporary workers in many companies.[8] This segmentation of the workforce has direct consequences for the employment rights and social protection of the affected groups. It has also been accompanied by major changes in the organisation of companies that have led to the fragmentation of the corporate entity as a result of the subcontracting and outsourcing of its activities or as a result of its consolidation into corporate groups with fragmented corporate responsibility. This fragmentation in which the organisation of companies is transformed from a purely bilateral relationship between employer and worker into a complex structure where the company's economic function is split among several people is frequently accompanied by the use of atypical forms of employment, especially in connection with subcontracting and other similar outsourcing mechanisms.[9] These changes in companies' structure can also be understood as a consequence of the decline of Fordism—seen as the epitome of industrialised civilisation—and the associated consumption patterns. The 'new way' of organising production in the post-industrial world is to replace hierarchical structures with collaborative, coordinated networks and streams. This new organisational structure of companies allegedly calls for the use of flexible, atypical forms of employment in preference to standard employment relationships.

The rise in the number of atypical jobs prompted action by the European trade unions and employers' organisations to regulate them through collective agreements. They succeeded in doing so for fixed-term and part-time contracts, but not for the use of temporary employment agencies. These instances of European collective bargaining (even though no collective agreement was concluded in the last of these areas, the topic was subsequently taken up by the Commission) resulted in three directives on atypical work whose regulatory principles are essentially based on the notion that these employment relationships should receive equal treatment and be voluntary in nature. Based on the principle of equal treatment, these directives—especially the Fixed-term Work Directive—have been used in the rulings of the European Court of Justice as a key means of modifying the employment regulations of certain European countries where the use of fixed-term contracts is particularly widespread, such as Italy and more recently Spain.[10]

Although the topography of temporary work in Europe is not uniform, fixed-term work has combined with the decentralisation of production and the privatisation of public services to cause significant damage to the regulatory paradigm of stable employment, notwithstanding the collective countermeasures and mechanisms that have sought to mitigate some of the most harmful impacts of this division of the workforce into groups with unequal rights. Something similar has happened with part-time work, especially intermittent, short-term part-time work that is not usually chosen voluntarily by the workers in question. Furthermore, atypical forms of employment are dominated by vulnerable groups, particularly women, young people and immigrants, whose vulnerability is heightened by this form of work. The fact that these groups alternate between periods of unemployment and atypical work means that quite apart from the precarious nature of their work, their living conditions also become progressively more precarious.

This slide towards precarious work was exacerbated in Europe primarily as a result of the processes triggered by the economic and financial crisis of 2008 and in particular the onset of the eurozone crisis in 2010. These events led to the adoption of 'austerity measures' which politically determined the structural reforms and public spending cuts imposed on the nations of Greece, Italy, Spain, Portugal and Ireland which had become over-indebted as a result of having to prop up their national financial systems and the uncertainty about the solvency of their governments on the financial markets. These measures would subsequently spread to other countries under the pretext that they were an essential policy response for delivering economic and social modernisation. This open-ended policy approach amounts to saying that the level of protection and the extent of the rights granted to working people are directly dependent on a country's economic development and financial stability. The same reasoning has repeatedly been used to inform reforms of countries' social security systems and justify the possibility of adopting regulations that reduce their scope. It emphasises the relationship between labour and employment by adopting a strictly economic understanding of the cost of labour as the factor that determines a worker's employability and a company's ability to succeed in a free market.

This exacerbates the segmentation of the workforce because vulnerable groups are far likelier to slip into precarious jobs, i.e. employment 'which does not comply with European Union, international and national standards and laws and/or does not provide sufficient resources for a decent life or adequate social protection'.[11] The creation of precarious jobs that has been justified on the grounds of the high unemployment levels in some southern and eastern European countries where between one fifth and one quarter of the population are unemployed—described as the 'long path of the deterioration of work' (Guaman and Trillo 2015)—makes it possible to blur the boundaries between regular and irregular work and to some extent establish a continuum between the two. Real-term wage cuts, the exponential growth in involuntary part-time work, the precariousness caused by exceptionally high levels of temporary work used primarily to replace permanent, full-time jobs, increased flexibility with regard to working time and the availability of workers, and the fact that it has become easier and cheaper to make people redundant are all factors that are causing the conditions responsible for social exclusion and vulnerability traditionally associated with undeclared work to become 'assimilated' into certain forms of work that are formally recognised by the law.[12] The rise in poverty and social exclusion is also affecting a proportion of the working population, and these "working poor" are included in this typology.

Nevertheless, this 'weak employment' deployed as part of a culture of flexibility (Alonso 2000) has not as yet replaced the political and democratic model based on the value of work as a contributor to social cohesion and an arena for fighting for citizens' rights. All the same, the fact that it is clearly becoming more prevalent is a worrying trend for European policies confronted with lower protection standards for workers and the accompanying loss of social legitimacy. According to a recent European Parliament resolution, in the last ten years (i.e. more or less since the onset of the global financial crisis) typical forms of employment—regular, voluntary full-time and part-time jobs with permanent contracts—have fallen from 62 to 59%. If this trend continues, it may well become the case that standard contracts will only apply to a minority of workers, since the rise in employment since the adoption of austerity measures has mainly occurred in atypical forms of working. The Parliament resolution provides a non-exhaustive list of these atypical forms that includes fixed-term contract work, involuntary and especially marginal part-time work, casual labour, seasonal work and on-demand work.[13] To this, we can also add the different forms of self-employed and freelance work that will be discussed in the next section. Notwithstanding these concerns and the Parliament's proposals to the Commission and the member states, unequal treatment and inequality regarding the employment rights of both groups of workers is now a fact that informs both the structure of employment relationships and the importance within this structure of having a corresponding range of different protection standards. It is a situation that has come about despite collective bargaining efforts to oppose this trend and the adoption of mechanisms to try and reduce the disparity in the levels of recognition and implementation of employment rights between the two groups.

The segmentation of the workforce and fragmentation of comparable, homogeneous types of work are not the only reasons for the consolidation of this diversification. It is also promoted in geographical terms by cross-border movements of workers and service delivery that fuel social dumping based on the wage differential between the different EU member states and the resulting offshoring, made possible thanks to freedom of establishment and above all the freedom to provide services. Indeed, this second freedom does not guarantee that workers who move from one country to another will enjoy the same employment conditions as workers in the destination country, although Directive 96/71 does establish a 'hard core' of minimum protection standards focused in particular on minimum rates of pay (Orlandini 2017). However, the Directive has been interpreted in a diverse and elastic manner in the ECJ's rulings, although a detailed analysis lies outside the scope of this paper.

The dismantling of the symbolic figure of the employment relationship (Romagnoli 1995, 205) has come about as a result of the differentiation of atypical jobs. These types of contract have often been stripped of their original economic function and used as a form of employment that lacks the guarantees of a 'standard' employment relationship. In some industries, atypical employment (temporary and irregular part-time work) and precarious work are by far the most common forms of work. In these instances, things are turned on their head and temporary, irregular work becomes the 'standard' employment relationship, causing precarious employment to become disproportionately widespread in these industries.[14] Moreover, since the available figures point to a 60/40 split between typical and atypical employment, it is also difficult to find a formula for an 'unequal law' that would provide a sliding scale of employment standards based on the recognition of minimum basic rights covering all working people regardless of which form of employment their job involves.[15]

THE COMMODITISATION OF WORK, SELF-EMPLOYMENT AND NEW FORMS OF EMPLOYMENT IN THE DIGITAL AGE

The world of work is not exclusively confined to employees with different standards of treatment depending on how they are categorised. Working for oneself on a freelance or self-employed basis is becoming an increasingly widespread alternative. This type of work is not subject to employment law and the corresponding standards for working and employment conditions. It entails the worker organising the work they do by themselves and managing it as they see fit. In legal terms, the self-employment category has traditionally been governed by civil or commercial contracts covering the services or production of goods carried out by the self-employed worker. It is primarily the distinction between this type of work and the concept of subordinate employment that judges have been asked to clarify in cases concerning the employment status of a particular job.

Two phenomena may be observed in this context. On the one hand, there is the rather predictable trend involving attempts to commoditise work by labelling it as self-employment. This employs the simple mechanism of arguing that the work in question should be governed by a civil or commercial contract, meaning that the fee and working hours are agreed voluntarily by the parties to the contract and the self-employed worker is liable for any social security contributions, tax, etc. The phenomenon of 'false self-employment" leads to a deterioration in working conditions and a reduction in social security protection. Consequently, ever since ILO Recommendation 198 concerning the employment relationship (2006), a range of minimum criteria for determining the existence of an employment relationship have been employed in order to distinguish between genuine and bogus self-employment.

At the same time, however, there has been widespread discussion of a new category of self-employment, with significant regulatory consequences. Although technically still self-employed, the workers in this category are in practice highly dependent on one or more major clients. While this economic subordination to another company does not invalidate their 'self-employed' status, it may qualify it. To account for this situation, some regulatory solutions have created a special category of self-employed worker.[16] The workers in this category—either as part of a network or through various forms of subcontracting—have a permanent relationship with companies or customers who exert some measure of control over their work. They may be prone to replicating forms of collective organisation, for instance in trade unions, leading to the emergence of a form of collective bargaining. This is, in fact, specifically called for in the European Parliament resolution referred to on several occasions in this paper.[17]

But self-employment is more than just a form of economic activity that has become more widespread following the mass redundancies of the most recent crisis and another 'atypical' form of work compared to stable employment relationships that in practice now accounts for a significant share of the labour market.[18] It also ties in with the discourse that has been repeated time and again in the context of austerity measures, promoting entrepreneurship as a key concept that will allow the notions of work and employment to be replaced by appealing directly not to companies but to the individual's independent capacity to create wealth and thus become an efficient driver of economic growth. A discourse based on risk, promotion of the individual and above all the entrepreneurial capacity to organise a world from which the waning concepts of work and employment are gradually disappearing. To a greater or lesser extent—and to a particularly extreme degree in Spain— entrepreneurship is intuitively linked to the figure of the self-employed worker as an individual entrepreneur capable of organising the world. The flip side is that this idea allows its proponents to make negative value judgements about the economically inactive or unemployed. Despite being framed as a rhetorical discourse with few concrete repercussions beyond a handful of government subsidy programmes, it, in fact, entails a very specific ideological shift.

This exaltation of self-employed workers is being accompanied— through a different channel—by the emergence of new ways of working in the context of digitalisation, new technologies and the collaborative economy, the vast majority of which take the form of self-employment. This has revived the old debate on the relationship between skills, technology, cognitive work and subordination. However, the idea of digital working as 'subjectified working where the time/work exchange is not objectified', i.e. almost as a post-capitalist form of work (Bavaro 2018), bears little relation to the very real issues that it poses in terms of the key criteria for determining who the employer is, the criteria for establishing whether the people providing these services are subordinate employees or self-employed, and ultimately the extent to which these relationships can acquire a collective dimension as a potential counterbalance to an economic system that isolates workers and places them in direct competition with each other (Trillo 2016). There have already been a number of landmark legal rulings around the globe in this area, since the transition of workers to self-employed status is not always clear-cut and the trend towards this type of work could lead to an increase in false self-employment. In terms of EU law, we can be sure that there will be some form of legislative initiative concerning 'collaborative platforms' as online labour market intermediaries. There is also likely to be a review of the information given to employees on the conditions applicable to the employment relationship in order to take account of these new forms of employment and of the need to increase the protection afforded to workers in the collaborative economy sector by 'stepping up transparency with regard to their status, the information they are given and non-discrimination'.[19]

CONCLUSION

Although the constitutional model of the welfare state and its formal realisation based on work and citizens' rights have not as yet been formally modified, the underlying assumptions of this model of work are gradually being transformed. Nevertheless, it is a model deeply embedded in a political and civic culture that has become strongly established in order to provide social legitimacy and is shared by a variety of key social actors such as the trade unions and other civil society organisations. Consequently, our observations focus on the watering down of protection standards and citizens' rights, especially those connected with work, highlighting a significant increase in the power imbalance at the heart of the employment relationship and among the collective actors that govern it, accentuated still further by the recent structural reforms in many European countries. As a result of its segmentation and the spread of precarious jobs, work has largely ceased to be the axis around which people's social existence revolves.

The relative decline in traditional salaried employment and the emergence of precarious and weak alternatives is also blurring the comparatively solid boundaries that used to exist between other categories related to work and employment, particularly unemployment, precarious work, underemployment and self-employment. These categories have become more fluid, making it possible—especially for some conceivable types of worker—to move between them faster and in multiple directions.

The re-commoditisation of work that constitutes the most salient characteristic of recent regulatory processes in the European Union has resulted in a significant scaling back of social standards. Over and above this, it has led to the depoliticisation of work as a fundamental element of modern social democracies. There are those who are opposed to these trends, advocating a neo-regulatory approach instead. However, there is little institutional support for this among the member states or indeed at EU level, as demonstrated by the disappointing debate on the EU's social pillar.[20]

Notes

1. This is a recurring finding in studies of social constitutionalism and is reiterated in analyses of the welfare state through the "Keynesian connection" (Alonso 1999: 214 ff).
2. Vega and Martínez (2002).
3. Barretto (2001).
4. This trend has led to an interesting debate among labour lawyers around the world. Cf. Mundiak (2012), Bellace (2014).
5. The doctrinal work of European labour law culture, especially during the 1950s and 1960s, involved the development of these concepts in order to enable the administration of the trend towards recognition as employment of the professional activities involved in the production of goods and services (subordination in Italian and French legal doctrine, *ajenidad*—the concept of working on another's behalf—in Spanish doctrine, where it is the employer—the "other"—who owns the product of the labour and who assumes the risks associated with the market). However, this would be superseded by the debates that began during the 1980s regarding the fragmentation of the protection provided under the employment relationship.
6. Adams and Deakin (2014).
7. Art. 45 Treaty on the Functioning of the European Union (TFEU) cf. Giubboni and Orlandini (2007, 72 ff).
8. This has been accompanied by a progressive transformation in the internal understanding of the direction that should be taken by employment policy as the responsibility of the state. The central role that this new model ascribes to employability—with its twin subjective dimensions of unemployed people's availability for work and an employer's suitability to offer a job—has to a large degree been responsible for shifting the topic of employment from the level of state responsibility for formulating planning strategies for a country's overall employment system to the level of

relationships between private individuals, where the "contractual" and "organisational" dimension within companies and professions determines the basic options regarding the level of employment.

9. The discussion regarding the position of the employer in this bilateral relationship, and how it has changed, has occupied a prominent position in the debate among labour lawyers, almost on a par with the discussions concerning the different forms of atypical employment and their definition.

10. For a general overview, see Sciarra (2007); for the more recent case of Spain, see Pérez Rey (2016). For the United Kingdom, see Salvatori (2015).

11. European Parliament resolution of 4 July 2017 on working conditions and precarious employment [2016/2221 (INI)].

12. The available estimates for Europe are startling. According to Eurofound, undeclared work accounted for an average of 18.4% of GDP in Europe in 2012. The highest levels were found in Bulgaria (31.9%) and Romania (29.1%); only Austria, Luxembourg and the Netherlands were below 10%, while the figures for France and the UK were 10.8 and 10.1%, respectively. Spain (19.2%) and Portugal (19.4%) were both slightly above the average. A study of the informal economy in 28 European countries between 2013 and 2015 produced slightly different results, with a European average of 18%. While the top two countries are still Bulgaria (30.6% of GDP) and Romania (28%), the "undeclared" economy in Spain is estimated at 18.2% of GDP, while the figure for Italy is 20.6% and France and Germany are both above 12%. Either way, these figures account for a significant proportion of trade and production in a region where the institutionalisation of the economy and markets is particularly highly developed.

13. Temporary agency work accounts for 1%, fixed-term work for 7%, apprenticeships or traineeships for 2%, marginal part-time work (less than 20 h per week) for 9% and part-time permanent work for 7% (European Parliament resolution of 4 July 2017 on working conditions and precarious employment).

14. Agriculture, construction and arts have in recent years been joined by the aviation and hotel industries (European Parliament resolution of 4 July 2017).

15. This is the basis of a neo-regulatory approach that already has important doctrinal precedents dating back to the Suppiot Report of 1989. Its influence is apparent in a number of nation state initiatives.

16. This has occurred in Italy, where they are referred to as "parasubordinate" workers, and in Spain, in the shape of the "economically-dependent self-employed worker". In practice, however, little use has been made of this category in Spain—the vast majority of self-employed work continues to be performed by workers classified as self-employed workers with

employees or freelance workers, without any reference to whether or not they are economically-dependent (Cruz Villalón and Valdés Dal-Re 2008).

17. "Calls on the Commission and the Member States, within their respective competences, to ensure that individual self-employed workers who are legally considered a sole-member company have the right to collective bargaining and to freely associate" (European Parliament resolution of 4 July 2017).

18. According to the available statistics, 4% of total employment in the EU is accounted for by self-employment with employees and 11% by freelance work (European Parliament resolution of July 4 2017). There has been a pronounced increase in this type of work since the crisis of 2008/2010.

19. European Parliament resolution of July 4 2017.

20. Translation from the Spanish by Joaquín Blasco.

REFERENCES

Adams, Z., and Deakin, S. 2014. "Institutional Solutions to Precariousness and Inequality in Labour Markets." *British Journal of Industrial Relations* 52 (4): 779–809.

Alaluf, M. 2002. "La ciudadanía social erosionada por la moral." In *Trabajo, subjetividad y ciudadanía. Paradojas del empleo en una sociedad en transformación*, edited by E. Crespo, C. Prieto, and A. Serrano, 23–37. Madrid: Editorial complutense and CIS.

Alonso, L. E. 1999. *Trabajo y ciudadanía. Ensayos sobre la crisis de la sociedad salarial.* Madrid: Fundación 1 de Mayo and Trotta.

Alonso, L. E. 2000. *Trabajo y posmodernidad: el empleo débil.* Madrid: Fundamentos.

Barretto, H. 2001. "Concepto y dimensiones del trabajo decente: entre la protección social básica y la participación de los trabajadores en la empresa." *Boletín Informativo CINTERFOR* 151: 153–172.

Bavaro, V. 2018. "Questioni in diritto su lavoro digitale, tempo e libertà." *Rivista Giuridica del Lavoro e della Previdenza Sociale* 1 (forthcoming).

Bellace, J. 2014. "Human Rights at Work: The Need for Definitional Coherence in the Global Governance System." *The International Journal of Comparative Labour Law and Industrial Relations* 30 (2): 175–198.

Casas Baamonde, M. E. 2017. "Precariedad del trabajo y formas atípicas de empleo, viejas y nuevas. ¿Hacia un trabajo digno." *Derecho de las Relaciones Laborales* 9: 867–890.

Crespo, E., C. Prieto, and A. Serrano-Pascual, eds. 2009. *Trabajo, subjetividad y ciudadanía. Paradojas del empleo en una sociedad en transformación.* Madrid: Editorial complutense and CIS.

Cruz Villalón, J., and F. Valdés Dal-Re, eds. 2008. *El Estatuto del Trabajo Autónomo*. Madrid: La ley and Wolters Kluwer.

Galli, C. 2013. *Sinistra. Per il lavoro, per la democracia*. Milano: Mondadori.

Giubboni, S., and G. Orlandini. 2007. *La libera circolazione dei lavoratori nell'Unione Europea*. Bologna: Il Mulino.

Guaman, A., and F. J. Trillo. 2015. "Desempleo y precariedad: repensar el trabajo." In *El trabajo garantizado. Una propuesta necesaria frente al desempleo y la precarización*, edited by A. Garzón and A. Guamán, 26–52. Madrid: Akal.

Mundiak, G. 2012. "Human Rights and Labor Rights: Why Don't the Two Tracks Meet?" *Comparative Labor Law & Policy Journal* 34: 217–243.

Orlandini, G. 2017. "Desplazamiento transnacional y *dumping* salarial en la Unión europea." *Revista de Derecho Social* 78: 139–148.

Pavlou, V. 2016. "El potencial del Derecho laboral de la UE para luchar contra la vulnerabilidad de los trabajadores domésticos. Implicaciones para el ordenamiento jurídico español." *Revista de Derecho Social* 76: 83–106.

Pérez Rey, J. 2004. *Estabilidad en el empleo*. Madrid: Trotta.

Pérez Rey, J. 2016. "Por una reformulación de nuestro modelo de contratación temporal: reflexiones sobre las consecuencias de la Sentencia Porras en nuestro ordenamiento y la eficacia de la Directiva 99/70." *Revista de Derecho Social* 76: 219–252.

Romagnoli, U. 1995. *Il lavoro in Italia. Un giurista racconta*. Bologna: Il Mulino.

Salvatori, A. 2015. "The Effects of the EU Equal-Treatment Directive for Fixed-Term Workers: Evidence from the UK." *British Journal of Industrial Relations* 53 (2): 278–307.

Sciarra, S. 2007. *Il lavoro a tempo determinato nella giurisprudenza della Corte di giustizia europea. Un tassello nella 'modernizzazione' del diritto del lavoro*, WP C.S.D.L.E. "Massimo D'Antona". INT – 52, Universidad de Catania. En http://aei.pitt.edu/13690/1/sciarra_n52–2007int.pdf (última consulta 5 November 2017).

Trillo, F. J. 2016. "Economía digitalizada y relaciones de trabajo." *Revista de Derecho Social* 76: 59–82.

Vega, M. L., and D. Martínez. 2002. *Los principios y derechos fundamentales en el trabajo. Su valor, su viabilidad, su incidencia y su importancia como elementos de progreso económico y de justicia social*. Ginebra: OIT.

Wolmark, C. 2007. *La définition prétorienne. Étude en Droit du Travail*. Paris: Dalloz.

Zoppoli, L. 2006. *Lavoro, impresa e Unione Europea. La tutela dei lavoratori nell'Europa in trasformazione*, Franco Angeli. Milano Pubblicazioni DASES, Universitá degli Studi del Sannio.

CHAPTER 7

Self-Employment and the Transformation of Employment Relationships in Europe

Alberto Riesco-Sanz

INTRODUCTION

Throughout the course of contemporary European history, the configuration, mobilisation and utilisation of the productive capacity of the population have increasingly—albeit not exclusively—tended to be centred on one of the different forms of salaried employment. The conditionality, arbitrariness and indeed precariousness that a salaried employment relationship produces in the interaction between people and the work they do resulted in a long and often turbulent process of institutionalisation and stabilisation of labour relations. This process was necessary, not only for the protection of the people affected but also in order to guarantee the production process itself. The institutionalisation of employment led to the recognition of the political, social and economic rights of these people, albeit to varying degrees and

A. Riesco-Sanz (✉)
Unidad Departamental de Sociología Aplicada,
Facultad de Ciencias Económicas y Empresariales,
Complutense University of Madrid, Campus de Somosaguas,
Madrid, Spain

© The Author(s) 2019
A. Serrano-Pascual and M. Jepsen (eds.),
The Deconstruction of Employment as a Political Question,
https://doi.org/10.1007/978-3-319-93617-8_7

at different points in time in different countries. It also resulted in the establishment of a variety of mechanisms and institutions intended to minimise the risks associated with modern employment relationships, in many cases through their mutualisation. Fundamentally, these risks arose when people were unable to continue working as salaried employees due to factors such as illness, old age, unemployment, or the obsolescence of their skills and knowledge.

However, rather than automatically granting these new rights and guarantees to all of the potentially affected groups, the state introduced extensive selection and classification criteria for them. As a result, it can be argued that the establishment of the political, social and economic rights embodied in the 'salaried employment regime' was accompanied by the exclusion of these guarantees for other parts of the working population in Europe. These groups included people who worked only intermittently or irregularly and people engaged in forms of employment (self-employment) or industries (e.g. domestic service and agriculture) that did not conform to the formal definition of salaried employment based on the legal principles of subordination and working in the employ of another.

However, the extent of this exclusion should be qualified. Over the course of time, most European countries have at least to some degree extended the rights and institutions that were originally established for salaried employees (or certain groups of salaried employees) to groups of workers and types of employment that are wider and more diverse than initially envisaged. This substantial widening of the scope of the 'salaried employment regime' means that its original focus on the 'working class' has been superseded by a far more heterogeneous reality characterised by the convergence—not always with equal positions and rights—of groups with formerly conflicting interests such as industrial workers, agricultural workers, artists, domestic workers, middle management and even senior management, civil servants, sales executives and the liberal professions.

The fact that salaried employment is a widespread phenomenon in the world's leading economies today might cause us to erroneously assume that it is becoming more homogeneous. In actual fact, however, nothing could be further from the truth. Europe is currently witnessing a rise in the heterogeneity and multiplicity of models for utilising the productive capacity of the population. This applies both to formal salaried employment (subcontracting, temporary work, part-time work, casual work and zero-hour contracts, etc.) and its combination in various shapes and forms with different types of non-salaried work (self-employment, voluntary work, work placements, unpaid work, etc.) or even undeclared work. These unconventional ways of utilising labour frequently result in hybrid employment models and regimes that are often insufficiently or poorly formalised, but which nevertheless interact with the institutions and mechanisms of traditional salaried employment on a daily basis despite not fitting in very well with their structures. This wide range of employment models and regimes with different configurations presents significant challenges both with regard to the coordination and organisation of production and in terms of employment quality and protection. It also points to major changes in the structure of Europe's employment regimes. This chapter will focus on one of these unconventional ways of utilising labour in Europe: self-employment.

THE TWO DISTINCT TRENDS OF SELF-EMPLOYMENT IN THE EUROPEAN UNION[1]

In 2015, there were just over 35 million self-employed workers in the European Union (EU-28). The majority (67%) were self-employed workers without employees. Workers formally defined as 'non-salaried' thus accounted for a significant 16% of the EU-28s working population, although they were rather unevenly distributed across the member states, with the figures for some countries being well above or below the European average (see Fig. 7.1). On the whole, the geographical distribution of the data appears to point to higher levels of self-employment in southern and eastern Europe (22 and 19% of the working population respectively) compared to western Europe and Scandinavia (12.5%). In other words, at first glance, it would seem that there is a correlation between (lower) levels of economic development and (higher) levels of self-employment.

In actual fact, however, self-employment trends in Europe are not exclusively determined by differences in countries' level of development. Indeed, although self-employed work remains more widespread in southern and eastern Europe, if we consider its development over the course of time (see Figs. 7.2, 7.3, and 7.4) it quickly becomes apparent that it is, in fact, the richest countries in Europe that have recorded the strongest growth in the number of self-employed workers over the past two decades. During this period, the southern European countries and the former socialist republics that are now members of the European Union

Fig. 7.1 Non-salaried workers as a percentage of the total working population (aged 15–74) in the EU-28. 2015 (*Source* Author's own figures based on European Union Labour Force Survey (Eurostat). Annual figures for people aged 15–74)

actually experienced a significant fall in the number of self-employed workers. In southern Europe, this decline has been especially pronounced since the onset of the financial crisis in 2008.

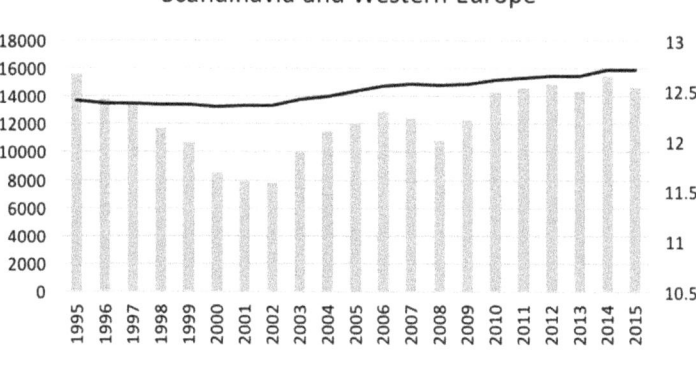

Fig. 7.2 Non-salaried workers in Scandinavia and Western Europe (Germany, Austria, Belgium, Denmark, Finland, France, Netherlands, Ireland, Luxembourg, UK and Sweden), total numbers (left), percentage (right), 1995–2015 (*Source* Author's own figures based on European Union Labour Force Survey (Eurostat). Annual figures for people aged 15–74)

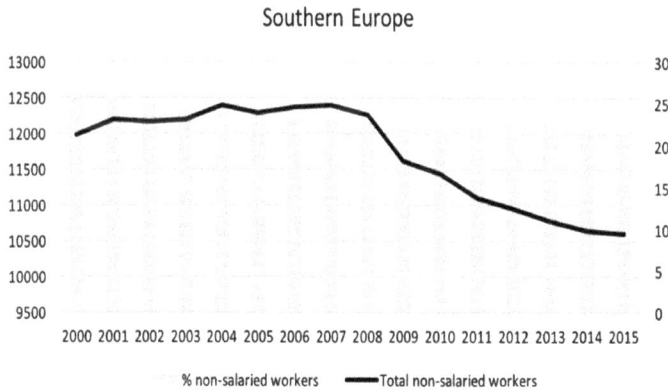

Fig. 7.3 Non-salaried workers in Southern Europe (Cyprus, Spain, Greece, Italy, Malta and Portugal), total numbers (left), percentage (right), 2000–2015 (*Source* Author's own figures based on European Union Labour Force Survey (Eurostat). Annual figures for people aged 15–74)

EU Former Socialist Republics

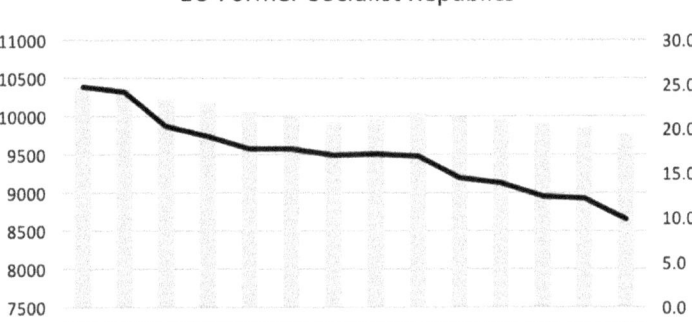

% non-salaried workers   ━━Total non-salaried workers

Fig. 7.4 Non-salaried workers in the EU's former socialist republics (Bulgaria, Croatia, Slovakia, Slovenia, Estonia, Hungary, Latvia, Lithuania, Poland, Czech Rep. and Romania), total numbers (left), percentage (right), 2002–2015 (*Source* Author's own figures based on European Union Labour Force Survey (Eurostat). Annual figures for people aged 15–74)

The aggregate data could, therefore, be providing an incomplete picture of how this form of employment is developing in Europe. Between 2002 and 2015, for example, the number of self-employed workers in the EU-28 declined by 749,000 (equivalent to a decrease of 3.4 self-employed workers per 1000 members of the working population). This was reflected in the proportion of self-employed workers in the total workforce, which fell from 17.5 to 16%. During this same period, however, the number of self-employed workers fell by around 1.4 million in southern Europe (28.2 self-employed workers per 1000 members of the working population) and 1.7 million in the former socialist republics (38.8 self-employed workers per 1000 members of the working population). In stark contrast, Scandinavia and western Europe recorded an increase of 2.6 million self-employed workers over this period (21 self-employed workers per 1000 members of the working population). Non-salaried work in Europe thus shows two distinct geographical trends: it has undergone significant growth in Scandinavia and western Europe (with a growth rate of 20% between 2000 and 2015, double the rate for salaried employment), whereas it has declined in southern and eastern Europe by 11.5 and 16.7%, respectively (see Figs. 7.5 and 7.6).

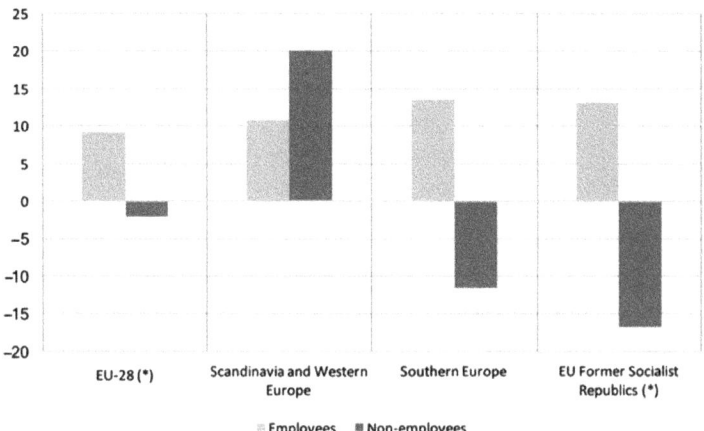

Fig. 7.5 Change in numbers of people employed in Europe by employment type (percentage), 2000–2015 (*Source* Author's own figures based on European Union Labour Force Survey (Eurostat). Annual figures for people aged 15–74. *Figures only available from 2002)

Fig. 7.6 Change in numbers of non-salaried workers in Europe (percentage), 2000–2008 and 2009–2015 (*Source* Author's own figures based on European Union Labour Force Survey (Eurostat). Annual figures for people aged 15–74. *Figures only available from 2002)

What is the explanation for these pronounced differences in self-employment trends across different parts of Europe? In order to try and answer this question, it is first necessary to make a small digression.

It is clear that there has been a strong decline in self-employment in the former socialist republics since the onset of the 2008 financial crisis (see Fig. 7.6). However, Fig. 7.6 also shows that self-employment levels in eastern Europe were already falling at a similar rate before the crisis, meaning that the crisis cannot be held solely responsible for the decline in this part of Europe. In southern Europe, on the other hand, the pronounced reduction in self-employment does appear to be closely linked to the onset of the 2008 financial crisis (see Fig. 7.6). However, if we consider a longer timeframe it becomes apparent that the decline in self-employment actually began before the 2008 crisis. Self-employment in Greece, for example, fell by 4.7% between 1983 and 2000 (declining from 51 to 42% of the working population). A similar phenomenon was observed in Portugal (where there was a 4.4% fall in self-employment between 1986 and 2000 and the proportion of self-employed workers declined from 31 to 25% of the total workforce) and, to a lesser extent, in Spain (a 1.7% fall in self-employment and a decline from 29 to 20% as a proportion of the total workforce).[2] Seen over a longer timeframe, the decline in self-employment witnessed in southern and eastern Europe could therefore be at least partly attributable to a single process that occurred at different times in these two different parts of Europe: the economic 'modernisation' driven by EU membership and the resulting restructuring of traditional industries (such as agriculture) that had been characterised by high levels of self-employment in the past (see Fig. 7.7).[3]

However, the strong decline in self-employment recorded chiefly in southern and eastern Europe is not the only significant self-employment trend witnessed across Europe as a whole. As indicated above, in other parts of Europe self-employment levels have increased as a spontaneous or institutionally driven response to rising unemployment and as a means of promoting labour market flexibilisation and cheaper labour (see European Commission 2016; 2015a, b; European Employment Policy Observatory 2014; European Parliament's Committee on Employment and Social Affairs 2013; Abdelnour 2013; Eurofound 2010, 2002; D'amours 2009; Muehlberger 2007).[4] Although this second trend is

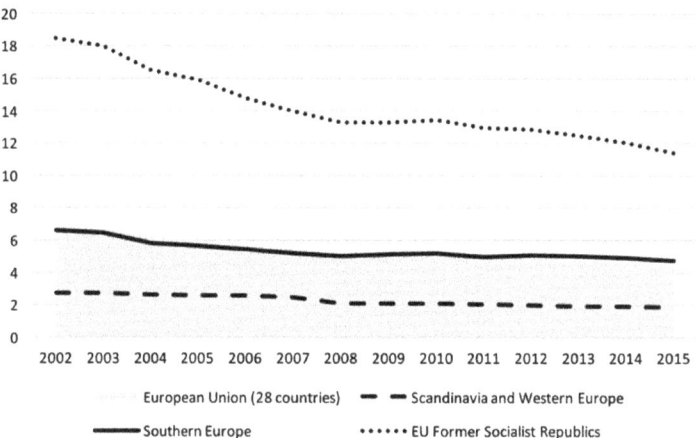

Fig. 7.7 Proportion of agricultural workers as a percentage of all workers in the European Union, 2002–2015 (*Source* Author's own figures based on European Union Labour Force Survey (Eurostat). Annual figures for people aged 15–74)

especially apparent in Scandinavia and western Europe, where the transformation of the economy's traditional structures occurred much earlier, we believe that it is not solely confined to these countries. For instance, if we consider the development of self-employment with and without 'agricultural jobs' (see Fig. 7.8), it becomes evident that 'non-agricultural' self-employment has risen across the whole of Europe, albeit to different degrees. In other words, the decline in self-employment in southern and eastern Europe resulting from the restructuring of the agricultural sector (and the impact of the 2008 financial crisis) has been accompanied by a simultaneous rise in self-employment in other industries and professions in these countries. This increase in self-employment throughout the whole of Europe points to wider changes in the field of employment. For several decades now, there has been an ongoing drive in Europe to make the labour market more flexible, resulting in various combinations of 'typical' and 'atypical' employment that go beyond the simple use of self-employed labour.[5] Accordingly, the different interventions and reforms affecting self-employment in Europe over the past few decades should be framed and analysed in the context of these wider changes.

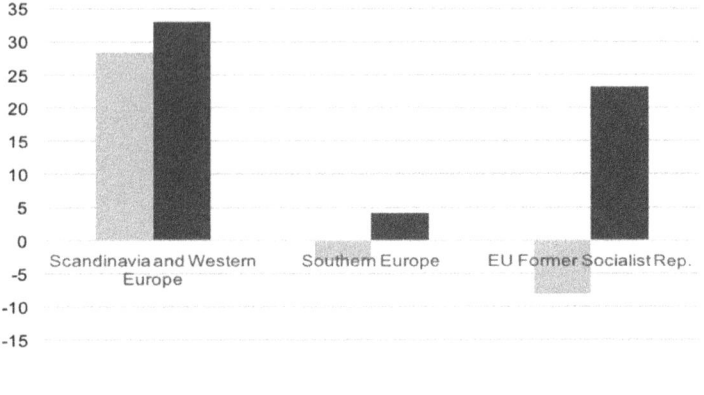

WITH AGRICULTURE   ■ WITHOUT AGRICULTURE

Fig. 7.8 Change in the number of self-employed workers in Europe with and without agricultural sector, 2000–2015 (The figures refer only to self-employed workers (with or without employees). The period covered for the former socialist republics is 2002–2015) (*Source* Author's own figures based on European Union Labour Force Survey (Eurostat). Annual figures for people aged 15–74)

SELF-EMPLOYMENT AS A TARGET AND INSTRUMENT OF EUROPEAN PUBLIC POLICY

Although *entrepreneurship* has been the subject of debate and public policy in Europe since at least the 1980s (Eurofound 2011a, 7), its importance has clearly grown in recent years.[6] Self-employment has ceased to be regarded as an indicator of economic backwardness and is instead now championed—under the guise of *entrepreneurship*—as a strategic instrument for promoting innovation and sustainable economic growth in the European Union (see European Commission 2010). At the same time, self-employment has attracted a lot of interest among policymakers as a potential means of creating employment. Although not the main one, it has certainly become one of the mechanisms that are regularly included in Europe's active employment policies. For instance, one recent study on the use of *entrepreneurship* as a means of combatting unemployment in Europe found that all of the European Union's member states had incentives (at national, regional or local level) for unemployed people to start their own businesses (European Employment Policy Observatory 2014).

Similarly, an earlier study (Eurofound 2011b) calculated that between 2008 and 2011 approximately 180 initiatives had been launched in Europe to promote self-employment as a means of creating jobs. These included measures facilitating access to finance, tax incentives, cutting red tape, the promotion of an 'entrepreneurial culture', advice services, help with recruitment, reforms of labour market and social security regulations, etc.[7]

The interest in self-employment and *entrepreneurship* as a tool for combatting unemployment is also reflected in the fact that many European countries now sanction or even promote part-time *entrepreneurship* and the simultaneous compatibility of employment regimes that could not have been combined in the past. In some cases, for example, unemployed people are provisionally allowed to do self-employed work while still drawing unemployment benefit. In total, at least 15 EU member states (Belgium, Bulgaria, Czech Republic, Germany, Estonia, Greece, Spain, Hungary, Lithuania, Poland, Portugal, Austria, Sweden, Slovakia and Finland) have introduced schemes providing non-refundable benefits and allowances to help unemployed people start a self-employed business. In some countries (Denmark, the Netherlands and France), these *entrepreneurship* allowances may even be claimed at the same time as (full or partial) unemployment benefit. However, it is more usual for the allowances to be granted either instead of unemployment benefit (Belgium, Germany, Austria, UK, Finland) or as a conversion (capitalisation) of unemployment benefits into a lump sum for setting up a business (Bulgaria, Spain, France, Luxembourg, Portugal) (European Employment Policy Observatory 2014, 16–21).

Just like the decline in non-salaried employment in Europe, many of these measures were not solely a product of the 2008 financial crisis and in fact often date back to the 1980s (although at that time they perhaps received less media coverage and institutional support than they do today). This was borne out by one of the author's previous studies of the situation in France and Spain (Célérier et al. 2016b) as well as other studies which found that one third of EU member states have launched *entrepreneurship* incentives for unemployed people since the mid-1980s (and that most of the remaining EU countries have done so since 2000) (European Employment Policy Observatory 2014, 14–15). While the employment crisis that followed the 2008 financial crisis may have revived interest in this type of measure, their existence and content are far from new in a European context.

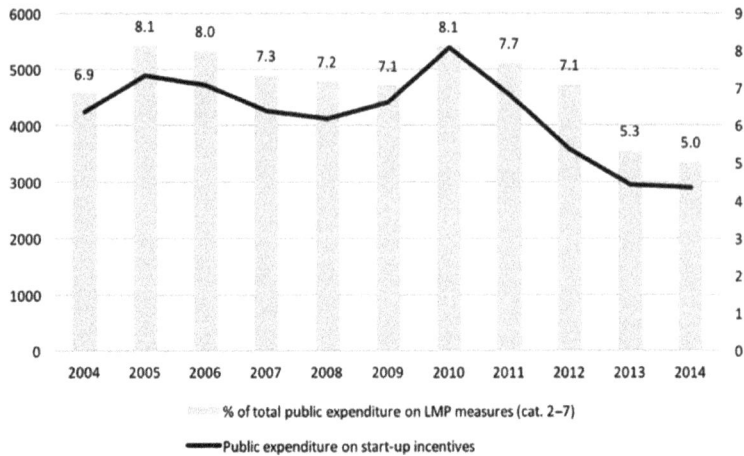

Fig. 7.9 Public spending on start-up incentive measures and as a percentage of total public spending on labour market policy measures (cat. 2–7) (*Source* Eurostat. Unit: Million EUR)

On the whole, these *entrepreneurship* measures have had little impact in terms of job creation since the onset of the crisis. Although there was an increase in public spending on this type of policy in Europe during the years immediately after the crisis (2008–2010), spending on them has fallen significantly since 2010. As a result, their share of total public spending on employment measures fell from 8.1% in 2010 to 5% in 2014 (see Fig. 7.9). A similar trend can be observed for the number of participants in European *entrepreneurship* programmes. While their numbers and relative weight compared to other employment measures increased throughout the 2000s (an increase that thus predates the financial crisis), they have declined in absolute terms since 2010 and in relative terms since 2012, falling from 11% of the total number of participants in employment measures in 2012 to 9% in 2014 (barely 800,000 workers across the whole of Europe) (see Fig. 7.10). Even in those countries with a stronger tradition of policies to promote self-employment among the unemployed, initiatives of this type usually affect little more than 1–2% of people officially registered as unemployed. Furthermore, they create very few additional jobs over and above the job of the self-employed individual themselves (European Employment Policy Observatory 2014, 38–42).[8]

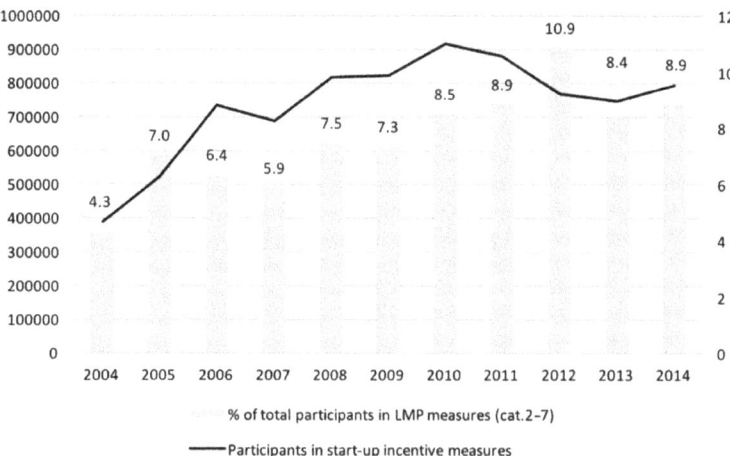

Fig. 7.10 No. of participants in start-up incentive measures and as a percentage of total participants in labour market policy measures (cat. 2–7) (*Source* Eurostat. Unit: Annual average stock)

The underwhelming results of these *entrepreneurship* measures in terms of job creation are compounded by the extensive list of risks associated with them: fluctuating and often inadequate income; the fact that there is less or in some cases no social protection for self-employed workers; their tendency to promote 'false self-employment' and the use of weakly protected forms of self-employment such as 'economically dependent self-employed work'; the displacement of salaried employees into a high-risk form of employment, etc. (European Commission 2016; European Employment Policy Observatory 2014; Eurofound 2011a). In view of the above, how can we explain the apparent enthusiasm that Europe's political leaders and policymakers have shown for these types of measures over many years?

Part of the explanation is undoubtedly to do with the fact that some political leaders and public bodies have been seduced by the purely ideological elements of the *entrepreneurship* discourse (individualism, free enterprise, private initiative, independence, innovation, etc.) and that these principles are similar to those driving other reform processes in Europe (e.g. social welfare reforms, the boom in active employment policies, the shift from welfare to workfare, etc.) (Barbier 2011; Serrano

Pascual and Magnusson 2007; Kosonen 1999). Be that as it may, the increased prevalence of 'entrepreneurship' initiatives on the European agenda should also be seen in the light of more pragmatic considerations. Other studies (European Employment Policy Observatory 2014, 11) have pointed out that although *entrepreneurship* programmes have little impact on unemployment figures, they are cheaper for the public purse than many other widespread measures such as income transfers to unemployed individuals and households. In other words, *entrepreneurship* programmes allow Europe's leaders and institutions to placate public opinion by being seen to be doing something about the politically important issue of unemployment without placing an excessive burden on the public finances.[9]

In short, these measures—together with others that can be described either as massaging the figures (use of narrower definitions of 'unemployed' by various institutions and statistical reports) or masking the real situation in society (using the proliferation of part-time work, short-term contracts, mini jobs, etc., to boost the official number of people in work)—allow Europe's political leaders and policymakers to put off any attempt to tackle the real causes and effects of Europe's employment crisis. It should be noted that the causes of this job crisis cannot be solely attributed to the current economic crisis and will therefore not necessarily disappear once Europe returns to a path of stable growth. This strategy makes it possible to avert any public discussion of the de facto job sharing that is already occurring in Europe under the worst possible conditions for its citizens: lower incomes (often even below the poverty indicators); irregular, erratic career paths; increasing precariousness and loss of rights; 'involuntary' switching between periods of activity and inactivity, the proliferation of 'atypical' forms of employment with fewer rights, etc. Seen through this lens, one might conclude that Europe's *entrepreneurship* policies have been more successful in terms of their impact on public opinion and in the political arena than in terms of actually combatting unemployment and that they have thus been better at influencing people's views than at creating jobs.

Nevertheless, it would be wrong to suggest that self-employment interventions in Europe are simply a reflection of the ideological obsessions, political strategies or concerns of Europe's leaders. The use of *entrepreneurship* as an instrument for combatting unemployment is not the only significant aspect in the debate on self-employment in Europe, nor is it the only type of public intervention in this area. Of equal or even greater importance to the debate on the transformation of employ-ment in Europe are the reforms being introduced by many European countries to regulate and protect the self-employed.

THE REFORM OF SELF-EMPLOYMENT IN EUROPE: TOWARDS THE ESTABLISHMENT OF HYBRID EMPLOYMENT REGIMES?

At the beginning of this chapter, we explained that the transformation of self-employment in Europe is characterised by two distinct trends. On the one hand, it is becoming less common in some countries due to the decline of industries such as agriculture where this form of employment had traditionally been widespread. On the other hand, however, self-employment is becoming more prevalent in many other industries due to the flexibilisation of the European labour market, the emergence of platform capitalism and the changes in the organisation and operation of companies as one of the actors responsible for procuring and com-bining different production factors. We have also seen how the rise in certain forms of self-employment in Europe is not an isolated phenome-non and should be understood in the context of a wider diversification of ways of utilising labour, of which the use of self-employment is just one expression (International Labor Organisation 2016). It is in this context that we should frame and analyse the growing number of reforms of self-employed work being introduced by many European countries, in par-ticular with regard to certain ambiguous forms of self-employment that fall somewhere between independence and subordination, such as 'eco-nomically dependent self-employed work'.[10]

In recent years, many of the European Union's member states have in some form or other debated what the correct legal definition of self-employment should be. In practice, these debates have really been about whether or not the different and increasingly heterogeneous forms of labour market participation should be incorporated into the salaried employment regime and covered by the corresponding institu-tions, and about the principles, assumptions and mechanisms for doing so. The debates have been accompanied by discussion of the rights of self-employed workers (and workers engaged in other unconventional forms of employment) and potential ways of improving their protection. However, the scale of the changes that such reforms would involve (not only to each country's employment law but also to their tax regimes, social security systems, unemployment benefits, etc.) has in many cases limited the extent to which these discussions have translated into concrete initiatives (Eurofound 2010, 14). As a result, the legal distinction between independence and subordination that has traditionally shaped the definition of salaried employment has remained in place as the basis of employment regulation in most countries. Despite this underlying continuity, however, it is possible to discern two different strategies or approaches to addressing the challenges posed by self-employment—and in particular forms of economically dependent self-employed work—to Europe's employment and social welfare regimes.

On the one hand, countries like Germany (Eurofound 2010, 16 ff.) have tried to tackle the growing diversity and ambiguity in the ways that labour is utilised through the consolidation of the salaried employment regime, i.e. by assimilating as many atypical forms of employment as possible into this established regime. They have done this by adopting a more flexible definition of salaried employment (it is now only necessary to fulfil at least three of the criteria on a much wider list of conditions rather than complying with a strict, closed definition[11]) and by giving the labour courts a greater role when it comes to interpreting these more flexible concepts. We do not deny that other mechanisms may be resulting in precarious employment conditions in Germany (promotion of part-time work, erosion of salaried employees' rights, longer working hours, loss of purchasing power, etc.). Nonetheless, Germany and other countries such as France and Belgium seem to have taken a fundamental decision to maintain salaried employment and the corresponding regulations (although admittedly the content of these regulations has been progressively 'watered down') as the basis of employment regulation and protection, and to fit in other less conventional forms of labour utilisation around this model.

In contrast—or more accurately in parallel—to this type of approach, several European countries are opting to formalise and regulate some of these 'atypical' forms of labour utilisation. Instead of watering them down or assimilating them into the established salaried employment regime, this second type of approach recognises—with considerable variability in the extent to which they are formalised—forms of labour utilisation that fall somewhere between subordination and independence, creating hybrid employment regimes that share many of the dependencies that characterise salaried employment but frequently lack their basic protection mechanisms (Martín Puebla 2012; Schmid 2011; European Economic and Social Committee 2010; Perulli 2003; Supiot 2000).[12]

Austria, for example, introduced the 'free service contract' in 1997 with the aim of extending the social insurance coverage of certain types of self-employed workers. These contracts are aimed at workers who formally perform their work without a relationship of subordination but who often work for a single or principal employer and with fixed working time schedules. The contracts recognise the existence of a certain degree of dependence or subordination, notwithstanding the independence that characterises self-employment, and provide self-employed workers with some of the basic statutory protection afforded to salaried employees (health, occupational accident and pension insurance). However, they exclude other important forms of protection such as unemployment insurance (Eurofound 2010, 28). Until their recent abolition in 2016, Italy had what was known as the *contratto di collaborazione a progetto* (co.co.pro), a type of employment contract aimed at economically dependent freelance workers. To qualify, a self-employed worker had to meet at least two of the following conditions over a two-year period: to have worked with the client for more than eight months, to have received 80% of their income from the client during this period, or to have a permanent workplace on the client's premises (Terrasse et al. 2016, 92).[13]

The example of Spain is one of the most notable and ambitious instances of this second type of approach (Riesco-Sanz 2016) and thus merits closer examination. In 2007, Spain adopted the *Ley 20/2007, de 11 de julio, del Estatuto del Trabajo Autónomo* (LETA) (Jefatura del Estado 2007), an act introducing a Self-Employed Workers Statute. The act established a professional regime specifically for self-employed workers that would become the regulatory framework of reference. This regulatory framework was unanimously adopted by the Spanish parliament and remained virtually unchanged when the Right returned to power in 2011, except for the largely symbolic shift in emphasis from (the protection of) 'self-employed workers' to (the empowerment of) 'entrepreneurs'.[14] In other words, as well as recognising economically dependent self-employed work like other countries had done, Spain also introduced a specific regime for self-employed work. The framework for the regulation and protection of this modern form of employment is not based on the principle of legal subordination and adopts a positive definition of self-employment rather than simply defining it as anything that is not salaried employment. But has Spain's adoption of a specific employment regime for self-employed work actually resulted in a clearer differentiation of this type of work from formal salaried employment? We would argue that it hasn't and that if anything the opposite is true.

The adoption of the *Estatuto del Trabajo Autónomo* in Spain has resulted in the (admittedly only partial) convergence of two employment forms and regimes that have historically been treated as separate. This convergence is for example apparent in the fact that the LETA grants self-employed workers a range of individual and collective basic rights typically associated with employees: the right of association, representation and collective defence of their professional interests; the right to an appropriate work-life balance; the right to health and safety at work, etc. The LETA and its subsequent updates (Jefatura del Estado 2010; Ministerio de Trabajo e Inmigración 2009) also grant self-employed workers various types of protection and monetary benefits that have traditionally been associated with salaried employment: healthcare for pregnant women and people suffering from common illnesses or occupational diseases, death, accident and retirement benefits, and the opportunity for self-employed people who have ceased trading to claim a monetary benefit funded through the social security contributions of self-employed workers.

The convergence of the regimes for self-employed work and salaried employment is even more apparent in a new category of self-employed worker established by the LETA, referred to as *Trabajadores Autónomos Económicamente Dependientes* (TRADEs—Economically Dependent Self-Employed Workers).[15] For instance, the LETA makes it mandatory for a written employment contract to be concluded between economically dependent self-employed workers and the companies contracting their services, specifying (among other things) the self-employed worker's weekly/annual working hours and rest periods. The LETA also grants this category of self-employed worker the right to a form of pseudo collective bargaining that can in theory lead to the conclusion of 'agreements of professional interest' between the self-employed workers' trade unions or professional organisations and the companies to which they provide their services—although the effectiveness of these agreements has been questioned (Castro 2011; Cairós 2008). Last but not least, the LETA stipulates that the labour courts shall be responsible for resolving TRADE workers' employment disputes—in other words, the employment law for salaried employees also applies to them.

However, the regime convergence hypothesis described above should be qualified, at least in terms of its current extent. The new regulatory framework for self-employment in Spain maintains a separate tax regime for self-employed workers, as well as a special social security regime—the Régimen Especial del Trabajo Autónomo (RETA—Special Regime for Self-Employment). Ever since it was established in 1970, and despite undergoing a series of reforms, the RETA has been characterised by lower social security contributions and consequently also by lower benefits and more limited protection mechanisms. In 2013, for example, the average contribution base for workers registered under the General Social Security Regime was calculated at €1739/month, whereas the average contribution base under the RETA was €1030/month (CEPYME 2013, 35). This is hardly surprising given that, according to figures from the Ministry of Employment and Social Security (2016), as of December 31, 2015, 67.3% out of a total of more than 3 million self-employed workers registered with the RETA were paying the minimum social security contribution base of €884.40. The pensions paid to self-employed workers by the social security system remain modest and are significantly lower (38%) than the pensions under the General Regime that covers the majority of salaried employees (Unión de Profesionales y Trabajadores Autónomos 2012). Furthermore, in 2012, just 21% of self-employed workers registered with the social security system were covered by the cessation of trading insurance established by the LETA—which is compulsory for TRADEs but voluntary for all other self-employed workers (Unión de Profesionales y Trabajadores Autónomos 2012)—whereas 38% of the working population as a whole was covered by this insurance (or 78% if we do not count only contributory unemployment benefits) (Instituto Nacional de Estadística, *Indicadores Sociales* 2011). Figures such as these make it clear that self-employed workers do not yet fully enjoy the same rights as salaried employees. Consequently, the employment regime convergence and establishment of hybrid employment regimes postulated in this chapter should be understood as a long-term trend that forms part of the evolution of Spain's social employment protection systems. As we have seen, this trend is also occurring in other parts of Europe, albeit at different levels and to differing degrees.

Indeed, the countries that have adopted one or other of the two approaches described above have in practice not done so to the exclusion of the other. Countries such as Germany and France, where the assimilation of new forms of employment into the traditional salaried employment regime still predominates, have nonetheless also begun to recognise some of the abovementioned hybrid employment categories. Germany, for example, has formally recognised the category of the *arbeitnehmeränliche person* for economically dependent self-employed workers (defined as self-employed workers who work for or receive more than 50% of their income from a single client), granting such workers a (limited) number of protection rights traditionally enjoyed by salaried employees (Terrasse et al. 2016, 91). Meanwhile, the *auto-entrepreneurs* regime introduced in France in 2009 establishes a category of entrepreneurs who operate on a self-employed basis but are entitled to a number of basic employee benefits such as sickness benefits, pensions, maternity/paternity benefits, etc. (Célérier et al. 2016b). By the same token, even though—unlike France and Germany—Spain seems to have chosen to create a specific employment regime for some of these new forms of employment that is formally distinct from the regime for salaried employees, this hasn't prevented it from also constantly reinterpreting the ever-shifting formal boundaries of salaried employment. The rulings of Spain's labour courts have resulted in types of work that were originally classified as self-employment being redefined as 'salaried employment' and thus being covered by the established employment law and institutions for salaried employees.[16]

Despite the differences in their motivation, content and implications, all of these reforms point to an ongoing transformation of the traditional salaried employment regime. They also suggest that Europe's nations are finding it necessary to intervene in response to a global transformation in the mobilisation and utilisation of labour that they themselves have contributed to. This transformation is resulting in workers becoming increasingly decoupled from particular jobs, leading to the emergence of more complex methods and structures for utilising their labour. This begs the question of whether this increased complexity should not also be reflected in the study methods used by researchers to try and explain it.

SELF-EMPLOYED WORK: AN OPPORTUNITY TO ADOPT A BROADER UNDERSTANDING OF THE WAGE-BASED SOCIETY

In spite of the reforms that have been introduced, in most European countries the legal definition of salaried employment continues to be based on the existence of an employment contract, i.e. of a relationship in which the worker is dependent on their employer (Rodríguez-Piñero 1999; Montoya 1999). In this context, however, 'dependence' has a very specific meaning. The legal definition does not refer to the social and economic dimensions of dependence. Instead, it is the legal construct of subordination (the power of one of the parties to direct the work performed by the other) that is employed to distinguish between salaried employment and 'non-subordinate' types of work (Lefebvre 2009; Rodríguez-Piñero 1999).

The principle of legal subordination has thus traditionally played a pivotal role in defining the boundaries of salaried employment and also, indirectly, in the definitions of other forms of work (Lefebvre 2009; Didry and Brouté 2006; Chauchard and Hardy-Dubernet 2003; Supiot 2000; Cruz Villalón 1999). This is not a trivial matter, since the definitions in question have informed the establishment of criteria for access (or denial of access) to the rights, regulatory mechanisms and institutions of protection provided for by the salaried employment regime that has progressively developed since the second half of the nineteenth century. In other words, it is the application of the legal principle of subordination that has led to the traditional treatment of salaried employment and self-employment as two formally distinct—one might even say diametrically opposed—forms of employment, despite the fact that the differences between the two are in fact not always that clear. For instance, the principle of legal subordination is often blurred in *new forms of work organisation* where (salaried) workers are habitually required to show initiative and the ability to act autonomously in the performance of their duties and in terms of how their work is organised (quality circles and semi-autonomous work groups, project work, etc.) (Durand 2012; Lahera Sánchez 2005; Boltanski and Chiapello 2002). Meanwhile, there has been a rise in the use of subcontracting and outsourcing, which involves the contracting of workers and companies that despite being formally independent are in practice often forced to comply with the organisational imperatives and schedules, instructions and strategies of the contracting companies (e.g. with regard to quality standards, manu-facturing processes, working hours, etc.) (Perraudin et al. 2013; Lebeer and Martínez 2012).

Just like all the other social sciences in the field of employment, legal theory, too, has had to recognise that it is difficult to maintain clear dis-tinctions between the different employment regimes when dealing with the 'grey areas' in the labour market (Martín Valverde 2009; Cairós 2008; Alonso 2004; Supiot 1999). In legal practice, it is frequently nec-essary to take a range of very different factors into account in order to establish whether or not certain employment relationships constitute sal-aried employment. This has led to a progressive shift in the boundaries of salaried employment which have proven to be more porous and dynamic than anyone could have imagined at the time when they were first for-mally established. Furthermore, the institutions associated with salaried employment (for instance the contract of employment and the system of social contributions and benefits that eventually led to the creation of a social security system) now cater to a far wider range of users than the specific segments of the working population that they were origi-nally confined to (Friot 2012; Castel 1997; Martín Valverde 1990; Rolle 1988). As well as expanding their coverage to new groups of workers—domestic and agricultural workers, artists, management executives and professionals, sales executives and certain liberal professions such as lawyers, doctors and architects—these institutions are also no longer restricted to people who are in active employment (e.g. they also cover students, pensioners, people suffering from illness, etc.). Consequently, these structures have the potential to affect large parts of the popula-tion, if not the evolution of society as a whole. One might, therefore, ask whether rather than limiting our analysis to the formal definition of salaried employment we should not instead talk about a wage-based soci-ety (referred to in French as *salariat*). Is the legal definition of modern employment relationships really adequate for investigating the global changes currently occurring in the field of employment?

The state use different types of institutions—not least the social security system—to implement interventions that go beyond the strict confines of the relevant employment regime, extending some of the protection and rights traditionally associated with (the formal definition of) salaried employment to all types of workers. In doing so, they cre-ate an apparently contradictory situation where the constant proliferation of new forms of employment and employment regimes coexists with a (relative) tendency to homogenise the 'conditions of use' for large parts of the workforce. This situation is perhaps less surprising if we consider the requirement for coordination and combination associated with modern networked production methods, where the involvement of large numbers of individuals in the production process does not necessarily require them to belong to an organisational structure in the mould of a company.

The regulation and reform of self-employment in Europe briefly described in this chapter serves to illustrate how the state actively participates in the establishment of common criteria for the utilisation of labour that are applicable to different employment regimes. The state thus regulates the conditions for entering and exiting the new employment regimes, formally recognising them and defining their potential compatibility with other existing employment regimes. It also intervenes with regard to the cost, duration and different forms of utilisation of these legally non-subordinate workers, as well as the definition of many aspects of their career paths and working conditions. Furthermore, it intervenes with regard to the disposable income—and thus ultimately the social reproduction and welfare—of these groups through the introduction of a range of fiscal measures and the institutionalisation of compulsory contributions and insurance against certain risks that are common to the labour activity of the wage-based society.

Seen from this perspective, the legal definitions of self-employment and salaried employment do not provide an adequate basis for their analysis—indeed, the formal distinction between these two types of work is of limited relevance. As well as undoubtedly pointing to major transformations and ruptures in the traditional salaried employment relationship, the trends shown by self-employment in Europe also indicate a diversification of the ways in which people participate in the creation and benefits of the wealth produced by society and, more generally, a diversification of ways of participating in the institutions that perpetuate and renew the wage-based society. If, as we argue here, self-employment is, in fact, nothing more than one of the possible models within the wider wage-based society for the (temporary) interaction between human productive capacity and activity, then any attempt to propose a tentative explanation of the current developments in and transformation of self-employed work should be framed within this wider transformation trend. In other words, we believe that in order to advance our understanding of the transformation of employment, the changes affecting self-employment should be treated as part of the changes occurring within the wage-based society as a whole, regardless of the formal distinctions drawn between different forms of employment or employment categories and regimes. There is no doubt that the wage-based society has been transformed and that the modern reality of self-employed work is one of the many factors responsible for this transformation. However, the suggestion that it may have disintegrated completely has yet to be demonstrated (from a theoretical perspective) and explored in a practical setting (from a political and social perspective).[17]

NOTES

1. The statistics used in this section are taken from Eurostat's *European Union Labour Force Survey* (annual averages for persons aged 15–74). Unless explicitly stated otherwise, the term "self-employment" is used generically to refer to all the different forms of non-salaried employment. Wherever possible, the statistics on self-employment are based on data for "non-salaried employees". "Northern", "southern" and "eastern" Europe are employed here as political rather than geographical categories.

2. In some respects, Italy constitutes an exception, since although the number of self-employed workers also fell by 1.7% between 1983 and 2000, their number as a proportion of the total workforce remained relatively stable (falling from 29 to 28%).

3. In Spain, for example, the number of jobs in agriculture fell from 2.7 million in 1976 (21% of the working population) to just 737,000 in 2015 (4% of the working population). Almost 1.2 million jobs were lost between 1987 and 2015, the vast majority of which (894,000, or 72%) belonged to self-employed workers. As a result, the proportion of salaried employees as a percentage of the industry's total workforce rose from 27 to 61% between 1987 and 2015 (National Statistics Institute-INE, Economically Active Population Survey). Furthermore, there is a strong positive correlation across the EU-28 between the "relative weight of agricultural work" and the "relative weight of self-employed work" ($r=0.537$, $p=0.01$). This supports the plausibility of the suggestion that a close link exists between self-employment and agriculture in Europe.

4. The Pearson correlation coefficient indicates a strong negative correlation ($r=-0.632$; $p=0.01$) between the prevalence of self-employment in the labour market and the development of labour costs in Europe since 2010 (in other words, an increase in one of these two variables causes a decrease in the other). The Pearson coefficient also reveals a slightly weaker but nonetheless significant positive correlation ($r=0.474$; $p=0.05$) between

the prevalence of self-employment and the level of unemployment (in this instance, an increase in one of the variables leads to an increase in the other). However, this simple statistical test does not in itself provide evidence of a causal relationship between the two variables.

5. We addressed some of these phenomena in more detail—albeit still provisionally—in another recent paper. For further details, see Célérier et al. (2016a).

6. This is illustrated by the numerous recent EU initiatives geared towards promoting and supporting small and medium-sized enterprises and entrepreneurship: the *European Charter for Small Enterprises* (2000), the *Modern SME Policy for Growth and Employment* (2005), the *Small Business Act for Europe* (2008), the *European SME Week* (2009), the *European Progress Micro-Finance Facility* (2010), the *Europe 2020 Strategy* (2010), the *Employment Package* (2012), the *Entrepreneurship 2020 Action Plan* (2013), the *Green Action Plan for SMEs* (2014), etc. (European Commission 2016; European Employment Policy Observatory 2014; European Employment Observatory 2010).

7. For a more detailed country-by-country breakdown of the content and characteristics of many of these *entrepreneurship* measures, see OECD/ European Union (2015), European Employment Policy Observatory (2014), and Eurofound (2011b).

8. For instance, the European Commission's report on employment in Europe (European Commission 2016, 42) found that just 2.7% of people registered as unemployed in Europe in 2013 had become self-employed (without employees) in 2014 (the equivalent figure for the economically inactive population was 5 and 4.5% for salaried employees). The figures are even lower for people who became "self-employed with employees": 0.7% of unemployed persons, 1.2% of the economically inactive and 3% of salaried employees.

9. In 2011, public spending on *entrepreneurship* measures came to just 0.036% of Europe's GDP (European Employment Policy Observatory 2014, p. 11).

10. Based on the data in Eurofound's 5th *European Working Conditions Survey* (2010), it can be estimated that economically dependent self-employed workers (who receive at least 75% of their income from a single client) accounted for 22% of all self-employed workers in the EU-28. This figure rises to 39% if "economically dependent" self-employed workers are defined as those who depend on a single client for at least 50% of their income. Using this definition, economically dependent self-employed workers make up 16.5% of the total workforce in the agricultural sector and 6.6% of professionals and artists. These figures demonstrate that this is not just a residual employment category in Europe.

11. For example: the worker does not employ other employees, the worker usually works for only one contractor, prior to this job, the worker concerned carried out the same work as an employee, the same job is also performed by regular employees, the worker has not initiated any entrepreneurial activities, etc. (Eurofound 2010, pp. 16–17)

12. A recent research note prepared for the European Commission (Fondeville et al. 2015, p. 39) found that all the EU member states provided some form of old-age pension for self-employed workers, all but 4 provided sickness benefits, and 17 provided some form of unemployment benefit. These figures do point to a certain awareness of the need to protect self-employed workers in Europe, although as we know the problem is often in the level of the benefits, which are either inadequate or voluntary in nature. This point is amply illustrated by the case of Spain which is examined in more detail below.

13. However, this new regulatory framework which provided slightly more protection for economically dependent self-employed workers did not apply to highly-skilled work, to people whose income exceeded a threshold of €18,000, to members of professional bodies (such as lawyers), or if the client could prove that the worker was genuinely self-employed (Terrasse et al. 2016, p. 92).

14. The new, conservative Spanish People's Party government has primarily focused on introducing complementary measures to promote *entrepreneurship*, tax incentives, and recruitment allowances for self-employed workers and small businesses. Many of these measures are set out in the *Ley de Apoyo a los Emprendedores y su Internacionalización* (Act of Support for Entrepreneurs and their Internationalization) (Jefatura del Estado 2013) and the subsequent *Ley de Fomento del Trabajo Autónomo* (Act for the Promotion of Self-Employed Work) (Jefatura de Estado 2015).

15. The LETA defines economically dependent self-employed workers (TRADEs) as workers who "usually carry out, personally and directly, an economic or professional activity for financial gain and predominantly for one physical or legal person, referred to as the 'client', on whom they are economically dependent in that they receive at least 75% of their income from said client in return for their work or economic or professional activities". However, this new category has had very limited success: according to Ministry of Employment and Social Security figures for the number of people registered with the social security system, just 9851 TRADE contracts had been registered as of December 31, 2015. This is despite the fact that more than one study (Agut and Núñez 2012; Asociación de Trabajadores Autónomos 2006) has estimated that around 300,000 self-employed workers (approximately 14% of all self-employed

workers) could potentially be included in this category and benefit from the corresponding protection mechanisms.
16. For an analysis of Spanish case law between 1980 and 2008, see Martín Valverde (2002, 2009).
17. Translation from the Spanish by Joaquín Blasco.

REFERENCES

Abdelnour, Sarah. 2013. "L'entrepreneuriat au service des politiques sociales: La fabrication du consensus politique sur le dispositif de l'auto-entrepreneur." *Sociétés contemporaines* 89: 131–154.
Alonso, Luis Enrique. 2004. "La sociedad del trabajo: debates actuales. Materiales inestables para lanzar la discusión." *Revista Española Investigaciones Sociológicas* 107 (4): 21–48.
Asociación de Trabajadores Autónomos. 2006. *Informe del trabajo autónomo dependiente.* http://www.ata.es.
Agut, Carmen, and Cayetano Núñez. 2012. La regulación del trabajo autónomo económicamente dependiente en España: un análisis crítico comparado con Italia. Working Paper 124, Associazione per gli Studi Internazionali e Comparati sul Diritto del Lavoro e sulle Relazioni Industriali.
Barbier, Jean Claude. 2011. "Activer les pauvres et les chômeurs par l'emploi? Leçons d'une stratégie de réforme." *Politiques Sociales et Familiales* 104: 47–58.
Boltanski, Luc, and Eve Chiapello. 2002. *El nuevo espíritu del capitalismo.* Madrid: Akal.
Cairós, Dulce. 2008. "Acerca de la denominada crisis del contrato de trabajo tradicional y la aportación española: el estatuto del trabajo autónomo." *Gaceta Laboral* 14 (2): 193–219.
Castel, Robert. 1997. *Las metamorfosis de la cuestión social. Una crónica del salariado.* Buenos Aires: Paidós.
Castro, María Antonia. 2011. "Los acuerdos de interés profesional: un balance de la negociación llevada a cabo al amparo del Estatuto del Trabajo Autónomo." *Anales de Derecho* 29: 34–80.
Célérier, Sylvie, Alberto Riesco-Sanz, and Pierre Rolle. 2016a. "Figures de travailleur—figures d'entrepreneur? Tentatives de caractérisation au niveau européen." *XV Journées Internationales de Sociologie du Travail,* Athens (Greece), 11–13, May.
Célérier, Sylvie, Alberto Riesco-Sanz, and Pierre Rolle. 2016b. "Une indépendance équivoque: les nouveaux statuts des indépendants espagnols et français." *Revue Française de Socio Economie* 17: 21–41.

Confederación Española de la Pequeña y Mediana Empresa. 2013. *Análisis del Régimen Especial de Trabajadores Autónomos en el sistema nacional de la Seguridad Social.* Madrid: CEPYME.

Cruz Villalón, Jesús, ed. 1999. *Trabajo subordinado y trabajo autónomo en la delimitación de fronteras del Derecho del Trabajo.* Madrid: Tecnos.

Chauchard, Jean Pierre, and Anne-Chantal Hardy-Dubernet, ed. 2003. *La subordination dans le travail.* Paris: La Documentation Française.

D'amours, Martine. 2009. "Travail précaire et gestion de risques: vers un nouveau modèle social?" *Lien social et Politiques* 61: 109–121.

Didry, Claude, and Rémi Brouté. 2006. "L'employeur en question, les enjeux de la subordination pour les rapports de travail dans une société capitaliste." In *Les nouvelles frontières du travail subordonné,* edited by Héloïse Petit and Nadine Thèvenot, 47–70. Paris: La Découverte.

Durand, Jean Pierre. 2012. *La cadena invisible. Flujo tenso y servidumbre voluntaria.* Mexico: Fondo de Cultura Económica.

Eurofound. 2002. *Economically Dependent Workers, Employment Law and Industrial Relations.* Dublin: Eurofound.

Eurofound. 2010. *Self-Employed Workers: Industrial Relations and Working Conditions.* Dublin: Eurofound.

Eurofound. 2011a. *Emerging Forms of Entrepreneurship.* Dublin: Eurofound.

Eurofound. 2011b. *Public Measures to Support Self-Employment and Job Creation in One-Person and Micro Enterprises.* Dublin: Eurofound.

European Commission. 2010. *Europe 2020. A Strategy for Smart, Sustainable and Inclusive Growth.* Brussels: European Commission [COM(2010) 2020].

European Commission. 2015a. *Policy Brief on Informal Entrepreneurship. Entrepreneurial Activities in Europe.* Brussels: European Commission/OECD.

European Commission. 2015b. *Recent Changes in Self-Employment and Entrepreneurship Across the EU.* Social Situation Monitor, Research Note 6/2015. Brussels: DG for Employment, Social Affairs and Inclusion, European Commission.

European Commission. 2016. *Employment and Social Developments in Europe 2015.* Brussels: DG for Employment, Social Affairs and Inclusion, European Commission.

European Economic and Social Committee. 2010. "New Trends in Self-Employed Work: The Specific Case of Economically Dependent Self-Employed Work." Soc/344—cese 639/2010. Brussels: European Economic and Social Committee.

European Employment Observatory. 2010. *Self-Employment in Europe 2010.* Brussels: DG for Employment, Social Affairs and Equal Opportunities, European Commission.

European Employment Policy Observatory. 2014. *Activating Jobseekers Through Entrepreneurship: Start-Up Incentives in Europe*. Brussels: DG for Employment, Social Affairs and Equal Opportunities, European Commission.

European Parliament's Committee on Employment and Social Affairs. 2013. *Social Protection Rights of Economically Dependent Self-Employed Workers*. Brussels: European Parliament, DG for Internal Policies [IP/A/EMPL/ST/2012-02].

Fondeville, Nicole, Erhan Ozdemir, Orsolya Lelkes, and Terry Ward. 2015. *Recent Changes in Self-Employment and Entreprenership Across the EU*. Brussels: European Commission, Research note n° 6/2015.

Friot, Bernard. 2012. *Puissances du salariat*. Paris: La Dispute.

International Labor Organisation. 2016. *Non-standard Employment Around the World: Understanding Challenges, Shaping Prospects*. Geneva: International Labor Organisation.

Jefatura del Estado. 2007. "Ley 20/2007, de 11 julio." *Boletín Oficial del Estado* 166: 29964–29978.

Jefatura del Estado. 2010. "Ley 32/2010, de 5 de agosto." *Boletín Oficial del Estado* 190: 68526–68551.

Jefatura del Estado. 2013. "Ley 14/2013, de 27 de septiembre." *Boletín Oficial del Estado* 233: 78787–78882.

Jefatura del Estado. 2015. "Ley 31/2015, de 9 de septiembre." *Boletín Oficial del Estado* 217: 79824–79848.

Kosonen, Pekka. 1999. "Activation, incitations au travail et workfare dans quatre pays scandinaves." *Travail et Emploi* 79: 1–15.

Lahera Sánchez, Arturo. 2005. *Enriquecer el factor humano. Paradigmas organizativos y trabajo en grupo*. Barcelona: El Viejo Topo.

Lebeer, Guy, and Esteban Martínez. 2012. "Trabajadoras del sector de la limpieza: precariedad en el empleo, desigualdades temporales y división sexual del trabajo." *Laboreal* VIII (1): 28–41.

Lefebvre, Philippe. 2009. "Subordination et 'révolutions' du travail et du droit du travail (1776 2010)". *Entreprises et Histoire* 57: 45–78.

Martín Puebla, Eduardo. 2012. *El trabajo autónomo económicamente dependiente. Contexto europeo y régimen jurídico*. Valencia: Tirant lo blanch.

Martín Valverde, Antonio. 1990. "El discreto retorno al arrendamiento de servicios." In *Cuestiones actuales del Derecho del Trabajo*, edited by Alfredo Montoya, 209–236. Madrid: Ministerio de Trabajo y Seguridad Social.

Martín Valverde, Antonio. 2002. "Fronteras y 'zonas grises' del Derecho del Trabajo en la jurisprudencia actual (1980–2001)." *Revista del Ministerio de Trabajo y Asuntos Sociales*, 38: 21–50.

Martín Valverde, Antonio. 2009. "Fronteras y 'zonas grises' del contrato de trabajo: reseña y estudio de la jurisprudencia social (2002–2008)." *Revista del Ministerio de Trabajo e Inmigración* 83: 15–40.

Ministerio de Trabajo e Inmigración. 2009. "Real Decreto 197/2009, de 23 de febrero." *Boletín Oficial del Estado* 54: 22048–22062.

Montoya, Alfredo. 1999. "Sobre el trabajo dependiente como categoría delimitadora del Derecho del Trabajo." In *Trabajo subordinado y trabajo autónomo en la delimitación de fronteras del Derecho del Trabajo*, edited by Jesús Cruz Villalón, 57–72. Madrid: Tecnos.

Muehlberger, Ulrike. 2007. *Dependent Self-Employment. Workers on the Border Between Employment and Self-Employment*. London: Palgrave Macmillan.

OECD/European Union. 2015. *The Missing Entrepreneurs 2015: Policies for Self-Employment and Entrepreneurship*. Paris: OECD.

Perraudin, Corinne, Nadine Thèvenot, and Julie Valentin. 2013. "Subcontratación y evitación de la relación de trabajo en la industria francesa entre 1984 y 2003." *Revista Internacional del Trabajo* 132: 585–611.

Perulli, Adalberto. 2003. *Economically Dependent/Quasi-Subordinate (Parasubordinate) Employment: Legal, Social and Economic Aspects*. Brussels: European Commission.

Riesco-Sanz, Alberto. 2016. "Trabajo, independencia y subordinación. La regulación del trabajo autónomo en España." *Revista Internacional de Sociología* 74 (1): e26.

Rodríguez-Piñero, Miguel. 1999. "Contrato de trabajo y autonomía del trabajador." In *Trabajo subordinado y trabajo autónomo en la delimitación de fronteras del Derecho del Trabajo*, edited by Jesús Cruz Villalón, 21–38. Madrid: Tecnos.

Rolle, Pierre. 1988. *Travail et salariat. Bilan de la sociologie du travail*. Grenoble: Presses Universitaires de Grenoble.

Serrano Pascual, Amparo, and Lars Magnusson. 2007. *Reshaping Welfare States and Activation Regimes in Europe*. Brussels: Peter Lang.

Schmid, Günther. 2011. "Non-standard Employment in Europe: Its Development and Consequences for the European Employment Strategy." *German Policy Studies* 7 (1): 171–210.

Supiot, Alain. 1999. *Au-delà de l'emploi. Transformations du travail et devenir du droit du travail en Europe*. Paris: Flammarion.

Supiot, Alain. 2000. "Les nouveaux visages de la subordination." *Droit Social* 2: 131–145.

Terrasse, Pascal, Philippe Barbezieux, and Camille Herody. 2016. *Rapport au Premier Ministre sur l'économie collaborative*. Paris: La Documentation Française.

Unión de Profesionales y Trabajadores Autónomos. 2012. *Anuarios del Trabajo Autónomo en España, 2011–2012*. Madrid: Ministerio de Empleo y Seguridad Social.

CHAPTER 8

The Blurring of Employment Boundaries: A Social Economy Perspective

Sarah de Heusch

WHY IS TRADITIONAL EMPLOYMENT DECLINING?

Many people will say that the steady decline in traditional jobs—those with full-time, permanent contracts—is the result of neoliberal policies. Although employers and above all shareholders are now undoubtedly the big winners both on the labour market and in what passes for 'social dialogue', they are not the only ones responsible for the situation. New lifestyles, career aspirations and technological progress have also had a lot to do with the diversification of forms of salaried employment, which is still the form of contract that largely dominates the European employment market, particularly in the services sector which is the focus of this article.

Market Developments

In recent decades, changes on the labour market have severely tested the social protection models introduced by European countries in the postwar period. First of all, the financialisation of the economy has made

S. de Heusch (✉)
Development & Strategy Unit of Smart, Bruxelles, Belgium

© The Author(s) 2019   179
A. Serrano-Pascual and M. Jepsen (eds.),
The Deconstruction of Employment as a Political Question,
https://doi.org/10.1007/978-3-319-93617-8_8

shareholders greedier, demanding large returns on their investments and putting pressure on production costs. First, there was just-in-time management, where production depends on orders. This contributed more generally to the extension of project-based management. Next, since there was already serious pressure on the cost of raw materials, the only option left was to reduce the workforce to an adjustment variable. This was easily done by outsourcing and the possibility of taking on a certain number of temporary workers. However, it was not just the private sector which adopted this approach: because of the pressure on public spending and the liberalisation of many public services, governments too have joined the race to reduce costs of all types. They pursue short-term policies, financing projects but less and less of the actual work needed to keep structures that depend on public funding.

While a substantial proportion of jobs used to be internalised within the undertaking (private or public), the race to reduce costs (in order to increase profits, thereby attracting investors) has mainly involved concentrating long-term employment on the core business. Other activities are outsourced to the self-employed or cheaper external undertakings.

It should also be noted that the growth of small and medium-sized enterprises also depends on the growth of the services sector, precisely because of this outsourcing and the development of 'new' sectors such as tourism, well-being and the media (Bologna 2015). A series of new jobs is emerging in these sectors, involving seasonal work carried out by project workers or those working fragmented hours.

Profound Societal Transformations

These new sectors have developed particularly as a result of the collective reduction in working time and the appearance of paid leave. By the end of the twentieth century, people were working fewer hours annually than they did in the previous century (Cette and Taddei 1994). This has freed up time (and money) for them to travel, take care of themselves, go out and enjoy themselves.

Technological progress is obviously another factor behind the emergence of these new sectors. Think of the media and the many different types of new technologies: these have particularly helped to boost workers' productivity (both long- and medium-term), which also helps to increase firms' financial profits. Technological advances have also profoundly transformed the way we consume: we can finance a project even before the product is on the market, we can create short consumption chains, we can give our time to a project we support. When we make skills available for a project, the time is not regarded as work (because it is not paid). However, when we look at what civil society has achieved in recent years, with initiatives like community gardens or support for immigrants, we can see that these citizens' initiatives have sometimes been more effective than public measures in responding to societal challenges. Yet individuals' involvement in this voluntary work, which does so much to benefit society, has not been recognised, either as work (and has thus not given them social rights) or as a public interest activity.

Having said that, some collaborative platforms provide work and are not necessarily in the public interest. There are cases of abuse too, such as platforms like Uber, which make millions in profit, force drivers to be self-employed in order to keep staff costs down, but do not redistribute profits to the drivers creating the wealth.

This type of platform is successful because it allows individuals to choose when and when not to work (by contrast with 'office hours'). Some workers prefer instead to be involved in meaningful economic projects and activities. And more and more workers with a good level of education are rejecting the daily commuter grind and hierarchies. Many explain that they prefer to live with smaller (and less stable) incomes if it allows them to develop interesting activities or to be in control of their time. Work for them is no longer experienced as the only or main place for socialising, we all have different identities and different social circles (family, places of learning, personal development activities, social networks, activism, etc.).

A Particular Political Atmosphere

The government response, however, is still a policy of full employment (the Member States even jointly adopted this in the Europe 2020 Strategy), a policy tied to a view of the typical world of work of the industrial era. In the absence of an adequate supply of jobs, governments are using various incentives (start-ups, incubators, etc.) to encourage people to start their own businesses. This helps to get both the unemployment figures and benefit spending down. It remains to be seen whether these activation policies are cheaper over the short and longer term than paying social benefits.

The State itself, as an employer, uses outsourcing and many different types of contracts for those it employs: fewer and fewer people are employed as civil servants. This is explained by the pressure on public spending felt by the EU Member States because of the stability pact and the resulting austerity policies. In response to the 'crisis', governments see social spending as a cost to be cut. In order to do so, they most often limit actual access to social protection by tightening up the eligibility conditions (think of the retirement age, for example, or access to unemployment benefit), or by shortening the period for which it is provided.

These political changes have, of course, gone hand in hand with a change in the concept of the individual and the social relationship: while, in the post-war period, social protection was regarded as a form of solidarity against the vicissitudes of life and the labour market, today those receiving social benefits are seen as people playing the system. It is as if, contrary to all the sociological evidence,[1] individuals were entirely responsible for their fate and therefore for whether they can find work or not.

With this world view, it is hardly a surprise that individuals are encouraged to take out supplementary (private) insurance. This tends to mask the fact that those most in need of cover are very often the ones who cannot afford to pay for private insurance, particularly as they are seen as a risk (of non-payment) by insurers, who therefore charge more to cover them.

Innovative policies are starting to emerge (in France, for example, there are new regulations setting up Activity and Employment Cooperatives (AECs) and Personal Activity Accounts[2]) that are comprehensive and inclusive responses. However, these proposals are still under discussion and have to accommodate the wishes (and sometimes even the privileges) of certain stakeholders. They often still view individuals as free and equal on the market. Even worse, between employment flexibility and security of career paths, the political scales all too often come down on the side of flexibility, bringing a greater risk of precarity for workers.

DIFFERENT FORMS OF EMPLOYMENT

How are all these changes being reflected in the world of work? Many institutional stakeholders like to argue that paid employment still dominates in Europe. Although it is true that paid employees account for 85% of the working population, a closer reading shows that traditional jobs (employees working full-time on permanent contracts) accounted for less than 60% of the active population in Europe. 17.17% of employees were working part-time (whether on permanent or fixed-term contracts), 8.13% were on fixed-term contracts and 16.44% were self-employed (Eurostat 2014). More than 40% of Europe's workers are therefore not in a 'traditional' employment situation; calling them atypical is a refusal to acknowledge the scale of this situation in the world of work.

Of course, some people will say that there is double counting in these figures, because very often workers not on full-time, permanent contracts have a number of different employment situations. But it can also be said that some workers counted as on permanent contracts are actually not traditional workers at all, because they are working through umbrella companies ('portage salarial') or through Activity and Employment Cooperatives, and have to generate their own income.

The diversification of contractual forms of employment (and above all discontinuous careers) has had a major impact on access to social protection for workers. The conditions for accessing social protection were designed around typical jobs in the period when solidarities were created by the State: from the late nineteenth century to the 1940s and 1950s the standard ideal worker was a white man who was the family's sole breadwinner, with a wife who stayed at home and looked after the children (Vielle 2014). Careers tended to be linear and workers often stayed within one company. But the world of work (and much else besides) has changed a great deal since then.

Regulatory Adjustments

Legislators have not been blind to the changes in the world of work, which have largely resulted from the way work is organised and employment relationships. Various European countries have adjusted their legislation to take account of the specific features of different work situations even within the contractual forms that now exist: commercial contracts (for the self-employed) and employment contracts (for employees). In most cases, legislative responses have been implemented piecemeal to facilitate access to labour law and social protection for workers. But these responses are still at a very early stage and tend to be linked to certain sectors (such as the performing arts), certain ways of working (such as seasonal and temporary work), or certain jobs (such as writers, fishermen, etc.), and they never give workers access to all the rights associated with a full-time permanent contract.

These ad hoc measures create exceptions to the core statuses (employee and self-employed), with individuals ending up being not entirely employees nor entirely self-employed. Artists are a good example here. Take two contrasting cases, France and Germany. For a long time now, and particularly since the 1980 UNESCO Recommendation on the Condition of the Artist, recognition that the sector has a particular, time-limited production method and the increased need for these workers to have social protection have forced a number of States to introduce special rules. In France, performing and audiovisual artists are regarded as employees covered by special rules governing casual workers. The rules give them access to unemployment benefit when they are not working (under certain conditions which are more straightforward than those for traditional employees). Performing artists in Germany, on the other hand, are classified as self-employed but are protected, under certain conditions, by a specific fund, the Künstlersozialkasse. This allows them to pay contributions and 'to enjoy the same health, pension and dependants protection as is provided for employees' (D'Amours 2012). The fact that these workers are covered by special employee/self-employed rules means that they are in a sort of hybrid situation, adding to their confusion about their actual employment status.

Furthermore, because those working part-time or intermittently have irregular incomes, they often develop different skills and know-how in order to improve their job prospects. But depending on the country and sector, workers with multiple activities will have to perform their different jobs under different forms of contract. If we go back to the example of a French actor, when he is on stage he will be covered by the intermittent regime, but if he also writes (plays, for example), he can only be paid for these works as a self-employed worker (artist-writer). The fact that workers with multiple activities combine and juggle with different employment statuses makes it even more difficult for them to know their actual rights and obligations. Some countries have introduced thresholds for accessing rights (for example, temporary workers having to work a certain number of days to be entitled to paid leave), which is contributing to these workers being under-protected socially, particularly if they have multiple activities.

The Development of Grey Forms of Employment

What do these various employment situations mean? And what impact do they have in terms of access to social protection? There are different ways of approaching this issue. The one below classifies the various employment situations along two axes (Grégoire 2016): access to social protection (i.e. in relation to the assumed level of subordination) and the extent to which occupational income depends on the individual's ability to find contracts. The resulting figure shows that between the 'typical' employee and 'traditional self-employed' workers there is a whole range of employment situations (Fig. 8.1).

This figure requires a few words of explanation.

Top left are employees (part-time or full-time, permanent or fixed-term contracts). Immediately below are the self-employed whose work is supplied by companies (like press groups).

Next, come work situations that are more varied because of the changes described earlier in the article. Project-based management has significantly altered the way that work is organised (Boltanski and Chiapello 1999). Within and around businesses we are starting to see people working on a project basis and autonomous workers. Project managers within companies may be either employees (such as permanently employed consultants) or self-employed workers (for instance, architects working for an architects' office or lawyers working for a law firm). Their work comes as a succession of projects (i.e. single, non-repeated commissions circumscribed by time, budget and resources limitations and by performance specifications) (Kerzner 2001), but their income is not (or is only partially) linked to their ability to find contracts. Those working on a project basis, by contrast, work for private

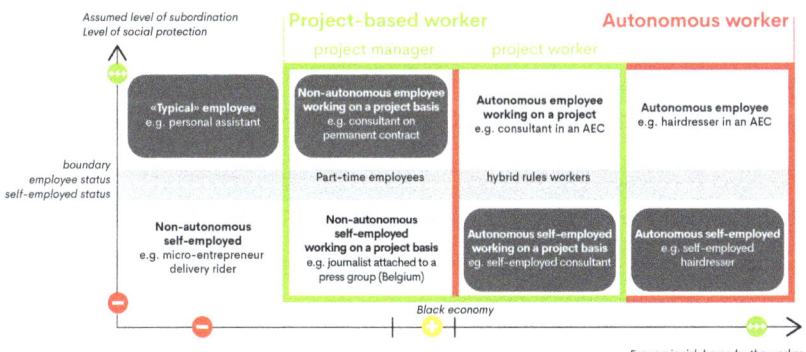

Fig. 8.1 Employment situations [*Source* Grégoire et al. (2016)]

individuals or public or private undertakings. Their work comes as a succession of projects and their income is directly linked to their ability to find contracts. For employees, these are people working in something like an AEC or through an umbrella company structure (artists, consultants, etc.). These workers are on the interface between project-based work and autonomous work.

Autonomous workers, on the other hand, are in a situation where they have to find work opportunities on their own, and their work does not necessarily fall into a series of projects. Among employees, these are once again people working in something like an AEC or through an umbrella company structure (such as hairdressers, masseurs, etc.), while for the self-employed there are the same occupations, including many liberal professions. In each case, these are employment situations rather than set forms of employment. The workers may switch from one situation to another during their career, or combine different situations at the same time. This is why the term 'patchwork worker' coined by Eva Van Ooij seems a particularly apt way to describe these 'non-traditional' employment situations. The expression 'atypical jobs' is not appropriate given how many such jobs there now are on the labour market (40%), nor is 'new forms of employment', given that a variety of forms of employment have existed for decades and some even date from a time we think of as the past (such as on-call work, for instance).

In the figure, the dotted line is the theoretical line separating employees from self-employed workers. The grey band surrounding it, which extends horizontally right across the middle of the figure, shows the risk of the appearance of 'false self-employed' or 'economically dependent self-employed' workers.

Various types of intermediary structures can start to be seen. In simple terms, some supply work (like press groups or temping agencies), while others aim instead to improve workers' employment status and give them greater career security (like the Activity and Employment Cooperatives).

As we can see, the same occupation may be carried out under different employment statuses, with or without the involvement of intermediaries (these tend to be mainly involved in the case of paid employment). There is no clear cut-off between employed status and self-employed status, which raises the question of whether a relationship of subordination is relevant for distinguishing those who are entitled to social protection from those who are not.

A number of situations are ambiguous, to the point where it might legitimately be asked whether some people classified as in a subordinate relationship should really be so. For example, some employees (such as university researchers) are totally independent in carrying out their work. No-one tells them what to do, and office hours are meaningless because in actual fact they work when and where they want (except when giving classes). Supervision by their employer is entirely relative here, yet they are regarded as subordinate because they are in paid employment.

At the other end of the spectrum, the terms 'economically dependent self-employed' and 'false self-employed' are appropriate in many cases, but can present problems for many autonomous workers. Take someone who has a client that provides him with over 50% of his earnings, but only a few months' work in total: the client may be self-employed or a micro-business that cannot afford to employ the worker permanently, and also the worker may want to be free to work for other people.

Between self-employed workers looking to make money and employees looking for security (Corsani and Lazzarato 2008) we are seeing the emergence of active workers wanting to earn a living from their own skills, free from hierarchies, free to decide on their working time and very keen on solidarity, whether mutualist or State-provided (such as access to social protection).

Focus on Autonomous/Freelance Workers

Independent workers receive little attention as such in the literature (one of the few comprehensive approaches in Corsani and Bureau 2014) and are clear evidence that distinguishing between employee/self-employed for access to social protection is now irrelevant. In this article, independent workers are those who have to find their own work opportunities (whatever their employment status) and who usually have a specific occupation or skills (intellectual or manual). We will not be discussing all the variables of independence, such as freedom to negotiate prices or to carry out work, etc. The main aim of independent workers as defined here is not so much to develop a lucrative business as to make a living from their own skills. To make their activities economically viable, they often develop related skills around their main know-how in order to improve their employability. These multiple activities can mean that they have to adopt various employment statuses, as we saw with the example of the French actor-writer who has to deal with two statuses, that of intermittent worker and that of artist-writer.

Independent workers also have changing roles, since they may have to work in teams led by others or to create teams for a project they themselves are leading. They may thus be taking workers on or taken on themselves. In addition, they work for a number of clients (or contractors). In the creative and intellectual sectors especially, working abroad (for very short or longer periods) is a normal and even desirable practice to obtain greater exposure and professional recognition.

When we talk about independent workers we are usually thinking of (highly) skilled workers. Having said that, these workers sometimes take unskilled jobs, such as bartending in cafes, for financial reasons. However, there is a new form of work that some freelances are also turning to, involving digital platforms, and particularly home deliveries of meals (via Foodora, Deliveroo, etc.). This fairly recent phenomenon suggests that developments in the labour market (and social protection) need to look beyond workers' skills levels.

Regardless of the employment status they adopt to do their job(s), the main occupational problems identified for these workers who have to find their own work opportunities are: finding clients, tight cash flow, legal and administrative issues, access to training and social protection. At an individual level, the occupational situation of independent workers often results in irregular or low incomes, which means that they, much more so than workers in stable employment, are in need of social protection.

Problems in Establishing Representation

There seem to be two main factors in these workers being overlooked: first, their special characteristics compared with the institutional referent, and second, the connection between the business fabric and social dialogue.

It is difficult for independent workers to demonstrate their specific assets, for a number of reasons. First, they have a combination of different employment situations and statuses. This often means that these workers are unable to define their employment status(es) or, even worse, no longer know what their rights and obligations are. Second, they tend to work in isolation and it is therefore difficult for them to get together (although co-working spaces and social networks provide opportunities to meet). Third, obtaining representation is difficult given that they are stuck between two models that are not appropriate for them.

The first model regards these workers as people who should be classified as employed (which is tantamount to regarding them as false self-employed). But aside from the fact that many independent workers like not being in a hierarchical relationship, they particularly value the diversity of experiences and learning that having a range of different clients brings. Secondly, independent workers often own their work tools (PC, GSM, software, instruments, etc.). They also work in different locations, very often at home. Finally, they have great intellectual freedom and freedom to organise the way they work. It, therefore, cannot really be said that they are in a subordinate position to the people they are working for.

The second model into which people try to shoehorn these freelancers is the self-employed model. The problem here is the preconceptions surrounding self-employed workers, which are the legacy of the early twentieth century (Bologna 2015). The first of these has to do with their income level. They are supposed to be well-off, in profitable occupations (like the liberal professions) and aiming to make as much money as possible (the entrepreneur is the dominant figure here). This preconception is shown to be wrong today when we see just how much many of them earn, even in the liberal professions. Many figures and studies (such as Conaty and Bird 2016) show that self-employed incomes are falling and a growing number of self-employed workers are living below the poverty line. They are also often taxed on the basis of a hypothetical or minimum income which is assumed to be much higher than their actual earnings. And do not forget that the self-employed have little or no social protection (no unemployment benefit, for example).

As regards the work supply situation, small (10–50 employees) and medium-sized (also known as SME, 50–250 employees) enterprises represent 99.8% of businesses in Europe, 92.7% of which are microenterprises (employing fewer than 10 workers). SMEs account for 67.1% of jobs in Europe, 30% in microenterprises, 20% in small enterprises and 17% in medium-sized enterprises. When we look at their contribution to value added, however, SMEs contribute only 57.3% (including 25% from microenterprises). This graph shows the distribution of the figures quoted (Fig. 8.2).

These figures are important in shedding light on two issues: trade union representation and businesses' financial resources. On the subject

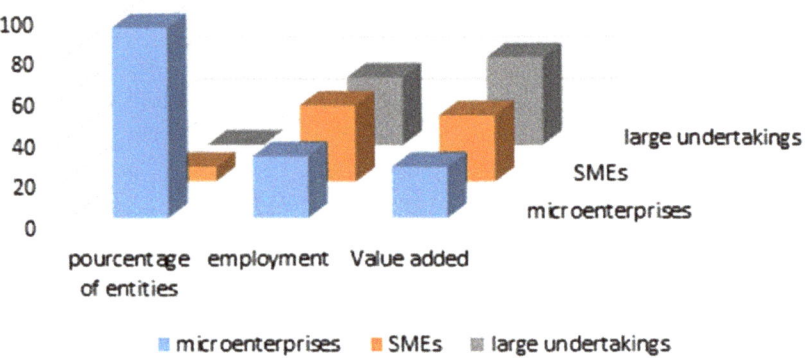

Business fabric EU28 (2012)

Fig. 8.2 Business fabric EU28 (2012) [*Source* Eurostat (2012)]

of representation, in several European countries (such as Belgium, France and Austria) union representation in undertakings is compulsory only if they employ more than 50 permanent staff (Fulton 2013) This means (according to the data gathered) that almost 50% of employees in these countries (working in small and microenterprises) are not systematically represented by trade unions in their undertaking. And the figures do not even take account of the self-employed workers working for those undertakings. It also means that over 90% of undertakings in these countries are not required to hold trade union elections, and so the specific needs of these workers are less well recognised.

Small and medium-sized enterprises are (in proportion to their quantitative importance in terms of employment) those that are least involved in creating value added in Europe. This means that they do not have the same economic clout or the same ability to employ as other businesses, even though they have done the most to create jobs in recent years (Leighton 2013). It is, therefore, easier to understand why SMEs are disinclined to employ long-term, and why they need to be able to outsource a number of services, some provided by other SMEs, others by independent workers.

So independent workers can certainly have large undertakings as their clients, but they are statistically more likely to work for SMEs or other self-employed workers. This world of small economic entities is a fragile ecosystem which needs social and political representation that understands their particular situation, which is very different from medium-sized and large undertakings both economically and in terms of employment.

Making Freelancers Employees

Given the difficulties faced by independent workers, the question is whether it is appropriate to classify them as self-employed, in view of the lack of social protection provided by this status, despite efforts by many States to offer the self-employed greater social protection.[3] Intermediary structures such as umbrella companies and cooperatives are seeking to remedy this situation by offering independent workers the option of working as employees in order to have access to better social protection. But making freelance workers employees does not necessarily mean in the traditional sense, on permanent, full-time contracts. Although, in some countries, these intermediary structures are obliged to give independent workers at least a permanent contract, in others (and particularly in certain sectors) fixed-term contracts may be used if necessary. In every case, the cooperative is the statutory employer in a tripartite relationship with the independent worker and his client.

SMart is one example of a cooperative that is recreating solidarity between workers and trying to give independent workers greater social protection. A social enterprise set up in Belgium to help artists (SMart is short for Société Mutuelle pour artistes -Artists' Mutual Society-), it is now open to all independent workers. Its aim is to support them in developing their activities. It is a shared enterprise that members are free to use according to their needs. It enables them to edit contracts and order forms online, to deal with administrative issues and social contribution and tax declarations, to obtain informed advice from a support network and to access a whole range of mutualised services. In Belgium, where over 75,000 workers have used these services since 1998 and with a turnover of 136 million in 2016, SMart has been able to develop a whole range of mutualised services to help independent workers to deal with the most commonly experienced work-related problems. To tackle legal complexity, SMart simplifies the legislation by asking users simple questions from which a computer programme can calculate social contributions, taxes and net earnings. To deal with cash flow problems and late payments, SMart has set up a wage guarantee fund which allows independent workers to be paid within seven days of completing their work (SMart recovers what it is owed at a later point). In order to professionalise independent workers and help them in their careers, SMart provides cross-disciplinary training courses (such as 'How to negotiate a contract') and negotiates reduced prices with specialised training bodies. In addition, to overcome isolation, SMart has opened third places where freelancers from different sectors can meet and arrange to work together. This non-exhaustive list gives some idea of the professionalising services that can be provided at lower cost by mutualising the costs and risks involved.

This model was created to help artists, and SMart has no contracts with workers' clients and does not pair them up. The only commercial contract with clients was with Deliveroo and Take Eat Easy. When hundreds of bicycle couriers appealed to SMart, the social enterprise decided, rather than refusing to help these workers, to negotiate better employment conditions and rights for them. The agreement provides for wholly paid shifts of a minimum of three hours (whereas previously the couriers were only paid by the delivery), makes it compulsory to provide safety training and to check equipment before the courier first starts work, and to cover the courier's costs of using his own bicycle and mobile phone (essential tools for the job). This is one example of giving workers greater security and professional status.

The purpose of the structure is to simplify legal and administrative procedures, which has reassured many workers who had previously not declared their activity. SMart has helped independent workers to regularise their situation and has encouraged their professionalisation. Unfortunately, budget cuts in the arts and culture sectors (which are still well represented among users), the economic slow-down and reductions in social allowances have led to a drop in individuals' income compared with previous years.

Now, cooperatives create solidarity between members and tend to be the best representation of the relationship between workers and a shared enterprise. With cooperatives, members are both workers and owners of the enterprise from which they generate income, and whose profits are redistributed in the form of services. This is why SMart became a cooperative in 2016.

It was its spinning off into 8 European countries that encouraged SMart to become a cooperative. Its experience showed that the employment problems faced by artists (and creative professionals more generally) are similar in countries with different legislation, even for those working under different statuses. And, as certain authors have already explained (Menger 2002; Capiau 2014), the situation faced by artists is an extreme example of what a growing number of people are experiencing or going to experience on the employment market. In fact, people from increasingly different sectors (such as well-being, language teachers, consultants, etc.) are contacting SMart, which was why the social enterprise decided to take a leap and open itself (in Belgium at least) to all freelancers.

Providing independent workers with mutualised services and giving them the employment status of salaried workers has allowed SMart to give these workers more secure careers and greater access to social protection than if they were self-employed and working in isolation. But because they are not traditional employees (the figure on which social protection funding mechanisms and conditions of access are based), they are in a grey area when it comes to accessing social protection. They cannot take special leave, for example, or have access to training paid for by their employer, or sometimes even take paid leave because their contributions are scattered across different social schemes. This is why, in addition to developing services, SMart is endeavouring to work with academics and economic and social stakeholders to promote social policies that include different forms of employment, including independent workers.

Is Employment the Cure-All in the World of Work?

Looking at the picture we have drawn and particularly the fact that many people aspire to earn a living from their own skills, by developing a meaningful occupation without an oppressive hierarchy, employment at any cost (both in terms of pay, conditions of employment and the work to be performed) no longer appears to be THE solution. Though it certainly cannot be claimed that a patchwork career or independent working is suitable for everyone, anyone wanting to develop this type of career must at the very least acquire skills, and should ideally be able to build and use a social network, and, for some people, rely on other sources of income.

That does not mean, however, that patchwork workers do not include some who are well-off or have considerable cultural capital. There are also less skilled profiles such as bicycle couriers or Uber drivers who either want to boost their income, or else purely and simply to work when they want. However, saying that these aspirations have to be met is no excuse for the way in which some employers evade responsibility and unilaterally and unreasonably impose flexibility (such as with zero hours contracts).

The traditional employment model is interesting for some of the things it brings with it, such as a stable income and access to social protection. But does this have to be linked to employment? Is it not conceivable to create an inclusive social protection model that takes account of the wide range of employment forms and situations? It is not about calling for employment to end: businesses will still need a certain proportion of permanent employees, and the *aquis* of those workers must certainly be preserved. But refusing to consider other forms of employment and how to include them in social protection is contributing to the segmentation of the labour market.

If the many different contractual forms of employment are to be more sustainable, including the careers of freelancers, account must be taken of patchwork workers. We must make sure that they do not lose social rights and benefits because the different employment statuses they adopt or the different collective agreements that apply impose access thresholds or fragment their rights. The idea of portable personal rights (relating to unemployment, retirement, special leave, access to training) is a very compelling one. There remains the issue of legislation on occupational safety in the broad sense (including occupational accidents and illnesses). Measures adapted to those working in different locations must be improved, and particularly the question of cover and compensation for occupational accidents and illnesses. How do we organise compensation for those working intermittently? In AECs or umbrella companies, can the employer (i.e. the intermediary structure) be held responsible for the way in which an independent worker does his job? And from the opposite perspective, can we knowingly require independent workers to take out private insurance to cover those aspects?

More generally, in a society where work and economic dynamism mean that not all individuals of working age can make a living by working, it is courting disaster to push for full employment. Moreover, some authors[4] argue that full employment has never existed because many activities have never been recognised as work. Think of housework, caring for family members or voluntary activities of all kinds. The register of invisible work also includes work upstream (e.g. drawing up a quote or submitting a project proposal) and downstream of services provided (e.g. disseminating/raising the profile of a job done in order to improve chances of further work) which, with independent working and project-by-project financing, is rarely paid. Better redistribution of work is a good idea (such as by a collective reduction in working time), but is not enough to be inclusive.

Would not the introduction of a socialised income be even more directly inclusive? By 'socialised income' I mean income generated by contributions collected by the State and distributed unconditionally to all inhabitants. The term avoids going back to the thorny question of which model to adopt: universal income, revised welfare benefits, living wage, or something else. If it is to be inclusive, a socialised income must not take the place of services of general interest like health, education or culture; it must be in addition to them. However, it would replace some existing allowances and benefits, provided that recipients do not end up being paid less than they currently receive. It would be a huge step forward if we could agree on the fact that work, as it is currently organised, does not provide for everyone's needs.

Of course, there is the question of how this new model would be financed. Labour income is already highly taxed and supports most of the funding for social protection, even though the share of labour income in GDP is steadily declining (OECD Employment Outlook report 2012). The contribution to GDP of other types of income (property, moveable assets and others), on the other hand, is steadily increasing, as are overall income inequalities (Piketty 2013). So there is plenty of wealth in our European countries to fund an inclusive social model. All that is missing is the genuine political will to harness and tax this income to finance a new social pact that fairly combines work flexibility (so that workers have a real choice) and genuinely inclusive social protection. This should be the key battle, and if it is to be effective, it can only be fought at a European level.

Clearly, although this means changing the way that trade unions operate, it will, above all, be an opportunity to improve working conditions and the quality of work for everyone, to open up union membership, to gain greater power in negotiations on social protection and rights, and above all to guarantee fair wealth distribution. The price for this will be having to rethink how the unions operate and some of their objectives. The European Trade Union Confederation resolution *Towards new protection for self-employed workers in Europe* adopted on 14 and 15 December 2016 is an excellent step in this direction. Thinking that the biggest problem facing the world of work is the diversification of contractual forms of employment is a legalistic approach based on familiarity. It is a mindset that is based on a nostalgic view of work derived from an exceptional period in history (the 'glorious 30' years between 1945 and 1975), the basic premises of which (demographic growth, strong industry, strong economic growth and a world in need of reconstruction after the War) no longer exist. By looking at the world of work and social protection from the point of view of workers' aspirations and practices, we can seek solutions that are suited to our increasingly diversified lifestyles. It is not just the world of work that has changed: families, education, means of production and consumption are also multifaceted.[5]

NOTES

1. Think of traditional sources, from Marx's class struggle to Bourdieu's social reproduction…
2. In the draft El Khomri Law, there a number of very questionable aspects, but the section on personal activity accounts (TITLE III—making career paths more secure and laying the foundations for a new social model for the digital age) puts forward some interesting proposals that are worth considering.
3. Among others, the ILO's social protection floors, and the European Commission's maternity directive which, although not entirely accepted by the Member States, extended social cover for the self-employed in a number of countries.
4. For example, Philippe De Feyt, Jean-Claude Barbier, Pascale Vielle.
5. Translation from the French by Julie Barnes.

REFERENCES

Bologna, Sergio. 2015. *The New Workforce. Il movimento dei freelance: origini, caratteristiche, sviluppo*. Trieste: ed Asterios.
Boltanski, Luc, and Eve Chiapello. 1999. *Le nouvel esprit du capitalisme*. Paris: Gallimard.

Capiau, Suzane. 2010. *L'artiste, entrepreneur de l'incertain*. Bruxelles: L'art et le droit, Éditions Larcier.

Capiau, Suzane. 2014. *Sécurité sociale: portrait de l'artiste en contorsionniste*. SMart. Source http://smartbe.be/media/uploads/2015/01/Portrait-de-lartiste-en-contorsionniste.pdf.

Cette, Gilbert, and Dominique Taddei. 1994. *Temps de travail et modes d'emplois, vers la semaine des 4 jours?* Paris: Éditions la découverte.

Conaty, Pat, and Alex Bird. 2016. *Not Alone: Trade Union and Co-operative Solutions for Self-Employed Workers*. Source http://www.uk.coop/sites/default/files/uploads/attachments/not_alone_-_trade_union_and_co-operative_solutions_for_self-employed_workers_3.pdf.

Corsani, Antonella, and Marie Christine Bureau. 2014. «*Du désir d'autonomie à l'indépendance*». *La Nouvelle Revue du Travail*, n°5/2014 Indépendance et salariat.

Corsani, Antonella, and Maurizio Lazzarato. 2008. *Intermittents et précaires*. Paris: Ed. Amsterdal.

D'Amours, Martine. 2012. *La Protection Sociale des Artistes et Autres Groupes de Travailleurs Indépendants*. Québec: Université de Laval. Source https://www.mcc.gouv.qc.ca/fileadmin/documents/publications/Protection__sociale_artistes_Cadre_analyse_synthese.pdf.

Fulton, Lionel. 2013. *La représentation des travailleurs en Europe*. Labour Research Department and ETUI. Source http://fr.worker-participation.eu/Systemes-nationaux/Pays/Italie/Representation-sur-le-lieu-de-travail.

Grégoire, Maude, et al. 2016. Evolution et diversité des situations de travail: une analyse à travers les notions de «travail autonome» et «travail au projet». *Journées Internationales de Sociologie du Travail*. Athènes.

Kerzner, Harold. 2001. *Applied Project Management*. New York: Wiley.

Leighton, Patricia. 2013. *Future Work: The Rise if Europe's independent Professionals (iPros)*. Edited by EFIP. Source http://www.um.es/prinum/uploaded/files/Future_Working_Full_Report-2%20final%20subir%20web.pdf.

Menger, Pierre-Michel. 2002. *Portrait de l'artiste en travailleur. Métamorphoses du capitalisme*. Paris: Ed. Seuil.

Piketty, Thomas. 2013. *Le Capital Au XXIe Siècle*. Paris: Les Livres du Nouveau Monde.

Van Ooij, Eva. 2016. Présentation lors de la Task For Culture of the European Border Region Association, Mons. Page 33. Source http://www.aebr.eu/files/publications/TF_CB_Culture_Mons_AEBR_Report02_Def.pdf.

Vielle, Pascale. 2014. *Sustainable Work: The Role of Social Systems with Regard to Men and Women's Careers, Including Cover for Risks Over Their Life course*. Brussels: Eurofound.

SOURCES WEB

UNESCO: http://portal.unesco.org/fr/ev.php-URL_ID=13138&URL_DO=DO_TOPIC&URL_SECTION=201.html.

OECD: Rapport de l'OECD EMO. 2012, chapitre 3: *Partage de la valeur ajoutée entre travail et capital: Comment expliquer la diminution de la part du travail?* Source: https://www.oecd.org/fr/els/emp/EMO%202012%20Fra%20_Chapitre%203.pdf.

ETUC: https://www.etuc.org/fr/documents/towards-new-protection-self-employed-workers-europe#.WbqbLrJJaUk.

European Union: https://ec.europa.eu/info/strategy/european-semester/framework/europe-2020-strategy_fr, http://ec.europa.eu/eurostat/statistics-explained/images/0/0a/Labour_status_of_persons_aged_15_years_and_older%2C_EU-28%2C_2014.png, http://ec.europa.eu/eurostat/statistics-explained/index.php/Statistics_on_small_and_medium-sized_enterprises.

Eurostat. 2012. http://ec.europa.eu/eurostat/statisticsexplained/index.php/Statistics_on_small_and_medium-sized_enterprises.

French Government: http://www.economie.gouv.fr/ess-economie-sociale-solidaire/loi-economie-sociale-et-solidaire.

CHAPTER 9

The Marketisation of Public Employment and Public Services and Its Impact on Civil Servants and Citizens

Jean-Michel Bonvin

INTRODUCTION

The Fordist employment contract, prevailing in the so-called 'Thirty Glorious Years' after the Second World War, has been characterised by an exchange between subordination and security. More precisely, workers were expected to accept a subordinate role at work, which would result in increased productivity that would, in turn, produce more gains and benefits to be redistributed between the various stakeholders; in exchange, they were entitled to more material security in the form of secure employment, regular wage increases (based on seniority rather than performance) and guaranteed access to social benefits in cases where predefined social risks, such as illness, disability, old age or unemployment, would lead to job loss or temporary suspension. According to this approach, employment was intended to provide support for entitlements, rights and social protection, which were, for the most part, associated

J.-M. Bonvin (✉)
Université de Genève, Geneva, Switzerland

© The Author(s) 2019
A. Serrano-Pascual and M. Jepsen (Eds.),
The Deconstruction of Employment as a Political Question,
https://doi.org/10.1007/978-3-319-93617-8_9

with the status of wage earner. Public employment, that is the status of civil servants working in public administration, is certainly one of the most emblematic examples of this Fordist model of employment: public employees were expected to perform their work in accordance with precise specifications, managed by strict rules and hierarchical superiors (laying down, in great detail, the terms and conditions of employment), and access to any public positions was subject to strict entrance examinations. This model of public administration is in line with Max Weber's description of bureaucracies as 'iron cages' (Weber 1968): indeed, in such a system, public employment is not the realm of individual initiative or improvisation; it is rather characterised by the competent implementation of standardised rules that apply to all citizens. In exchange for their loyalty and obedience, civil servants receive appropriate remuneration with regular pay increases throughout their career (based on seniority), and they enjoy extensive guarantees in terms of job security (by means of a lifetime contract that can be broken only in cases of serious misconduct), as well as significant protection, very often at a higher level than that of their private counterparts, in cases such as illness or retirement. Accordingly, public employment emerges as a paradigmatic case of exchange between wide-ranging subordination at work and extensive guarantees of material security. Public employment is thus defined as a secure and subordinate status. It clearly departs from a contractual situation in which labour would be defined as a commodity to be bought under specific terms and conditions (in terms of wages, work content, timetables, etc.) defined in a sovereign manner by the contractual parties; indeed, this is a statutory view of employment, where working terms and conditions refer to a status defined by law and imposed on all actors of the employment relationship.

The second feature of this specific approach towards public employment and public services is the link between public administration and citizens. Public services are designed in a standardised way, which implies that citizens are seen as users who are entitled to the same quality of services (e.g. water, electricity, social services) and/or subject to the same duties or obligations towards public institutions (for instance the tax system). They are not considered as consumers or customers who need to be offered a choice of a variety of services and providers, or who have to be enticed into consumption of public services rather than their private counterparts. Public services are not deemed to be a market where supply needs to find its demand; instead, they are compulsory for (for instance taxation) or available to (e.g. public transport, electricity, social services, etc.) all citizens. Therefore, the link between citizens and public administration is designed along very different lines from that between producer and consumer on private markets for goods or services. Here again, there is a clear distinction between the consumer on the market and the citizen in the field of public administration.

Since the mid-1980s, these two aspects of public employment and public services have been undergoing a significant transformation that is leading towards a blurring of two divides: that existing between contract and status (and, as a consequence, between the public and private sectors) in so far as the public sector is required to operate along the same lines as those of private companies, in particular, multinational companies (Saint-Martin 2000), on the one hand; and that existing between the citizen and the consumer, with a view to creating the paradoxical figure of the citizen-consumer (Clarke et al. 2007), on the other hand. This paper is devoted precisely to the investigation of these two developments and their impact on the deconstruction of public employment; this impact will be examined both with regard to civil servant status and in terms of the transforming expectations placed upon the beneficiaries of public services. Obviously, owing to the high proportion of public employment (20–30% depending on the country) and the significant share of public expenditure in overall GDP, these transformations have implications that go far beyond public administration and public services themselves (Bach et al. 1999). Indeed, such challenges to the public sector can be interpreted as challenges to the Fordist model of employment based on an exchange between subordination and security and to the Weberian model of public administration and public services. Part 1 presents the two main critical approaches to the Fordist and Weberian models of public employment, while Part 2 goes on to address both the evolution of public employment (2.1)—how it is organised and managed, what the status of civil servant implies, etc.,—and the renewed place of the citizen in relation to the supply of public services (2.2)—what services are on offer, what scope there is for choice, what kinds of rights and duties are entailed, etc., Part 3 summarises the main findings and offers a conclusion.

PUBLIC EMPLOYMENT UNDER SCRUTINY: PUBLIC CHOICE AND PRINCIPAL–AGENT THEORIES

The challenges to public service employment as defined in the introduction coincide with the rise of the managerial State (Clarke and Newman 1997), which is strongly inspired by public choice and principal–agent theories. Since both of these critical approaches have wide-ranging consequences for redefining the terms and conditions of public employment, they are reviewed briefly in the following paragraphs.

PUBLIC CHOICE CRITICISMS LEVELLED AGAINST PUBLIC EMPLOYMENT

According to public choice theorists, civil servants have a natural tendency to exaggerate their budgetary needs in order to maximise the importance and prestige of their respective departments (Niskanen 1971). In their view, whenever public agents are given the discretion to decide on their budget (the resources they need) and their output (what they should produce), this results in inefficiencies and overproduction, that is excessive quantity and quality of the goods, benefits and services produced by the public administration. This increases bureaucracies' tendency to be inefficient and overly expensive. If the corporatist interests of civil servants are allowed to prevail, then they will—so public choice theorists claim—quite naturally ask for an ever-increasing amount of budgetary resources and insist on the necessity to provide consistently better services, even though these might be very expensive or unnecessary. According to such theorists (e.g. Tullock 1965; Niskanen 1971), the remedy for this inefficient and expensive situation that undermines the competitiveness of national economies and threatens the overall balance of public accounts is to break the monopoly of State actors over the provision of public services. In other words, if competition is allowed to flourish in the realm of public services, this will break the undue privileges that public agents hold in a monopolistic context. By opening up the competition to other potential providers, public agents are required to prove their efficiency; more precisely, they have to produce clear evidence that they are able to do better and cheaper than their competitors. In the eyes of public choice theorists, there is no reason why public agents should be automatically accorded more trust than private actors. In particular, they cannot invoke supposedly higher professional competences in order to justify their monopoly over public services; quite the contrary, they have to be subjected to a market test, in just the same way as private firms or actors are. This implies bringing the State into market competition with other non-public actors, be they for-profit (firms) or not-for-profit (NGOs or associations).

With regard to the terms and conditions of public employment, this has the significant implication that statutory privileges such as guaranteed lifetime contracts or wage increases based on seniority ought to be abandoned and that public service employees have to demonstrate that they are performing in precisely the same way as do workers in private firms. The 'security' aspect of the Fordist employment contract, one of the most accomplished examples of which is certainly public employment as defined in the introduction of this chapter, needs to be thoroughly reformed or even fully abandoned, as it is an essential part of the explanatory diagnosis as to why public administrations are inefficient and expensive. To break the bureaucratic vicious circle that leads to ever-increasing costs and an ever-expanding scope of public services (Crozier 2010), one also needs to break with the traditional model of public employment. The appropriate scope and substance of public interventions and public services should not be decided by civil servants or bureaucrats alone, but should be subjected to a market test. In the same way, public administration should not have the monopoly over the provision of public goods or services, but should be required to compete with other non-State actors (via public tenders) or, at the very least, to demonstrate that they fare better than other public services completing the same tasks (through benchmarking practices, for instance, where the results of various public agencies delivering the same public services are assessed against each other). Such competition should have a tangible impact such as financial bonuses or penalties, or the loss of the public service mandate. According to public choice theorists, breaking up the monopoly of the public sector over the delivery of certain goods and services, together with the in-depth reform or the abandonment of civil service status, will lead to better value for money in the realm of public action. In short, job security is made responsible for impeding efficiency and needs to be challenged in order to create room for a risk-taking public administration inspired by a more entrepreneurial spirit. In Gingrich's words, introducing competition in the public sector in this way aims at taking 'power away from incumbent professionals. Hospitals and the doctors who work in them, schools and the teachers who teach in them, [...]

must now compete for resources that used to be guaranteed on a non-competitive basis' (2011, p. 3). Markets are conceived as devices to discipline egoistic and corporatist bureaucrats into a more efficient and qualitative delivery of public services.

This view of public administration considers public agents as utility-maximising actors looking out for their own interests, and the only way to 'tame' them is to subject them to the test of market competition. The very fact that public agents may be moved by altruistic motives such as the pursuit of the common good is negated in this perspective. In other words, this approach denies the existence of any form of public service motivation (for instance Perry and Hondeghem 2008) and sees the market as the only device to move necessarily egoistic people in the direction of the common good. To use Le Grand's famous distinction, public agents are not considered as knights or public-spirited altruists, but as self-interested knaves (Le Grand 2003). This implies that, alongside the changing concept of public employment, the assessment of the public agent has changed, and the logic of the cost/benefit analysis is considered as also prevailing in the public sector: agents in public administration are *homo economicus*, just like any other economic actor. Therefore, public employment as a means of supporting extensive rights and entitlements is interpreted by public choice theorists as necessarily favouring the pursuit of egoistic interests by those enjoying such a privileged position; by contrast, public employment ought to be conceived not as a status but as a contract where rights or entitlements are not automatically guaranteed but are dependent on the performance of public agents.

THE CHALLENGES RAISED BY PRINCIPAL–AGENT THEORIES

This first line of criticism is complemented by another, based on the principal–agent theory (Ross 1973). According to this second line of thought, any principal delegating the accomplishment of a task to one or more agents (in this case, the State or, more specifically, certain public agencies such as those responsible for healthcare delivery, welfare benefits or electricity provision) needs to find an efficient way to supervise this task in order to ensure that it is achieved in the manner prescribed and that it yields the expected results. This is made all the more difficult by the fact that public service mandates cannot be fully exhaustive; that is, they cannot foresee and plan every event that may arise in the accomplishment of a task, as is emphasised by the theory of incomplete contracts according to which it is impossible for the parties to a contract to specify all relevant contingencies (Hart and Moore 1988). This necessary incompleteness can be illustrated by the situation of relational public services (e.g. social services) and all 'street-level bureaucracies' (Lipsky 1980). In such cases, the delivery of public services is based on a face-to-face relationship between a public agent and a potential beneficiary, and, unless this were to involve the creation of a panoptic-like society where all agents were subject to computerised or other forms of oversight, it is impossible to observe all the details of this relationship. Moreover, this non-observability of public agents' behaviour can result in practices that are not in line with the principals' expectations, especially with regard to cost containment and efficiency. In this context—the impossibility of foreseeing all contingencies and of observing all that is happening in street-level bureaucracies—the issue raised by principal–agent theories can be summarised as follows: how is it possible to control and supervise agents so that they act in the prescribed manner in a context that is characterised by extensive non-observability of practices; in other words, how is it possible to implement efficiently the 'subordination' element of the Fordist employment contract and ensure that public agents act in a loyal manner?

Principal–agent theories take full account of the impossibility of designing complete contracts which would supposedly be able to foresee and plan every possible contingency and thus fully implement the Weberian 'iron cage'. Nevertheless, they claim that control and supervision are necessary, since agents cannot be trusted, and that it is possible to implement them, albeit on a different basis. Indeed, although work processes cannot be fully supervised (by means of precise specifications regarding the task to be performed) in relational public services, the results or performance of public agents or public services can be rigorously checked and measured. In this way, supervision shifts from processes to outputs or outcomes. In other words, what matters is not the way agents work and the methodologies they use to reach the targets that are assigned to them; rather, it is the end result that will be the focus of the supervisory activity. Therefore, principal–agent theories do neither consider agents to be reliable and professional, nor that they should be trusted. Quite the contrary: they clearly recommend not to place excessive trust in the agents' or incumbent professionals' competences and to continue supervising them, but in a different way. What they suggest is not government by compliance (with rules or specifications concerning work methodologies), which would precisely define the best way to accomplish a given task, but governance by results, which leaves agents free to choose their working methods while still compelling them to achieve predefined outcomes. Public agents are considered to be responsible for their performance in relation to predefined targets. In this way, subordination has not been eliminated but has been reorganised along different lines based on governance by outcomes, indicators or numbers.

What principal–agent theories do not address, however, is the appropriateness of the outcomes to be achieved by agents. In their view, what matters is that agents comply with expectations in terms of results or outcomes; it is not the reasonableness or adequacy of such targets. In other words, the crucial issue of 'what is the appropriate outcome to be achieved through public action' is disregarded by this approach. Hence, public action is envisaged as a matter of efficiency (devising efficient tools to ensure that public agents act loyally) and not of appropriateness. However, the fact that this issue is not tackled by principal–agent theorists does not mean that it is irrelevant or unimportant. Quite the contrary: depending on the selected targets or indicators, the work content and the degree of subordination of public agents will vary significantly. In certain cases, targets mainly involve outputs directly produced by the public administration (for instance the number of interviews that agents in public employment services should conduct with unemployed people every month; the number of beds a hospital operates or the number of customers served by each public agent in a post office); in other cases, the focus is rather on societal outcomes that do not depend solely on the action of public agents, for example a reduction in the unemployment rate, a reduction of child mortality or an increase in the level of well-being of the overall population. Whatever the focus—be it outputs or outcomes—its appropriateness and its feasibility in terms of available resources do have an impact on the degree of subordination imposed on public agents. However, principal–agent theories do not include this aspect in their rhetoric and concentrate only on the issue of efficiency; in other words, regardless of the targets or the available resources, what matters is that the principal's expectations are efficiently implemented by the agents.

Both lines of criticism—public choice and principal–agent—converge in the recent public administration reforms. It is both a matter of making public services more efficient and responsive, and of ensuring that public agents achieve the targets they have been set. This implies a deep-seated reconfiguration of the 'subordination vs. security' nexus underlying the public employment contract, though in directions that are not necessarily convergent: on the one hand, public choice theorists insist on increased commodification of labour and on the introduction of the market logic in the public sector (which implies rethinking the 'security' component of the public employment relationship); on the other hand, principal–agent theories emphasise the importance of public agents' loyalty towards their principal (which entails a reconfiguration of the 'subordination' aspect of public employment).

MAKING MARKETS IN THE PUBLIC SECTOR

Actual public administration reforms can be achieved in a plurality of ways and pursue a variety of objectives such as efficiency or value for money, motivation of public agents and improved quality. Although the literature distinguishes between various models or types of managerial states (e.g. Ferlie et al. 1996), it is commonly accepted that the introduction of market-like mechanisms will help reach all three targets of increasing efficiency in the use of public money, enhancing the commitment of public agents and improving the quality of public services. This introduction of the market logic in the public sector can be achieved in two ways: first, the State is considered an employer just like any other; it enjoys no privileges or monopoly with regard to the accomplishment of certain tasks. In other words, open competition should prevail everywhere: if the State can prove that it provides better value for money and is more competitive, then it will remain responsible for public service delivery; if not, this responsibility will be delegated to private (for-profit or not-for-profit) actors. Public tenders or outsourcing to 'preferred' private suppliers are the main tools used. Second, the State operates just like any other market actor in that public employees must demonstrate their performance and are recompensed accordingly. All forms of management, whether based on objectives, provision agreements, performance indicators, annual evaluations, etc., pursue the same goal of rewarding efficiency and penalising poor performance. The job security enjoyed by public employees is presented as an undue privilege that should be abolished; as a consequence, public employees should be exposed to dismissal just like any private-sector worker. In both cases, what is required is a blurring of the divide between public and private employment conditions and a subsequent homogenisation of the employment terms and conditions based on market criteria for performance and productivity. In other words, the purpose of employment should be one and the same for both the public and private sectors.

These developments are in line with the recommendations of public choice and principal–agent theorists. Indeed, both lines of criticism advocate that the divide between the public and private sectors, and their operational procedures, should be blurred, as a result of which market management modes should prevail in all sectors and all sectors should be competing along these lines. However, such transformations are not implemented homogeneously across all sectors and in all countries. The marketisation of public administration occurs to varying degrees and at a very different pace depending on the country and the sector of public action (Pollitt and Bouckaert 2004); indeed, some countries take a very strong and clear managerialist stance, while others are more resistant to such reforms and still others follow the path of the 'Neo-Weberian State', combining a focus on efficiency and quality with a reaffirmation of the role of the State in the present context (Lynn 2008).

Gingrich likewise emphasises that the introduction of the market logic in the public sector can occur in very different ways. In her view, actual reforms vary greatly according to (a) how control over service delivery is organised (in other words, who is considered as the principal to whom public agents are accountable) and (b) the basis on which access to benefits and services is granted (is universal access guaranteed as a matter of collective responsibility, or is it an issue of individual responsibility, thus depending on individual choice and resources?). With regard to control over service delivery, we will focus here on two of the three ideal-typical situations identified by Gingrich[1]: on the one hand, the principal to whom public agents are accountable is the State; on the other, it is the citizen-consumer who plays this role.

Empowering the State: Management by Numbers and by Incentives

In the first instance, the State retains control over service delivery: it precisely defines the outputs or outcomes to be achieved by the public agents and puts in place appropriate incentives and supervisory mechanisms. In this case, the principal is the State, and the agent is constituted by either the public service employees or the subcontracted agents in the private for-profit or not-for-profit sector. This is what Gingrich (2011) calls the 'managed market' characterised by less security (in that it is conditional on achieving predefined targets) and a high degree of subordination. In the vast majority of such cases, the outputs or outcomes to be achieved are defined in quantitative terms, mainly because their implementation is more easily verified and monitored if the outcomes can be precisely identified and measured. The most appropriate solution is seen to be the institution of a government (or governance) by indicators (Bezes et al. 2016) or by numbers (Supiot 2015), both of which specify precisely the outcomes or level of performance to be achieved. The work of public agents is not verified on the basis of its day-to-day content or the work practices used, but on the basis of its outcomes as specified in terms of quantitative targets to be achieved. Market mechanisms such as benchmarking and competition with other providers (be they private for-profit or not-for-profit, or public) are used to discipline public agents into complying with the official targets set. This is an essential component of the managerial state as it emerged in most EU and OECD countries from the mid-1980s on.

According to Supiot's analysis (2015), such developments by no means imply that subordination is no longer imposed, but rather that it has been transformed. The supervision of public agents' work is not achieved through a Taylorian scientific organisation of work that governs its processes and methodologies, which would be more akin to the 'iron cage' described by Weber; rather, it is provided in other ways. Indeed, the mechanical clockwork model, where work organisation is perceived as a machine in which the workers or employees are merely cogs, is substituted by what Supiot calls a cybernetic model. The aim is to design public administration as a programmable system, the components of which (the public agents) react appropriately to the signals given to them. Thus, governance becomes a matter of giving the right signals, in the form of incentives or threats of sanctions, in order to encourage public agents to act in the expected way. In this connection, it is important that such signals are clear and unambiguous, which is the reason why, according to Supiot, numbers are the preferred tool: a quantitative target gives a clear signal about what is expected and leaves very little room for interpretation. In this way, the margin of manoeuvre of street-level bureaucrats is strictly limited: not everything is possible, but only those steps or methods that allow targets to be met are permitted. Another claimed advantage of using numbers in the governance of people is that they make it possible to reduce or even negate the complexity of public action: potential conflicts between the various objectives of public action (e.g. being efficient while delivering high-quality public services) are occulted where single and clear targets are set. In the same way as private firms pursue clear-cut objectives such as an increase in turnover or sales revenue, public agents are required to pursue clearly identified objectives. When used in this way, numbers aim at making public action mimic corporate action (Saint-Martin 2000), providing simple and measurable objectives in order to ensure that the agents' action is properly targeted. In this manner, the use of numbers aims at reducing the complexity of public action and preventing any discussion about the relevance of the targets set. For instance, the quality of a public employment service is measured based on its results in relation to specific indicators, such as the proportion of beneficiaries that are reinserted in the labour market or the number of interviews conducted with them. This implies that employees who perform well in relation to such indicators are considered to be good employees, irrespective of the methods they used to achieve the objectives set. Brodkin's work (e.g. 2011) has provided plenty of evidence about the potential perverse effects of focusing on quantitative indicators: she demonstrates, among other things, how the objective of reintegrating as many unemployed persons as possible into the labour market may induce public agents to pay more attention to those recipients who are more likely to find a new job quickly or to do their utmost to remove the least employable individuals from their caseload.

Alongside the emergence of numbers and indicators, another development in the management of public administration, recommended by public choice theorists and principal–agent approaches alike, involves the use of incentives rather than disciplining tools. To ensure that targets and performance indicators are taken seriously, financial incentives are put in place. If targets are met or, better still, exceeded, then financial bonuses are awarded. However, if they are not met, penalties will be applied such as loss of wages or, in extreme cases, dismissal or non-renewal of contracts with inefficient subcontractors. Incentives work in a different way than disciplining tools: they aim at the self-internalisation of official norms by agents. In other words, the principal does not need to go to great lengths to check the agents' work—not because s/he trusts them, but because s/he can be sure that the agents have endorsed the targets and will do their utmost to meet them, since it is in their best interest to do so. In this connection, it is not the agents' professionalism or their sense of the public or common good that drives them to do their best; rather, it is their own self-interest or their desire to secure a financial reward or to avoid penalties that offers the best guarantee that they will perform appropriately. In this way, the employment relationship undergoes a deep-seated transformation. Rights and material entitlements are no longer a matter of status but of performance: both civil servants and private (for-profit or not-for-profit) agents need to meet the targets if they are to maintain their wage level or even to keep their job. They are governed by a market logic (Boltanski and Thévenot 2006) that insists on their individual merit and performance measured against quantitative predefined targets, rather than by a civic logic that emphasises their contribution to the development of the common good. Government by compliance still prevails, albeit not based on rules or work methodologies but on targets and performance indicators. The introduction of mechanisms such as performance pay, bonuses or penalties follows this logic. Again, such mechanisms do not encourage public agents to voice their viewpoints or participate in public deliberations about the aims and objectives of public action. Instead, the objective is to persuade them to act in the expected way.

With the adoption of management by numbers and by incentives, it could be said that the Weberian concept of the 'iron cage' has not been abandoned altogether but has simply been reformed along new lines. The bars of the cage are no longer represented by the precise specifications for the tasks to be accomplished by civil servants but by the performance indicators, the quantitative targets or, as Supiot indicates, the signals. The main issue, then, is how these signals are devised and constructed; in other words, who decides on the targets and quantitative indicators to be reached. The more this decision is monopolised by policymakers or the heads of public administration in a top-down way, the more the resulting public administration will replicate Supiot's cybernetic model. According to this model, compliance is pursued not through the imposition of rules but by means of precise and inescapable signals accompanied by appropriate incentives that convince public agents that compliance is in their best interest. In such cases, the managerial model cannot be differentiated from the bureaucratic model in terms of how it interprets the 'subordination' aspect of the public employment relationship (Giauque 2004). Indeed, the yardstick or criteria used to direct and shape public action are not negotiable by public agents or incumbent professionals; instead, they are imposed on them. According to

Hirschman's typology (Hirschman 1970), this ought to be interpreted as a model of loyalty with no room left for voice.[2] Public employment is envisaged here as a matter of calculus (offering the right incentives) and behavioural economics, not of democracy and public debate. By contrast, if targets or indicators are defined in collective negotiations involving all relevant stakeholders, especially incumbent professionals and users, thus leading to a co-construction of what a high-quality public service should be, then the result is a much more complex elaboration of the 'subordination' aspect of the public employment relationship. Indeed, public agents, together with other actors, are engaged in this elaboration. Employees are not simply required to comply with rules or targets defined by others; they are involved in the definition of these targets. This is a model of loyalty that leaves some room for voice.

Therefore, numbers can be used in two very different ways: to reinforce subordination and provide it with an objective and unquestionable basis, preventing any contestation or democratic debate about the legitimacy of objectives (targets) on the one hand; and to open a wide and inclusive public debate about the mission and terms of public employment on the other. Actual reforms of public administration tend towards the introduction of management by numbers in order to make public action more efficient, but they can be distinguished by their specific use of numbers. The partisans of new public management, the 'marketisers' identified by Pollitt and Bouckaert (2004), envisage the introduction of market mechanisms in the public sector (such as contracting-out, public tenders, contractual appointments, performance pay, all of which point towards a blurring of the divide between the public and private sectors), with the objective of increasing the efficiency of public action in meeting predefined targets. By contrast, other reformists, the 'modernisers' identified by Pollitt and Bouckaert, insist on the important role of public agents, professionals and users in the definition of targets. For the former, the use of numbers is a matter of efficiency, while for the latter, it raises issues of both efficiency and appropriateness. In both cases, however, the purpose of public employment is not to provide support for rights and entitlements, but to recognise merit and performance. Accordingly, merit replaces solidarity as the underlying principle of public employment, which tends to be increasingly governed according to a market order of worth rather than a civic one (Boltanski and Thévenot 2006).

EMPOWERING THE CONSUMER OF PUBLIC SERVICES
OR CREATING CITIZEN-CONSUMERS

Another important turning point in the way we view public administration, particularly emphasised by New Labour in the UK, can be seen in the reforms of public services that aim at empowering citizens to make their own choices from among a range of publicly funded services on offer. Here too, this implies reorganising services according to a market logic, where supply is driven by the demand of consumers. Since the State has proven its inability to provide public services in adequate quantity and quality (in line with public choice theorists' criticism that highlights both the excessive quantity and quality of public services, that is their excessive cost and the disconnection between the services provided—according to a bureaucratic logic—and citizens' needs), it appears necessary to find other ways to provide appropriate public services. This is achieved by putting the citizen centre stage. As Tony Blair put it, 'I believe people do want choice [...]. But anyway, choice isn't an end in itself. It is one important mechanism to ensure that citizens can indeed secure good schools and health services in their communities. [...] Choice puts the levers in the hands of parents and patients so that they as citizens and consumers can be a driving force for improvement in their public services' (Blair 2004, quoted in Clarke et al. 2007, p. 1).

The explicit aim of such reforms is to ensure that the quality of public services is not regulated by the State or by public administration but directly by users. By the same token, users are envisaged both as citizens and consumers: in other words, it is not the citizen-voter who is being asked to take a leading role, but the citizen-consumer. What is purported here is that the most efficient way to organise public services and ensure that they correspond to people's actual needs is by means of market mechanisms. Not only do traditional 'command-and-control' mechanisms give way to the newly introduced market logic, but this market logic is also presented as being more appropriate than democratic mechanisms through which citizens are asked to voice their concerns and participate in the collective discussion about what an adequate public service should be. In short, citizenship does not emerge through deliberation or participation in public debates ('voice' in Hirschman's terms) but through consumer choice. According to Clarke et al. (2007), there is a 'tendency to treat the consumer as an organising figure for policies, processes and practices' (ibid., p. 6). As a consequence, the divide between citizens (functioning according to a political or civic logic) and consumers (motivated by an economic or market logic) is blurred, creating the paradoxical figure of the citizen-consumer. In this connection, the issue of public services becomes a matter of individual choice and no longer one of collective deliberation, thereby transforming policies into a collection of individual consumer decisions that together send clear signals about how providers of public services should behave and what kinds of intervention or services should be funded by the State. This also has an impact on how we view public employment, in so far as it means that customer satisfaction becomes the key criterion used to define a good public service. Subordination has therefore not been eliminated but has been redeployed towards the users of services rather than towards the holders of public authority in public administration. In this way, the customer is viewed as a disciplining figure in the face of potentially unruly professionals (Giauque 2003). All these changes are justified by the aim of increasing the quality and responsiveness of public services.

Dowding and John (2012) analyse this evolution in relation to the 'exit-voice-loyalty' triptych proposed by Albert Hirschman (1970) more than 40 years ago. They demonstrate how the introduction of consumer choice as a governing principle of public services gives rise to unintended effects. To that end, they draw on the teachings of the original example developed by Hirschman, who showed how and why the privatisation of the Nigerian railways had led to a reduction in the quality of publicly provided services. Indeed, in order to emphasise the importance of consumer choice, the State must support or allow the creation of alternatives to its monopoly over public services, making that choice effective for citizen-consumers. However, when alternatives are made available through the promotion of competition in the realm of public services (i.e. the introduction of market mechanisms that allow private providers to compete with public agencies), consumers tend to move away from public services of poor quality and turn to alternative providers, rather than attempt to pressurise the government into making improvements to the delivery of public services. According to Hirschman, citizen-consumers choose exit over voice, which leaves the government with no incentive to improve public services and creates a negative spiral of declining quality in the services provided by the public sector. Thus, the new figure of the citizen-consumer implies that political decisions are not made based on voice mechanisms (i.e. complaints about the quality of services) but on a collection of exit decisions. In the Nigerian case, the government did not receive complaints and therefore did nothing to improve the quality of the public railways; as a consequence, their quality continued to decline steadily.[3] This example shows that governing public services by exit (consumers' decisions to turn to alternative providers) rather than by voice (citizens' complaints about the poor performance of services) can be extremely detrimental to their quality.

In addition to this issue of exit and voice and their respective adequacy to govern public services, Dowding and John (2012) point to another significant problem. Consumer choice cannot be postulated as a universal capacity: for choice has a cost, and this cost cannot be borne equally by all citizens. Only those who can afford to pay the price for privately provided services will be able to choose this option. For instance, in a situation where public schooling is considered to be of poor quality, disadvantaged people will have no choice but to send their offspring to these schools, while the middle- and upper-classes have the choice of better alternatives even when these prove to be more expensive. Even if the State provides means such as vouchers to guarantee that all citizens can exercise the same degree of consumer choice (or at least have access to a minimum threshold of consumer choice), other issues may arise such as asymmetrical information, as illustrated by Sol and Westerveld in the field of employment services (Sol and Westerveld 2005). Indeed, citizen-consumers are not equally informed or knowledgeable about the quality of the services supplied, and the least informed among them can easily be induced to make choices based on misleading consumer information. Unless extensive public action is deployed in a bid to reduce such inequalities in terms of purchasing power and access to information, governing public services through the figure of the customer may well result in reinforcing existing inequalities, effectively reserving high-quality public services for the most advantaged and informed citizens.

In point of fact, consumer choice does not naturally coincide with democratic forms of decision-making: while citizens may be considered to be equal at least formally (according to the democratic principle of 'one voter, one voice'), wide-ranging inequalities persist between consumers. What matters, therefore, is what action is taken by the State to ensure that all citizens can become consumers in their own right, so that all of them are effectively given the power to choose from among a wide range of providers of public services. Equalising consumers' capacity to make their decisions is then a key task that requires extensive public intervention if the figure of the citizen-consumer is to result in a fair and equitable society. Gingrich (2011) emphasises precisely this point when she distinguishes between 'consumer-driven markets', on the one hand, where service users are empowered with a view to enhancing their ability to choose their provider, and 'two-tiered markets', on the other hand, where higher-income or lower-cost individuals are privileged. In the former, asymmetries of information or inequalities in terms of disposable income or other material resources are reduced through the action of the State; in this way, the attractiveness of customers to suppliers is equalised, thereby preventing adverse selection practices. In contrast, inequalities are not corrected in two-tiered markets where suppliers are free to choose the most attractive customers and discard all others, i.e. the most vulnerable and least solvent customers. Therefore, while consumer-driven markets in which all citizens enjoy effective consumer choice may enhance their access to quality public services, two-tiered markets governed by the invisible hand of the market (i.e. not corrected by State intervention) impede access to quality services for the most disadvantaged citizen-consumers.

CONCLUSION

In summary, the rise of the managerial State coincides with a blurring of the private and public sectors with regard to the terms and conditions of the employment relationship and the various ways of managing it. Public employment is no longer to be seen as a status that provides rights and social protection but as a contract where entitlements are not guaranteed but made conditional upon reaching certain targets or performance indicators (as evidenced by the increasing introduction of mechanisms such as bonuses or performance pay in the public sector). In this way, the very concept of public employment has been thoroughly transformed: it is no longer to be interpreted as a support for collective solidarity, for it is increasingly devised as a means of measuring individual performance and merit. The emphasis is therefore placed on individual responsibility. However, in most cases, this does not coincide with greater autonomy in the accomplishment of civil servants' work, since the Weberian 'iron cage', with its precise specifications, is substituted by government by numbers and by incentives. In such a framework, civil servants are not considered as partners (whose voice should be taken seriously) in the conception and delivery of public action but as self-interested professionals who need to be induced to behave in an appropriate manner.

In much the same way, the blurring of the citizen-consumer divide requires that public services are designed just like any other kind of private service that needs to compete for its customer base. As a result, public services are seen as commodities or market transaction objects: they need to be attractive enough in order to convince potential customers (citizen-consumers) to buy them. This, in turn, implies that the quality of public services is pursued first and foremost through exit mechanisms: if citizen-consumers decide to opt out of a public service in favour of a private one, then it is to be interpreted as a clear signal that the publicly provided service is inadequate and needs somehow to be adjusted. For this to happen, however, the consumer's decision to exit must have financial consequences for public providers, in the same way as it does for market actors. Indeed, if public funding is guaranteed independently of their performance, then exit decisions will have no effect on public providers. Thus, the blurring of the citizen-consumer divide requires the blurring of the public and private sectors.

In this way, a market logic is being introduced in the public sector: the State must function like private firms in that it is required to provide evidence of its superior performance if it wants to preserve its prerogatives over public services; civil servants are to be viewed in the same way as any other category of worker and are subject to the same set of rights and duties in terms of performance and merit; public services are to be organised according to a market logic where the best providers should be allowed to prevail, be they public or private, for-profit or not-for-profit and citizens are to be seen as consumers who are given the effective choice among a wide variety of options. Accordingly, most of the boundaries that were characteristic of public employment and public services in the Fordist period (States vs. firms, civil servants vs. private economy workers, public services vs. private goods or services, citizens vs. consumers) are becoming blurred, which poses the complex challenge of what regulatory mechanisms are needed for such marketised forms of public administration and public services to work in not only an efficient but also an equitable and appropriate manner.

NOTES

1. Gingrich also refers to a situation where it is the producers themselves who control the conditions of service delivery.
2. This obviously does not prevent public agents from finding ways other than using their voice to contest or even circumvent the official expectations placed upon them.
3. This was further reinforced by the fact that the public railway service had no incentive to respond to exit signals as a market firm would have done.

REFERENCES

Bach, Stephen, Lorenzo Bordogna, Giuseppe Della Rocca, and David Winchester. 1999. *Public Service Employment Relations in Europe. Transformation, Modernization or Inertia?* London: Routledge.
Bezes, Philippe, Eve Chiapello, and Pierre Desmarez. 2016. "Introduction: La tension savoirs-pouvoirs à l'épreuve du gouvernement par les indicateurs de performance." *Sociologie du travail* 58 (4): 347–369. https://doi.org/10.1016/j.soctra.2016.09.024.
Boltanski, Luc, and Laurent Thévenot. 2006. *On Justification. Economies of Worth.* Princeton and Oxford: Princeton University Press.
Brodkin, Evelyn. 2011. "Policy Work: Street-Level Work Under New Managerialism." *Journal of Public Administration Research and Theory* 21: 253–277. https://doi.org/10.1093/jopart/muq093.
Clarke, John, and Janet Newman. 1997. *The Managerial State.* London: Sage.
Clarke, John, Janet Newman, Nick Smith, Elizabeth Vidler, and Louise Westmarkland. 2007. *Creating Citizen-Consumers, Changing Publics and Changing Public Services.* London: Sage.
Crozier, Michel. 2010. *The Bureaucratic Phenomenon.* London and New Brunswick: Transaction Publishers.
Dowding, Keith, and Peter John. 2012. *Exits, Voices and Social Investment. Cititzens' Reaction to Public Services.* Oxford: Oxford University Press.
Ferlie, Ewan, Lynn Ashburner, Louise Fitzgerald, and Andrew Pettigrew. 1996. *The New Public Management in Action.* Oxford: Oxford University Press.
Giauque, David. 2003. "Le client, nouvelle figure disciplinaire de l'administration publique." *Pyramides* 7: 89–104.
Giauque, David. 2004. *La bureaucratie libérale, Nouvelle gestion publique et régulation organisationnelle.* Paris: L'Harmattan.
Gingrich, Jane. 2011. *Making Markets in the Welfare State, The Politics of Varying Market Reforms.* Cambridge: Cambridge University Press.

Hart, Oliver, and John Moore. 1988. "Incomplete Contracts and Renegotiation." *Econometrica* 56 (4): 755–785. https://doi.org/10.2307/1912698.

Hirschman, Albert Otto. 1970. *Exit, Voice, and Loyalty: Responses to Decline in Firms, Organizations, and States*. Cambridge, MA: Harvard University Press.

Le Grand, Julian. 2003. *Motivation, Agency, and Public Policy: Of Knights and Knaves, Pawns and Queens*. Oxford: Oxford University Press.

Lipsky, Michael. 1980. *Street-Level Bureaucracy: Dilemmas of the Individual in Public Services*. New York: Russell Sage Foundation.

Lynn, Lindsay. 2008. "What Is a Neo-Weberian State? Reflections on a Concept and Its Implications." *The NISPAcee Journal of Public Administration and Policy* 1 (2): 17–30.

Niskanen, William. 1971. *Bureaucracy and Representative Government*. Chicago: Aldine & Atherton.

Perry, James, and Annie Hondeghem (eds.). 2008. *Motivation in Public Management, The Call of Public Service*. Oxford: Oxford University Press.

Pollitt, Christopher, and Geert Bouckaert. 2004. *Public Management Reform, A Comparative Analysis*. Oxford: Oxford University Press.

Ross, Stephen. 1973. "The Economic Theory of Agency: The Principal's Problem." *American Economic Review* 63 (2) (May): 134–139. http://www.jstor.org/stable/1817064.

Saint-Martin, Denis. 2000. *Building the New Managerialist State, Consultants and the Politics of Public Sector Reform in Comparative Perspective*. Oxford: Oxford University Press.

Sol, Els, and Mies Westerveld, eds. 2005. *Contractualism in Employment Services. A New Form of Welfare State Governance*. The Hague: Kluwer Law International.

Supiot, Alain. 2015. *La gouvernance par les nombres, Cours au collège de France 2012–4*. Paris: Fayard.

Tullock, Gordon. 1965. *The Politics of Bureaucracy*. Washington: The Public Affairs Press.

Weber, Max. 1968. *Economy and Society*. New York: Bedminster Press.

PART III

The Redefinition of Work and Unemployment *Qua* Reference Category

CHAPTER 10

The Boundaries of Unemployment Institutional Rules and Real-Life Experiences

Didier Demazière

INTRODUCTION

Any definition of unemployment spurs debates on the issue of measurement: precisely how many unemployed are there, who should be considered unemployed and what criteria apply? This leads to discussions on how to measure unemployment: some ask how do we quantify unemployment according to the source, with particular regard to survey and administrative data (Lemoine 2007); others point out that the figures depend on which indicators are used, calling for a diversification of the instruments used to measure unemployment (Castel et al. 1997); while others still warn that the scope of international harmonisation is limited if specific national and institutional features are not taken into account (Desrosières 2003). It is now accepted that there is 'no "correct" figure for the number of unemployed; on the contrary, there are as many statistics as there are sources and ways of conventionally – not

D. Demazière (✉)
French National Center for Scientific Research (CNRS), Paris, France

© The Author(s) 2019
A. Serrano-Pascual and M. Jepsen (Eds.),
The Deconstruction of Employment as a Political Question,
https://doi.org/10.1007/978-3-319-93617-8_10

arbitrarily – defining unemployment' (Marchand 1991, 8). Therefore, this is not just a matter of statistics but of the very definition of unemployment: what is to be understood by the term; is there any consensus on the category of unemployed; where should the line be drawn between unemployed and not unemployed; who decides who is to be called unemployed and who has authority over the different meanings?

Where do the boundaries of unemployment lie and what characterises them: is it clarity, sharpness, stability, obviousness, finesse and precision or, on the contrary, is it obscurity, ambiguity, instability, fragility, density and approximation? Tracing a border consists in making a separation and a distinction within the context of continuity. It is a social and political act, because it creates classifications that may then shape the functioning of groups and societies (Durkheim and Mauss 1903). Unemployment is also one of those operative categories (Demazière 2003) that are both shared representations of the social universe and resources for taking action in and on that universe. That being so, who are the actors capable of mobilising the categories for action, and who is able to modify and adjust the scope of that action? In formulating such questions, the analysis is oriented towards the work involved in producing boundaries (Gieryn 1983; Evans 2009). Our hypothesis is that, in the case of unemployment, working on boundaries—taking them into account even while modifying or displacing them—is an activity carried out by institutional stakeholders who define the rules for managing the unemployed, as well as by those who actually experience joblessness.

Therefore, the boundaries—of this category—are not limits drawn by experts, taken to be self-evident and immutable. Boundaries cause phenomena to emerge and to become visible, and boundaries redesign and recompose them when they have been displaced (Degenne 2005). Those phenomena do not pre-exist the boundaries, rather it is the boundaries that make them materialise: 'we should not look for boundaries of things but for things of boundaries' (Abbott 1995, 857). Boundaries are thus where definitions are worked out, a fact that was masterfully demonstrated with regard to emerging unemployment at the turn of the twentieth century: unemployment is neither the reflection of an existing social reality, nor even the realisation of an emerging reality, it is an invention involving a great number of actors (Salais et al. 1986; Topalov 1994). Initially, the notion of boundary allowed us to consider social or ethnic groups not as objective and substantial entities but as the historical and conventional result of demarcation (Barth 1969). Over time, the concept gradually separated itself from the notions of group or territory (Silber 1995; Jeanpierre 2010) and spread to other collective or symbolic bodies. The reasoning remains constant: it is relational because differences are always produced with reference to another whose identity is reinforced by the tracing of the boundary. It is a process, because differences are always the temporary crystallisation of entities whose relationships change. Boundaries thus imply working on the relationships and processes that define them.

The aim of this chapter is to propose an analysis of contemporary unemployment by describing the movements of its boundaries: its boundaries with employment because it emerges historically on the negative side of salaried employment, and its boundaries with inactivity because it has been differentiated from poverty and idleness. To explore how the boundaries of unemployment function, we will focus here mainly on two aspects: public action—since unemployment is a codified status—and the persons concerned—given that unemployment is a subjective experience. Two types of boundaries correspond to these two aspects. In the first case, the boundaries are institutional: they define various status-bound situations and regulate the access to material resources (benefits, public employment services) or immaterial resources (recognition by the public employment service). In the second case, the boundaries are 'symbolic' (Lamont and Fournier 1992; Lamont 2001): they influence the meanings attributed to personal experience (of unemployment but also atypical forms of employment and work) and affect categories of identification (affiliation, identity claims) and future projections (accessible and valued positions). We will analyse each of these two aspects in turn and attempt to show that boundary work is heterogeneous both in its orientations and in its consequences.

INSTITUTIONAL STATUS BOUNDARIES

Unemployment is not an economic issue comparable to balancing the supply and demand percentage of employment. Moreover, 'in a purely commercial world, unemployment does not exist' (Eymard-Duvernay 2001, 292). Unemployment is defined by institutional boundaries that disconnect it from other social positions involving activity or inactivity. To see how these boundaries have developed, we will focus on the rules governing unemployment coverage and the distribution of replacement incomes, for they are at the heart of the categorisation process.

CODIFIED BOUNDARIES: UNEMPLOYMENT IS EMPLOYMENT

Sifting Out the Poor

Historically, joblessness is the result of new ways of considering the poor and of a stabilised partition delimiting three groups, each associated with a specific approach (Castel 1995): the infamous 'idle poor' who must not be helped but, on the contrary, suppressed, locked up and forced to work; those unfit to work, marked by an infirmity or other handicap, who must be afforded minimal assistance, though with no hope of their returning to work and the involuntary poor who are physically fit, searching for ways to survive, and who must be helped and assisted in their quest. At the start of the twentieth century, the invention of unemployment spurred the establishment of relief organisations initiated by workers or municipalities, subsequently taken over by the State. Very early on, the benefits allocated were matched to the job search which—before the role of the intermediary became more widespread—targeted specific occupations (Luciani 1990; de Larquier 2000). This response to the financial precariousness generated by the scarcity of jobs traced a border between those workers who had fallen victim to a bad economic situation and the poor, considered unemployable or lazy, thus between the good and the bad jobless (Topalov 1987), between the unemployed and the inactive. In that sense, the meaning of unemployment has evolved considerably: 'seen as a catastrophe today, being called "unemployed" at the turn of the century meant an enhanced social image' (Mansfield et al. 1994, 16).

Inventing unemployment was intended to improve production by stimulating the factors that constitute it—here, the labour factor—with the aim of producing more wealth (Gautié 2002). It signified organising the labour market, controlling the employment relationship and disciplining workers' behaviour. For, in the industrial economies of the late nineteenth century, workers were still marked by discontinuity, fragmentation, irregularity and unpredictability: in rural areas, many workers still farmed and worked in the fields when the season required it, while in the towns, people changed jobs frequently because of poor working conditions or salaries. Against this background, replacing a service contract by an employment contract rendered the relationship of subordination official in the long term and strengthened the tie between worker and employer. Over the decades, that legal development has spread and evolved with the result that unemployment is now anchored to salaried employment as its complement, its corollary, 'its negative face, but also its *raison d'être*' (Lefresne 2008, 3).

Identifying the Potential Workforce

However, although the unemployed are potentially wage earners, what are the criteria for identifying them, and what principles apply when setting up their benefits or accompanying them on the road to employment? The main criterion is the involuntary nature of being jobless. Once this is established, we must then focus on verifying the authenticity of that involuntary quality, which is no easy task. The first criterion to be applied for such verification was a person's work history. For instance, in 1895, the French Supreme Labour Council (*Conseil Supérieur du Travail*, the Ministry of Labour at that time) defined unemployment as 'the situation of a worker who usually makes his living in a specific occupation but is presently out of work in that profession' (Daniel and Tuschzirer 1999, 44). Unemployment signified 'professional unemployment', and the fact that a person exerted a professional activity regularly was taken to indicate that he was forcibly and undeservedly being deprived of work. That sort of logic still underpins the activities of employment agencies, which refuse to help or present job offers to casual workers who are perceived as lacking in both discipline and merit—also known as the 'sham unemployed' (Marpsat 1984).

In the second half of the twentieth century, the will to work was disassociated from a person's work history and linked instead to the job search. As of the 1960s, when the International Labour Office made the will to work an essential criterion, that approach became standard: any person over the age of 15 with no waged or unwaged employment, actively looking for a job and immediately available was considered unemployed. That definition enlarged the scope of unemployment, since a simple job application was enough to be officially recognised as unemployed. However, the positive side of the status of unemployment was only temporary, partial and conditional: temporary because the application had to be renewed on a regular basis and because the job search was monitored, which might have led to loss of the status; partial, since the acknowledgement of a job application did not automatically make a person eligible for benefits and conditional, since each individual claim to the status of unemployed depended on social and regulatory conditions—such as being considered as legitimately occupying that status from a gender point of view (Maruani 2002)—and also depended on the use of the resources made available as a result of that status (Marchand and Thélot 1983).

It should be added that not all population groups are equally entitled or prepared to enter the world of unemployment. If one considers a large spectrum of countries—Europe and the United States—three lines of reasoning emerge concerning the distribution of resources which, when taken together, point to 'national activity and employment systems' (Barbier and Gautié 1998): first, resources may consist of participation-based production (wage labour, employment); second, they may be linked to the redistribution of social transfers (replacement incomes) or third, they may be associated with interpersonal relationships in the private sphere (family solidarities). The category of unemployment was invented so as to isolate those who are involuntarily excluded from the primary resource base, i.e. employment. To understand that boundary, one must take any related categories into account. However, in many Western countries, the second two lines of reasoning concern mainly women, who are encouraged in many ways *not* to enter the labour market—pro-family policies, the sexual division of household labour, social norms governing the distribution of jobs—or to leave it when they are laid off (Maruani 1996). During the period known as the Economic Miracle (*Les Trente Glorieuses*), a time when the scope of unemployment was consistent and very clearly delineated, those boundaries had selective effects to the detriment of women (but also to the detriment of individuals at both extremes of the working life cycle). If unemployment is the opposite of employment, it concerns the breadwinner first and foremost. In the period following this, a structural surplus of manpower caused employment—in different ways depending on the country—to undergo significant transformations; the realm of unemployment shrank considerably, while the volume of joblessness continued to grow.

Reinforced Boundaries: Shrinking Unemployment

Indemnifying Unemployment

The erosion of employment standards and the growing 'precariousness of the labour contract' (Ghesquière 2014) are powerful trends in Western societies. They take different forms depending on national trajectories (Lefresne 2005), but atypical forms of work—compared to the Fordist model of wage employment—crop up everywhere: short-term contracts, part-time or segmented work, service contracts, multiple employer contracts, subleasing of employees, independent entrepreneurs working for a single contractor, solo work and even work in the informal labour market. All these developments have an impact on the institutional boundaries of unemployment.

Since the 1990s in Europe, public deficits, a reduction in statutory contributions and a restructuring of welfare systems, have made access to unemployment benefits more difficult (Freyssinet 1998). The pace and magnitude of reforms differ, as do their justification and implementation, but a certain number of shared key orientations can be observed (Clasen and Clegg 2006). The criteria for eligibility have become more stringent, and consequently, the area covered by unemployment insurance has shrunk. Of course, coverage rates vary from one country to another, but in all countries, the length of time a worker must pay into the plan—i.e. the number of months' payment required for a given period of reference—has been extended. Allowances are becoming smaller, and the replacement rate based on the last salary received is diminishing (in Europe, it varies between 30 and 80% during the first six months of unemployment). Despite differences between countries in minima and maxima, or in the conditions sometimes placed on access to benefits (income level, family status, etc.), the trend remains the same. The length of time a worker can be in receipt of compensation is becoming distinctly shorter as well, even though the permitted maximum length can vary considerably (from six months to five years). Overall, changes in patterns of employment and increasing transitions between employment and unemployment have had the effect of reducing the cumulative benefits and subsequently shortening the periods during which allowances are paid. This is still the case regardless of changes in legislation, except in a few countries where the duration of benefits is not dependent on the length of time that contributions have been made (Denmark, Italy, UK).

A second feature common to Western countries is the tighter checks carried out on the jobless, all the more salient in the light of simultaneously evolving social representations, making joblessness and its duration a matter of individual responsibility. There is a strong tendency towards that 'rigorous turn' (Dubois 2007) in European policies, which promote and support closer supervision of the unemployed, especially those who are in receipt of benefits. In all areas, the link between allowances and supervision is becoming stronger, although activation standards—a dubious, prescriptive term, since benefits are considered passive expenditure, thus *ipso facto* obligatory—fluctuate between two, variously attractive poles depending on the country. On the one hand, allowances are seen as discouraging people from looking for work; benefits should, therefore, be kept to a minimum and beneficiaries monitored so as to speed up the process of finding a job. On the other hand, allowances are seen as a resource that provides access to employment, so the amount and duration should be adequate regardless of the fact that the individual's earnestness in their search for a job must be verified. Variously combined, these two lines of reasoning have brought about an ideological transformation in European countries (Serrano-Pascual 2007) in support of activation policies that have given rise to a wide variety of interpretations (Barbier 2009). It can at least be observed that more stringent follow-up of unemployed in receipt of benefits is in place (constrained by institutional limits), as well as closer supervision of the job search, and that the notion of an adequate and reasonable job offer places greater demands on the unemployed. The procedure involving the signing of a contract by the individual and the public employment service is widely used (Willmann 2001), facilitating checks and, in particular, penalties; the obligations stated in the terms of such a contract do not cover the job search but concern specific points that are deemed better tailored to individual circumstances and are accepted by the unemployed person (salary level, percentage of working time, distance from residence to place of work, etc.).

Alternative Systems of Coverage

All these changes whittle the perimeter of unemployment down to the criteria that obtained when the category was first conceived: an allowance directly dependent on a person's work history and its duration, and the job search, subject to tighter checks. Consequently, unemployed persons whose work history is deemed lacking and who are not sufficiently active in their search for a job risk being driven to the margins of unemployment or even beyond its institutional boundaries. In these times of persisting instability in terms of employment and unemployment, boundaries have shifted and begun to oscillate between benefits and other systems of social protection that define the status of inactivity. Moreover, inactive persons are widely called upon to substitute for the jobless or to fill positions that make it possible to reclassify individuals who were initially recognised as unemployed. That trend takes specific forms in different countries, depending on the status they wish to emphasise.

Early retirement packages have been widely implemented as part of workforce reduction plans in order to prevent older laid-off employees from being classified as unemployed (Palier 2003). Despite injunctions from Brussels aimed at raising seniors' employment rate, these systems persist, and, most importantly, there is little likelihood that those affected would be able to move from unemployment to employment, given that they are provided with easier access to benefits or are exempted from looking for work. In this way, many seniors find themselves in a hazy, peripheral area of unemployment, on the fringes of inactivity (Demazière 2002). In some countries, occupational incapacity and invalidity systems are often used to regulate patterns of activity and reduce the number of long-term unemployed. In the Netherlands, for instance, there is widespread social support for the implementation of extensive early retirement programmes—in the 2000s, those individuals in receipt of an invalidity pension were three times more numerous than the registered unemployed (Wierink 2002). In the United Kingdom, in line with the dominant logic of activation, those entitled to invalidity benefit and declared apt receive reduced allowances (Angeloff 2011). Admittedly, transfer policies promoting a shift from unemployment to assistance schemes, aimed at the least employable unemployed, became less popular during the 1990s. However, other movements lead many unemployed persons to various ill-defined situations of inactivity. This concerns, first and foremost, those who are unable to escape the condition of being unemployed: for example the 'discouraged unemployed', who wish to work but do not search for jobs and are therefore classified as inactive; or those vulnerable and disoriented young people whom the European Commission labels as NEETs (Eurofound 2012); or even lone mothers who are targeted by redistributive policies (specific income support or allowance for the education of children) that encourage their inactivity (Demazière 2017).

Such policies of transferring those unemployed deemed to be the least employable towards specific assistance systems—which may also include social protection such as that provided by the minimum wage—displace individuals from one social status to another and are instrumental in redistributing their identities. However, in the 2000s, the obligation to search for a job began to extend beyond the boundaries of unemployment, placing an increasingly heavier burden on social minima recipients. This does not, however, suggest a reversal of flows at the boundaries of unemployment, since this extension concerns the obligations associated with unemployment status but not entitlements such as unemployment benefit or career guidance. More and more inactive people are thus subject to obligations associated with unemployment but without being fully established as having this status. Therefore, the dissemination of job-search standards does not open up the boundaries of unemployment.

The difficulty in eradicating unemployment through inactivity is compounded by systems where the relationship between employment and unemployment encourages or forces a person to accept any job, even an undesirable one (Huyghues-Despointes 2001). Legal mechanisms vary, with some transferring a portion of the benefits to any employer who takes on an unemployed person, who in turn continues to receive a fraction of his entitlements on condition that he accepts a low-paid job. As a result of these public policy systems, the active—or 'activated'—unemployed person is facing a new and somewhat paradoxical situation: on the one hand, the person is nearing employment, even if it means taking a less than desirable job; on the other hand, he remains aloof for fear of falling into the 'trap of precarious employment' or temporary work that such systems entail (Lefresne and Tuchszirer 2001).

In a context marked by the tendency towards activation common to many countries—albeit to varying degrees—the institutional boundaries of unemployment shift. Whether or not a person is unemployed (or acknowledged as such) hinges increasingly on how close they are to employment, which is assessed on multiple levels: the intensity of the job search, the likelihood of securing a job, the identification of factors that might prolong the period of unemployment, the existence of possible stigmas (age, health issues), etc. Implementing these selective and discriminating criteria causes the realm of unemployment to shrink. The unemployed themselves play hardly any role in this: they do not participate in defining the rules or the systems, and they have very little leeway in applying them to their own personal situation. Nevertheless, the boundaries of unemployment are not only institutional and do not boil down to being merely instruments for managing statuses and a means of assigning people to those statuses: they also shape the actual, real-life experiences of unemployment which in turn modify and reconfigure those boundaries.

THE SYMBOLIC BOUNDARIES OF AN EXPERIENCE

Unemployment is not only a status contained within institutional boundaries, it is also an experience that is lived through subjectively (Demazière 2006). The ways one considers one's social situation or interprets events that occur (and behaves in consequence) also define the boundaries of unemployment—its symbolic boundaries, which determine feelings of belonging and identity. Experiencing unemployment raises questions about how one relates to employment, determines how the status is perceived and furthers the process of interpreting work as a goal that is achievable by the unemployed. In order to grasp the ways these boundaries move, it is necessary to adopt a comprehensive approach that focuses on an understanding of what it means to be unemployed.

MOVING BOUNDARIES: IS UNEMPLOYMENT EMPLOYMENT OR WORK?

The Essential Place of Employment and the Job Search

The job search occupies a crucial place in the experience of unemployment because it is perceived as the counterpart of a person's right to financial assistance: it is 'where the unemployed person's legal identity is most securely anchored' (Willmann 1998, 248). Recent research based on approx. 60 biographical interviews with persons officially unemployed in France confirms this (Demazière et al. 2015).[1] It represents a salient trait in the condition of being unemployed: given that unemployment is a state of deprivation, it is oriented towards employment. A significant amount of research shows that the daily life of an unemployed person revolves to a certain extent around employment in its various forms, involving, on the one hand, strong personal commitment and active use of networking, and, on the other, discouragement and withdrawal (Bakke 1940; Schnapper 1981; Bartell and Bartell 1985; Gallie and Vogler 1994). Efforts to make sense of unemployment are not intended to be inward-looking but are aimed at producing different outlooks, coming up with ways out of overcoming obstacles or developing alternatives, and, in order to give these perspectives credit and substance, they also devise rapid responses and experiment with different solutions. Unemployment seeks to eradicate itself, an obliteration that can be perceived as being far-off or immediate, probable or uncertain, total or partial.

However, the erosion of contractual standards has had a particular impact on jobs, which have changed considerably over the past few decades. The unemployed person who seeks access to work or applies for a job is the most exposed to atypical contracts. For the unemployed, employment is a moving target, uncertain or remote. The person becomes caught up in the flow of life, buffeted by the hopes or disillusions that are triggered by the steps they have taken to find work and by their share of failure. Employment explodes into a myriad of situations, all more or less plausible, acceptable, desirable or accessible, all converging towards a vanishing point. And experiencing unemployment, as related by the interviewees, consists in evaluating interpretations and finding solutions to an undervalued and humiliating condition. But employment is too narrow a concept to account for the variety of prospects envisaged by jobseekers. A larger entity is at stake, as indicated by the expressions used: 'work; something to do; anything; a permanent contract; even moonlighting; just to be able to eat; a project; money; to be employed; even undeclared would be all right; I dream of setting up my own business; an odd job; a real job; earn a living; stay in my profession; just put me somewhere; a salary, that's all I ask'.

This sample of expressions gathered during the interviews illustrates the broad spectrum of outlooks. Rather than employment per se, they relate to activities that are both sources of income and a support for some sort of status—not in the legal sense of the word but in the sense of conferring a social existence and an identity—what we call *accessible work*. Thus, when real-life experiences are taken into consideration, unemployment does not boil down to being the opposite of employment—or to the act of looking for employment—it is reshaped in a process of reinterpreting work as an achievable goal for the unemployed. The issue is not about being more or less attached to work or having a greater or lesser will to work; it is about the conceptions of work itself, and therefore of unemployment.

Accessible Work in Its Different Forms

An analysis of the interviews made it possible to identify four contrasting conceptions of work, all related to unemployment—points of view that condense specific conceptions that we have summed up according to the place, the contract, the project and 'bricolage'.

The first way in which accessible work (the place) is conceived is defined by the statutory conditions imposed by social protection.

Certain specific jobs represent safe places to work where one is lastingly protected from unemployment, serving as a fortress, an impregnable citadel. The full-time permanent contract (CDI) is the legal translation of that form of accessible work, though the expressions used are more diverse ('real work', *vrai travail*; 'safe job', *emploi sûr*; 'a place for you', *une place où tu es collé*; 'security', *sécurité*; etc.). The experience of unemployment is structured around the job search, and unemployment is interpreted according to its official definition. Employment is given a restrictive meaning, which indicates that being employed remains the norm and is the focal point in a person's aspirations. However, an assessment of the likelihood of securing that place was expressed in a variety of ways. Some respondents were confident, backing themselves up with the argument that they were carrying out an active and proficient job search. Others simply expressed their preference for one of several possible outcomes. Still others mentioned the obstacles and constraints that reduce the possibilities of securing a place. For many of them, that place seems out of reach, and so the notion of accessible work must be readjusted.

Accessible work is also defined by various statuses that denote participation in production, a participation that is governed by official rules and regulations. This leads us to apply the term 'contract' to such a perspective, even if not all are backed up by a labour contract in the strict sense of the term, i.e. short or fixed-term contracts (CDD), interim contract work, integration or state-assisted contracts, internships, industrial training, one-off contracts, etc. Although these are not all considered to offer the same level of reward or security, they are all considered possibilities for finding one's way out of the unemployment tunnel. The projections take on different meanings, depending on whether they are experienced as temporary or as controlled arrangements, as an acknowledgement of one's entourage and the institutions that advise seizing upon the tiniest opportunity, or endured as the only possibility to counter the relatively serious risk of finding oneself in limbo. A contract is a marker that blurs the boundaries of unemployment, because it may mean exiting unemployment or, on the contrary, being trapped in unemployment disguised as work. Unemployment brings to bear a pressure that enlarges the definition of salaried employee and slackens the norms defining work.

Accessible work can be consolidated by promoting a specific activity that can be used to visualise the future—a craft (*métier*); a passion; a qualification; skills (*compétences*); 'doing something with your hands' (*quelque chose dans les mains*), etc. We called this approach 'the project' in order to designate a work objective and indicate the series of preparatory tasks that would allow the person to advance in that direction: tests, training periods, one-off jobs, occasionally unpaid or even informal work. The project directs the person towards the margins of salaried employment: often fragile forms of working alone (such as self-employment, carrying out autonomous tasks, subcontracting for a one-time employer, becoming an independent actor or artist, freelancer or freelance journalist), less often the classical forms of independent labour (such as setting up one's own business, creating a company or forming a partnership in a small firm). Such projects are very ambivalent. In some cases, the rewards associated with the work are good enough to erase the stress of unemployment. In other cases, the prospect of a self-fulfilling activity is hazy and unsure, or even fades into a vague dream that fails to eliminate unemployment. In still other cases, the person is not very enthusiastic about his project because it is seen as nothing more than a last resort after other possibilities have fallen through, or because it hinges on forms of employment that are considered degrading or worthless. Typically, the project alters the opposition between the status of jobless and that of employed worker.

Finally, accessible work may also signify informal or unofficial activities that confer recognition, meaning and financial resources: 'I make do' (*je me débrouille*); 'it's not declared' (*c'est pas declaré*); 'only a couple days' work' (*quelques chantiers*); 'lending a hand' (*des coups de mains*); 'we help each other' (*on s'entraide*), etc. As in the above examples, the forms it takes vary in terms of amplitude, regularity, stability, profitability and legitimacy. However, it represents actual practice rather than a projection into the future, which is why we call it 'bricolage'. The meanings of these activities also vary: they may indicate a discreet sort of resourcefulness ('making do') that relies on a well-stuffed address book; or they may indicate a weak capacity to act that relies on family and friends and leads to becoming dependent; they may also reflect a way of life based on expediency, despite personal efforts to avoid the risk of exclusion. For a number of unemployed, such bricolages are fragile and not very far-reaching, but they determine their attitudes towards work and orient their future towards relatively informal activities. Given that unemployment and work seem so closely associated as to be almost blended into one another—only the importance attributed to the chosen activity may allow the use of one or the other term in order to qualify a given situation—bricolage dilutes the boundaries of unemployment.

An analysis of experiences of unemployment in France shows that the relationship between unemployment and employment, traditionally complementary due to the institutional codification of social statuses, has deteriorated. This degradation amounts to more than a reduction in occupational claims and aspirations in terms of wages, employment status, working time, etc. It goes far beyond these declining expectations that are already well observed (Schnapper 1981; Bartell and Bartell 1985; Gallie and Vogler 1994), as it tends to replace the targeted job (even a degraded one) by more imprecise activities that, despite being informal and having no status, are deemed to be 'accessible work'. It reveals how employment—as a goal for the future—has broken down into countless interpretations of accessible work. That diversity translates a certain vagueness surrounding the symbolic boundaries of the experience of unemployment and shows how they differ from the institutional boundaries.

Fuzzy Boundaries: Unemployment Is Vulnerable

International comparisons confirm that the fragility of unemployment and the haziness of its boundaries are not seen only in France, as illustrated by a survey carried out among 199 individuals in situations of unemployment (administratively speaking) in three metropolitan areas— Paris, Sao Paulo and Tokyo (Demazière et al. 2013).[2] In this survey, the meanings of unemployment are quite heterogeneous: it all boils down neither to the job search nor to expecting to find a job; on the contrary, it removes itself from that institutional definition. Its relationship to employment is tenuous. The diverse ways in which unemployment is experienced follow two of the approaches identified above: projecting oneself into the future and anticipating accessible and rewarding solutions, on the one hand; and developing activities while being unemployed and devising ways of inhabiting that joblessness, on the other.

Anticipating Accessible Solutions

The first approach differentiates the ways in which unemployment relates to the possible alternatives and the expectations that give them meaning and colour subjective experiences. On the one hand, unemployment leans towards securing formal and official employment, a job that would hone in on a person's aspirations and focus on their individual behaviour patterns. On the other hand, unemployment is defined by a quest that turns its back on employment, hungers for alternatives and considers withdrawing into an often devalued inactivity. The anticipated solutions may be thought of as definitive (e.g. a stable position, a protective status such as retirement or invalidity) or transitory (e.g. temporary contracts, replacement incomes such as single-parent benefits). Such anticipations rely on fairly elaborate official codifications, depending on the context— retirement is less widespread in Sao Paulo where informal labour is more frequent; a status linked to motherhood or health affords greater protection in the Paris region, etc.

The two extremes may also correspond to prospects that are blurred and not very codified. The spectrum introduces a gradient into the interviews which runs from arguing that securing a job is a guaranteed outcome to tracing precise paths that lead to withdrawal, through projects peppered with uncertainty or ambivalence. Some anticipations bear the stamp of discouragement, a half-hearted job search or the decision simply to give up quietly. Others are oriented towards the margins of salaried employment, largely unregulated forms of working solo and survival activities. Others are also directed towards cursory, barely legible projects, dreams allowing a person to escape from an impossible situation, or mysterious, dramatic occurrences. Whatever they may be, these anticipations represent the experience of unemployment. They blur the boundaries between unemployment and employment, making their relationship a tenuous one.

Inhabiting Unemployment

The second approach involves activities developed while being unemployed and the various means of inhabiting that condition. On the one hand, the job search is the main—albeit not necessarily exclusive—activity and gives unemployment its meaning; it is experienced as a deprivation of employment, which calls for focus to be placed on the job search. On the other hand, there is the ability to 'make do', corresponding to activities that procure an income, or offer hopes for one, and are dependent on personal and reciprocal support networks. These two ways of inhabiting unemployment refer to opposite ways of relating to the official definition of unemployment. In the first case, the experience corresponds to its standard definition and to the obligations associated with the status—more usual in countries where systems for servicing, supervising and supporting the unemployed are most developed. In the second case, unemployment causes the regulatory framework to break up, the impact of which is tempered by the creation of systems of redistribution that offer an income or by a codification of labour that reduces the legitimacy of informal activities.

The many ways of experiencing unemployment combine the two models in different forms. The ordeal of finding a job is punctuated by difficulties, uncertainties, disillusionment and failures that may cause a person to flag in their efforts to find a job and undermine their belief in their usefulness. Other types of investment may then balance out these negative aspects in the form of alternative activities such as informal work in a private home, for friends or for an occasional employer. At the same time, a resourceful 'getting along' attitude may give rise to fairly consistent, lucrative and regular source of income, and may coexist alongside the job search. Both activities are often fragile: the job search is vulnerable to the signals received—and interpreted—in response to a person's efforts; while the 'getting along' achievements depend on the opportunities close at hand and on the place occupied by that person in the various networks likely to provide such opportunities. The experience of unemployment consists of adjustments and adaptations that combine situations that are clearly distinct on an institutional level, i.e. carrying out a job search and an activity simultaneously. Unemployment has therefore developed into a mixed category.

By extending the analysis of how unemployment is experienced to the international level, the observations made during the French study can be confirmed. The boundaries of unemployment thicken and become hazy, whether seen from the perspective of unemployed people's actual activities (oscillating between the job search and 'making do') or of their projections into the future (fluctuating between anticipating a job and withdrawing into inactivity). However, these modifications, which have an impact on the real-life experience of unemployment, remain clandestine or are ignored by the institutions.

CONCLUSIONS

Ultimately, it might be said that unemployment both changes subjectively and remains the same institutionally: its symbolic boundaries are full of holes while its institutional boundaries remain codified;

the experience of unemployment stretches out over new areas while the status of unemployment is becoming increasingly restricted. Is unemployment still a shared reference for social representation and action? Unemployment is a distinct category that makes sense in societies where formal labour is sufficiently widespread, and yet it is also a vague concept, despite simultaneously being the result of considerable formal investment (conventions to measure it, surveys to count the unemployed, legal codifications, institutions to manage the populations concerned, systems to monitor individual situations, etc.).

How then can one visualise the boundaries of unemployment? We have brought to light their diversity, each historical period being characterised in terms of the distance between—or proximity to—those boundaries. Two forms of performativity of the border can be distinguished (Gottmann 1980) that apply the metaphors of 'the door' and 'the bridge' (Simmel 1988). On the one hand, the border dissociates, separates, divides, selects and partitions. It includes and excludes, and in so doing corresponds to the function of the line, or door. It was this rationale that prevailed when unemployment was first invented in order to break with a non-differentiated treatment of the poor. The contemporary dynamics of the institutional boundaries consist in displacing those barriers, in a move that restricts the domain of unemployment but also preserves that entity, whose boundaries are reaffirmed by being tightened. On the other hand, the border allows one to pass, it crosses, connects, links and conveys. It thus permits circulation and is more like a zone: not a line but a bridge. That is the rationale underlying unemployment as it is experienced: an uncertain condition with unclear limits, for the unemployed are not only jobseekers, they experience and develop a great variety of expectations (unemployment, inactivity and all possible forms of accessible work). The dynamics of symbolic boundaries consist in exploring and extending the border zones.

Two autonomous, dynamic processes thus coexist on the boundaries of unemployment. Uniting them does not lead to confrontation, conflict or contradictions, for they unfold on different levels and are served by unequal capacities to express the realities of the world. Unemployment, therefore, remains immutable, or rather tightens around its normative core, while, at the same time, a growing number of real-life experiences are taking place further and further from that core. One might well wonder up to what point those contradictory tendencies can coexist without challenging the very category of unemployment.[3]

NOTES

1. The aim was to ask interviewees to explain what their experience of unemployment was and to relate the events that had occurred during that period, how they interpret them, their endeavours to remain resilient as well as their understanding of what it means to be unemployed. Interviews were conducted according to a semi-directive method (without a grid), each one lasting from 1 hour to 2 hours 40 minutes; at the time of the interviews, 57 people were registered with the French National Employment Agency (*Pôle Emploi*). The sample was built with a view to demonstrating a diversity of situations, and was controlled by duration of unemployment, age and level of education.

2. The biographical interviews aimed to gather narratives of experience in order to grasp interpretations of unemployment from the point of view of the people who actually live through it, to understand the meanings it holds for them and to seek explanations for their subsequent behaviour. The overall sample was subdivided into three subsamples of equivalent size for each of the three cities: Paris, Sao Paulo and Tokyo. In order to study a diversified population while controlling its diversity and avoiding dispersion, four categories defined by specific combinations were targeted: women whose career path had been interrupted by a period of inactivity ('mothers'); workers and employees with families who were experiencing an unplanned hiatus in their career ('workers'); poorly educated young people seeking occupational integration ('young people'); and members of middle management whose upward mobility had been thrown off course after losing their job ('managers'). Each of the three subsamples includes the four categories in similar proportions.

3. Translation from the French by Gabrielle Varro.

REFERENCES

Abbott, Andrew. 1995. "Things of Boundaries." *Social Research* 62 (4): 857–882.

Angeloff, Tania. 2011. "Des hommes malades du chômage? Genre et (ré-)assignation identitaire au Royaume-Uni." *Travail et Emploi* (128): 69–82.

Bakke, E. Wight. 1940. *Citizens Without Work: A Study of the Effects of Unemployment upon the Worker's Social Relations and Practices.* New Haven: Yale University Press.

Barbier, Jean-Claude. 2009. "Le *workfare* et l'activation de la protection sociale, vingt ans après: beaucoup de bruit pour rien? Contribution à un bilan qui reste à faire." *Lien Social et Politiques* (61): 23–36.

Barbier, Jean-Claude, and Jérôme Gautié. 1998. *Les politiques de l'emploi en Europe et aux États-Unis.* Paris: Presses Universitaires de France.

Bartell, Marvin, and Riva Bartell. 1985. "An Integrative Perspective on the Psychological Response of Women and Men to Unemployment." *Journal of Economic Psychology* 6 (1): 27–49.

Barth, Fredrik. 1969. "Introduction." In *Ethnic Groups and Boundaries. The Social Organization of Culture Difference*, edited by Fredrik Barth, 1–23. Londres: Allen & Unwin.

Castel, Robert. 1995. *Les métamorphoses de la question sociale Une chronique du salariat.* Fayard: Paris.

Castel, Robert, Jean-Paul Fitoussi, Jacques Freyssinet, and Henri Guaino. 1997. *Chômage: le cas français.* Paris: La Documentation française.

Clasen, Jochen, and Daniel Clegg. 2006. "Beyond Activation: Reforming European Unemployment Protection Systems in Post-industrial Labour Markets." *European Societies* 8 (4): 527–533.

Daniel, Christine, and Carole Tuchszirer. 1999. *L'Etat face aux chômeurs. L'indemnisation du chômage de 1884 à nos jours.* Paris: Flammarion.

Degenne, Alain. 2005. "Penser, faire bouger les catégories et leurs frontiers." In *Les catégories sociales et leurs frontières*, edited by Alain Degenne, Catherine Marry, and Sylvie Moulin. Québec: Presses de l'Université Laval.

de Larquier, Guillemette. 2000. "Émergence des services publics de placement et marches du travail français et britannique au XXe siècle." *Travail et Emploi* (84): 33–45.

Demazière, Didier. 2002. "'Chômeurs âgés', chômeurs 'trop vieux'. Articulation des catégories gestionnaires et interprétatives." *Sociétés Contemporaines* (48): 109–130.

———. 2003. *Le chômage. Comment peut-on être chômeur?* Paris: Belin.

———. 2006. *Sociologie des chômeurs.* Paris: La Découverte.

———. 2017. "Les femmes et le chômage." *SociologieS.* Mis en ligne le 21 février 2017. http://sociologies.revues.org/5966.

Demazière, Didier, Nadya Guimarães, Helena Hirata, and Kurumi Sugita. 2013. *Être chômeur à Paris, Sao Paulo, Tokyo. Une méthode de comparaison internationale.* Paris: Presses de Sciences Po.

Demazière, Didier, Fabien Foureault, Claire Lefrançois, and Aranud Vendeur. 2015. *Affronter le chômage. Parcours, expériences, significations.* Paris: Centre de Sociologie des Organisations.

Desrosières, Alain. 2003. "Comment fabriquer un espace de commune mesure? Harmonisation des statistiques et réalisme de leurs usages." In *Stratégies de la comparaison international*, edited by Michel Lallement and Jan Spurk, 151–166. Paris: CNRS éditions.

Dubois, Vincent. 2007. "État social actif et contrôle des chômeurs: un tournant rigoriste entre tendances européennes et logiques nationales." *Politique Européenne* (21): 73–95.

Durkheim, Emile, and Marcel Mauss. 1903. "De quelque formes primitives de classification. Contribution à l'étude des représentations collectives." *L'Année Sociologique* (6): 1–72.

Eurofound. 2012. *Les jeunes et les NEET en Europe. Premiers résultats.* Dublin: Fondation Européenne pour l'amélioration des conditions de vie et de travail.

Evans, Michael. 2009. "Defining the Public, Defining Sociology: Hybrid Science Public Relations and Boundary Work in Early American Sociology." *Public Understanding of Science* 18 (1): 5–22.

Eymard-Duvernay, François. 2001. "Principes de justice, chômage et exclusion: approfondissements théoriques." In *Les marchés du travail équitables? Approche comparative France/Royaume Uni*, edited by Christian Bessy, François Eymard-Duvernay, Guillemette de Larquier, and Emmanuelle Marchal, 271–299. Brussels: Peter Lang.

Freyssinet, Jacques. 1998. "L'indemnisation du chômage en Europe. Entre l'activation des dépenses pour l'emploi et la garantie de minima sociaux." In *Pauvreté et exclusion*, 69–92. Paris: La Documentation Française and Conseil d'Analyse Economique.

Gallie, Duncan, and Carolyn Vogler. 1994. "Unemployment and Attitudes to Work." In *Social Change and the Experience of Unemployment*, edited by Duncan Gallie, Catherine Marsh, and Carolyn Vogler, 115–153. Oxford: Oxford University Press.

Gautié, Jérôme. 2002. "De l'invention du chômage à sa deconstruction." *Genèses* 46 (1): 60–76.

Ghesquière, François. 2014. "Précarité du contrat de travail et risque de perte d'emploi en Europe." *Sociologie* 5 (3): 271–290.

Gieryn, Thomas. 1983. "Boundary-Work and the Demarcation of Science from Non-science: Strains and Interests in Professional Ideologies of Scientists." *American Sociological Review* 48 (6): 781–795.

Gottmann, Jean. 1980. "Les frontières et les marches: cloisonnement et dynamique du monde." In *Geography and Its Boundaries. In memory of Hans Boesch*, 53–58. Berne: Kummerly & Frey.

Huyghues-Despointes, Hervé. 2001. "Avoir un emploi et en rechercher un simultanément: types d'itinéraires passant sur la frontière de l'emploi et du chômage." *Revue de l'IRES* (35): 125–153.

Jeanpierre, Laurent. 2010. "Frontière." In *Dictionnaire des concepts nomades en sciences humaines*, sous la direction de Olivier Christin, 157–169. Paris: Métailié.

Lamont, Michèle. 2001. "Symbolic Boundaries: Overview." *International Encyclopedia of the Social and Behavioral Sciences* (20): 15341–15346.

Lamont, Michèle, and Marcel Fournier. 1992. *Cultivating Differences: Symbolic Boundaries and the Making of Inequality.* Chicago: University of Chicago Press.

Lefresne, Florence. 2005. "Les politiques d'emploi et la transformation des normes: une comparaison européenne." *Sociologie du Travail* 47 (3): 405–420.

Lefresne, Florence. 2008. "Regard comparatif sur l'indemnisation du chômage: la difficile sécurisation des parcours professionnels." *Chronique Internationale de l'IRES* (115): 3–22.

Lefresne, Florence, and Carole Tuchszirer. 2001. "Stratégies d'activation par les activités occasionnelles et normes d'emploi. La situation française confrontée aux expériences belge, danoise, néerlandaise et anglaise." *Travail et Emploi* (87): 47–65.

Lemoine, Matthieu. 2007. "Chômage: débattre de la mesure." *Lettre de l'OFCE* (286): 1–4.

Luciani, Jean. 1990. "Logique du placement ouvrier au XIXe siècle et construction du marché du travail." *Sociétés Contemporaines* (3): 5–18.

Mansfield, Malcolm, Robert Salais, and Noël Whiteside, eds. 1994. *Aux sources du chômage, 1880–1914. Une comparaison interdisciplinaire entre la France et la Grande-Bretagne.* Paris: Belin.

Marchand, Olivier. 1991. "Statistiques du chômage: les écarts se creusent depuis cinq ans." *Économie et Statistique* (249): 7–4.

Marchand, Olivier, and Claude Thélot. 1983. "Le nombre des chômeurs." *Économie et Statistique* (160): 29–45.

Marpsat, Maryse. 1984. "Chômage et profession dans les années trente." *Économie et Statistique* (170): 53–69.

Maruani, Margaret. 1996. "L'emploi féminin à l'ombre du chômage." *Actes de la Recherche en Sciences Sociales* (115): 48–57.

———. 2002. *Les mécomptes du chômage.* Paris: Bayard.

Palier, Bruno. 2003. *La réforme des retraites.* Paris: Presses Universitaires de France.

Salais, Robert, Nicolas Baverez, and Bénédicte Reynaud. 1986. *L'invention du chômage. Histoire et transformation d'une catégorie en France des années 1890 aux années 1980.* Paris: Presses Universitaires de France.

Schnapper, Dominique. 1981. *L'épreuve du chômage.* Paris: Gallimard.

Serrano-Pascual, Amparo. 2007. "Activation Regimes in Europe: A Clustering Exercise." In *Reshaping Welfare States and Activation Regimes in Europe*, edited by Amparo Serrano-Pascual and Lars Magnusson, 275–316. Brussels: Peter Lang.

Silber, Ilana. 1995. "Space, Fields, Boundaries, the Rise of Spatial Metaphors in Contemporary Sociological Theory." *Social Research* 62 (2): 323–355.

Simmel, Georg. 1988. "Le pont et la porte." In *La tragédie de la culture*, edited by Georg Simmel, 159–166. Paris: Payot (First Edition, 1909).

Topalov, Christian. 1987. "Invention du chômage et politiques sociales au début du siècle." *Les temps modernes* (496–497): 53–92.

———. 1994. *Naissance du chômeur, 1880–1910.* Paris: Albin Michel.

Wierink, Marie. 2002. "La réforme du régime de l'inaptitude au travail." *Chroniques Internationales de l'IRES* (76).

Willmann, Christophe. 1998. *L'identité juridique du chômeur.* Paris: Librairie Générale de Droit et de Jusrisprudence.

———. 2001. "Le chômeur cocontractant." *Droit Social* (4): 384–392.

CHAPTER 11

Can We Still Speak the Language of Unemployment? Some Reflections Based on the French Experience

Michel Lallement

INTRODUCTION

François Hollande, invited to speak on the French television news on 9 September 2012 while President of the French Republic, promised to do his utmost to reverse the trend of French unemployment over the coming year. Five years later, he was forced to concede failure with respect to this promise: by the first quarter of 2017 unemployment was affecting 9.6% of the French working population (Mayotte excluded), a 0.4 percentage-point increase on 2012. This figure places France in sixth position among the countries of the European Union, and a very long way behind Germany with its score of 3.9%. Among the 28 EU countries taken as a whole, the average unemployment rate is 7.8%. In 2017, therefore, unemployment remained a sensitive topic for François Hollande who had repeatedly linked a decision to stand for a second presidency to his ability to contain this scourge to which our society has fallen prey. For this reason, alongside several others, he threw in the towel.

M. Lallement (✉)
Conservatoire national des arts et métiers, Lise-CNRS, Paris, France

© The Author(s) 2019
A. Serrano-Pascual and M. Jepsen (Eds.),
The Deconstruction of Employment as a Political Question,
https://doi.org/10.1007/978-3-319-93617-8_11

The unemployment rate is, alas, much more than one ingredient of the numerous political psychodramas so relished by the media. Above all else, the lack of a job represents a painfully distressing existential drama for the vast majority of the men and women suffering enforced exclusion from the world of labour.

Unemployment may quite legitimately be approached in a number of different ways. I propose here to analyse it as a category. In the critical tradition of transcendental idealism, it could be defined as a basic form that enables a link to be established between representation and apperception. For a sociologist, this way of seeing is not sufficient, and Emile Durkheim was one of the first thinkers to supply arguments enabling us to move beyond the traditional Kantian approach. For the author of *The Elementary Forms of the Religious Life* (1912), the notion of time is irreducible to an a priori form of intuition; it is, above all, an abstract and impersonal framework issuing directly from social life. Exactly the same thing can be said of unemployment. This concept, regarded widely today by many social and economic actors as a 'natural phenomenon', utterly lacks the features of an 'external reality' that impacts our lives in the manner of sunshine or rain.

It is to Didier Demazière (1992, 2003) that we owe an in-depth study of the processes of categorisation by which unemployment is shaped, at the crossroads between the logic of institutions and the interplay of actions among individuals. While I do not aim here to produce anything so exhaustive, my approach is intended to be similar in that it will emphasise, above all, the cognitive implications of the category of unemployment. I adopt to this end the hypothesis that, as a commonly accepted noun in the French language, unemployment—*le chômage*—lends itself to analysis by means of linguistics or, more modestly, by bringing into play some of that discipline's founding categories: semantics (the relationship between signs and what they designate); syntax (the relationship of signs among themselves); and pragmatics (the relationship between signs and their user). These are the three registers I shall—by way of analogy—examine here, in order to consider whether in France today the language of unemployment retains any meaning. The question itself becomes meaningful once it is accepted that, as from the institutionalisation—around the turn of the nineteenth/twentieth centuries—of the category of unemployment, we have witnessed a step-by-step calling into question of the various criteria that, initially, enabled a distinction to be drawn between unemployment and other forms of labour-related status such as 'of no occupation'.

UNEMPLOYMENT: THE WORD AND THE THINGS
THAT IT SHAPES

In *L'invention du chômage*, which appeared some thirty years ago, Robert Salais, Nicolas Baverez and Bénédicte Reynaud hypothesised that 'the current crisis is, at bottom, a crisis of formerly established representations and categories' (Salais et al. 1986, 20). This diagnosis has acquired no wrinkles; and yet unemployment remains a category to which politicians in government, statisticians and social scientists, and also the vast majority of French citizens, continue to attach meaning. In spite of criticism and warnings concerning the weaknesses and biases of this category and the main indicator that embodies it (Gautié 2002), in spite of recommendations aimed at diversifying the ways in which unemployment is defined and measured, in spite also of alternative proposals (Malinvaud 1986), such as that of recourse to the notion of non-employment (Laroque and Salanié 2000), the category of unemployment remains in use as a widespread tool and significant mode of reference.

The crisis of 2008–2010 failed to definitively dislodge this category which is now close on a century and a half old. Unemployment, as we understand it still today, is in fact a convention laid down at the end of the nineteenth century at a stage of economic and social development marked by the growth of industry, development of trade unions and institutionalised upsurge of a socialist movement avid for recourse to the scientific tools required to describe a social world in the throes of transformation. The term '*chômage*' was no longer used, as formerly it had been, to designate 'all those situations in which a worker was neither working nor earning a wage: Sunday rest or strike action, sickness or old age, lack of customers or of tasks to be performed in the workshop' (Topalov 1994, 24)—a wide-ranging set of situations that could be designated, in French, by recourse to the plural form of the word—*les chômages*—or in various alternative ways. In the public sphere, in France, the terms '*chômage*' (as from 1871) and '*chômeurs*' (as from 1876) gradually acquired visibility and legitimacy as the means of designating, respectively, the fact of being out of work and the workers who were affected by this situation (Topalov 1987).

In spite of this innovative shift in vocabulary, use of the terms in question continued to be rather imprecise up until the beginning of the twentieth century. As from the 1890s, there were some efforts to clarify their meaning, attributable, above all, to the *Conseil supérieur du travail* ('supreme labour council')—the predecessor of the current employment ministry—which proposed tightening up the definition of *chômage* to make it mean involuntary unemployment attributable to one precise cause, namely, lack of work. The term designating the unemployed worker, *le chômeur*, underwent similar development and, in differing quarters, various alternative designations came to be preferred: *'ouvrier sans ouvrage'* ('worker without work'), or, in the world of welfare assistance, *'nécessiteux valide sans travail'* (able-bodied out-of-work person in need). Whether in order to promote or to object to one or other designation, contributions to the reform came from a diversity of quarters (civil servants, politicians, economists, statisticians, trade unionists, representatives of professional bodies, philanthropists, etc.) triggering something like a battle for the establishment of terminology.

One specific development constituted a decisive stage that helps to explain and understand how and why, in France, the term *'chômage'* became the hegemonic category for analysis and action. The issue at stake was the need for a satisfactory distinction between, on the one hand, able-bodied workers involuntarily deprived of work for a period of variable duration and predictability and, on the other, the 'mass of customarily indigent persons prone to regular periods of destitution on grounds of occupational incapacity, physical or moral weakness such that the only help forthcoming will be from charitable bodies set up for that purpose' (Conseil supérieur du Travail 1896, 188, quoted by Salais et al. 1986, 49). The development in question dates from 1896 when the French census, for the first time, established a distinction, among the jobless, between an 'unemployed' person and one who was 'of no occupation'. Two decisive parameters were used for this purpose, namely, age and the period of suspension from work.[1]

There was, it is true, some variation from one census to the next in terms of the exact criteria used: for example, in 1896 and in 1901 a 65-year-old could no longer be counted as unemployed. Nor was the minimum period of suspension from work specified prior to 1906, from when, until 1936, it was one week. The maximum duration was specified in 1901: 'in general, persons declared as jobless for more than a year are not genuinely unemployed; with some exceptions, for example long-term sickness, wage-earners remaining out of work for more than a year have frequently chosen to give up work or are in possession of resources that would permit of their being placed in a category other than that of wage-earners in the strict sense' (1901 census, volume 4: 332, quoted by Salais et al. 1986, 39).

From 1906 to 1936 the distinction was finalised by distinguishing, among the ranks of the jobless, between, on the one hand, the unemployed (those aged below 60 and out-of-work for a period of at least a week and less than two years; those aged above 60 and out-of-work for more than a year and less than two years) and, on the other hand, persons 'of no occupation' (those aged above 60 and out-of-work for more than a year and less than two years; elderly persons out-of-work for more than two years, whatever their age) (Reynaud-Cressent 1984). While the classification criteria did continue to evolve, the category of unemployment became, as from the twentieth century, clearly established as the equivalent of a period spent out-of-work that met the following conditions: (1) temporary; (2) involuntary; (3) measurable; (4) applicable to able-bodied workers; (5) not able to be equated with any other socially accepted use of time (leisure, housework, education, etc.); and (6) referable, as from 1958, to an insurance (and not a welfare benefit) regime.

Classification is not an operation that consists in passively recording an already constituted reality. This remark, which in sociology would tend to be considered rather obvious, is nonetheless frequently disregarded in numerous quarters, starting with the media. To classify is to devise tools that serve, at one and the same time, to produce a judgement about the world, to put it into practice and to act upon it. Statistical indicators are thus 'conventional signs by means of which a society represents itself and acts upon itself' (Desrosières 2008, 203). The classification criteria of which the category of unemployment is the product thus come to be implemented *qua* values. While we cannot enumerate here the myriad concrete implications entailed by the notion of unemployment invented at the turn of the nineteenth/twentieth century, it will at least be worth mentioning two of them. The first is that, insofar as the situation of the unemployed person is regarded as temporary, protection against the risks inhering in this situation (in terms, first and foremost, of income) is to be provided by insurance and not welfare assistance. Considerable thought was devoted to this point when the category of unemployment was first forged, in order to determine how a replacement income was to be provided for workers who involuntarily found themselves out of work.

In fact, throughout the first half of the twentieth century, several systems of cover gradually built up alongside each other, some of them more successful than others: trade union assistance funds (late nineteenth and early twentieth century); state-subsidised trade unions funds (1904–1914); national unemployment fund (1914–1930) (set up to compensate for the inability of the trade union funds to cover all workers); rationalisation and extension of the system (cover of short-time work, for example) (1930–1935); administrative involvement of the *départements* in the provision of unemployment benefits (1935–1939); subsequent disappearance of the trade union unemployment funds under the Vichy regime; introduction of a *dirigiste* policy for the supervision of labour; and minimal attention accorded after WW2 to unemployment benefits during a period when the numbers of people out of work were low. In 1958, under General de Gaulle, an unemployment insurance regime was set up for workers in industry and trade. It had thus taken more than half a century for unemployment insurance to become compulsory. Alongside Unedic (*Union nationale interprofessionnelle pour l'emploi dans l'industrie et le commerce*), responsible for unemployment insurance, other bodies subsequently came into being to consolidate the institutionalisation of a public employment system. The most important was the national employment agency—*Agence nationale pour l'emploi (ANPE)*— set up in 1967 for the pooling of job offers, production of unemployment statistics and accompaniment of jobseekers (Muller 1991). In 2008 The ANPE was merged with the network of Assedics (associations for employment in industry and trade)[2] to become the *Pôle Emploi*. The chequered history of the provision of unemployment benefits, of which I have recalled merely a few important stages, was marked by two recurrent tendencies: the temptation, above all at times of crisis, to take its distance from the principle of insurance,[3] on the one hand; the tendency to regard the unemployed as idle individuals to be placed under supervision and issued with incentives to return to work, on the other.

The second implication of the initial conventional mode according to which the category of unemployment had been shaped may be read in terms of gender. The definition of unemployment that gradually gained sway in France at the end of the nineteenth and beginning of the twentieth centuries relates essentially to men (employed in large-scale manufacturing industry) as distinct from women (who worked in the home). For the women, indeed, it was extremely difficult objectively to establish periods spent out of work, given the extent to which their occupational labour in the home was intimately bound up with their domestic duties, to the point where they themselves found it quite impossible to differentiate.[4] Pierre Bourdieu recorded a similar phenomenon in his studies of workers in Algeria.

As long as work is defined as a social function, the notions of unemployment or short-time work cannot be formed. Appearance of an awareness of unemployment thus marks a conversion in terms of attitude towards the world. The natural adherence to an order that is regarded as natural because it is traditional is suspended; customary forms of work are seen in a new light and are judged in relation to a new system of reference, namely the notion of full employment deriving from the experience of work in an industrial society. It is thus that, in the presence of real activity levels that are extremely close to one another, the rural Kabyle populations will readily declare themselves to be unemployed if they consider that they are not working enough, whereas the farmers and shepherds of southern Algeria will tend to describe themselves as working. (Bourdieu 1963, 303)

Following a similar line of reasoning, it is not difficult to understand that, in the 1896 census, persons working in the home were classified as '*isolés*' and that, whether or not they were regularly out of work, such persons could not claim the status of unemployment (Lallement 1991). By virtue of a similar rationale which (1) basically associates unemployment with the involuntary absence of waged work and (2) grants no status, no recognition and no rights to women who perform the bulk of domestic tasks and/or work in co-operation with their self-employed husbands (farmers, traders, etc.), large numbers of women were—and still are—classified as 'inactive' (alongside students, retired persons, etc.). This was particularly the case during the 'historic parenthesis' of the years 1950–1970 when the 'male breadwinner model' reigned supreme (Giraud 2014). Conducting research within a register that is of direct relevance to the language of unemployment and employment, Margaret Maruani and Monique Méron (2012) have demonstrated how the new measurement of labour activity adopted by the French national statistics and economic studies institute (INSEE) in 1954 had a decisive impact on the recognition, or rather the non-recognition, of women's work. By adopting a new instrument, the statisticians wiped out from the French manufacturing landscape about one million working women. All in all, it is impossible not to corroborate Margaret Maruani's claim that:

unemployment is not the opposite of employment; it is the flipside of the right to employment. And it is precisely here that men and women diverge fundamentally: we live in societies where the entitlement to gainful employment, the right to be occupationally active or inactive, is not always the same for one sex as for the other. (Maruani 2002, 17)

In other words, the invention of unemployment can be shown to have contributed also to making women's work invisible and to the introduction of structural inequalities in terms of social protection.

SEMANTICS: LABOUR MARKET DEVELOPMENTS AND THEIR IMPLICATIONS FOR THE CATEGORY OF EMPLOYMENT

Over the decades, and with the crisis the first symptoms of which became apparent in the mid-1970s, the links between the categories of unemployment and unemployed persons, on the one hand, and the features of the labour market and population to which they refer, on the other, were becoming increasingly loose. The first reason for this was, almost paradoxically, the steady increase in the number of persons who were involuntarily out of work. To take the measure of this phenomenon, a first approach—and certainly the simplest—is to observe the development of the unemployment rate which is the ratio between the numbers of the unemployed and of the working population (whether actually working or not). As from the mid-1970s the trend was indeed a rising one. According to the International Labour Office (ILO) definition,[5] the number of unemployed in France in 1975 was 740,000. In 1985 it was 2,078,000; in 1995 2,442,000, in 2005 2,321,000 and in 2017 2,700,000. This means that one in ten members of the working population is unemployed at the current time.

This quantitative development has qualitative effects that undermine the semantic foundations of the category of unemployment. The first consequence is thus to call into question the 'temporary' nature that had been attributed to the situation of unemployment at the turn of the nineteenth/twentieth centuries. In parallel with the considerable increase in the *numbers* of unemployed, a lengthening of the *periods* spent in unemployment can indeed be observed. The INSEE employment survey thus indicates that the average period rose from 7.6 to 14.6 months between March 1975 and March 1995. In 2013 the average period was 14 months. At the end of 2014 the percentage of long-term unemployed (those out of work for more than 12 months) within the unemployed population was 43.2% (as compared with 16.7% in 1975). Something like half of these long-term unemployed are 'very long-term unemployed' whose period out of work has lasted two years or more (Lê et al. 2014). Still in 2017, 1.2 million people stated that they had been seeking a job for at least a year (Insee 2017). This calling into question of the 'temporary' nature of the period of unemployment, which was further exacerbated by the crisis of 2008–2010, goes hand in hand with the systematic promotion of employment flexibility policies which call into question, in turn, the permanent nature of the employment contract as it had been formalised since the beginning of the twentieth century. Evidence of the surge in precariousness is the predominance of 'reaching the end of a fixed-term contract' as a circumstance to justify the status of jobseeker. This was the reason stated by 45.3% of the unemployed in 2012, others being dismissal (18%), resignation (7.5%) and 'miscellaneous' (29.2%).

French unemployment is characterised, what is more, by strong elements of inequality: women and young people (those who have left school) are particularly affected. In the first quarter of 2017, the unemployment rate among 15–24-year-olds regarded as belonging to the working population was 21.8% as compared with 8.7% among the 25 to 49-year-olds and 6.6% among those aged 50 or more. Gender inequality is equally striking. In the third quarter of 2009 the rate of unemployment among men nonetheless caught up—for the first time since the 1970s— with that of women. Over and above certain medium-term trends (job creation in services benefiting women more than men; gradual reduction of the gap between the sexes in terms of educational qualifications), the crisis during the first decade of the new millennium is not unrelated to this trend because it massively affected sectors (such as building and public works) and forms of employment (such as temporary work) that were predominantly preserves of male workers. Since then, however, the effects of the crisis have spread to the rest of the economy, and the employment rate among women has grown at a rate comparable to that of men. In 2017 the latter are once again in the less unfavourable situation, the unemployment rate among men being 9.2%, while among women it is 9.4%.

Socio-professional category is another discriminating variable. In 2015 the unemployment rate among unskilled manual workers was 20.3%, as compared with 11.4% among the skilled, 10.2% among white-collar workers, 5.8% for intermediate occupations, and 4% among managers. In a word, the growth in unemployment does not reduce disparities but, on the contrary, actually exacerbates them. The explosion of unemployment, what is more, has in common with the growing number of those in education that, overall, it least penalises those groups already best endowed with qualifications and cultural capital.[6]

> **Box 1—Unemployment benefits in France**
>
> Since 1984 the system of unemployment benefits in France has been structured in two distinct regimes:
>
> - An unemployment insurance regime, operating according to the principle of contributions and entitling persons involuntarily out-of-work and with a proven work record to, for a certain period, an allowance depending on their past income from employment. The name of this allowance, since July 2001, has been 'return-to-employment benefit' (*allocation de retour à l'emploi—ARE*).
> - A national solidarity regime (*régime de solidarité nationale—RSN*) that provides benefits to specific categories: jobseekers whose entitlement to unemployment benefit has expired and who receive a 'specific solidarity allowance' (*allocation de solidarité spécifique—ASS*); persons who have been working from a very young age who are entitled to a 'retirement-equivalent allowance') (*allocation equivalent retraite—AER*); former prisoners; expatriate workers; and asylum-seekers who may be entitled to a 'temporary waiting allowance' (*allocation temporaire d'attente—ATA*).
>
> Unemployment assurance is financed by worker and employer contributions to Unedic, while the national solidarity regime is financed by the State via a solidarity fund.
> *Source* http://travail-emploi.gouv.fr/etudes-recherches-statistiques-de,76/statistiques,78/chomage,79/les-mots-du-chomage,1413/les-demandeurs-d-emploi-inscrits-a,9576.html

A final point to be stressed here is that the unemployed population is currently more diverse than ever. Generally speaking, everyone is aware that categorisation takes place subject to standardised criteria which, whatever they may be, never actually remove the differences between the persons, objects, etc. subsumed within the same set. It seems legitimate, nonetheless, to question the operational validity of a category such as unemployment which appears, as the decades pass, to be increasingly forfeiting whatever claim to coherence it may formerly have possessed. For, setting aside a bureaucratic label, what common features can possibly be discerned between an unemployed worker of 55 prepared to take up an early retirement option, a young unemployed person with virtually no work experience and whose skills as recorded on paper are already considered obsolete, and a 'clever guy' able to fend for himself thanks to familiarity with all the tricks-of-the-trade in terms of undeclared labour?

The confusion has worsened still further with the gradual shift of large numbers of unemployed toward a welfare assistance regime. On account of the structural difficulties encountered by an economy that is no longer on a growth path, large numbers of jobseekers are pushed out of the labour market once and for all and no longer entitled to claim unemployment benefits. Since the beginning of the 1990s this has been the situation of, on average, something like one in two of all unemployed workers. Those no longer entitled to unemployment benefits can claim basic welfare allowances like the *allocation solidarité spécifique* (introduced in 1984) or the *revenu minimum d'insertion* introduced in 1988 which in 2009 was renamed the *revenu social d'insertion*. The *revenu de solidarité active*,[7] and then the *prime d'activité* (introduced in 2016), today complete an evolving panoply of welfare allowances generating extremely marginal employment effects. An additional consequence of the increase in the average length of periods of unemployment will thus have been to erode another pillar of the original institutional set-up, by loosening the link between having lost one's job work and entitlement to insurance.

Syntax: Classifying the Unemployed, Getting the Number(s) Right

How are the unemployed counted in France?[8] The first source that can be used for this purpose is the census of the French population which records persons who spontaneously give their status as unemployed. The difficulty here, however, is that among these persons—even though they may state that they are looking for a job—some belong to the category of what, in ILO terminology, are referred to as the 'economically inactive' (who include 'full-time mothers', 'housewives', 'early retired', 'students', etc.). The census, accordingly, is rarely used to provide figures intended to assess the extent of unemployment. For this purpose, systematic recourse is made, by contrast, to two alternative sources, the first of which enables the compilation of 'monthly labour market statistics' in relation to jobseekers. The data in question is compiled by extracting information from the files of *Pôle Emploi*, and the resulting figures are made available to the public on the 18th working day of each month. The quality of the data thus circulated depends largely on the information supplied by the jobseekers registered with *Pôle Emploi*, who are required to update their status by submitting a monthly statement of their situation. If they fail to do this by the stipulated closing date, they are automatically removed from the lists, in which case they receive notification of this step and are entitled to re-register immediately if they so desire.

An administrative act of 5 February 1992 defined five categories of unemployed person: category 1 (jobseekers at the end of the month) included jobless persons, immediately available for work and seeking full-time permanent employment; category 2 included jobless persons, immediately available for work and in search of a part-time permanent job; category 3 included jobless persons, immediately available for work and in search of fixed-term, seasonal, or temporary work; category 4 included jobless persons, not immediately available for work, in search of work, fixed-term or not, whether full- or part-time; category 5 was for persons who had a job but were looking for another one. By an administrative act of 5 May 1995, three additional categories were created to allow for separate classification of unemployed persons who had worked on a 'reduced or occasional' basis for 78 hours or more during the previous month (cf. Table 11.1).

Following recommendations issued in June 2008 by the national statistics council (*Conseil national de l'information statistique*), a new set of categories was adopted, supposedly intended to enhance the relevance of the statistical analysis of the data concerning jobseekers registered with *Pôle Emploi*. Since 2009, *Pôle Emploi* and the Employment Ministry have accordingly been using the following categories: category A: out-of-work jobseekers required to take positive steps to seek employment; category B: jobseekers required to take positive steps to seek employment, who have worked 'short reduced' hours (i.e. 78 or less) during the previous month; category C: jobseekers required to take positive steps to seek employment who have worked 'long reduced' hours (i.e. more than 78) during the previous month; category D: out-of-work jobseekers not required to take positive steps to seek employment (because of

Table 11.1 Categorisation of the unemployed in France between 1992 and 2008

Type of contract sought	No work during previous month or work of less than 78 hours	Reduced or occasional work of more than 78 hours in previous month
Permanent full-time contract	Category 1	Category 4
Permanent part-time contract	Category 2	Category 5
Fixed-term or temporary agency contract	Category 3	Category 6

Source French Employment Ministry

Table 11.2 Administrative and statistical categories of unemployment in France

Statistical category	Administrative category
Category A	Categories 1, 2, 3 without reduced work
Category B	Categories 1, 2, 3 with reduced work
Category C	Categories 6, 7, 8
Category D	Category 4
Category E	Category 5
Categories A, B, C	Categories 1, 2, 3, 6, 7, 8
Categories A, B, C, D, E	Categories 1, 2, 3, 4, 5, 6, 7, 8

Source French Employment Ministry

training schemes or courses, sickness, etc.); category E: jobseekers not required to take positive steps to seek employment, who actually are in employment (i.e. beneficiaries of assisted contracts, etc.). Table 11.2 shows how these new categories correspond to those that had been in force since 1992.

Even if they have been improved in order to refine our knowledge of unemployment, it must not be forgotten that these categories are, above all, instruments designed for administering a population of job-seekers. Proof of this is supplied by the reasons for which jobseekers may be removed from the *Pôle Emploi* files. The reasons fall into four types: (1) failure to update their job-search details; (2) statement of a change in situation; (3) the conditions for registration at *Pôle Emploi* are no longer fulfilled (for example, a residence permit has expired); and

(4) removal from the register by administrative decision (on account, for example, of failure to meet the requirements incumbent on registered jobseekers) (Dares 2015). The second source that can used to count the unemployed population is thus one that is *not* associated with administrative concerns and their surrounding apparatus and which is therefore, in principle, better adapted to meeting the demand for 'disinterested' knowledge. This source is the INSEE employment survey, the first issue of which dates back to 1950. The criteria used by this source for defining an unemployed person are those stipulated by the ILO in 1982. It will be readily understood that, depending on the source used, the unemployment figure may vary. For example, an unemployed person listed in the employment survey will not be automatically recognised as such in the monthly labour market statistics if s/he is not registered at *Pôle Emploi*. On the other hand, there will be registered persons who are not recognised as unemployed under the ILO criteria: some may classed as inactive even though they are working (albeit probably only some of the time and in a precarious labour situation) and others will be genuinely inactive (in many cases as a result of discouragement). Nor can the information and totals obtainable from one or other of these two sources be expected to serve the same purposes. Until 2017, the figures issued each month by *Pôle Emploi* were, for example, subject to public comment by the French employment minister and, in the light of such comment, to immediate media coverage. One advantage of the employment survey figures is that they allow of international comparison with other countries which classify the unemployed along similar lines.

On account, in particular, of the major changes in the size and morphology of the unemployed population, the French public authorities are regularly tempted to devise a 'thermometer' that would allow labour market trends and developments to be more accurately reflected. Thus, in 1986, Edmond Malinvaud, a French economist of international repute, drafted a report that had a lasting impact. After examining some of the most strikingly ambivalent features of the overall situation, such as the practice of early retirement, or schemes situated mid-way between training and employment, Malinvaud stressed the need to preserve measurements based on international recommendations, while suggesting that these be enhanced by complementary indicators that would better reflect the diversification in the uses of labour. To this end, four complementary notions were analysed: visible under-employment (the situation of persons 'engaged in waged or non-waged employment, whether currently working or not, who, involuntarily, work at their job for less than normal working hours and who, during the reference period, were searching for, or available for, additional work'); on-the-job-training formulae; job creation and destruction; and, finally, disaffected workers (people who, while not actively seeking work, would in fact work if offered the possibility).

Without entering into all the debates and improvements linked to this delicate question of measurement, it is important to mention the most recent reform of significance, adopted in 2009 at the point when the economic crisis was really beginning to pinch in Europe and the United States. This reform put into effect proposals issued by the authors of a report entitled '*Emploi, chômage et précarité: mieux mesurer pour mieux débattre et mieux agir*' (employment, unemployment and precariousness: better measurement to facilitate debate and action). Chaired by Jean-Baptiste de Foucault, former Commissioner to the French Plan, the working group consulted members of the official statistics bodies, representatives of the trade unions, employer associations and other associations for which unemployment was a matter of concern (Conseil national de l'information statistique 2008). The points raised and the intentions stated related invariably to the need to put in place indicators better suited to reflecting the diversity of situations within, and on the fringes of, the labour market. With a view to gaining a 'richer view of the realities', the group issued thirty proposals, two of which led to immediate action: the first of these called on the Employment Minister and the public employment services to draw up new categories so as to make it perfectly clear that the indicators related to jobseekers registered at the end of each month with the national employment agency (which subsequently became *Pôle Emploi*). This recommendation was very quickly implemented, as we saw earlier (cf. Table 11.2).

A second suggestion was along the same lines as the renewal promoted in 1998 by the ILO which proposed putting in place new indicators that would enable the precarious aspects of employment to show up more clearly. To this end, the French working group proposed seeking objective measure of the unemployment 'halo' (i.e. inactive persons who would actually like to work), of under-employment (those employed part-time and wishing to work longer hours), and of unsatisfactory employment (persons dissatisfied with their current job who would like a different one). INSEE thus began to use the notion of 'unemployment halo' to classify jobless persons wishing to work but not classified as unemployed (persons not actually seeking a job; those currently una-vailable for work because of studies, childcare responsibilities, etc.). The numbers of those falling into this 'halo' category are far from insignifi-cant: during the first half of the 2000s the figure was almost 1.1 million, and the crisis manifestly served to exacerbate the phenomenon so that, in 2017, the 'halo' contained an additional 400,000 persons.

Today INSEE also provides information on under-employment, a phenomenon it describes along the lines of the ILO definition of 1998, namely, persons working part-time and who would like to work longer hours and who are either seeking a job or are available to work longer, as well as persons who have involuntarily worked less than usual (because of lay-offs, for example) whether employed full-time or part-time. Here too, the numbers of persons concerned are far from negligible. In the first quarter of 2017, 6.2% of employed persons were under-employed according to the above definition.

While statistical refinements of this kind do appear to enhance accuracy, the risk is that the overall category of 'unemployed person' will be divested of all statistical and social significance. In 1996, in an official report to the Prime Minister (Castel et al. 1997) and at a time when France had 3 million unemployed, some attempts had been made to amplify the counts by adding to the 'official unemployed' all those whose jobs were in any way insecure. This calculation led to a total of almost seven million persons affected, more or less directly, by the condition of unemployment.

The difficulty of seeking to adjust an instrument of measurement by relaxing the conventions that governed the initial formulation of the cat-egory of unemployment, while at the same time increasing the numbers of indicators, here becomes clearly apparent. This difficulty is, at bottom, epistemological. As Alain Desrosières correctly pointed out, the

'pressure to supply the "right figure", and the metaphors used to draw attention to inaccuracies, result from the fact that social statistics have been constructed, legitimised and disseminated on the basis of the realistic met-ronomic methods of the natural sciences. Reality exists prior to its observa-tion, just as the polar star existed long before the astronomers came along. But the epistemology applicable to the definition and measurement of the working population and of unemployment is not the same as that applica-ble to the polar star. The former endeavour entails conventions (compa-rable with the general principles governing legislation and codes voted by Parliaments) and decisions (comparable to those of a judge) concerning the placing of a given case in a given category'. (Desrosières 2008, 159)

It is appropriate, therefore, to alter one's analytical lens if the aim is to understand changes in the category of unemployment. The first, and perhaps most important, implication is to take seriously the political stakes of unemployment figures and, as a result, to divest oneself of all the rhetoric about 'correct measurement' in order to cast light on the myriad decisions, small and large, that have affected unemployment figures over recent decades.

Pragmatics: The Politics of Figures, the Stakes and the Strategies

In France, unemployment figures, because they constitute a first-order indicator of the success of the current government, are a regular focus for media coverage. The political character of the unemployment rate serves to explain why the authorities have, for a very long time already, fallen prey to the regular temptation to juggle with the counting rules. It was thus not totally by chance that in 1985, when important elections were imminent, a rule was introduced exempting elderly unemployed persons from job searches. During similarly politically sensitive periods, training courses have been offered to the long-term unemployed (in June 1985 and summer 1987). Whatever benefits they may have entailed for their beneficiaries, one salient feature of such schemes was that, at the outcome of the course, participants' days-of-unemployment count was put back to zero. History repeated itself yet again only recently. On the occasion of the Presidential new year wishes for 2016, François Hollande, whose party had just suffered a painful defeat in the regional council elections, promised a 'jobs of the future'[9] training plan that would benefit half a million unemployed persons. An immediate objection voiced by Jean-Claude Mailly, confederal secretary of *Force Ouvrière*, one of the most important trade union confederations in France, was that a strategy of this kind was a convenient means of shifting jobseekers registered in Category A to Category D. 'The government had promised to reverse the rising unemployment', Mr Mailly pointed out, 'and as the presidential election was coming up, a way had to be found of pushing down the figures'.[10]

These petty strategies are not always effective. In 1994 the ANPE (later the *Pôle Emploi*) was reprimanded by the Council of State which revoked a set of measures adopted by the employment agency to achieve an artificial reduction in the unemployment figures. The Council of State initially contested the fact that unemployed persons had been removed from the lists before they had been given a chance to submit their observations; it also judged it excessive to regard a person engaged in voluntary work as not immediately available to take up employment (a woman jobseeker employed as a volunteer in a food bank had on these grounds been deprived of her unemployment benefit). The Council of State further contested the ANPE practice of asking persons of European origin resident in France for more than three years to provide proof of their EU-national status.

Another means of bending the figures, especially at a critical juncture, is to exempt certain categories of jobseeker from the active job search requirement on the grounds of their low employability (because of age, state of health, etc.). This happened in 2016 in relation to almost 26,000 persons aged over 60 in receipt of allowances in the ARE, ASS or AER categories (see Box 1). The public authorities can also achieve reductions in numbers by increasing the constraints on those registered and then removing from the lists any who fail to comply with the bureaucratic rules or, alternatively, failing to count those who do not re-register in time. Between 1996 and 2006, as indicated by the monthly ANPE statistics published by the Employment Ministry, the risks of being removed from the lists were increasing, having risen from 0.2% at the beginning of the period to 1.4% with the introduction of the 'Plan to assist a return to employment' (known as the Pare[11]) in 2001. The explanation for this increase was that since the Plan in question entailed a tightening of the contractual relationship between the jobseeker and the public employment services, it simultaneously boosted the risks of being removed from the lists. In 2006 a new stage was entered with the introduction, as from the fourth month of unemployment, of 'personalised monthly monitoring' (the previous basic frequency of meetings having been quarterly). At this point, the risk of removal from the lists rose to 1.7%. Yet, very quickly, the system revealed its limits, in particular because the staff of the national employment agency—some of whom had to keep track of more than 200 jobseekers at any one time—found it materially impossible to organise all the meetings. For this reason, in 2010, the arrangement was relaxed.

In 2008 *Pôle Emploi* came up with a new reason for removing jobseekers from the lists: refusal of two 'reasonable offers of employment'. Now, what is to be regarded as a 'reasonable offer of employment'? The answer depends solely on the'personal project for access to employment' initially signed by the jobseeker on registering with *Pôle Emploi* (which may have been amended in the meantime).[12] Specifically, the reasonable offer of employment takes account of the following criteria: type of work sought; permanent, fixed-term or other type of contract preferred; part-time or full-time preferred; geographical area in which work is sought; minimum acceptable gross pay.

History has taken it upon itself to give renewed topicality to this recurrent temptation to place the unemployed under supervision on the grounds that they might be tempted to abuse the benefits system. On 2 September 2014, during a period when the high unemployment rate was a menacing cloud in the French political sky, François Rebsamen, the Minister of Employment, asked *Pôle Emploi* 'to step up supervision to check that jobseekers are genuinely taking steps to seek employment'. Supported by some trade unions, such as the CFDT (which sees it as a means of stepping up contact when necessary to improve *Pôle Emploi*'s efforts in assisting the unemployed[13]) the idea was rejected in other quarters, above all when, a few months later, it was put into action. Some jobseekers who were members of the CGT did not mince their words:

> The decision has been taken. At the board meeting on 15 April 2015, *Pôle Emploi* decided to go the full hog in policing the unemployed: "All job-seekers are liable to be subject to supervision, whether 'targeted', in the form of 'random checks' or following receipt of incriminating informa-tion." 200 agents will be recruited in the near future for this noble task, for implementation throughout France in August. The purpose of the mis-sion? To remove one in seven from the lists, as has already happened in Poitou-Charentes, a "pilot region" in policing of the unemployed. And also, of course, to put pressure on the unemployed to get them to accept increasingly precarious and ill-paid jobs.[14]

More recently still, during the 2017 presidential campaign, future President Emmanuel Macron promised, if he were elected, to extend unemployment insurance to all who had a work record (including the non-waged and those who had resigned their jobs) and, as a counter-measure, to suspend the benefits of all unemployed persons who had refused more than two 'decent' jobs (in relation to the criteria of pay and qualifications). To 'punish and then make the culprits invisible' would seem, decidedly, to represent a recurrent liberal temptation.

CONCLUSION

By means of whatever register it is approached, the language of unemployment seems today quite obsolete. On the semantic level, between the conventions initially adopted to define unemployment and the realities that attempts are today being made to pinpoint, name and measure, the gap has been growing, in recent decades, at an accelerated pace. On the syntactic level, the unending quest for the *right* figures—in the *plural*—reveals, without the need to look any further, the difficulty of devising coherent indicators for unemployment. A form of metronomic realism, by virtue of which unemployment is believed to be an external reality lending itself to objective measurement (always provided the right tools can be found) is a persistent feature of the French mentality. It is, in any case, in the name of such a belief that, just after the 2008 crisis had struck, new indicators were forged to account, with a finer accuracy and in greater detail, for the changes in unemployment, employment, and inactivity, and to describe the numerous grey areas—or 'halos'—surrounding them. Even if their ploys actually fool no one, it is nonetheless remarkable to witness, this time on a pragmatic register, the frequency with which the public authorities are tempted to adjust the measuring instrument in an attempt to mitigate the politically disastrous impact of escalating unemployment figures. The effects of strategies of this kind are—at least in appearance—never neutral: in 1995 the introduction of categories 6, 7 and 8 automatically produced a 200,000 drop in the numbers of the unemployed, translating into a 5% reduction in the unemployment rate.

The permanent gap between the phenomenology of unemployment and the mode in which it is categorised comes as no surprise. As pointed out by Reinhart Koselleck,

> as in the domain of history as it is happening, the gap between action and discourse retrospectively prevents social "reality" from ever converging with the history of its manifestation in language. Even if language acts and actual acts remain entwined in synchrony – which is itself an abstraction –, the diachronic evolution – which itself remains a theoretical construction – does not follow the same rhythms or the same chronology in "real" history as in the history of concepts. It sometimes happens that reality has changed well before its evolution has been conceptualised, and it can also turn out that concepts were devised that opened up the way to new realities. (Koselleck 1997, 156)

This thesis is perfectly illustrated by the observations we have recorded here. The constant to- and fro-ing observed in France between the search for the right figure—or figures—and the strategic use made of indicators should not serve to obscure, more generally, the structural transformations that have led, decade after decade, to erosion of the pillars that underpinned the category of unemployment. The new elements used today to classify the jobless population hardly lend themselves to the construction, with any degree of confidence, of a new category of unemployment. This observation receives further confirmation—as testified by the rise in the numbers of 'working poor'[15]—from the increasingly porous nature of the boundaries between employment, activity and unemployment. One lesson to be learned might lead to doing away entirely with the terms 'unemployment' and 'unemployed', in favour of new semantic forms. Yet, as we are still wading through these muddy waters, whatever may lie on the other side remains to be invented.[16]

NOTES

1. An alternative option originally featured also, distinguishing forms of unemployment on the basis of their cause (sickness or disability, off-season, accidental lack of work, other cause), but this was dropped in 1901.
2. The Assedics, of which there were twenty before the merger with the ANPE, were set up in 1958 and headed by the Unedic.
3. In 1931, for example, the unemployed whose entitlement was about to expire and who were thus deprived of a minimum income, were directed to welfare offices that could provide assistance after a means-testing procedure. The effectiveness of this arrangement was, in reality, very limited.
4. The census distinguishes outworkers and homeworkers from other wage-earners and in practice prohibits them from being described as 'unemployed' because they are not subject to orders or supervision.
5. The definition adopted by the ILO in 1982 was as follows: an unemployed person is one of working age (15 or above) who simultaneously fulfils three conditions: to be jobless, that is, not to have worked even for one hour during a reference week; to be available to take up work within a fortnight; to have actively sought a job during the preceding month or to have found one that begins in less than three months.
6. In 2016 the French unemployment rate broken down according to level of educational achievement was as follows: without school-leaving qualification 17.9%; school-leaving qualification (10.7%); school-leaving qualification +2 or more (5.7%).

7. The *revenu de solidarité active* (RSA) is a minimum income that was paid to almost 2.5 million persons in 2016. Since its experimental introduction in 2007, receipt of the RSA entails the obligation for the beneficiary to seek work or to draw up an occupational plan intended to improve her/his financial situation.

8. For a clearer understanding of the answers to this important question proposed before the 1980s, see, in particular, F. Michon (1975) and J. L. Besson et al. (1981).

9. This was no new idea: in 2013 the Socialist government had already adopted a priority training plan for 30,000 jobseekers, with the promise that it would be extended to cover 100,000 a year in 2014 and 2015.

10. 'Le plan de formation de 500,000 chômeurs de Hollande, à peine annoncé et déjà critiqué', *Le Monde*, 5 January 2016.

11. The Pare is a binding contract between the unemployed person and the public employment service. The jobseeker must have a 'project', in return for which the public employment service undertakes to accompany him/her more closely in the effort to carry it through.

12. Article L5411-6-2 of the French Labour Code stipulates that 'the nature and the characteristics of the job or jobs sought, the preferred geographical area and expected pay level, as stated in the personalised project for access to employment, are constitutive of the reasonable offer of employment'.

13. 'Supervision in the service of better accompaniment of the unemployed', CFDT press release, statement by V. Descacq, 15 October 2014.

14. http://cgtchomeursrebelles56.blogspot.fr/2015/05/renforcement-des-controles-pole-emploi.html.

15. Attributable in large part to the development of precarious forms of work and to the 'success' of part-time jobs, the explosion in the numbers of working poor affects between one and two million persons, depending on the definition adopted.

16. Translation from the French by Kathleen Llanwarne.

References

Besson, Jean-Louis, Paul Rousset, and Maurice Comte. 1981. *Compter les chômeurs.* Lyon: Presses universitaires de Lyon.

Bourdieu, Pierre. 1963. "Etude sociologique." In *Travail et travailleurs en Algérie*, edited by Pierre Bourdieu, Alain Darbel, Jean-Paul Rivet, and Claude Seibel, 257–389. Paris: Mouton.

Castel, Robert, Jean-Paul Fitoussi, Jacques Freyssinet, and Henry Guaino. 1997. *Chômage: le cas français.* Rapport au Premier ministre. Paris: La documentation française.

Conseil national de l'information statistique. 2008. "Mieux mesurer pour mieux débattre et mieux agir. Présentation du rapport du groupe présidé par Jean-Baptiste de Foucauld." *Chroniques* 8, 6 pages.

Conseil supérieur du Travail. 1896. *Rapport sur la question du chômage.* Paris: Imprimerie Nationale.

Dares. 2015. "Statistiques sur les demandeurs d'emploi inscrits et les offres collectées par Pôle emploi. Documentation pédagogique." 24 juin, 9 pages.

Demazière, Didier. 1992. *Le chômage en crise. La négociation des identités des chômeurs de longue durée.* Lille: Presses universitaires de Lille.

Demazière, Didier. 2003. *Le chômage. Comment peut-on être chômeur?* Paris: Belin.

Desrosières, Alain. 2008. *Pour une sociologie historique de la quantification. L'argument statistique.* Paris: Presses de l'école des Mines.

Durkheim, Emile. 1912. *Les formes élémentaires de la vie religieuse.* Paris: Alcan.

Gautié, Jérôme. 2002. "De l'invention du chômage à sa déconstruction." *Genèses* 46 (1): 60–76.

Giraud, Olivier. 2014. "Dynamique des normes d'emploi et citoyenneté des femmes en France. De l'entraide conjugale à la reconnaissance du travail, de l'emploi et des droits sociaux des conjointes d'indépendants." *Les Cahiers du Lise* 7.

Insee. 2017. "Le taux de chômage diminue de 0,4 points au premier trimestre 2017." *Informations rapides* 131.

Koselleck, Reinhart. 1997. *L'expérience de l'histoire.* Paris: Seuil.

Lallement, Michel. 1991. *Des PME en chambre. Travail et travailleurs d'hier et d'aujourd'hui.* Paris: L'Harmattan.

Laroque, Guy, and Bernard Salanié. 2000. "Une décomposition du non emploi en France." *Economie et statistique* 331 (1): 47–60.

Lê Jérôme, Sylvie Le Minez, and Marie Rey. 2014. "Chômage de longue durée: la crise a frappé plus durement ceux qui étaient déjà les plus exposés." *France—Portrait social,* 41–54. Paris: Insee.

Malinvaud, Edmond. 1986. *Sur les statistiques de l'emploi et du chômage.* Paris: La Documentation française.

Maruani, Margaret. 2002. *Les mécomptes du chômage.* Paris: Bayard.

Maruani, Margaret, and Monique Méron. 2012. *Un siècle de travail des femmes en France.* Paris: La découverte.

Michon, François. 1975. *Chômeurs et chômage.* Paris: Presses universitaires de France.

Muller, Martine. 1991. *Le pointage ou le placement: Histoire de l'ANPE.* Paris: L'Harmattan.

Reynaud-Cressent, Bénédicte. 1984. "L'émergence de la catégorie de chômeur à la fin du XIXème siècle." *Economie et statistique* 165 (1): 53–63.

Salais, Robert, Baverez Nicolas, and Reynaud Bénédicte. 1986. *L'invention du chômage*. Paris: Presses universitaires de France.

Topalov, Christian. 1987. "Invention du chômage et politiques sociales au début du siècle." *Les Temps Modernes* 496 (497): 53–92.

Topalov, Christian. 1994. *Naissance du chômeur 1880–1910*. Paris: Albin Michel.

CHAPTER 12

Counting Working Women in France: The Figures Are Political

Margaret Maruani and Monique Meron

Figures are political. We know this is true of the unemployment rate and the prices index. Do people realise it might also apply to the female employment figures? Yet it is sociologically self-evident, because every society, every era and every culture produces its own forms of female employment and shapes how it is viewed and represented. And statistics play a very active role in this social construct.

COUNTING WOMEN'S WORK: BY NO MEANS STRAIGHTFORWARD!

Counting the number of working women in twentieth-century France and recounting the story behind those figures is what *Un siècle de travail en France 1901–2011*[1] *(A century of work in France 1901–2011)* sets out to do. It so happens that counting (= telling numbers) and recounting

M. Maruani (✉)
National Center for Scientific Research (CNRS), Paris, France

M. Meron
Center for Research in Economics and Statistics (CREST), Paris, France

© The Author(s) 2019
A. Serrano-Pascual and M. Jepsen (Eds.),
The Deconstruction of Employment as a Political Question,
https://doi.org/10.1007/978-3-319-93617-8_12

271

(= telling a story) come from the same Latin word *computare*. No coincidence, then…

By analysing sociologically how statistics and their definitions have changed with time and between population censuses, we can see how women's work has often raised doubts: it has been miscalculated, underrated and sometimes recalculated in the light of optical illusions created by changes in statistical boundaries.

There is also the question of the visibility of women's work. What types of work were not measured, and when, and why? Where is the dividing line between an identifiable job and informal work? What is the difference between a farmer's wife and a female farmer? Between a maid and a domestic worker? Between a doctor's wife and a medical secretary? How have they been counted, omitted, recalculated, deleted or recognised over the years? How is female labour counted? What do people mean by activity, work and employment for women?

The problem of defining what people call and count as 'work' for women is a common thread that runs through past censuses: 'the classification of women is often a matter of interpretation', 'we do not have a specific criterion for classifying women…' is something you can read in every volume of French population censuses in the early twentieth century.

Because as well as problems with reading the figures, there are also questions about the visibility of women's work. Women are always implicitly suspected of being inactive: if a female farmer is standing in a field, is she working or just looking at the countryside? If a female worker is made redundant, is she unemployed or 'returning home'? These recurring and regrettable questions, which are only ever asked about women, show the contrast between male employment, which is taken for granted, and female employment, which is seen as incidental.

At the start of the century, most women worked at home, whether as farmers or 'on their own', such as seamstresses paid piece rates, etc. In the twenty-first century almost all women are employees and work outside the home, even if it is just 'for a few hours'. As wage earning has become more widespread, their labour has now become visible and independent of their family status. Female employees are working and earning a living, regardless of their family situation and their husband's occupation. Wage earning confirms the divorce between occupational and family status, and that changes everything. For a number of decades now it has no longer been the 'unworthy and wretched' situation whose history is described so clearly by Robert Castel in *Les métamorphoses de la question social* (Transformation of the social question). For women, in the second half of the twentieth century, it has been a stepping stone to financial independence—a big step towards freedom.

Declaring or not declaring a paid activity or an occupation, separating the social function associated with work, employment or a job from other more domestic or strictly family functions, means establishing oneself as a member of an economic society. They are acts which are symptomatic of the way women's work and, more broadly, their role in society have been viewed at various times. By looking at how statistics have been drawn up on the occupational activity of women over the years, we can tell something about the history of their status. Women's work is a key theme for understanding the position of women in society, in all societies today. In that sense, defining the boundaries of women's work is a highly political issue.

EXAMINING HOW STATISTICS ARE PRODUCED

As we know, the procedures used to collect and process data influence how their results are interpreted.

In the early twentieth century, data were already mechanised, centralised and relatively homogeneous from one census to the next (previously, censuses were processed at the *département* level and were much more irregular). The 'statistics ladies' at the *Statistique générale de la France*, forerunner of Insee (the French National Institute of Statistics and Economic Studies), used Lucien March's classifier-counter-printer from 1901 to 1940. Next came the development of mechanised accounting, to be replaced by data processing from 1968.

Our aim here is to take the basic figures and look at how and why their meaning changes over time, to quantify and decipher, and to examine how statistics are produced. Without seeking to judge yesterday's world by today's values, we will try to identify the approaches adopted when each period's figures were produced, and to use the statistics on and definitions of activity to understand the stories and social codes that defined the boundaries of 'women's work'.

Taking every population census since 1901, it is useful to look at the various wrinkles and cracks without trying to gloss over them, and without recalculating women's work throughout the twentieth century using today's definitions.

This approach of re-emphasising how definitions have changed allows us to debunk a few myths, answer recurring questions and ask a few questions ourselves (Table 12.1). Between 1901 and the start of the twenty-first century the active population grew from just under 7 to 15 million for women and from 13 to 16 million for men: a huge leap for women, a small step for men. This might have been the result we expected, but we had not imagined just how big the increase would be for women, or how big a difference there would be between the increases for men and women. Then there were other surprises...

Table 12.1 Active population in France 1901–2012 (in millions, taken directly from population censuses)

	Men	Women	Together	Proportion of women in the active population (%)
1901	12.91	6.80	19.71	34.5
1906	13.03	7.69	20.72	37.1
1911	13.21	7.72	20.93	36.9
1921 (87 départements)	12.53	8.31	20.84	39.9
1921 (90 départements)	13.11	8.61	21.72	39.6
1926	13.56	7.84	21.39	36.7
1931	13.71	7.90	21.61	36.6
1936	12.94	7.32	20.26	36.1
1946	12.67	7.85	20.52	38.3
1954 (1946 concept)	12.74	7.61	20.35	37.4
1954 (1954 concept)	12.71[a]	6.64	19.35	34.3
1962	13.17	6.59	19.76	33.4
1968	13.55	7.14	20.69	34.5
1975	13.97	8.25	22.22	37.1
1982	14.25	9.63	23.88	40.3
1990	14.23	11.04	25.28	43.7
1999	14.38	12.18	26.55	45.9
2007[b]	15.19	13.78	28.97	47.6
2012[b]	15.51	14.42	29.93	48.2

Coverage Active employed population + unemployed population, including conscripts, in mainland France
Source Population censuses 1901–2012
[a] recalculated adding conscripts (leading to double counting in some cases, since conscripts who had already worked were sometimes already counted in their former occupation)
[b] the twenty first century censuses are the product of five years of surveys, so the "2012" census is actually a weighted compilation of the years 2010–2014

A STATISTICAL OPTICAL ILLUSION: 1954

Some questions seem fairly simplistic: are women working a lot more in 2010 than in 1950, 1920 or 1901? What changes mark the development of their activity?

In actual fact, however, these questions are anything but simple! The curve showing the development of women's contribution to economic activity, constructed from gross figures taken from each of the population censuses throughout the century, is highly informative—and full of surprises (Fig. 12.1).

The first thing to note is that women's work has undoubtedly made a major and remarkably consistent contribution to the functioning of the economy, despite various crises and recessions, and long after the wars and the years immediately following had gone by. Women's share of the world of work in twentieth century France has never been less than a third and now amounts to almost half of the active population.

Having said that, if we compare the definitions and concepts used in the past with those of more recent times, we can identify a few 'statistical illusions' that have resulted from reconstructing data in order to eliminate changes of definition.

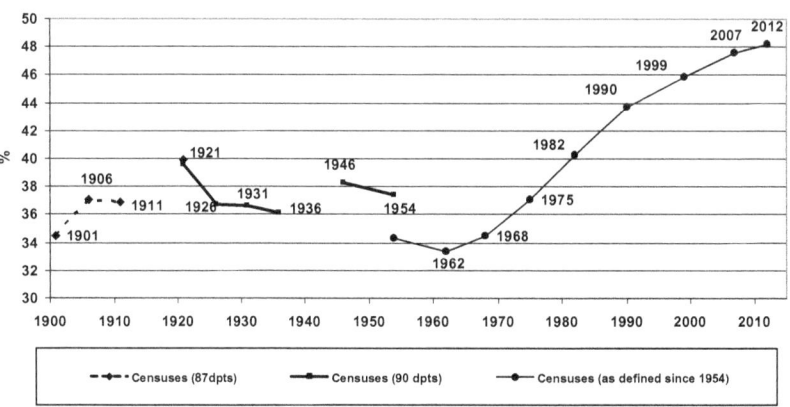

Fig. 12.1 Proportion of women in the active population from 1901 to 2012 [Key: Censuses (87 dépts). Censuses (90 dépts) Censuses (as defined since 1954)] *Coverage* Mainland France (87 then 90 départements in 1921) (*Source* population censuses)

1954 is a particularly striking example of this. The usual story about women's work in twentieth century France is that their activity declined from 1901 to 1962. This idea has been widely repeated by historians and sociologists (including women). Yet if we take account of changes in the definition of agricultural activity, it seems clear that there was no general downward trend in female activity in the first half of the century.

The so-called 'decline in female activity between 1901 and 1962' is quite simply a statistical illusion caused by a change of definition.

So what happened? At the start of the century, all adults (aged 14–70) living with a farmer and with no other declared occupation were classified as being farmers themselves. This mainly involved their wives, who were then defined as female farmers. In 1954, it was decided that only those who explicitly declared that they were farmers should be counted. Many women were suddenly classified as inactive even though, up to that point, the opposite had been assumed. So all of a sudden farmer's wives became 'inactive', watching the cows go by as they did the washing up.

The economists Jean Jacques Carré, Pierre Dubois and Edmond Malinvaud (1972) in *la croissance française* (*French growth*), along with Olivier Marchand and Claude Thélot (1991) in *Deux siècles de travail en France* (*Two centuries of work in France*), contributed to this false impression. Their decision to 'backward-extrapolate', in other words to recalculate female activity in the first half of the twentieth century on the basis of the new 1954 definition, created the illusion of a drop in female activity. This was not the view of Jean Daric who, in a work produced by Ined (the French Institute for Demographic Studies) in 1947 on *L'activité professionnelle des femmes en France* (*Women's activity in France*), had not detected any reduction in female activity at the start of the century but, on the contrary, found that their presence on the labour market was fairly constant.

In one fell swoop the change of definition in 1954 removed 1.2 million people—including nearly 1 million women—from the active population. And then the numbers of active women throughout the whole of the first half of the twentieth century were recalculated and remodelled on the basis of the new 1954 definition. So the number of working women seemed to decline inexorably between 1901 and 1954.

This schism played a major part in the spread of the myth that female activity declined in the early twentieth century: between 1901 and 1954, women's work was recalculated downwards on the basis of this new definition.

IN THE TWENTY-FIRST CENTURY THE STORY CONTINUES...

After the change of definition in 1954, the rise in female activity seen since the 1960s started from an artificially low point (since many farmers' wives were not counted as active). This therefore appears to have boosted the growth in female activity, which is still happening now, particularly as, since the start of the twenty-first century, statistics have focused on 'employment at all cost': one hour of paid work per week is enough to count students, the unemployed or retired people as having 'a job'. For women, a few hours of childcare or cleaning are enough to classify them as being in employment. These traditional definitions (activity, employment and unemployment are still defined according to criteria established in 1982 by the International Labour Office) are now applied to the letter, much more strictly than before, and this artificially increases the employment rates. EU targets have been set on this basis: increasing the employment rate at all cost. Female activity is more widespread than ever, but what sort of jobs or low-grade work are involved?

Other phenomena—secular trends relating to work done by young people and the elderly—have now been reversed. The disappearance of child labour and the reduction in work by young people as more and more attended school, on the one hand, and more widespread access to pension rights on the other, explain why the activity of the youngest and oldest fell throughout the twentieth century. But these trends too have recently been thrown into reverse. Young people have stopped extending their studies and reforms have increased the retirement age, and both of these turnarounds have been accentuated by the new focus on increasing employment rates advocated by the European Union. Changes to the procedures and particularly the questionnaires used in the census and then the Employment Survey have encouraged responses reporting, more so than previously, employment in two situations. These changes are altering the official view of the labour market.

UNEMPLOYMENT AND ITS HALO

The unemployment figures are increasingly being used as social policy indicators. For decades, women were more affected by unemployment than men. But now a recent phenomenon is becoming established: with the economic crisis that began in 2008, the unemployment curves for men and women have met and then crossed, so that the number of men out of work is now higher than the number of women and, since 2012, the male unemployment rate is higher than the female. In 2015 the gap widened, with the female unemployment rate falling while the male rate increased.

The reasons for this reversal have to do with the type of jobs that have disappeared with the crisis: industry and construction, both sectors that were particularly badly hit, employ mainly men, whereas services, which employ more women, have fared a little better, or survived more unscathed.

However, we must not forget that women are much more likely to work part-time than men, and many women end up inactive, particularly where they are unskilled and expect to be on a low wage, in an insecure job and paying a lot for childcare, for instance.

These findings raise the question of how recognised unemployment is defined, and the fairly arbitrary boundaries between the various concepts. For inactivity, the 'halo' around unemployment is measured,[2] which includes those close to the labour market, potential but deterred workers, those deemed to have not tried hard enough to find work, or those not available to take a job. For employment, underemployment is evaluated by counting those working less than normal hours involuntarily and who would like to work more. Although there are fewer women than men in 'official' unemployment, there are clearly more women than men in these invisible reserves of potential workers.

The 'official' (international) definition of the unemployment count was set out by the International Labour Office in 1982, but has been adjusted several times since then.

To be unemployed, a person must not have a job or have worked in the reference week 'even for an hour'. He or she must be 'available' to start work within the next two weeks, and have either found a job that they are waiting to start or have 'actively sought' work in the previous month, all steps which are very precisely listed in the Employment Survey questionnaire, the source of the official (annual and quarterly) unemployment figures. These 'actions' are controversial and are changing: for instance, internet jobseeking is now counted. However, in 2007 and 2013 some changes were made as regards interpretation and the questions asked.

In 2007 for example, some actions were suddenly deemed insufficient for a person to be counted as unemployed. For instance, complying with the conditions for registration with the job centre (in order to be kept on its files) is no longer viewed as an actual action. This slight variation in definition alone has cut the French unemployment rate by 0.7%! The various different[3] adjustments have resulted, all in all, in a sizeable reduction in the unemployment rate (1% on around 10% in 2007, which is significant). The impact has been greater for women, with the number of female unemployed falling more than the number of men (Fig. 12.2).

In 2013, the definition of unemployment was adjusted again in a further attempt to ensure that the definitions advocated by Europe were better applied to national concepts. These changes of criteria, procedure and questions asked in the Employment Survey have meant that many of those previously counted as unemployed ended up in the 'unemployment halo', or in other words were classified as inactive: in 2013, the new definition increased the halo from 841,000 to 1.294 million people, a difference of 463,000, half of them due to the change of concept (EU harmonisation) and half due to the change of questions in the Employment Survey. Thus, this 'halo' made up of people lacking one of the criteria for being 'unemployed' in the eyes of the ILO has grown to represent over half of those officially unemployed: in

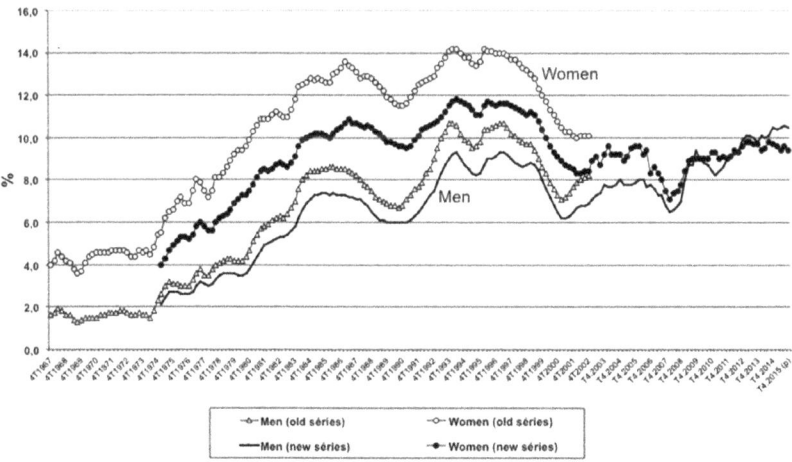

Fig. 12.2 Unemployment rate by sex, 1967–2002 and 1975–2015 *Coverage* Mainland France (*Source* Insee Employment Surveys [quarterly results])

2013, the unemployment halo covered 1,294,000 people (compared with 841,000 previously), out of the 2,813,000 unemployed counted with the new definition. Here again, the impact was greater on women than men. These findings provide food for thought on the differences between an unemployed man and an unemployed woman. The two sexes do not necessarily take the same sort of actions to look for work; the availability criteria do not have the same impact. It is women who are more often in the unemployment halo because of their lack of availability.

Thus, the 2015 Employment Survey counted an average of 1.560 million unemployed men and 1.308 million unemployed women. However, at the same time, 636,000 men and 790,000 women were in the unemployment halo. These were people without a job and wanting to work but not available to take a job in the next two weeks, or who had not actively sought work in the month prior to the survey.

While 45.5% of those out of work were women, they accounted for 55.4% of the unemployment halo. There were no doubt more who were not immediately available (in the next two weeks) to take a job, or who had been deterred to the point where they were not looking for work, or who, according to the recent changes of definition, had not taken the 'right'[4] actions to be counted as unemployed. For example, women are perhaps more likely to go to Pôle Emploi (the French national employment agency) to find a job, without actively looking elsewhere. But merely registering and remaining registered with Pôle emploi or even going there regularly to look at the job advertisements no longer counts as actively seeking employment—no matter what the people concerned think.

However, the number of men counted in the unemployment halo is tending to increase more quickly than the number of women (between 2010 and 2015: + 145,000 men and + 52,000 women) (Table 12.2).

The Blurred Boundaries of Underemployment

Underemployment is another way of recording some of the effects of the jobs shortage. This indicator supplements the unemployment and unemployment halo indicators.

The concept of underemployment has been used in Insee surveys since 1990. Underemployment 'as defined by the ILO' and interpreted by Insee covers those working part-time who would like to work more hours and are available to do so, and those who have involuntarily

Table 12.2 Population in the unemployment halo (thousands)

	Men	Women	Together
1990	373	877	1251
1991	344	844	1189
1992	378	871	1250
1993	411	895	1306
1994	424	924	1348
1995	410	906	1316
1996	421	843	1264
1997	419	865	1284
1998	447	851	1298
1999	443	820	1264
2000	402	836	1238
2001	390	776	1166
2002	408	778	1186
2003	428	743	1171
2004	444	780	1224
2005	461	715	1176
2006	437	765	1203
2007	426	730	1156
2008	430	710	1140
2009	472	744	1216
2010	491	740	1231
2011	491	743	1234
2012	505	719	1224
2013	546	743	1289
2014	592	779	1371
2015	637	791	1429

Coverage Mainland France, persons aged 15 or over living in households

Source Insee, Employment Survey (annual average)

worked less than usual in the survey reference week (because of short-time working or bad weather).[5] This is what is known as visible underemployment, in other words, people who declare themselves and are counted as such. In fact, most of those who are underemployed are simply women who are working part-time and want to work more. Those who are in short-time work, both men and women, are far fewer. In 2015 France had almost 1.7 million underemployed, of whom over 1.2 million were women and almost 500,000 were men. Temporary lay-offs involved only 67,000 jobs.

Underemployment concerns 6.6% of all jobs, but almost one in 10 women (9.7%) and 3.7% of men.

Women thus make up the vast majority of the underemployed (71.1%). However, since the crisis, it is slightly more common for men to work part-time, and underemployment is growing more quickly for men (+95,000 since 2011) than for women (+70,000).

The jobs concerned are most often employees (12% of jobs), particularly in certain services (hotels and restaurants, personal services, etc.), sometimes blue-collar workers (5.8% of jobs), often unskilled, and only rarely management posts (2.6%) (Fig. 12.3; Table 12.3).

In 2008, France's interpretation of the definition of underemployment was changed to bring it into line with the ILO concept. First, the desire to work a greater number of hours was now expressed, as with the ILO measurement of unemployment, for a given week rather than within a particular time frame. This change made it impossible to compare

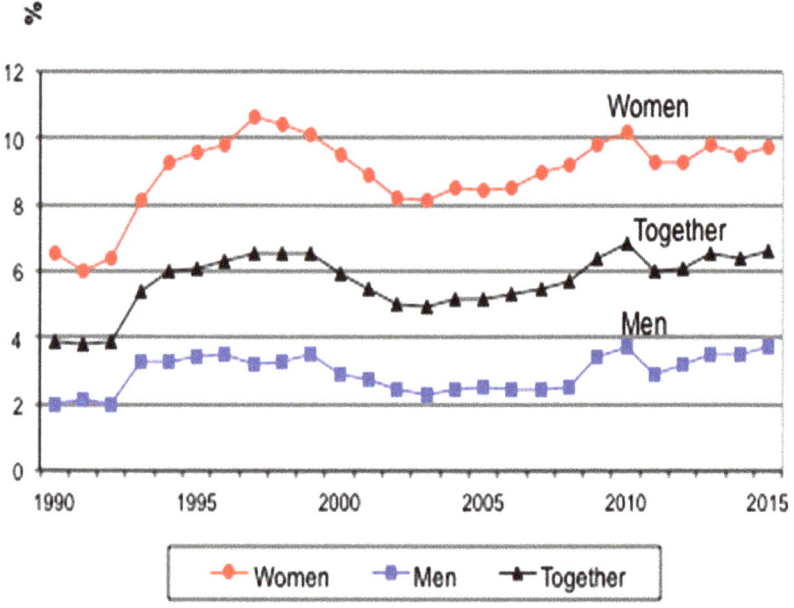

Fig. 12.3 Share of underemployment among those in employment *Coverage* Mainland France, population living in households, persons aged 15 and over (*Source* Insee, Employment Surveys 1990–2008 [corrected data for the breaks in series in 2002 and changes of definitions in 2008 and 2013])

Table 12.3 Underemployment, 1990–2015 (thousands)

	Population in underemployment (thousands)				
	Women	Men	Total	Total (2008 definition)	Difference
1990	638	264	902		
1991	594	274	867		
1992	638	261	898		
1993	805	420	1226		
1994	934	412	1345		
1995	974	433	1407		
1996	1000	452	1452		
1997	1087	410	1498		
1998	1087	415	1502		
1999	1067	452	1518		
2000	1036	378	1413		
2001	983	356	1339		
2002	923	319	1242		
2003	917	303	1220		
2004	980	315	1296		
2005	978	329	1308		
2006	1005	324	1329		
2007	1084	331	1416		
2008	1122	343	1465	1247	−218
2009	1198	452	1650	1380	−270
2010	1245	494	1739	1560	−179
2011	1137	396	1533		
2012	1147	433	1580		
2013	1206	476	1682		
2014	1178	464	1642		
2015	1207	491	1698		

Coverage Mainland France, population living in households, persons aged 15 and over
Source Insee, Employment Surveys 1990–2008 (corrected data for the breaks in series in 2002 and changes of definitions in 2008 and 2013)

the figures with previous levels. Second, those working part-time who wanted to work more hours, were looking for a job but were not available immediately were no longer counted as underemployed. The change of definition in 2008 had a very direct effect on the measurement of underemployment: all those who were not immediately available to work longer hours were no longer counted as underemployed. Between 2007 and 2008, the number of people recorded as underemployed fell dramatically, from 1,416,000 to 1,247,000. Almost 170,000 people were thus removed from the underemployment figures by a simple change of statistical definition. This completely artificial 'fall', you will not be surprised to learn, affected women much more than men: 136,000 fewer women, 32,000 fewer men.

Clearly, this change of definition was made for bureaucratic reasons (the need to harmonise international definitions), but confused the sociological understanding of underemployment: why did the fact of not being immediately available to work more hours cancel out the objective situation of being underemployed? According to these 'new standards', a check-out assistant working a few hours a week for pay that was well below the monthly guaranteed minimum wage and desperately wanting to work more to earn a decent living was no longer counted as underemployed if she did not immediately have suitable childcare arrangements in place for her children, or if she had no transport. However, making 'non-availability' such a key demarcation line for underemployment seemed sufficiently absurd for the rules to be changed again in the 2013 reforms. The dramatic drop that appeared in 2008 has since been removed from the long-term graphs. Recently, young people have more often been underemployed (12.5% of the working population aged 15–24 in 2015, compared with 6.3% aged 25–49 and 5.5% of those aged 50 or over), and their share is increasing more quickly than that of other groups. Employees with few qualifications (10.4% of those with no qualifications or with a basic school leaving certificate) are more likely to be underemployed than others.

Unemployment, part-time work and underemployment have at least one thing in common: their evaluation is uncertain, controversial and political. They are increasingly used as social policy indicators, and the successive revisions of their definitions have not been purely technical. They are political, and produce a view of the labour market where differences according to gender, age, occupation, qualifications and so on can be accurate, blurred or distorted, depending on the angle from which they are seen.

As far as gender is concerned, things are actually extremely complicated. For a number of decades unemployment has affected women more than men, even though reversals in recent years suggest that the trend is being turned around. Yet the female unemployment figures are extremely tricky, uncertain and shaky: for women and women alone worklessness always carries with it the shadow of inactivity. The dubious and ambiguous closeness between these two situations, and the fact that they can be confused (and that this is allowed), make analysis much more complicated, no matter what the period under consideration. When the definition of unemployment becomes more restrictive, more women than men end up in its 'halo'. However, in the present crisis period, given the position now held by women on the labour market, they appear to be faring better: it now tends to be men entering the ranks of the unemployed and its halo, or underemployment, even though the vast majority in these two latter categories are still women.

For underemployment and part-time work things remain relatively simple: since they have been covered by the surveys, it has been clear that these mainly concern women.

Of course, part-time work has changed substantially over the period under consideration. It already existed in the early twentieth century in some sectors (particularly retail), where both women and men worked part-time.[6] The part-time work that emerged from the 1970s onwards, however, was a specifically female form of employment. 'It's great for women' was the justification given for all the legislation and schemes designed to develop part-time work. With hindsight, we are starting— belatedly—to realise the lasting damage caused by this women-only form of employment: the development of part-time work has seen the growth of underemployment, low wages and in-work poverty. The rather dated idea of additional income is coming back into fashion. And part-time wages lead on to miserly pensions.

Part-time work grew from the ashes of full-time employment, pro- moted by public policies granting tax and social security concessions on part-time jobs. Between 1975 and 2008, of the 3,831,000 jobs created, two thirds (2,663,000) were part-time. For women, of the 3,762,000 jobs created, 2,287,000 (almost 70%) were part-time.[7]

The reduction in working hours and the abolition of specific conces- sions encouraging employers to take on part-time workers have slowed the progress of part-time working, for women at least. Because male jobs have been particularly affected by the crisis, the proportion of men in part-time jobs has increased: of women who had a job in 2015, 31% worked part-time, and this share has remained virtually unchanged throughout the 2000s; for men, the share of part-time jobs was over 7% in 2015, 2% more than in the early 2000s (Fig. 12.4; Table 12.4).

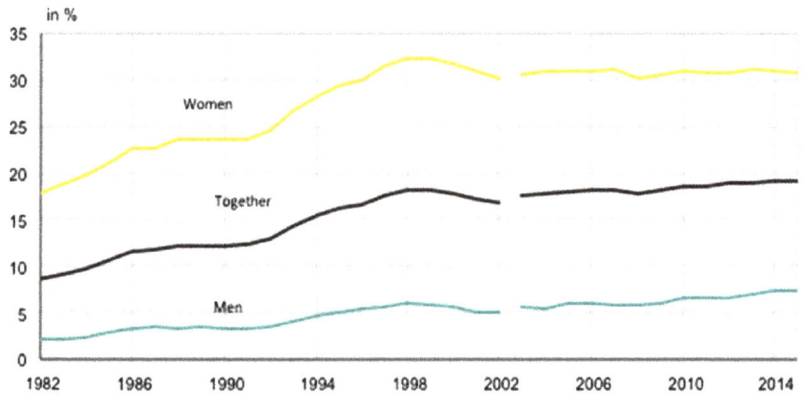

Fig. 12.4 Share of part-time work in paid employment 1982–2015 *Coverage* Mainland France, population living in households, persons aged 15 or over in paid employment *Note* Break in series in 2003, with the move from the Annual Employment Survey to the Continuous Employment Survey (*Source* Insee, Employment Surveys)

Like unemployment, underemployment and part-time work are symptoms of the jobs shortage. However, in the history of work in the twentieth century, part-time work presents a particular problem: it was a specifically female form of work that ran counter to the trend towards the homogenisation of male and female patterns of activity seen since the 1960s. It was actually created for women—'tailor-made' for them, as it were. Even though men are slightly more involved in part-time work— for want of anything better—than they were before the crisis, in 2015 81% of those working part-time were women. But going from that to saying that it suits women is another story. That would be creating a fable, a myth, a legend—or perhaps a social lie.

The main reason given by those working part-time is that they cannot work more hours in the job they occupy (50% of men and 42% of women, according to the Employment Survey). 26% of women say that they are part-time in order to look after children or a dependant (6% of men), which shows that family situation affects female activity, but much less than was thought: it concerns only a quarter of women working part-time.

Table 12.4 Share of part-time work in paid employment (in %)

	Together	Men	Women
1982	8.6	2.1	17.8
1983	9.0	2.1	18.7
1984	9.7	2.4	19.8
1985	10.6	2.9	21.0
1986	11.6	3.3	22.6
1987	11.7	3.4	22.6
1988	12.1	3.3	23.5
1989	12.2	3.5	23.6
1990	12.2	3.2	23.6
1991	12.3	3.2	23.6
1992	12.9	3.5	24.6
1993	14.4	4.1	26.7
1994	15.4	4.6	28.3
1995	16.2	5.1	29.4
9196	16.7	5.4	30.0
1997	17.6	5.7	31.5
1998	18.1	5.9	32.3
1999	18.1	5.8	32.2
2000	17.7	5.6	31.7
2001	17.2	5.1	31.0
2002	16.9	5.1	30.2
2003	17.6	5.6	30.6
2004	17.7	5.4	31.0
2005	18.0	5.9	30.9
2006	18.1	5.9	31.0
2007	18.2	5.8	31.1
2008	17.7	5.8	30.1
2009	18.2	6.0	30.6
2010	18.6	6.6	30.9
2011	18.6	6.6	30.8
2012	19.0	6.6	30.7
2013	19.0	6.9	31.2
2014	19.2	7.3	31.0
2015	19.1	7.4	30.7

Coverage Mainland France, population living in households, persons aged 15 or over in paid employment

Note Break in series in 2003, with the move from the Annual Employment Survey to the Continuous Employment Survey

Source Insee, Employment Surveys

PROFESSIONAL WORK AND DOMESTIC WORK: SHOULD THEY BE CLASSIFIED AS THE SAME?

The issue of the links between family structure and female activity is one that is often raised. For those aged between 25 and 49 the activity rate in mainland France is high (88% in 2015). It has stagnated for all women since 2010 (83% in 2015) after several decades of growth, and has fallen slightly for men (93%). Without children, activity rates among women (88%) and men (90%) in this age group are very similar; with children, and depending on their age, the gap increases: in large families[8] where the youngest child is under 3, fewer than one in two mothers (42%) and most fathers (93%) are on the labour market. The recurring question, given that this continues to be how responsibilities are shared, is whether those outside the labour market should continue to be regarded as 'inactive', particularly those who are taking time out to bring up their children and look after the home, who are far from being of no use to society. The International Labour Office, at its latest International Conference of Labour Statisticians (October 2013), advocated extending the measurement of work to include activities generally outside the labour market.

That raises a number of questions, which Pierre Concialdi (2014) among others addressed. Extending the conceptual framework of activity to encompass the concept of 'work', including paid employment but also voluntary work and domestic work, is part of the political determination to produce a better evaluation of living standards and 'well-being', and a better comparison of countries' economic performances. The traditional economic indicators (GDP, employment rate and unemployment rate, for example) ignore a large part of the work done by households, in the domestic context in particular.

The traditional boundary between 'active' and 'inactive' concealed a lot of domestic or voluntary 'work' done mainly by women. The ILO's discussions on the profile of what should be counted as 'work' and the resulting decisions—now or in the future—are clearly not going to be neutral on the question of the sharing of responsibilities between men and women in society.

In terms of terminology, it is good that those people (mainly women) who do not have and are not seeking paid work are no longer referred to as 'inactive'. The concept of 'labour force' is replacing 'active population', with 'inactive' now being called 'out of labour force' ('hors de la main-d'œuvre'), even if that presents translation problems. However, the question of the methods used to measure these new concepts is very important: in France, 'time use' surveys, the only accurate measurement of 'domestic work', are conducted only every 12 years, whereas the 'employment' survey, which monitors employment and unemployment, produces quarterly results.

Ultimately, the risks of confusion remain. Someone doing one hour's paid work per week is part of the 'labour force' and the labour market. The problems of boundaries have not been resolved for unpaid trainees, and the definition of payment for voluntary work remains blurred. As Pierre Concialdi points out, it is certainly commendable to survey all forms of work that contribute to people's 'well-being', but this new conceptual framework needs to be supplemented. With the lack of progress on defining inadequate employment, the new provisions are not entirely unambiguous. It is more than likely that, here again, as with underemployment now, women would be particularly affected by the clarification of these concepts. Should professional work and domestic work be classified as the same?

* *

In the world of work, women are anything but a 'minority'. The contribution made by their labour force has, over the years, been a huge and vital one. Their work has never been incidental for society, just as their wages are not just extra income for their families: women have never accounted for less than one third, and now represent just under half, of the workforce in the twentieth century. Despite crises and recessions, long after the wars and the years immediately following had gone by, women in France have really worked hard, in every period of the century.

But their work has often been viewed sceptically—is what they are doing really work? Throughout the twentieth century their labour has been recalculated, recalibrated and redefined.

Whether to recognise their activity as professional work or to dismiss it as inactivity is a political or perhaps even ideological decision, going beyond statistics. Whether or not to acknowledge the contribution made by women's work to the functioning of society is a significant choice that has huge implications.[9]

NOTES

1. Maruani Margaret and Meron Monique, *Un siècle de travail en France 1901–2011*, Paris, Ed. La Découverte, 2012.
2. The "unemployment halo" covers those without a job (or any link with an employer, and who have not worked during the reference week) and who would like to work, but do not meet all the criteria to be counted as unemployed: they have not "actively" sought employment in the previous 4 weeks or are not available to take a job in the next 2 weeks.
3. These adjustments relate to technical changes to the survey: weightings, criteria taken into account to be classified as "available" (15 days' illness may be regarded as being unavailable and switch a person's classification from unemployed to inactive). These changes have had less impact than the changes to the unemployment "actions".
4. I.e. the recognised actions on a precisely worded list in the Employment Survey.
5. Official definition since 2013. Before that they were persons "involuntarily working less than the normal duration of work determined for the activity, who were seeking or available for additional work".
6. Anne-Sophie Beau (2004) describes this very well in her book *Un siècle d'emplois précaires* (A century of insecure jobs), Payot, Paris 2004
7. Insee, long series, 2010.
8. "Large" families are those with 3 or more children at home.
9. Translation from the French by Julie Barnes

REFERENCES

Beau, Anne-Sophie. 2004. *Un siècle d'emplois précaires.* Paris: Payot.
Carré, Jean Jacques, Dubois Pierre, and Malinvaud Edmond. 1972. *la croissance française.* Paris: Le Seuil.
Castel, Robert. 1995. *Les métamorphoses de la question sociale.* Paris: Fayard.
Concialdi, Pierre. 2014. "Quand les statisticiens du travail définissent le travail." *Chronique internationale de l'IRES*, n° 145, mars 2014.
Marchand, Olivier, and Thélot Claude. 1991. *Deux siècles de travail en France.* Paris: Etudes Insee.
Maruani Margaret, and Meron Monique. 2012. *Un siècle de travail en France 1901–2011.* Paris: Ed. La Découverte.

CHAPTER 13

Transformation in the Meaning of Work Beyond the Institutional Sphere: The View from the Standpoint of Gender Relations and Differences

Carlos Prieto and Sofía Pérez de Guzmán

INTRODUCTION

We propose in this article to approach the question of 'the deconstruction of employment' and its condition as a 'floating signifier' from one specific angle. We set out to show that, although the origins of the current 'floating' quality of employment can be located in large measure in the institutional ramifications of the neoliberal order, its practical constitution—the specifically *social* aspect of employment as currently configured—can be fully understood only if the—hierarchically organised—moment of *reproduction* of the social order is brought into play and, in particular, the social

C. Prieto (✉)
Complutense University of Madrid, Madrid, Spain

S. Pérez de Guzmán
University of Cadiz, Cadiz, Spain

© The Author(s) 2019   291
A. Serrano-Pascual and M. Jepsen (Eds.),
The Deconstruction of Employment as a Political Question,
https://doi.org/10.1007/978-3-319-93617-8_13

ordering of the production and reproduction of life as it is manifested in gender relations. Such, then, is the principal subject of our article. For the purposes of our argument, we will follow the 'analytical deconstruction' approach and begin by recalling/explaining the meaning, significance and value attributed to work and employment in the current social order inspired by neoliberal convictions and practices. However, while this is an unavoidable starting point—and one that is also dealt with in other chapters of this book—our main interest will focus on deconstructing the meaning of the fabric of hierarchical relationships as they unfold in the *social order of the reproduction of life*, in order to demonstrate, at a subsequent stage, how this links up with the meaning and significance of *employment as placed within the institutional order of production*. We believe that it is essential to take account of these two worlds and of the interplay between them in order to reach a full and multidimensional understanding of the social configuration of employment. In the course of our arguments it will become apparent how the possibilities of altering the meaning of work—in our case, and more concretely 'down-grading' it—have as a necessary correlate a consideration of the meaning of *care*, currently ill understood at policy level, which continues to be based on a strong asymmetry in gender relations.

Weak Employment as a Starting Point

The descriptor that probably best sums up the meaning and value of labour and employment at the present time is 'weak' (Alonso 2001). This 'weakness', while inducing us to focus on the precarious character of jobs, actually goes far beyond this aspect. For it is not only precarious employment that is inherently weak; the adjective is applicable to employment taken as a whole. At the present time, there is *no* employment of which 'weakness' is not an attribute. To understand the meaning and value of employment today, there can be no better way than to reconstruct, albeit briefly, its genealogy. The history and meaning of the changes in labour and the treatment of workers span a long period beginning in the eighteenth and nineteenth centuries with the establishment of the classic liberal social order and continuing over more than two centuries down to the present day. This history begins with the invention of labour as a fundamental component of the liberal social order of the New Regime. It is there that labour appeared as a necessary component for the birth—and conceptualisation—of the new order which would consist in a society of individuals (by contrast with the society of estates of the Old Regime) regarded as free, autonomous, animated by passions, and closed in each on him- or herself. This form of work, or labour, is not just any kind of productive activity but solely that which is performed in and for the market, the overall coordinating force (Adam Smith's 'invisible hand'). This consideration and treatment of labour purely as a commodity had a twofold consequence. It entailed, above all else, an unacceptable deterioration in the labourers' working and living conditions.

At the same time, however, and in large part as a consequence of this deterioration, the new treatment of labour was also the driving force behind the greatest organisation and movement for the voicing of social demands in modern history, namely, the labour movement. The constant pressure exerted by the working classes in support of their demands to improve their own working and living conditions was to have the effect of turning labour into the most regulated social activity and the worker into the most recognised and protected figure, thereby bringing into being a new social order based on the wage-earning classes. This society of wage-earners was to reach its culmination in the 1960s and 1970s. The 1980s saw the beginnings of a counter-reform movement, neoliberal in inspiration, that down-graded labour and began to deprive workers of various forms of protection during a period when the central role of labour was being supplanted by the pre-eminence of the market and corporate business entities (Bilbao 1999). We are, at the present time, in the epicentre of this development.

Table 13.1 shows, in schematic form, the history of this broad historical process, distinguishing the types of social order that have succeeded one another since the birth of first-wave liberalism, and indicating the contrasting labour and employment standards that have developed during each period.

The characteristic features of labour and employment at the present time are fully consistent with the specific labour standard regulation criteria—within the neoliberal social order—that we name 'flexible employer-led standard' and that are summarised in the last column of the above table. By comparison with the previous stage, state intervention in wage-earning relationships becomes more limited; labour once again becomes a market commodity; relations between companies and workers become individualised and non-unionised; company organisation becomes increasingly hierarchical and authoritarian; and social protection becomes a matter for workers who are left to fend for themselves and to cope single-handed with the risks associated with job loss.

Table 13.1 Types of social order and labour standards

Types of social order	Classic liberalism	Wage-earning order	Neo-liberalism
Labour standards	Market-led standard	Fordist-style wage-led standard	Flexible employer-led standard
Dimensions			
Treatment of labour	Labour force as commodity	De-commodification	Partial re-commodification
Treatment of the worker	Seller and manager of his/her labour power	Public social protection against risks	Falling away of protection and re-exposure to market forces
Relations between workers and employers	Seen as relationships between free and autonomous individuals	Seen as relationships between social classes: the 'two sides of industry' (i.e. employers and trade unions)	Return to individualism and weakening of trade unions
Organisation of labour within the company	Hierarchical system: all decisions concerning workers' activity taken by employer	Lessening of hierarchy, with employer respect for previously agreed working conditions and terms of employment	Return to more hierarchy: greater employer power vis-à-vis workers
How does labour marketwork	Local/national self-regulation without state intervention	Two-way regulation with some state interventionism	Globalised self-regulation
Period	Nineteenth century	Post-war 'economic miracle'	'Age of globalisation'

As these criteria for mobilisation of the labour force became increasingly a matter of practice, they began to result in substantial changes in the social configuration of employment in its most institutional sense. A comparison between the social configuration of employment in the 1960s and 1970s and the current situation in any European country would bring to light profound differences. In the former case, we would encounter a social configuration characterised by strong employment (with labour enjoying social and political protection), reduced segmentation, and a low unemployment rate. In the current situation, we encounter a configuration characterised by weak employment (a low degree of social or political protection for workforces), high segmentation (with a broad fringe of precarious employment), and a high unemployment rate. What we are contemplating is thus nothing less than a metamorphosis in the political and social treatment of labour and the figure of the worker (Castel 1995).

The Social Configuration of Employment in Terms of Its Articulation Between Employment Classes and Population Classes

Here then we have, broadly presented, the features that describe and characterise the current critical moment represented by the social configuration of employment in the institutional sphere of virtually all European countries, as well as the political values and rationale by which these developments are driven. Yet it cannot be said that consideration of this rationale will on its own suffice for a complete understanding of the process that gives rise to the configuration described. For the configuration in question is the result also of the dynamic that links together and governs the hierarchising factors operating within the sphere of social reproduction, and of the 'battles of ideas' being fought within this realm. Such factors include the separation, and relationship, between nationals and immigrants; the separation, and relationship, between different social classes; between one generation and another; and, above all, between men and women. Given the dynamic that governs these varying forms of nexus operating within the overall social fabric, and their relationship with the productive social order of employment, any social configuration of employment consists in the articulation of classes of employment, on the one hand, with population classes—or labour force classes—on the other.

It is not that researchers in the social sciences habitually fail to take account of this approach to the analysis of labour markets. It comes into play, for example, with the observation that precarious work (one category of employment) particularly affects women, more so than men, immigrants more so than nationals of the country in question, or young people more than adults (population classes). The concrete interplay between the factors belonging to the reproductive social order (population classes) and those of the productive social order (employment) is, precisely, the product of activation of the different hierarchical positions of the categories of population belonging to each reproductive category. It is thus that nationals, adult generations, social classes with a privileged social and economic capital, males, show a tendency to join the primary employment categories, while immigrants, youth, social classes with a poor social and economic capital, women, tend to enter the secondary classes of employment.

There is, nonetheless, one characteristic of the interplay between these hierarchical categories of the reproductive social order that is only rarely included in analyses of the social configuration of employment. Not only is this interplay among categories a constituent of the reproductive social order of a country that, through its own dynamic, ends up in interplay with the whole contrasting fabric of the institutional order of social production. It is the case, in addition to this, that each and every one of these contrasting sets of categories—nationals/immigrants, adults/youth, men/women—operates on the basis of an internal relational dynamic and logic that is peculiar to each set and that is invariably different from the dynamic operating in processes of employment configuration in the productive sphere. It is this aspect that we wish to investigate in more depth here, showing, first, in what this hierarchical interplay among categories, and the classes of population entailed, actually consists; and, secondly, how one of the features that characterise the distinction and relationship between the said classes—and the one that we are here most interested in stressing—is that of their differing conceptions of, and relationships with, work. Although, at any given time in any given society, the meaning of work has a homogenous character for its members taken as a whole, at the same time, within this hegemonic homogeneity, its significance and value are relatively distinct for each of these 'classes', and this difference turns out to be related, precisely, to the position occupied by individuals within the specific interplay between particular categories to which they belong. It is this twofold question that we wish to investigate here, taking as a particular focus for thought and analysis the current meaning of the difference between men and women and the gender relations that are operational within the interplay between production and reproduction of life. The deconstruction of the meaning of work and employment is thus enriched and rendered increasingly complex. For our approach will combine analysis of the political sphere of production with that of the gender relations that spring from the private sphere of production and reproduction of life, in other words, the sphere of everyday life.

We will order our argument as follows. As the starting point of our investigation we will adopt the problematic of the differing relationship of men and women with regard to work/employment. We will then look more deeply at the asymmetrical relations that bring together and separate the sexes in the reproductive social sphere that forms the social substratum upon which the aforementioned differences are enacted. And we will end by showing how the particular mode of operation of the labour market is projected over these relationships in a manner that entails negative discrimination against women as compared with men. Accordingly, if it can be said that employment and the figure of the worker are, at the present time, undergoing a serious process of deterioration and *de-gradation*, this *de-gradation* does not only affect women in a different way from that in which it affects men but, in so doing, reproduces and re-enacts some pre-existing differences and inequalities. Let us then look at how and why this happens.

Gender Inequality and Asymmetry in Relation to Employment: The Problem Posed by the Universality of This Phenomenon

That men and women occupy different positions in the social configuration of employment in any—and every—country is an empirically observable fact that no one will deny. Of all the facets of employment usually adduced to demonstrate that this is the case, two stand out particularly. Taken together, these are, in our own view, the aspects that best express the differing relationships of women and men with paid work. They are the following: on the one hand, the differential in terms of labour market participation, the best indicator of which are the activity (and employment) rates; on the other hand, the extent to which participation is part-time, which is, however ambiguously or indirectly, a sign of differing intensity in terms of effective commitment to paid work.

It is a well-known fact that the activity (and employment) rate of women is in all countries systematically lower than that of men. While the difference is not *equal* in all countries, it *is found* in all; and so it can be said, with complete certainty, that this difference is a universal phenomenon. If we take as a focus of analysis, for example, the countries of the European Union, the universality of gender differences is confirmed by the fact that these differences are found equally in countries with traditional gender policies that reserve different treatment for men and women, such as Italy and Spain (with a difference in activity rates between men and women of more than 10 percentage points), and in those that have implemented egalitarian gender policies like the Nordic Countries (where the difference is 4 percentage points) (see Table 13.2).

These differences are all the more significant in that, in all the countries in question, a stagnation point seems to have been reached. As can be seen from Table 13.3, and in contrast with the rising trend over previous decades, since 2011 almost all female activity rates, and the differences between these and the male rates, seem to have been stabilising.

The question becomes more complex and pressing when it is observed that there exists another dimension of employment in which the differences between women and men are just as systematic and universal as in the case of activity rates. Apart from their differing activity rates, men and women are distinguished by differing levels of part-time employment. In this case, the part-time employment rate of women is invariably much higher than that of men (Table 13.4). And, just as in the case of activity rates, this difference is common to all countries, making it, too, universal. In all the countries that belonged to the EU/15 in 2015, an average of 38.3% of all working women were employed on a part-time basis, as compared with only 10% of men. The fact that the difference in the part-time work percentages has been characterised by a tendency to rise in keeping with parallel increases in activity rates has led some researchers to conclude that labour market inequalities between women and men are not disappearing or significantly falling, but merely undergoing a pattern of shift (Maruani et al. 2000).

Analysis of the existence of large and persistent differences between men and women in terms of time devoted to work and employment raises a twofold problem: how to interpret the differences among countries, on the one hand; how to interpret the universal presence of the phenomenon, on the other. While a great deal of research has been devoted to the first of these problems, much less, as far as we are aware,

Table 13.2 Activity rates by sex (15–64 years)

	1975		1985		1990		2000		2005		2010		2015	
	Men	Women	Men	Women	Men	Women	Men	Women	Men	Women	Men	Women	Men	Women
EU-15	88.4	46.7	82.6	51.2	81.5	55.0	78.1	59.8	78.6	63.0	78.7	65.6	78.7	67.8
Spain	92.9	33.1	80.5	34.1	78.8	41.2	78.3	51.5	80.5	58.2	80.4	65.8	79.4	68.8
France	88.8	53.7	79.1	57.0	77.9	59.0	75.2	62.5	75.0	64.3	74.9	65.8	75.1	67.0
Italy	81.6	32.9	77.1	38.2	76.9	42.0	73.6	45.3	74.7	50.5	73.4	51.1	73.5	54.4
Sweden	88.7	67.4	85.4	77.8	85.1	80.9	77.0	72.9	78.2	73.6	80.5	75.2	82.8	78.9
United Kingdom	92.0	55.6	87.7	61.9	88.0	66.6	82.6	67.8	82.0	68.8	80.9	69.1	81.9	71.5

Source Eurostat and European Commission (2000)

Table 13.3   Activity rates by sex (15–64 years), 2011–2015

	2011		2012		2013		2014		2015	
	Men	*Women*	*Men*	*Women*	*Men*	*Women*	*Men*	*Women*	*Men*	*Women*
EU-15	78.5	65.8	78.6	66.5	78.7	67.2	78.7	67.5	78.7	67.8
Spain	80.2	66.8	79.8	68.2	79.8	68.8	79.1	68.8	79.4	68.8
France	74.5	65.5	74.8	65.9	75.5	66.5	75.1	67.0	75.1	67.0
Italy	72.9	51.4	73.5	53.3	73.4	54.0	73.5	54.4	73.5	54.4
Sweden	81.1	76.3	81.2	76.8	82.3	77.5	82.6	78.2	82.8	78.9
United Kingdom	81.1	69.4	81.5	69.7	81.5	70.7	82.0	71.1	81.9	71.5

Source Eurostat

Table 13.4   Part-time work (percentage among all employed) by sex, 2000

	2000		2005		2010		2015	
	Men	*Women*	*Men*	*Women*	*Men*	*Women*	*Men*	*Women*
EU-15	:	:	7.1	36.0	8.3	37.1	10.0	38.3
Spain	2.7	17.2	4.6	25.0	5.1	22.9	7.9	26.1
France	5.2	30.9	5.7	30.7	6.2	30.5	7.5	30.3
Italy	3.4	15.6	4.5	25.8	4.8	29.4	7.8	32.3
Sweden	:	:	11.3	36.8	13.0	41.2	13.3	37.7
United Kingdom	7.8	43.7	9.1	41.8	10.6	42.2	11.1	41.2

Source Eurostat and author's own input

has been expressly concerned with the second, probably because it is by far the more complex. It is not easy to understand, in particular, why these differences persist in countries with egalitarian gender policies, such as, for example, the Nordic Countries (Sweden has a female part-time employment rate of 37%).

ANALYSIS OF PUBLIC GENDER POLICIES AS A MODE OF APPROXIMATION

One frequent research approach to tackling this question examines the relations between labour market and gender through recourse to statistical analysis of data in which women and men are regarded as individuals distinguishable by their personal characteristics. One example, among many others, is the contribution by Marta Ibáñez Pascual (2008) in her article on 'occupational segregation by gender' which has as its subtitle, precisely, 'associated personal, job, and workplace characteristics'. This type of approach has frequently cast new light on the problem of gender inequalities in employment. At the same time, this mode of analysis has been consistently subject to criticism from a feminist theoretical standpoint: according to critics, gender differences cannot be understood simply as differences between, so to speak 'gendered individuals', because the differences themselves are rooted, on the contrary, *within* the very sphere of gender relations—most particularly within the institution of the family—and it is in this setting that they are defined and acquire meaning (Hochschild and Machung 2012; Naldini and Saraceno 2011; Prieto and Pérez de Guzmán 2013; Sánchez Mira 2016). Against the background of this type of focus, the most habitual and interesting path followed by researchers—above all if they are women—in seeking to understand the differing relationships of women and men with regard to work is that which examines public gender policies, which in turn are regarded as a constituent of welfare policies. More precisely, and in practical terms, these investigations focus attention on the way in which states seek to introduce measures and devote resources to the achievement of compatibility between work, family life and gender equality (Crompton et al. 2007).

The comparative analysis of the public policies designed to achieve compatibility of work, family life and gender equality devises and employs, for the analysis and evaluation of the relationship between gender and work, criteria that are absent from other approaches and that definitely seem to contribute greater intelligibility to the problem. These three criteria are the following: (1) work is no longer regarded in *isolation* as an activity that men and women have to perform but instead as one that has to be evaluated *alongside care* with which it simultaneously has to be made compatible; (2) the unit of observation and analysis is no longer the relationship among individuals (men and women) and work; instead the focus is shifted to bring into play, and even give priority to, the relationship between work, care and the family-type household unit habitually constituted by men and women (Sánchez Mira 2016); (3) the approach entails the idea that the *whole* constituted by work, care and gender relations consists of a system of patterning within and by means of which an important part of the social order is produced and within the framework of which women and men have to be regarded and treated as equal human beings; at the root of the problem thus lies the question of gender equality.

If the normative principle of gender equality is one of the keys, or even *the* key, to explaining the existence of public gender policies for the promotion of a fair interplay between work and care, it seems necessary to deconstruct its meaning in order to achieve a full understanding of the problem that concerns us here. The very fact that gender equality is an express political goal of all these policies means that all states recognise, as a starting point, the existence of manifest instances of gender difference and *inequality* (observable and encountered above all in the family setting) that, from a normative point of view, are unjustified. These gender differences and inequalities are no negligible concern, for they have behind them a long and fraught history that has to be taken into account—and remembered—if they are to be understood according to their true measure. Initially—in the nineteenth century and up to the middle of the twentieth—an asymmetrical and unequal model of gender relations was firmly in place in which the role of the male—as husband and father—was to work and bring into the household the necessary economic resources, while that of the woman—as wife and mother—was to tend to the needs of all members of the household, a well-known model usually referred to as traditional or *patriarchal.* Entailed in this model is not only the *obligation- or duty- of the male,* husband and father, to *work* and, by means of his work, to bring into the home all requisite economic resources and the *obligation- or duty- of the female* to attend to all needs *within the home,* but also the exclusion of the former from any involvement in household activities and of the latter from any involvement in gainful employment. If, as has frequently been the case in the course of history, the woman nonetheless 'goes out to work', her presence on the labour market is occasioned by *family need* and is not the enactment of a normative obligation. And the same is true in the—much less frequent—event of the male being drawn into household concerns and activities; should this ever be the case, it would arise from *sheer necessity* and not obligation.

In comparison with the patriarchal model of the nineteeenth and first half of the twentieth centuries, the current standard reference in the countries of Europe concerning a fair distribution of, and interplay between, work, family and gender relations is to an order in which not only can work/family be performed/provided for in a balanced manner but in which also this balanced outcome is to be achieved under conditions of equality between the sexes. The transition from a patriarchal conception of the family to an egalitarian conception of gender relations within the family—generally referred to as the 'dual earner and dual carer' model—began, inspired and promoted by the feminist movements, in the 1960s and 1970s and continues still today. By contrast with the patriarchal model, an egalitarian model signifies that, within the family, the male has, *in addition to the duty to work, the duty to provide care and to perform housework*, and that the woman, *in addition to the duty to care for members of the household and attend to the home, has the duty to work*, with each member of the couple performing each of the two roles on equal terms.

The appearance of a regime in which (paid) work and care are equally shared/must be shared between women and men will have a twofold effect on the meaning of (paid) work and of care. On the one hand, the meaning and value of work become relative insofar as they are contrasted with the meaning and value of care, the contrast being, what is more, not merely conceptual but also subject to the test of feasibility (above all, among women). The consideration of care as a practice of especial social relevance, in itself and by contrast with paid work, has given rise to an abundant sociological literature that has shown how complex and rich a dimension of life it is and how this qualitative dimension fails to be accorded adequate recognition in the institutional sphere (on all these aspects, see Carrasco et al. 2011). On the other hand, paid work and domestic work are becoming—in referential terms at least—de-gendered. Work is no longer regarded as *men's business* but as of equal relevance to men and women; similarly, care and housework are no longer *women's concerns* but are seen as being activities for performance by both women and men.

The model of combination of work and family based on an egalitarian conception of the genders and their interrelationship is the assumed reference—more or less enthusiastically adhered to—by all the states of Europe. There is none that expressly denies it, while all pay lip-service to it in public statements. Even so, it is equally certain that conceptions of the model, and measures taken to convert a conception into a real and genuinely practicable model, differ from one country to another. And what is important here is not the degree of similarity in the ways in which men and women are considered and treated in relation to work but the ways in which they are considered, by the same token, equal in relation to care. This is where the existence of welfare regimes and gender regimes comes into play, for these, in spite of having a common basis, also have their distinguishing features. The ultimate formal goal of all these policies may be invariably the same but the means selected for implementing their own particular conception of the desirable articulation between work, family and gender relations is in each country different from the arrangements found in other countries. With few, albeit significant, variations, social scientists have tended to reduce this variety of policy practices to just a few types of welfare and gender regime. Thus, Den Dulk and van Doorne-Huiskes (2007), among many others, have distinguished, in Europe, four types of regime: social democratic; corporatist; mediterranean; and post-communist.

At the beginning of this section we stressed that large and persistent differences are to be observed in the relationship of men and women to work. In what we have just said, we have made a significant step towards understanding these differences. They are attributable to—or at least can, in the first instance, be plausibly explained by—the introduction of different public measures geared not just to regulate the relationship with work but also to achieve a regulation of men's and women's relationship with care and its distribution. Consequently, it will no longer be appropriate to seek to compare, separately, the relationship of men and of women with work; the comparison will, henceforth, cover work and care simultaneously (Table 13.5). Once this step has been taken and the differences in the amounts of time devoted by men and women to paid work and to care (including housework) are observed together, it becomes easier to understand why men spend less time in paid work than

Table 13.5 Distribution (in %) of average time devoted to paid work and to housework among men and women. Various European countries

Country	Paid work		Housework	
	Men	Women	Men	Women
Spain	39.0	23.0	24.4	44.8
France	37.4	23.2	20.4	38.4
Sweden	40.2	29.6	23.6	34.0
United Kingdom	40.2	23.8	22.2	40.4
Italy	41.6	19.8	14.8	48.8
Germany	34.8	20.0	22.4	37.8

Source OECD, Family database, and authors' own input
N.B. Population: adults between 20 and 74 years. Years: 2000–2003. The percentages are based on total time devoted to paid work activities, housework, free time and associated activities. Housework includes care and household tasks

do women. The latter are seen to devote much more time than men to housework and it appears only reasonable to assume a link between the two findings. To some extent at least, women devote less time to paid work because they devote more time to domestic tasks.

Observation of the data in this table brings clearly to the fore two aspects of relevance to our concerns: (a) in all the countries in question, women devote less time than do men to paid work while, at the same time, devoting much more time than men to work in the home, making it logical to assume the existence of a direct link between these two facts; (b) gender differences between countries would appear to be linked to their welfare and gender regimes; the country with the least differences is Sweden (a country distinguished by its egalitarian gender policies) and the one with the greatest differences is Italy (a country with a Mediterranean gender regime).

FROM PUBLIC GENDER POLICIES TO THE INTERPLAY BETWEEN THE SEXES IN EVERYDAY LIFE

In spite of the clarification contributed by analysis of gender equality policies to an understanding of the different relationships with work (and also, at this point, with care) between men and women, it would appear that there is no linear relationship between institutionalised welfare and gender regimes and distribution of time spent in the performance of paid work and domestic work (we know that there are countries in which men fail to take up their statutory entitlement to parental leave). What is particularly surprising is to observe the differences in time spent by men and by women in paid work and in domestic work that are observable also in countries with fully established gender equality regimes like Sweden. This critical observation leads us to raise, directly and explicitly, the question of the universal nature of such differences.

In order to understand this key point, it is necessary to move beyond public gender policies and to enter the realm of private gender relations as they are practised and can be observed in everyday life. It might seem reasonable to assume that the different welfare and gender regimes tend to reflect the way in which these relations are predominantly considered among their populations, in the public sphere as well as in private. Yet it can in no way be assumed that the conception of the relationship between work, care and gender relations implicit in public policies is a straightforward reproduction of the private conceptions of relations in this sphere held by members of these populations. In actual fact, on moving empirically down into this area it becomes evident that the diversity of conceptions of this particular nexus of relationships is far broader than might have been expected. In this empirical approximation to how everyday life is and/or ought to be lived, the egalitarian model ceases being *the* reference in order to become no more than *one* reference model among others. Alongside this particular reference model, the populations of European countries also favour others, including the traditional model. And, at the moment of truth, any type of combination other than that of strictly equal roles results in women being removed further from paid work and brought closer to care, while at the same time removing men further from care and bringing them closer to paid work, thereby serving, overall, to reproduce asymmetrical gender relations. The problem with this approach is thus that empirical findings fail to match rational expectations.

There exist, to our knowledge, very few studies that have empirically tested the extent to which the various modes of conceiving of the relationship between work, family and gender relations are actually reflected, in all their complexity, among the populations of European countries. One study in which this point is tackled expressly in six European countries (France, Sweden, Great Britain, West Germany, Spain and Portugal) was carried out by the Portuguese sociologist Karin Wall (2007). The originality of her research is that it is not limited to two models of relationship between work, family and gender—i.e. the traditional and the modern egalitarian ones—but distinguishes as many as five different models and goes on to analyse their distribution among the populations of the countries in question. The five models distinguished, and their definition, are as follows:

1. *Strong traditional*: 'male breadwinner/female stay-at-home carer model';
2. *Strong traditional modified*: 'male breadwinner/female carer/stay at home with young children while advocating the increased participation of the male breadwinner in caring and household tasks';
3. *Modern unequal caring*: 'strongly supports women's work and maternal employment but does not endorse increased male participation in childcare and household tasks';

4. *Modern motherhood pattern*: 'individuals are strongly in favour of the dual earner/dual carer, but believe maternal employment has a negative impact on young children';

5. *Strong modern*: 'dual earner/dual carer/employment for mothers with children with no negative impacts' (Wall 2007, 105–107).

As can be observed, these five models do include the extreme models, the 'strong traditional' and the 'strong modern', but, in between these extremes, the researcher distinguishes an additional three intermediate positions. Just as interesting as her distinction between so many models are this author's fieldwork findings (Table 13.6). The 'strong modern' model, i.e. the model closest to the strictly egalitarian one, is fully endorsed in all six countries by less than 20% of the population (ranging between 10 and 17%). At the other extreme, the more traditional models, the 'strong traditional' and the 'strong traditional modified', appear to be endorsed by a percentage that varies from a minimum of 21% to a maximum of 48%. On the basis of these results, it becomes easier to understand the distribution of paid work and domestic work between men and women that we observed in Table 13.5. A traditional conception of the relationship between work, family and gender, endorsed by such a high percentage of the population, generates a low inclination to work among women, turning men into the sole providers for their families. A strictly egalitarian conception entails, by definition, an egalitarian inclination to work on the part of both sexes, but this is an ideal endorsed by less than 20% of the population. When it comes down to the facts on the ground, no conception of the ideal relationship between

Table 13.6 Distribution of the models of relationship between work, family and gender in the population of European countries

Models of relationship between work, family and gender	*% of population advocating each model*
Strong traditional	Between 6 and 12
Strong traditional modified	Between 15 and 36
Modern unequal caring	Between 5 and 10
Modern motherhood pattern	Between 15 and 37
Strong modern	Between 10 and 17

Source Authors' compilation based on work of K. Wall (2007, 105–107)
N.B. Countries included: France, Sweden, Great Britain, West Germany, Spain and Portugal

work, family and gender will automatically translate into real practice (there are also situations, it must be remembered, in which people work *out of necessity*). Even so, ideals do contribute to the beliefs, mentalities and attitudes that, to a varying extent, determine behaviour.

Observation of the diversity of conceptions, within a given population, of the relationship between work, family and gender is not only the proof that there exist more than two reference models but also a symptom of the fact that our conceptions, far from being clearly defined, are porous, controversial, frequently in conflict and, hence, unstable and subject to change. By using techniques of qualitative sociological analysis—listening, for example, to what men and women actually say—some sense can be gained of the immense complexity, and deeply nuanced quality, of people's mental constructs and opinions. In a research project on this topic conducted recently in Spain using this type of methodology, three points emerge clearly as arguments in support of such complexity. First, work is never defined or valued by women and men as if it were a separate activity with a value of its own, but is invariably represented and evaluated in juxtaposition with the activity of care. Secondly, its meaning is described in a manner that is expressly ambivalent and polysemic. And thirdly, the differences between men and women (of childbearing age) are profound: a majority of the former perceive themselves as, inseparably, 'woman, mother and worker'; of the latter, a majority see themselves as working men who, as a result of their partners' mass entry to the labour market, have begun to take an interest in, and to become involved in, childcare. And here we find a stark line of separation between the sexes: under circumstances in which work and care turn out to be strictly incompatible, the priority option of women will be care, while that of men will be work. In spite of a strong change of attitude compared with the preceding generation (that of their parents), the gender asymmetry is preserved (Prieto 2015).

All the indications, accordingly, are that the gender differences in relation to work observable in all European countries are not attributable solely to the fact that each state has put in place a specific welfare and a (theoretically) egalitarian (dual earner/dual carer) regime. They are attributable also—and probably much more so—to the private beliefs held by the populations of these countries as to what is and/or ought to be the relationship between work, family and gender; these beliefs are much more diversified and remote from the gender equality model and central role of work than we are accustomed to imagine. In nearly all of these countries, we continue to observe gender differences and differences in the value accorded to care as compared with work. If the personal is both political and public, it is obvious that the struggle of ideas within European citizenry in favour of an egalitarian conception of the relationship between work, family and gender, though it has indeed won ground over recent decades, is far from having achieved a final victory.

Such, then, is the configuration we encounter with regard to the hierarchy of relations between work, family and gender relations in everyday life and the features of its internal dynamic. It may be observed here that, however important the changes seen in recent decades in all countries on the path towards gender equality, the differences persist (Crompton et al. 2007). While differences do exist between countries, within all of them, at the heart of their families, women devote on average more time than their partners to caring for the family and less time to paid work, and men vice versa.

This gender division of labour affects the paid work of women in a twofold manner. First of all, since they generally have to make their paid work compatible with more hours of care and housework compared to men, their method of managing this double workload leads them to combine their roles in a different way. This was conceptualised, as long ago as 1978, by Italian sociologist Laura Balbo, as '*doppia presenza*' ('double presence') (Balbo 1979). This concept is vividly summarised by Cristina Borderías in the following passage that we quote here in full:

> Production and reproduction demand of women rationales of behaviour and acceptance of values that are radically opposed. For this reason, the double presence has entailed not only problems in combining two working schedules or in finding ways of being simultaneously present in the family and in the workplace, but also the need to combine and establish a *modus vivendi* between the unequal rationales as they prevailed in the two spheres of work. The ambivalence with which many women describe their relationship with their work is an expression of the difficulty of responding to and identifying with these contradictory rationales: the feeling of a split in one's life; the difficulty of thinking of oneself as inhabiting exclusively either one of the two spheres; the rejection of work by family and of family by work; and the subordination of one sphere to the other. The ambivalence sometimes manifested by women in relation to the presence of these dichotomies in their everyday lives can be interpreted also as a reaction against the masculine mystique of production that claims work as the central concern of life, and against the traditionally feminine mystique

that seeks to subsume one's own life to the lives of others and to forgo all personal autonomy. Yet it is, precisely and paradoxically, the continual to-ing and fro-ing between one aspect and the other, one rationale and the other, one culture and the other, that places women in the position of subjects capable of conceiving of social life as an overall whole. (Borderías 2003, 108)

This results in a mode of relationship with work that appears not to be found among men who, while having made major strides in the direction of an egalitarian gender relations regime within the family, continue to uphold, fundamentally unchanged, their conception of—and their relationship with—work.

This 'double presence' so characteristic of the paid work of women has a second effect that is of no less importance in determining the manner in which they actually perform their occupational activity. Women's 'double presence' means that, from the standpoint of the labour market and employers, their work is regarded as an activity imbued with ambivalence and ambiguity in contrast to the unequivocal meaning attributed to the work performed by men. Women continue to be regarded by many employers as a second-class workforce, less well suited than men to the performance of occupational activity in the workplace. This applies particularly in the case of jobs that, from the employer's point of view, require strong commitment and a high degree of availability, jobs which are found nowadays in ever-increasing numbers (Prieto and Pérez de Guzmán 2013). This circumstance means that, at a time like the present when, as shown in other chapters of this book, the 'atypical' nature of so many jobs has become the norm, women are worse affected than men by 'atypical' working situations and are subject, as such, to more unemployment, more fixed-term and/or part-time contracts, allocation to lower-skilled and lower-paid jobs, etc. (see Table 13.7).

While this data is reminiscent of that with which we started out this section, its sociological significance is rather different. The former drew attention to an issue concerning factual distribution: for whatever reasons, women's relation to (paid) work—the *magnitude* of their labour market commitment, expressed in terms of activity rate and part-time employment rate—was different from that of men, posing the sociological problem of how this discrepancy was to be understood. The information in the above Table is descriptive of the way in which, in the current framework of a neo-liberalised labour market as outlined in the first

Table 13.7 Gender distribution of socially significant employment situations

	Employment rate (2014)		% of fixed-term employment (2014)		% of part-time employment (2015)		Average hourly earnings (€) (2010)		% of managerial posts (2015)	
	Men	Women	Men	Women	Men	Women	Men	Women	Men	Women
EU15	70.6	60.6	13.3	14.4	10.0	38.3	17.66	14.54	74	26
Spain	60.7	51.2	23.6	24.6	7.9	26.1	12.43	10.41	74	26
France	67.7	60.9	15.0	16.9	7.5	30.3	17.54	14.80	67	33
Italy	64.7	46.8	13.1	14.2	7.8	32.3	14.82	14.04	74	26
Sweden	76.5	73.1	14.7	18.8	13.3	37.7	19.33	16.31	72	28
United Kingdom	76.8	67.1	5.8	6.8	11.1	41.2	19.20	14.72	78	22

Source For employment rates, part-time and fixed-term work percentages and average hourly earnings, Eurostat. For percentage of managerial posts, Grant Thornton (http://www.grantthornton.es/)

section of this chapter, employers tend to treat the female labour force, and of how, through this treatment, they give expression to their idea of women's capacity for work (irrespective of whether or not this judgement corresponds to the reality). The data in the Table 13.7 confirm, once again, that, although there are indeed differences among countries that can be explained by the differing gender policies that have been put in place, the unequal gender distribution of atypical work situations is a generalised phenomenon. As such, the labour discrimination against women that stems from the current mode of functioning of labour markets, while the outcome, on the one hand, of the inherently hierarchical fabric of gender relations present in everyday life, is, on the other hand, the discriminatory result of the market itself. It is only logical, therefore, that some (female) researchers should have stated that, 'to a considerable extent (...), all the facilitators of transformational change we have discussed are highly contingent upon other trends in the evolving global capitalist economy' (Crompton et al. 2007, 242–243).

It remains to pose one more question concerning the differing degrees of labour market commitment displayed by women and men, a question that would seem to be of comparable magnitude in terms of its implications. In every comparison between women and men concerning their relationship with employment, the *male parameters* are those used to set the standard. Thus, it is considered that the employment and activity rates of women are 'low' and that the gap between these rates and those of men is an indicator of discrimination. From this observation, it is assumed to follow that the situation of women will become fairer the more closely it approximates to that of men, and that women's aim should thus be to achieve activity and employment rates equivalent to those of men. Yet when it is observed that this difference in labour market participation rates serves to obscure the overall distribution of labour (i.e. including both paid employment *and* work in the home), a fundamental question arises that modifies the hegemonic mode in which the problem is conceived: what if the standard was to be *that set by women*, such that it became men's activity rates that should be regarded as excessively high (it is they, after all, that prevent men from devoting more time and energy to household tasks)? Might then the study of labour market differences between men and women perhaps be approached from the angle of their different 'care participation rates' and their greater or lesser commitment to this aspect of work, by establishing, from the outset, a distinction between 'full-time care' and 'part-time care'?

Conclusion

We began this contribution by recalling the characteristic features of the current state of employment and of the figure of the worker in Europe. We thus argued that, after a historical period during which both one and the other had come to occupy a central position in the overall social order of each country, since the 1980s European societies have been undergoing something like a social and political counter-revolution. Employment has ceased being the central activity around which the social order as a whole is constructed, and the worker is no longer the figure who, *qua* incarnation of the fully-fledged citizen, enjoys political protection via the recognition of social rights. The central position of employment has been displaced, in the institutional sphere, by the market to whose rules of play labour has been compelled to adjust its behaviour, thereby converting the worker into the self-sufficient individual bearing sole responsibility for provision of personal welfare and protection against labour-related risks. The result of these global transformations has been a radical change in the social configuration of employment. During the period of the 'post-war economic miracle', this configuration was characterised by strong (i.e. socially and politically protected) employment, reduced segmentation, and a low unemployment rate. At the current time, the configuration is characterised by weak employment (i.e. lacking social and political protection), high segmentation (with a broad fringe of precarious employment) and a high rate of unemployment. We argued that, correct as this interpretation undoubtedly is, its full understanding required inclusion of its interplay with the social configuration of the population classes resulting from the various forms of hierarchical nexus operating in the reproductive social order, among which we mentioned the nexus that brings together/separates immigrants and nationals, that which places generations in a relationship of complementarity/opposition, and, above all, that which brings together, while yet effecting a division between, men and women. We said something further. It was claimed that these forms of hierarchical nexus produced and reproduced the differences between their members according to an intrinsic logic that, in each case, was different from—and yet not utterly unlike—the logic characterising the operation of the labour market. This resulted in an overall situation whereby the final social configuration of employment in a country at any given time appeared as the outcome of the interplay of a twofold dynamic:

that of the labour market itself and that of the forms of hierarchical nexus operating in the social order of reproduction.

To demonstrate this general thesis with sufficiently elaborated arguments, we chose to examine in depth the dynamic that brings together while also dividing the components of just one such nexus, namely the relationship between men and women. It was shown, accordingly, that the differing relationship of men and women to employment stems from the asymmetry that characterises their relations in everyday life. In everyday life, these—asymmetrical—relations do not revolve exclusively around (paid) work but also around care and, in general, work performed in the home, with the value of one form of work being juxtaposed and invariably contrasted with the value of the other. Within this framework, and under all circumstances, women devote more time and attention to care than do men, while men devote more time and attention to work on the labour market than to care. This domestic asymmetry comes to be the argument used by employers on the labour market to discriminate against women in favour of men. At a time like the present, when the market is accorded the privilege—and, more specifically, within it, the employers—of operating according to the unilateral logic of private economic profit with (virtually) no limit imposed by law, the discrimination against women vis-à-vis men can be exerted unfettered by the constraints of a socially and politically regulated labour market.

It has been a question here solely of the articulation between the outcome of the logic operating on the labour market and that operating in the hierarchical nexus within which gender relations are enacted. Yet this approach sufficiently indicates that relations between the labour market and every other hierarchical nexus in the reproductive social order can hardly be expected to be substantially different—the only problem being that this is a type of question that the research community has barely begun to explore in any depth.[1]

NOTE

1. Translation from the Spanish by Kathleen Llanwarne.

REFERENCES

Alonso, Luis Enrique. 2001. *Trabajo y posmodernidad: el empleo débil*. Madrid: Fundamentos.

Balbo, Laura. 1979. "La doppia presenza." *Inchiesta* 32. In *Las mujeres y el trabajo. Rupturas conceptuales*, edited by Cristina Borderías, Cristina Carrasco, and Carme Alemany (1998). Madrid: Icaria.

Bilbao, Andrés. 1999. "La nueva regulación del mercado de trabajo en España." In *La crisis del empleo en Europa*, edited by Carlos Prieto, 65–82. Alzira: Germania.

Borderías, Cristina. 2003. "La feminización de los estudios sobre el trabajo de las mujeres: España en el contexto internacional (1969–2002)." *Sociología del Trabajo* 48: 57–122.

Carrasco, Cristina, Cristina Borderías, and Teresa Torns, eds. 2011. *El trabajo de cuidados. Historia, teoría y políticas*. Madrid: Los libros de la Catarata.

Castel, Robert. 1995. *Les methamorphoses de la question social*. Paris: Fayard.

Crompton, Rosemary, Suzan Lewis, and Clare Lyonette, eds. 2007. *Women, Men, Work and Family in Europe*. London: Palgrave Macmillan.

Den Dulk, Laura, and Anneke van Doorne-Huiskes. 2007. "Social Policy in Europe: It's Impact on Families and Work." In *Women, Men, Work and Family in Europe*, edited by Rosemary Crompton, Suzan Lewis, and Clare Lyonette, 35–57. Basingstoke: Palgrave Macmillan.

European Commission. 2000. *Employment in Europe 2000*. Luxembourg: Office for Official Publications of the European Communities.

Hochschild, Arlie Russell, and Anne Machung. 2012. *The Second Shift. Working Families and the Revolution at Home*. London: Penguin Books.

Ibañez Pascual, Marta. 2008. "La segregación ocupacional por sexo a examen. Características personales, de los puestos y de las empresas asociadas a las ocupaciones masculinas y femeninas." *Revista Española de Investigaciones Sociológicas* 123: 87–122.

Maruani, Margaret, Chantal Rogerat, and Teresa Torns, eds. 2000. *Las nuevas fronteras de la desigualdad: hombres y mujeres en el mercado de trabajo*. Barcelona: Icaria.

Naldini, Manuela, and Chiara Saraceno. 2011. *Conciliare familialavoro*. Bolonia: Il Mulino.

Prieto, Carlos, ed. 2015. *Trabajo, cuidados, tiempo libre y relaciones de género en la sociedad española*. Madrid: Cinca.

Prieto, Carlos, and Sofía Pérez de Guzmán. 2013. "Desigualdades laborales de género, disponibilidad temporal y normatividad social." *Revista Española de Investigaciones Sociológicas* 141: 113–132.

Sánchez Mira, Nuria. 2016. "El empleo femenino desde el hogar. Hacia un análisis comprehensivo de la articulación entre empleo y vida familiar." *Cuadernos de Relaciones Laborales* 34 (2): 385–403.

Wall, Karin. 2007. "Main Patterns in Attitudes to the Articulation Between Work and Family Life: A Cross-National Analysis." In *Women, Men, Work and Family in Europe*, edited by Rosemary Crompton, Suzan Lewis, and Clare Lyonette, 86–115. New York: Palgrave Macmillan.

CHAPTER 14

Conclusion

Amparo Serrano-Pascual and Maria Jepsen

NAMING AND DOING

We started this manuscript by saying that language constitutes a strategic space for expressing and structuring a political battle between different social groups and perspectives. The hegemonic connotation that notions such as work and employment, or related categories such as unemployment or inactivity, may acquire would be nothing other than a reflection of the battle between different social groups, in the linguistic sphere, over the meaning (Voloshinov 1992). The outcome of these battles is the plurality of connotations that harbour key concepts in our contemporary consciousness. Hence, political struggles between different social actors are also, to a large extent, battles over (and in) language (Fairclough 2000), struggles for the conquest of political constructs, that is to say rhetorical struggles.

A. Serrano-Pascual (✉)
Complutense University of Madrid, TRANSOC Research Institute,
Madrid, Spain

M. Jepsen
ETUI and Free University of Brussels, Brussels, Belgium

© The Author(s) 2019   317
A. Serrano-Pascual and M. Jepsen (Eds.),
The Deconstruction of Employment as a Political Question,
https://doi.org/10.1007/978-3-319-93617-8_14

The domestication of the market and socialisation of the risks associated with the condition of wage-earner at the end of the nineteenth and over the course of the twentieth century were achieved partly through semantic conquests. The politicisation of work leads to the naming of the vulnerability associated with wage labour within a politicising framework capable of revealing the connection between vulnerability, power relations and oppression. The political framework used to look at the social question of wage labour in industrial societies has served to bring to light various core assumptions of the new social order: that the exercise of autonomy requires recognition of heteronomy, that the necessary condition for individuals to be accountable is the institutionalisation of mechanisms of collective responsibility, and that workplace harmony depends on recognition of conflict as the constitutive backbone of the wage relationship (Serrano-Pascual et al. 2017).

The signifier for work therefore operates not only as a manner of describing and classifying social activities, but also as a necessary condition for regulating, visualising and transforming them. Even though the notions of work and employment appear obvious, numerous authors (Méda 1998; Gorz 1988; Topalov 1994; Salais et al. 1986; Prieto 2007, among others) have highlighted the culturally and geographically circumscribed character of what is taken for granted as regards these notions. Employment is not a self-evident fact of society that our eyes cannot fail to perceive; it is a matter of a social construct. This abundant literature has emphasised, on the one hand, the recent invention of these categories and, on the other, that their invention is performative.

The emergence of the category of (regular paid) employment and worker made it possible to establish connections (and divisions) between experiences of reality which would otherwise be imperceptible to us, and provides a framework for classifying the activities carried out and, independently, the individuals who perform them. Production activities become a synonym for activity, relegating to the sphere of 'inactivity' (and hence loss of social status and invisibility) those other activities that do not fit within a commercial framework, such as unpaid care. Thus there appear dichotomies of meaning, which become political classifications (domestic/productive, gainful/nurturing, masculine/feminine, work/caring). At the same time as classifying activities, they also classify the individuals carrying them out (see chapters by Maruani and Meron, and Prieto and Pérez de Guzmán). Hence naming does not mean only describing (organising reality), but also prescribing (classifying activities and groups of people). Thus not only is a hierarchy of names (productive as opposed to reproductive work) established, but also one of principles (space where these activities are performed: factory or firm as opposed to family or home; individuals performing these activities: males as opposed to females; criteria governing work: moral as opposed to economic; how it is conducted: expertise as opposed to emotion; skills: natural as opposed to acquired; rationales: life-sustaining as opposed to wealth-generating; environment: private and not open to political and public scrutiny, hence political). If the productive space is the epicentre from which one conceptualises one's life, the other semantic territories of non-work occupy a subordinate position, a step towards invisibility (inactivity) and/or possible stigmatisation (moral deficiency, as in the case of the invention of the NEETs—people not in education, employment or training) and depoliticisation. Not only are the criteria for classification of activities political, but so is the attribution and codification of a given activity (and, hence, its status) within one category or another (employment or inactivity, part-time or reduced working hours), according to the social group to which one belongs (gender), as discussed in depth by Maruani and Meron, in this volume, and Maruani (2000).

The exercise of delimiting the boundaries of the semantic field covering the notion of work, first, and (paid) employment, second, which classify activities according to their integration in the market, is relatively recent. Their modern semantic connotation, in other words their conception as activities that bestow meaning on[1] and express the identity and sociability of the individuals concerned, and, hence, a space where we demand fairness (expression of what 'ought to be'—see the contributions by Prieto and Pérez Guzmán, and Alonso, in this volume), is also recent. The *invention* of this concept led to the emergence of the individuals performing the work, that is to say the worker as a historical subject of collective action, making the wage-earning relationship the central focus of contradictions and conflicts. Employment therefore becomes a political matter, because the semantic frameworks according to which work has been named (dignity, equality, power, rationality, freedom) become problematic. This politicisation allowed the conflict (of the asymmetry between the two parties that characterise the wage-earning relationship) to be recognised, and made the interdependence and vulnerability and a socialised conception of risk visible. This context fosters the emergence of protected wage-earning status as the epicentre of our social consciousness. This benchmark model was underpinned by a social language characterised by the terminological proliferation of notions relating to security (social assistance, social protection, social security), bringing into play a collective representation of wage employment through three regulatory approaches: insurance, law and collective action and representation. Through these regulatory systems, we have been able to conceptualise work in terms of interdependence (the key to social relations).

RESEMANTISATION AND RECONTEXTUALISATION OF THE NOTION OF WORK

There have been numerous studies (Gorz 1988; Méda 1998; etc.) reconstructing the semantic journey of the notion of work through various enunciation frameworks reformulating its connotative force: in Romance languages from being an instrument of torture (tripalium), to divine punishment, from this to an object of piety, and finally to an expression of humanity. The history of the meaning of work reveals an archaeology of past struggles between different social groups to legitimise criteria for classification among different social groups.[2] This history and this resemantisation of the notion and the traces of its genealogical route are still present in the wide polysemy characterising the notion with intrinsically contradictory connotations: work in Spanish (*trabajo*) is simultaneously synonymous with sacrifice, progress, effort, punishment, dehumanisation, moral expression, dignification, etc.[3] From a rapid but revealing genealogical appraisal, in the light of existing studies, we could analytically identify four phases in its semantic journey.

In an initial phase (as also in other cultures) of evolution of the notion, employment and work could not be named and were therefore unimaginable. Productive activities were not placed within a specific category, as they were subsumed in broader or more specific categories. It was therefore not relevant to differentiate productive work from other human activities (Méda 1998; Prieto 2007; Sanchis 2004). The motivations of working individuals were not economic, but derived from social and community obligations (Polanyi 1944/1989).

In a second phase, the notion of work took shape in the Latin languages in the fourteenth and fifteenth centuries (Le Goff 2013) and in English in the Middle Ages (Williams 1983), with negative connotations (tripalium: torment and torture; toil: physical effort). However, from the eighteenth century onwards, work was invented as a central category in its modern sense, in so far as productive activities (labour) that could be traded became the source of all wealth (Smith 1776/2011).

These activities came to be named within a productivist economic framework which made them a commodity (abstract, measurable, quantifiable productive work) that was central to the social order of liberalism. The emergence of this category made it possible for one group of individuals (the bourgeoisie) to produce a social order (work societies) and to occupy a position of power.

At the end of the nineteenth century, work was resemantised through metonymic slippage, turning it into employment (metonymic appropriation of work by employment that was politically regulated, once the concept of market had been problematised and became subject to political intervention) as a central category of political thought of contemporary societies. The category of waged employee (working for someone else) would occupy a central role in modes of conceptualising (and regulating) subordination and dependence. Hence it is around this status that a politicising environment came into being, which would foster the construction of mechanisms and devices designed to protect the worker as the weaker party (Baylos, in this volume). This socialisation of the risk explains why the contractual work/wages exchange does not take place between two individuals, but between two social groups (Prieto 2007), and why part of the wage is received in terms of a social wage (unemployment and sickness benefits, etc.). This delimitation of the boundaries of waged employment also sets the limits determining access to institutionalised social protection mechanisms. It rules other activities out of this political territory, such as housekeeping, as it is not a commercial activity, or self-employment, since it does not conform to the principle of legal subordination (Prieto and Pérez de Guzmán, Riesco-Sanz, and Baylos, in this volume). The notion of worker emerges, alongside which are grouped, within the same classification, all individuals participating in production.[4]

Thus, work comes to be seen as a homogeneous, abstract, quantifiable commodity that invites us to think of ourselves in terms of equivalences. With money, the qualitative differences become quantitative ones, and this allows for comparability (principle of fairness), objectivity (principle of freedom) and calculation (principle of rationality) (Simmel 1907/1977; Bilbao 2007) and, therefore, comparability, equivalence and tradability among individuals. Work is understood as potential labour power traded on the market. For trade to be possible, there have to be comparable units. The metaphor of the market would shape the way in which this trade was understood: between equal individuals (desocialised, free, autonomous units) selling (entering freely into contracts) their potential labour power in exchange for money. This principle of tradability allows for visibility and political denunciation, based as it is on the principle of equivalence, which asserts equality in work, hence fairness (Boltanski 2000).

(Un)Employment as a Floating Signifier

The liberal revolution is, therefore, first and foremost, a semantic revolution that made it possible to change the nature of the feudal dependence relationships of the *Ancien Régime* (notion of human rights, equality, etc.), but, at the same time, it gives rise to new boundaries in the territory of what is thinkable, and new patterns of normalisation (productive/unproductive, active/inactive, etc.). Political dependence was replaced by economic dependence (individual owning his or her labour power). These transformations made it possible for new meanings and new political identities (from subject to citizen) to develop. Emancipation thus becomes thinkable and, therefore, desirable. The evolution of the liberal order and the contradictions it engenders explain the progressive politicisation acquired by work, which made it the central space for exercising and expressing social conflicts.

It is not only notions such as that of work that have been resemantised, but the category of market itself has also undergone a major semantic change. From being understood as the metonym for an economic activity (the market as a defined space where economic transactions take place and where, frequently, the institutions regulating this social space and responsible for the proper functioning of the market were located), with the advent of liberalism, 'market' became a metaphor: the expression, firstly, of a self-regulated entity subject to a homeostatic equilibrium through the operation of a providential 'invisible hand', and, secondly, the normalised manifestation of certain ungovernable forces and laws. This metaphor has compellingly tended to turn into a synecdoche, and this fosters a tendency to extend its rules and principles to areas other than the commercial sphere (Polanyi 1944/1989).

It is in the light of this tendency to colonise and extend its logic beyond those that are strictly commercial (Polanyi 1944/1989; Gil Calvo 2016) that one can understand the revision of the market metaphor made by various social groups in the late nineteenth and throughout the twentieth century, opening the way to decommodified spaces, and, with these, laying the foundations for the institutional conditions (Supiot 2010) that made the exercise of citizenship possible (Alonso, in this volume). This recognition of the market's shortcomings and the appropriation of new terms and classifications by the trade union movement and other political groups facilitated the establishment of legal and political guarantees for waged work, turning it into socially and politically safeguarded employment.

One example of this politicisation of employment (work designated within a political framework) is the emergence of the category of unemployment at the end of the nineteenth century. Before this appeared, deprivation of employment and a lack of economic resources formed part of a single catch-all category known as poverty, inactivity or vagrancy, which implied a moral judgement (Lecerf 2002). The category of unemployment came into being when boundaries were established, distinguishing, within the community of those without work, between those whose situation of incapacity/age made them unfit to work, those whose situation of poverty was due to a lack of will, and, finally, those victims of failures of the market, which had cast them out against their will, as described by Demazière and Lallement in their chapter. Distinctions began to be drawn between situations, within this heterogeneous group of workless individuals, based on whether the situation was voluntary or not. Unemployment came to form a category distinguishing people who were involuntarily deprived of work, giving rise to a perspective seeing this as a social phenomenon (a situation of risk, rather than of individual fault) (Rosanvallon 1995). The emergence of this category is performative: there is a shift from an intervention based on the moral perspective (charity designed to discipline the behaviours of those concerned) to another based on a (political) framework of fairness. The politicisation of work has been a key condition for naming workers' vulnerability and stressing collective responsibility for the existence of unemployment and the corresponding social protection of workers (Crespo-Suárez and Serrano-Pascual 2013).

Notions do not only shift over time; they also have effects. The emergence of liberal societies cannot be understood without the establishment of a series of concepts in political consciousness (Durand 2007). The symbolic efficacy of this semantic process made it possible to establish an economic and social model that has as its central axes the principle of capital accumulation and economic rationality (the market). It made for the reappraisal of the (formerly vilified) activities covered by this notion, and liberation from the moral restraints that had been placed on the spread of the capitalist ethic[5] (because of its link with cardinal sins, such as greed and envy). As postulated by Prieto and Pérez de Guzmán in their contribution to this book, there is a direct relationship between the common-sense view of work (wage employment as norm: something we take for granted as fair and to be expected) and a particular social order. When they come to be regarded as common sense, these categories are exempted from any process of challenge or justification. They are taken as they are. And they are construed as the hegemonic modes according to which a society conceives of itself and challenges itself.

SOCIAL, ECONOMIC AND POLITICAL CONDITIONS OF THE CRISIS OF THE CATEGORY OF EMPLOYMENT

The common-sense approach whereby work was named and regulated is, however, undergoing a thorough shake-up, leading to a severe crisis of employment as a category. This is not a sudden change, but the outcome of a long process, which started at the end of the 1980s, and for which the recent economic crisis was a powerful catalyst. As we held above, changes in the social grammar are an expression of the asymmetries that take shape in the political battles between different social groups, exacerbated after the crisis, while, at the same time, they help to legitimise those asymmetries.

The authors who have contributed to this collective work discuss the dimensions that have accelerated this process: economic (changes in the economic model and economic crisis—Alonso, Sánchez Jiménez), changes in the production model and its organisation—Valenduc, Drahokoupil and Fabo—social changes (Prieto and Pérez de Guzmán, Maruani and Meron, Lallement, Demazière, de Heusch), regulatory changes—reshaping of the model of welfare governance (Bonvin, Alonso), institutional changes (Riesco-Sanz, Baylos in this volume).

An initial kind of trigger factor for these social changes is linked to the changes in the production model and the increasing application of information and communications technologies (ICTs), which not only intensify the demand for adaptation to fluctuations in production but also radically reshape the relationships between producers and consumers (relocation and reorganisation of production). The increasing spread of digital platforms, processes of offshoring and outsourcing, bolstered by the use of ICTs, etc., are set to radically reshape the regulatory bases of wage employment, facilitating new forms of employment, as described in the chapters by Alonso, Baylos, Drahokoupil and Fabo, Valenduc, and de Heusch. Valenduc studies in depth the processes inherent in the digitalisation of the economy, which have led to the transformation of employment relationships: the fragmentation of the value chain, which upsets the power balance and produces a new division of labour; the blurring of the boundaries between producer and consumer (two-sided markets); the mining of consumer and employee data as a value-generation criterion; and the activation of the informal economy. An increasing fragmentation of production, the growing use of non-standard forms of employment or self-employment, the ability for companies to engineer production in this way, in order to neutralise market regulatory mechanisms, etc., explain the increasing deconstruction of regulated employment (Drahokoupil and Fabo).

A second kind of factor is linked to the reshaping of mechanisms for disciplining the workforce, and the diversification of contracting arrangements as a result of flexibilising practices which are contributing towards the reapportionment of responsibilities in respect of the vulnerability and depoliticisation of employment (see chapters by Alonso, Riesco-Sanz and Baylos). Indeed, as argued by Drahokoupil and Fabo, decisions by companies to shift their activities to other countries or sectors are not necessarily justified by criteria of economic profitability and productivity, since it is highly doubtful that they have that effect. Rather, this is a political decision: capacity to discipline and ability to neutralise the power resources—employment legislation, regulatory institutions, etc.—that are in workers' hands, and capacity to deconstruct the uniformising (differentiation of workers' conditions between a core sector and a peripheral one) and regulated (room for manoeuvre to implement measures promoting flexibility) character of the wage-earning status. Subcontracting and outsourcing also produce new forms of dependence with the contracting company, even if people are working under statutes of workers' rights, such as for self-employed people (Riesco-Sanz, and Baylos, in this volume).

The increasing internationalisation of the economy, which is playing a part in changing the role of the social state and other regulatory mechanisms for work, constitutes a third kind of factor. The imbalance of forces brought about by globalisation and the consequent loss of sovereignty of the nation state will substantially undermine the pillars on which social rights, the social state and national citizenship have been based, as analysed by Alonso, Bonvin, Sánchez Jiménez, and Drahokoupil and Fabo.

A fourth kind of factor relates to the recent economic crisis, which helped make it legitimate to challenge any instrument of social regulation of the waged status. This crisis has made private bodies and other institutions preaching the blessings of the market into veritable oracles, and turned austerity policies and fiscal adjustments into the expression of an ethically responsible attitude on the part of governments (from protection of the worker to protection of the—'single'—currency and the market). This economic crisis, which particularly affected countries on the periphery of Europe, rather than challenging the financial, speculative economy that triggered it, has brought discipline to it. It has benefited its economic elites, promoting, as discussed by Alonso and Bonvin, a growing delegitimisation of the public sphere, understood as the common good. This situation has accelerated the weakening of work as a political issue and the deconstruction of the three kinds of empowering resources in employment relationships (the right to strike, the right to form and become a member of a trade union and the right to collective bargaining), substantially undermining the contractual position of the weaker party, as analysed by Sánchez Jiménez, and Baylos.

Lastly, it is also important to stress, as de Heusch does, the role of the change in lifestyles and professional aspirations of some workers who have access to alternative means of working.

THE DECONSTRUCTION OF EMPLOYMENT AS A POLITICAL ISSUE: A SUMMARY OF SOME OF THE MAIN FINDINGS

The changes that have occurred in the categories of employment and unemployment are linked not only with their resemantisation (changes in their connotations) but also with the transformation of their category boundaries and the emergence of new boundaries. The authors contributing to this collective volume have identified various patterns in this process of semantic transformation: (a) changes in the criteria on which the establishment of categories is based (challenging the assumptions of wage employment); (b) reshaping of the semantic boundaries of categories; (c) dismantling of the semantic boundaries between categories; (d) diversification of occupational statuses within each category, and (e) reshaping of the enunciation framework.

a. *Challenging the assumptions of wage employment*

As has been mentioned above, the *common sense* that concepts embody contains both a referential (describing what things are) and a prescriptive (positing what things ought to be) dimension. This is the case with the notion of employment: it does not only delimit what is taken for granted in respect of work, but also provides a (d)enunciation of what it ought to be (Prieto 2007). The category of *wage employment*, the typical representation of work (Baylos), was constructed (and regulated), as argued above, on the basis of a series of assumptions: the stability of the wage-earning status (performance of the activity in a single company with an institutionally protected contract for an unspecified term), universalising homogeneity (the standard worker holds universal social rights), collectivised representation of workers' interests (the worker is a member of a broader community) and normalisation (political regulation by means of social rights). This set of criteria facilitated the standardisation and regulation of living and working conditions, framed by a reference category: full-time, continuous wage employment, working for another party, with a permanent contract, outside the home, legally governed by an employment contract and protected by collective agreements guaranteeing social rights. It is around this category that the institutions and mechanisms regulating vulnerability in work developed. These four principles formed the basis of the wage-earning society, wage institutions and a particular kind of individual: a secure, settled person integrated into an institutionalised network of interdependencies.

This category has been thrown into crisis, in so far as the principles on which it was based have been radically reshaped: access to wage employment with (relative) social insurance cover, at least for adult males; a certain stability and progression in one's working life and a sense of more or less regular, predictable working time; the possibility of forming social categories or groups that were relatively homogeneous (employed, unemployed, self-employed or inactive workers, or employers) and apparently dichotomous (employed people as opposed to the jobless, active as opposed to inactive, employers as opposed to workers, principle of profitability/axiological rationale of employment law, design/execution, producers/consumers, civil society/state) and, finally, the contrast between working time and 'life'.

New ways of working are deconstructing the pillars that formed the basis of how we conceived and regulated wage employment, as discussed by Valenduc in his chapter: its spatial (factory or company) and temporal (working hours) footing; its regulation on the basis of a reference condition (guarantee of stability and continuity in the company) and the allocation and distribution of responsibilities for safety and social protection between the employer and the employee (see also Alonso, Baylos, Riesco-Sanz, Sánchez Jiménez). The new work activities remove the temporal, material and spatial footing of employment—digital nomadism (discontinuous, flexible, unpredictable employment relationship depending on fluctuations in demand—on-call work), lead to fragmentation (deuniversalisation and differentiation of social rights between particular groups) of work, decollectivisation (weakening of collective frameworks and reformulation of responsibility in respect of vulnerability) and depoliticisation of the wage relationship (Valenduc, in this volume). Thus, work is losing its role as the backbone of collective solidarity and a means of rooting the individual in society.

The challenging of the axiological foundations that made employment into a political category (stability, homogeneity, regulation of heteronomy) has also led to a reshaping of the criteria for classifying the category of unemployment and of the pillars and assumptions around which its social regulation is organised: temporary nature (the unemployed person's fundamental purpose is to become the opposite, an employed person) (1), semantic opposition to employment (unemployment as the absence of work) (2) and homogeneity (society of equivalents) (3).

As regards the first axis, its transitory and temporary nature, exclusion from the labour market has ceased to be temporary as it extends over time, generating a new subcategory: the long-term unemployed. The plan for full (and relatively decent) employment has been reformulated with the impact of the successive economic crises since the 1980s, but the recent crisis provides a major stimulus. In turn, the new models of organisational management, which make flexibility a key dimension, are to a large extent challenging the stability and security of the organised employment relationship hinging on a contract protected by employment law. This prolongation and perpetuation of unemployment means that many vulnerable members of the insurance regime (and semantic framework) are driven into the assistance regime instead (Lallement, in this volume).

As far as the second axis is concerned, the increased precarity of employment renders the former common-sense association between the search for employment and its absence problematic. Many underemployed workers (involuntary part-time workers or people in inappropriate jobs due to insufficient use of their skills or inadequate income) can actively seek alternative work. From this point of view, a single individual may be included in both the employed (part-time) and the unemployed (part-time job-seeking) categories. Moreover, while regulated wage-earning societies had the aim of making work inconsistent with poverty (people were poor because they did not have access to work), we are currently seeing the proliferation of situations qualified with epithets in which work and poverty have become perfectly compatible (the working poor). The reduced share of wages in the economy, the drop in unit labour costs, the increase in the number of people living from income not specifically linked to work, the reformulation of the corporate profit ratio, etc. reveal the role that factors unrelated to work, linked to a speculative economy, are playing in the creation of value and wealth (see the chapters by Alonso and Sánchez Jiménez). In this semantic chaos, people can have a job and, even so, still be unemployed, and people can be poor and not necessarily unemployed.

Thirdly, the supposed homogeneity (with which unemployed people used to be conceived and unemployment tackled and which facilitated the shift from a moral attitude towards unemployed people to intervention on the labour market) is being challenged through a semantic process brought about by employment (now employability) policies. Employability presupposes a change in how unemployment is represented: there is a shift from treatment of social phenomena where differences between individuals are disregarded, to intervention on individual behaviours (Gautié 2002). Therefore, this logic of intervention introduces heterogenisation and individualisation into the treatment of unemployment (as opposed to the homogeneity of insurance).

b. *Reshaping of the semantic boundaries of categories*

A second axis of the crisis of social categories is formed by the shifting of boundaries between categories, such as that of unemployment and inactivity, in which employment policies have also played a part. In the semantic territory of non-work, a distinction has been drawn between unemployment, inactivity and poverty, depending, on the one hand, on the involuntary, imposed nature of the jobless status and, on the other, on the availability and attitude of the unemployed person (see Demazière and Lallement).

Activation policies have contributed to the increasing reshaping of the boundaries between unemployment and inactivity stemming from the development of a process of political challenges to the supposed involuntary nature of unemployment, making the expression of a moral commitment on the part of the unemployed person (rejection of a job offer, or not appearing sufficiently active in job seeking) a central axis when it comes to including an individual in the unemployed category, or excluding him or her from it (Serrano-Pascual 2004). In this way, activation policies are reshaping the relationship between unemployment and social protection (with a parallel redefinition of the 'worthy unemployed'), tightening up on the criteria for access to social protection that is increasingly represented as a disincentive to participation in the world of work (Demazière). The question of deservingness as a criterion for access to the unemployed category has translated into an ongoing inquiry into the jobless person's availability and attitude. The practice of expelling people into category limbo or into other categories, increasingly common since the economic crisis, is particularly noticeable in the case of the most underprivileged social groups (such as women, care workers, young people or other groups undergoing training, or voluntary workers) (Maruani and Meron, Lallement and Demazière, in this volume). In the case of unemployed women, they are banished to subordinate categories (part-time work, or 'female' jobs) or inactivity. This situation has given rise to the growth of what has come to be known as the 'unemployment halo', made up of the discouraged jobless, who are temporarily unavailable due to training, care duties, illness, etc. It involves those individuals who want to work but who do not meet the formal requirements to be deemed unemployed in statistical terms (in terms of immediate availability, or not having carried out the required job search procedures) (Maruani and Meron, and Prieto and Pérez de Guzmán). This reformulation of the criteria for access to a given category is the expression of, but also the condition for, the asymmetries among social groups. In the case of France, this intermediate space between inactivity and unemployment represents over half of all unemployed people (Maruani and Meron in this volume).

This reformulation of the criteria defining unemployment follows different logic depending on who draws them up. As postulated by Demazière, there is a clash between the statistical and legal criteria that employment institutions use to define unemployment, and the criteria used by individuals when they talk about their situation. The process of semantic expulsion of many social situations from the unemployment category by employment policies (more restrictive definition of the category of unemployed) goes hand in hand, conversely, with a process of expansion by those affected, with a progressive call for the inclusion of situations formerly excluded from this category. The reduction of the semantic space with which work is named (people do not only work: they also do a job, take something on, etc.), with a view to seeking alternative statuses, means that unemployment has ceased to act as a category that stands in opposition to employment, spanning a broad area of representation of a fragile condition with poorly defined limits. For this reason, Demazière posits that the nature and performativity of the boundaries of unemployment are being reshaped: it has ceased to act, as was the case after its emergence towards the end of the nineteenth century, as a door separating unemployment from other territories of non-employment (boundaries between categories that separate and divide) and has come to act as a bridge (an uncertain condition with unclear limits, with a delimiting criterion that propels people not only into employment, but also into inactivity or other kinds of activity).

Other situations also contribute to slippage of the boundaries between categories. On the one hand, there has been a proliferation of initiatives promoted by civil society, performing and supplementing public service tasks. In many cases, as de Heusch argues, these activities are carried out on a voluntary basis, excluded from the category of work and, therefore, access to social rights, which calls into question their semantic boundaries. On the other hand, this need to review the boundaries delimiting categories is a central axis of mobilisation for feminist movements. It is argued that domestic chores carried out by women fall within neither the category of employment nor that of voluntary work,[6] but of inactivity, and, therefore, their access to social protection is subsidiary (as spouses of a wage-earning worker), as discussed by Prieto and Pérez Guzmán. Since we see through words rather than with our eyes, political struggles are also, and above all, semantic battles.

c. *Dismantling of the semantic boundaries between categories*

The crisis in, and reappraisal of, the criteria around which the categories of social thought, employment and unemployment, are organised are, as we have argued, increasingly leading to the dismantling of the boundaries that have delimited the territories of these categories.

The binary, dichotomous logic whereby social and employment categories were organised is being remodelled into different sectors of society. The evolution of the economic model has led to the hybridisation and proliferation of statuses, which are reshaping the previous dichotomous categories formerly used to think of ourselves as a society (Bonvin, in this volume): social/instrumental rationality, state (power)/civil society, formal/informal. Hybridisation and overlapping of conditions (build-up of different employment statuses) are behind the appearance of a broad territory of intermediate working situations within the category of employment, as is the case with project-based management, which de Heusch analyses in her chapter, and these deviate from the reference model of the waged worker as regards the level of social protection and of subordination and dependence.

But perhaps the most eloquent example of these porous limits between categories is the blurred boundary that is forming between wage employment and self-employment. The differentiation between these conditions has crystallised, as highlighted by Riesco-Sanz, around three principles: continuity, formalisation and legal subordination. Changes in the production model, intensification of the processes of promoting flexibility and cost-cutting in production, and the increasing stress on the activation paradigm have led to a process of expansion of self-employment that takes different forms in European countries (see Riesco-Sanz, Drahokoupil and Fabo, de Heusch).

In this connection, Baylos, Riesco-Sanz, and de Heusch all reflect on the relevance of the criterion of subordination as the sole pivotal point between work and access to social rights. In the first place, because the ties of subordination and dependence are growing more complex as the production model evolves, making it difficult to establish a clear differentiation between employment statuses (intrapreneurs, quasi-wage earners, bogus self-employed people, workers in hybrid situations in terms of continuity and contractual wording) as well as to whom one is subordinate to (supply chains, subcontracting, and franchising). Drawing a straightforward distinction between regulation based on an employment contract (waged worker) and that deriving from a commercial contract (self-employed worker) has become problematic (Baylos and de Heusch). The self-employed person is becoming increasingly dependent, and the waged worker has to behave increasingly like an intrapreneur (new methods of business management and worker supervision). Embedded in new models of organisational management, many work activities are diverging from those characteristic of waged status (as regards the type of dependence that ensues, supervisory mechanisms employed, criteria for remuneration laid down), which has given rise to a debate on the criteria delimiting the boundaries of the category of employment.

Secondly, some of these workers do not identify with any individual category, and want the criteria for establishing employment statuses to be diversified. This means that being denied a category does not result in their being barred from access to social and political rights (de Heusch in this volume).

Thirdly, the status of (self-)employed and unemployed or inactive have ceased to be incompatible, as discussed by Riesco-Sanz, as is the case with the recent trends in employment policies, which make it possible to combine unemployment benefits with pursuing an economic activity or use unemployment benefits to start a new work activity.

This situation of category hybridisation calls for a reappraisal of the criteria for the legal delimitation of the various employment statuses, and entails a major challenge for employment law, the basic foundations of which have been substantially reshaped (see Riesco-Sanz). This remodelling process is heading in two opposite directions. On the one hand, there is a tendency to extend waged status to other kinds of non-wage employment conditions, and with this a convergence of employment statuses (self-employment, internship, domestic work, etc.), substantially reshaping the social (industrial workers) and axiological (standardisation of situations and clash with other contractual arrangements) foundations of the waged status. On the other hand, a greater heterogeneity, plurality and hybridisation of situations are causing the dichotomies formerly established between waged work/self-employment/informal work to be questioned (Riesco-Sanz, Baylos, de Heusch, Valenduc, in this volume).

This weakening does not only apply to the boundaries separating self-employment from wage employment, but is also to be found in other social spaces: dismantling of the borderlines between formal and informal work, as in the case of platform workers (Valenduc, and Drahokoupil and Fabo); between private and public sector and the spread of the conditions of commercialisation of task performance to non-commercial sectors, including public sector work (de Heusch, in this volume); between the producer and the consumer—prosumer work (Valenduc); between the customer and the citizen (Bonvin). This dismantling of the criteria around which the territory of employment revolves will also call into question the boundaries established between work and home space and time, which is a key dividing line in the emergence of the category of employment, with productive work possibly encroaching into the family space.

Hence one effect of this blurring of the boundaries between categories is the creation of new territories in the social sphere. Given the strategic role represented by the trend in the number of unemployed people, employment policies have made a major objective of creating new, intermediate statuses in the employment market, and alongside this, acting at the statistical frontiers of employment and unemployment, helping to blur the boundaries between training and employment (trainees, apprentices, etc.), and employment and inactivity (more restricted access to unemployed status). Therefore, the boundaries between categories (wage employment and self-employment, formal and informal economy, employment and unemployment, unemployment and underemployment) are being dismantled. This favours the expansion of intermediate categories between waged workers and self-employed workers dubbed 'bogus', as suggested by Alonso and Valenduc: bogus self-employment (economically dependent self-employed workers), bogus intern, bogus employee.

d. *Diversification of occupational statuses and situations within categories*

The proliferation of non-standard forms of work has helped to undermine the social and political foundations of employment regulation (employment law, social security and collective agreements). There has been a proliferation of legal statuses, giving rise to an increasing heterogeneity of contractual arrangements, which are calling into question the uniformity and homogeneity that have characterised the wage-earning status.

People's working lives and working conditions are becoming more diverse, workers move from one company (substantial labour turnover), employment status and contractual relationship to another. The benchmark for working (as an employed person, dependent, stable and on a full-time, exclusive contract) that has served employment law as a reference point for regulating the wage-earning employment relationship has been thrown into crisis, and the prototype of the worker is no longer expressed in the singular (the worker) but is now spoken of in the plural (Valdés Dal-Ré 2008).

There is a drive to include in the category of employment situations that diverge substantially from the reference category: proliferation of part-time and temporary working, self-employment, mini-jobs, under-employment, work placements, internships, etc. The economic crisis is, as described by Alonso in this volume, speeding up this process of frag-mentation of contractual situations, leading to serious divisions and rifts between the corporate nucleus with considerable negotiating power and the majority of subcontracted, peripheral workers in precarious situa-tions. In this context, there is a proliferation of employment situations which could not be captured under the traditional category of employ-ment, whereby employment was formerly measured and made visible (statistically). In the 1980s, this led the ILO to seek more suitable cri-teria, including the category of underemployment (Dooley and Joann 2005).

This normalisation of the non-standard is leading to deconstruction of the uniform legal treatment of a society of equivalents on which employ-ment law and collective bargaining were based and, accordingly, a con-sequent dejuridification of work (Baylos, in this volume). Employment conditions and social rights cease to be uniform, and there is a prolif-eration of contractual arrangements deviating from the prototype of wage employment. The increasing tendency to decentralise regulations at company level means that a broad, homogeneous perspective of employ-ment law and collective bargaining is ever diminishing in importance (see Sánchez Jiménez).

Not only are the ways of being employed becoming more diverse, but there is also an increasing heterogeneity forming within the unemployed community, as Lallement describes in his chapter, hindering any attempts at classification. Finally, the categories of non-employment, interme-diate and hybrid between work and inactivity (work placements, pre-retirement), unemployment and inactivity (the discouraged jobless), employment and unemployment (possibility of combining unemployment benefits with starting a work activity) are increasing. This situation is lead-ing to an interesting discussion, reported on in Lallement's chapter, about the obsolescence of the criteria that were used to define unemployment, and the need to include the spread of insecurity, precarity and heteroge-neity in our social categories. This is an issue which, as the author points out, is not a discussion to be conducted within the scientific environment alone, but above all in the political sphere.

e. *Reshaping of the enunciation frameworks*

The combination of the above circumstances explains why employment is losing its social footing. The legal pillars that made it possible to protect the worker (which was the basis of the emergence of employment as a social norm) were constructed on the basis of a nation state supervising and guaranteeing their effectiveness, and the company as a space where collective bargaining took place. ICTs have made it possible to dismantle the physical or temporal barriers that used to stand in the way of a demand for workers' constant mobilisation and adaptability. In a context of normative Darwinism that has turned the law into a 'market of legislative products' (Supiot 2010, 171), the notion of rights has been semantically transferred from a framework posited on social justice to a different, commercialist one, which turns them into barriers to production (labour costs, mismatch factors) and, accordingly, sees them as obstructive (Alonso in this volume). It is argued that social protection has ceased to be represented as an expression of collective solidarity and social justice, and is now construed as the expression of a parasitic lack of solidarity on the part of those who, while being responsible for their fate, enjoy the benefit of supposedly obsolete social measures (see de Heusch).

This combination of trends is fostering an increasingly fragmentary nature of work (absence of social protection, individualisation in terms of the pay-setting mechanisms, self-exploitation, etc.) and, hence, greater fragility of the mechanisms for collective representation of workers and socialisation of work. As Alonso describes, there is in progress a major deformalisation of the basic concepts and conventions underlying the social responsibility of governments. The role of the state, as highlighted by Alonso, has ceased to be the provision of spaces outside market logic, and it has become a facilitator of partnership relationships between social actors, in order to promote economic profitability and boost the operation of the economy. Thus, the market becomes the prime regulator of society, and the economy ceases to be an instrument of society, but society becomes an instrument of the economy. It is not the interventionist state, therefore, that regulates the economy, but economic and production rationale that will drive the privatised functioning of the state (Bonvin, in this volume). In this way, the universalising mission of the social state (the consequence of posing the social question in a non-individualising way) comes to be replaced by the privatisation of welfare, the individualisation of risk, the removal of disadvantaged groups—women, young people, migrants—to subordinate areas, and the focusing, on the basis of *de minimis* palliative policies, on particular groups of supposed losers, and co-responsibility of the citizen (user fees, indirect taxes, etc.) (see Alonso).

We are therefore moving from universalising rationales that served as the foundation of the welfare state (universal national citizenship) to hypotheses for mitigating the indirect effects of the market, focusing on at-risk groups. The welfare state is undergoing major redefinitions of its intervention philosophy, which go so far as to affect the very concept of regulation (from government to governance) (see Bonvin, in this volume). This new mode of social regulation makes the public, and, therefore, political nature of social regulation invisible. As Supiot (2010) appositely argues, the notion of governance stems from physics and biology, and refers to a mechanism inherent in the unit or organism, thus reinforcing its normalisation and justification. However, the concept of government, which is based on legal regulation, refers to a different connotation of 'regulating'. It consists in understanding regulation as inseparable from what 'ought to be', linked to a fair order defined in a manner that is external, not immanent, to society. Hence the importance of denormalising the market and restoring discussion of its regulation to the arena of public debate (placing the economy at the service of social justice).[7]

Notes

1. See the classic study by Jahoda et al. (1987) on the unemployed of Marienthal, which served as a major prompt for the conduct of studies revealing the drastic psychosocial consequences of unemployment (apathy, disorientation, deterioration in quality of life, loss of meaning, inability to organise time) and the consequent functions of work.

2. The analysis of the evolution of the meaning and role of work shows how class struggles are, to a large extent, struggles over classifications (Bourdieu 1985)—The evolution of the meaning of work demonstrates the reshaping of social and political relationships established between slaves and free men, aristocracy and bourgeoisie, men and women, etc. (Sanchis 2004).

3. This is particularly evident in proverbs, a good source for tracking the semantic evolution of hegemonic notions. An analysis of Spanish proverbs demonstrates the polysemy of *trabajo*: both essence of humanity and dehumanisation, both curse/penitence and blessing/happiness, both reciprocity/fair exchange and injustice/oppression, both dignification/recognition and humiliation/exploitation, both penitence and self-fulfilment, both means and end.

4. Williams (1983) posits that the notion of labour is a term which was consciously adopted by a political movement which asserted the dignity of labour. The notion of labour as effort associated with manual work shifted metonymically to come to designate a group of people who performed this effort (social class). Productive labour as part of the market thus emerges as a classification criterion between individuals. This semantic process is reinforced by the spread of another notion that has political effects: the concept of class, which, initially, was used only to classify objects, and subsequently came to designate divisions among social groups. This notion of class replaced the traditional concepts to describe social divisions of rank, order and estate, metaphors which implied continuity and social inheritance (Williams 1983). The notion of class was used politically by the middle classes to distinguish between the virtuous, productive classes and the unproductive ones. However, the working class later appropriated this notion to distinguish itself from the bourgeoisie.

5. Hirschman (1977/2014) posits that, from the sixteenth century onwards, the notion of profit was replaced by the euphemism of interest (combination of selfishness and rationality), with reassuring connotations of predictability, as against the passions associated with profit, which were deemed to be a social threat and condemned.

6. The differentiation among socially useful activities that would be classified in the category of voluntary work, compared with those that would fall under the category of inactivity, would be fundamentally based on a political criterion. Behind any classification operation, a political line has been drawn, which explains the arbitrary nature of the criteria for delimitation and classification: why are activities of an NGO conceptualised within the semantic framework of voluntary activities and solidarity—voluntary work—whereas activities carried out by women in a family context—housekeeping—are not?

7. Translation from the Spanish by Sally Blaxland.

REFERENCES

Bilbao, Andrés. 2007. *Individuo y orden social. La emergencia del individuo y la transición a la sociología*. Madrid: Sequitur.

Boltanski, Luc. 2000. *El amor y la justicia como competencias. Tres ensayos de sociología de la acción*. Buenos Aires: Amorrortu Editores.

Bourdieu, Pierre. 1985. *¿Qué significa hablar?* Madrid: Akal.

Crespo-Suárez, Eduardo, and Amparo Serrano-Pascual. 2013. "Las paradojas de las políticas de empleo europeas: de la justicia a la terapia." *Universitas Psychologica* 12 (4): 1113–1126.

Dooley, David, and Prause, Joann. 2005. *The Social Costs of Underemployment: Inadequate Employment as Disguised Unemployment.* Cambridge: Cambridge University Press.

Durand, Pascal, ed. 2007. *Les nouveaux mots du pouvoir. Abécédaire critique.* Bruxelles: Éditions Aden.

Fairclough, Norman. 2000. "Representaciones del cambio en el discurso neoliberal." *Cuadernos de Relaciones Laborales* 16: 13–35.

Gautié, Jérôme. 2002. "De l'invention du chômage à sa déconstruction." *Genèses* 46: 60–76.

Gil Calvo, Enrique. 2016. *Sociólogos contra el economicismo.* Madrid: Catarata.

Gorz, André. 1988. *Métamorphoses du travail: Critique de la raison économique.* Galilée, Debats.

Hirschman, Albert. 1977/2014. *Las pasiones y los intereses. Argumentos políticos en favor del capitalismo previos a su triunfo.* Madrid: Capital Swing.

Jahoda, M., et al. 1987. *Empleo y desempleo: un análisis socio-psicológico.* Madrid: Morata.

Le Goff, Jacques. 2013. *La bolsa y la vida. Economía y religión en la Edad Media.* Gedisa.

Lecerf, Eric. 2002. *Le sujet du chômage.* Paris: L'Harmattan.

Maruani, Margaret. 2000. "De la sociología del trabajo a la Sociología del Empleo." *Política y Sociedad* 39: 9–18.

Méda, Dominique. 1998. *Le travail, une valeur en voie de disparition.* Paris: Champs Flammarion.

Polanyi, Carl. 1944/1989. *La gran transformación.* Madrid: La Piqueta.

Prieto, Carlos. 2007. "Del estudio del empleo como norma social al de la sociedad como orden social." *Papeles del CEIC* 1: 2–27.

Rosanvallon, Pierre. 1995. *La nouvelle question sociale. Repenser l'Etat-providence.* Paris: Seuil.

Salais, Robert, Nicolas Baverez, and Bénédicte Reynaud. 1986. *L'invention du chômage. Histoire et transformations d'une catégorie en France des années 1890 aux années 1980.* Paris: Presses Universitaires de France.

Sanchis, Enric. 2004. "Concepciones del trabajo: de las ambivalencias medievales a las paradojas actuales." *Cuadernos de Relaciones Laborales* 22 (1): 37–65.

Serrano-Pascual, Amparo. 2004. "Are European Activation Policies Converging?" In *Labour and Employment Regulation in Europe*, edited by Jens Lind, Herman Knudsen, and Henning Jørgensen, 211–233. Brussels: Peter Lang.

Serrano-Pascual, Amparo, Maarten Keune, and Eduardo Crespo-Suárez. 2017. "The Paradoxical Ways of Naming Employment by European Institutions During the Crisis: The Weakening of Collective Frames." *Stato e mercato* 110: 223–246.

Simmel, G. 1907/1977. *Filosofía del dinero*. Madrid: Instituto de Estudios Políticos.

Smith, Adam. 1776/2011. *La riqueza de las naciones*. Madrid: Alianza Editorial.

Supiot, Alan. 2010. "Perspectiva jurídica de la crisis económica." *Revista Internacional del Trabajo* 129 (2): 1–14.

Topalov, Christian. 1994. *Naissance du chômeur: 1880–1910*. Paris: Albin Michel.

Valdés Dal-Ré, Fernando. 2008. "Contratación temporal y trabajo a tiempo parcial en España: La normalización jurídica de la precariedad laboral." Accessed December 1, 2017. http://www.ucm.es/data/cont/docs/183-2013-05-08-Ponencia_Fernando%20Vald%C3%A9s%20Dal-R%C3%A9.pdf.

Voloshinov, Valentin N. 1929/1992. *El marxismo y la filosofía del lenguaje*. Madrid: Alianza.

Williams, Raymond. 1983. *Keywords. A Vocabulary of Culture and Society*. New York: Oxford University Press.

INDEX

Lightning Source UK Ltd.
Milton Keynes UK
UKHW02n2339240718
326217UK00002B/14/P

9 783319 936161